*Aristotle's Chemistry*

# Aristotle's Chemistry

## On Coming to Be and Passing Away
## Meteorology 1.1–3, 4.1–12

Translated
With an Introduction and Notes
By

C. D. C. Reeve

Hackett Publishing Company, Inc.
Indianapolis/Cambridge

Copyright © 2023 by Hackett Publishing Company, Inc.

All rights reserved
Printed in the United States of America

26 25 24 23     1 2 3 4 5 6 7

For further information, please address
 Hackett Publishing Company, Inc.
 P.O. Box 44937
 Indianapolis, Indiana 46244-0937

www.hackettpublishing.com

Cover design by Deborah Wilkes
Interior design by E. L. Wilson
Composition by Aptara, Inc.

Cataloging-in-Publication data can be accessed via the Library of Congress Online Catalog.
Library of Congress Control Number: 2022938277

ISBN-13: 978-1-64792-098-2 (cloth)
ISBN-13: 978-1-64792-089-0 (pbk.)
ISBN-13: 978-1-64792-099-9 (PDF ebook)

The paper used in this publication meets the minimum requirements of American National Standard for Information Sciences—Permanence of Paper for Printed Library Materials, ANSI Z39.48–1984.

∞

*For*

Marc Cohen
friend and συνεργός

# Contents

*Preface* — ix
*Abbreviations* — xi
*Introduction* — xvii

## On Coming to Be and Passing Away

### Book 1

| | | |
|---|---|---|
| 1.1 | Unconditional coming to be and passing away, growth and withering, alteration. Monists versus pluralists: Empedocles, Anaxagoras, Leucippus. | 2 |
| 1.2 | Unlimited divisibility of magnitudes: Plato, Democritus. | 4 |
| 1.3 | Unconditional coming to be. | 8 |
| 1.4 | Alteration. | 13 |
| 1.5 | Growth. | 14 |
| 1.6 | Contact. | 18 |
| 1.7 | Affecting and being affected (1): like and unlike. | 20 |
| 1.8 | Affecting and being affected (2): Empedocles, Leucippus, Democritus. | 23 |
| 1.9 | Affecting and being affected (3): potentially versus actually. | 27 |
| 1.10 | Mixing. | 28 |

### Book 2

| | | |
|---|---|---|
| 2.1 | The elements of bodies (earth, water, air, fire) and their matter. | 32 |
| 2.2 | The primary contrarieties: hot and cold, dry and wet. | 33 |
| 2.3 | The contrarieties and the elements. | 35 |
| 2.4 | The change of the elements into each other. | 36 |
| 2.5 | Different ways in which the elements change into each other. | 37 |
| 2.6 | Against Empedocles. | 40 |
| 2.7 | How the simple bodies mix to form compound ones. | 42 |
| 2.8 | Each element present in every compound. | 43 |
| 2.9 | Material, formal, and final causes of coming to be and passing away. | 44 |

| 2.10 | Efficient cause of coming to be and passing away: the sun's movements. | 46 |
| 2.11 | Necessity in the sphere of coming to be and passing away. | 48 |

# Meteorology

## Book 1

| 1.1 | The scope and subject matter of meteorology and its place in the system of natural science. | 52 |
| 1.2 | The celestial element, ether, and the four sublunary ones. The efficient and material causes of natural phenomena. | 52 |
| 1.3 | The positions of air and fire relative to the celestial sphere. Why clouds and water do not form in the upper air. | 53 |

## Book 4

| 4.1 | Hot and cold as capable of affecting; wet and dry as affectable. Natural coming to be is due to these. Putrefaction. | 58 |
| 4.2 | Concoction and non-concoction. | 59 |
| 4.3 | Three kinds of concoction—ripening, boiling, broiling—and their contraries. | 60 |
| 4.4 | Wet and dry and their consequences—hard and soft. | 63 |
| 4.5 | Every body must be hard or soft and solid; solidification. | 64 |
| 4.6 | What things can be solidified. Kinds of solidification and dissolution. | 65 |
| 4.7 | Coarse-grainedness caused by heat and caused by cold. | 67 |
| 4.8 | The capacities and incapacities of homoeomerous bodies. | 69 |
| 4.9 | More capacities and incapacities of homoeomerous bodies. | 71 |
| 4.10 | Homoeomerous bodies. | 75 |
| 4.11 | Hot and cold liquids and solids. | 78 |
| 4.12 | Homoeomerous things, in which end and function are less clear, are composed of elements; non-homoeomerous ones, in which end and function are more clear than in the case of homoeomerous ones. Transition to biology. | 78 |

| *Appendix* Plato, *Timaeus* 48b–57d | *81* |
| *Notes* | *91* |
| *Further Reading* | *193* |
| *Index* | *195* |

# Preface

Everyone likely to read this book will have heard of Aristotle's physics and metaphysics, and also of his ethics, politics, rhetoric, and poetics. After all, these are in many cases the English titles of some of his treatises. But Aristotle's *chemistry*—who has heard of that? And yet the treatises collected here—*On Coming to Be and Passing Away* (the standard abbreviation *GC* comes from its Latin title, *De Generatione et Corruptione*) and *Meteorology* (*Mete.*) Book 4 (with 1.1–3 as an introduction)—seem to me to be best described as contributions to chemistry. For chemistry overlaps with physics, on the one hand, and biology, on the other, and that is more or less what these treatises do: they come right after the physical treatises and right before those dealing with the animate world (*De Anima, Parva Naturalia, History of Animals*, and the other so-called biological treatises). Moreover, physics—like Aristotle's *Physics*—deals with fundamental concepts such as causation, space, time, and movement, while chemistry deals more with the formation of molecules and compounds, including very complex organic ones, from atoms or elements, and with the processes by which they are formed, as—allowing for differences in background theories—do *GC* and *Mete.* 4.

To make the journey through these difficult treatises as convenient as possible, footnotes and glossary entries are replaced by sequentially numbered, cross-referenced endnotes, so that the information most needed at each juncture is available in a single place. These always appear at the end of the sentence to which they apply, so as not to interrupt the thought. The non-sequential reader, interested in a particular passage, will find in the detailed Index a guide to places where focused discussion of a term or notion occurs. The Introduction describes the book that lies ahead, explaining what it is about, what it is trying to do, how it goes about doing it, and what sort of audience it presupposes. It isn't a comprehensive discussion of every pertinent issue or an expression of scholarly consensus on the issues it does discuss. The same goes for many of the more interpretative notes. Both are a place to start, not a place to finish—a first step in the endlessly rewarding dialectical enterprise of coming to understand Aristotle for oneself.

I conceive of all my translations as aimed at enabling reasonably committed readers to read the work at issue for themselves, with a credible chance of really understanding it. Readers should think of this edition,

*Preface*

then, as one that will take them quite deeply into Aristotle's chemistry, while giving them some of the tools that will enable them to go deeper still. It can be used in any college or university class likely to include Aristotle's theoretical philosophy in its purview, but it can also be used by readers approaching these works on their own.

I have benefited greatly from previous translators and commentators, especially E. S. Forster, H. H. Joachim, Marwan Rashed, and C. J. F. Williams in the case of *GC*, and H. D. P. Lee, Pierre Louis, E. W. Webster, and Malcolm Wilson in the case of *Mete*.

István Bodnár, Stasinos Stavrianeas, and Malcolm Wilson did me the great favor of providing many useful corrections and suggestions. I thank them all very warmly, as I do Russ Dancy and Nathanael Stein.

I renew my thanks to ΔKE, the first fraternity in the United States to endow a professorial chair, and to the University of North Carolina for awarding it to me. The generous research funds, among other things, that the endowment makes available each year have allowed me to travel to conferences and to acquire books, computers, and other research materials and assistance, including in particular that of the eagle-eyed Sean Neagle, without which my work would have been much more difficult.

To all at Hackett, but especially Deborah Wilkes, I express again my enormous gratitude for their unparalleled support, as I do to my dear friend Pavlos Kontos for his.

# Abbreviations

## Aristotle

Citations of Aristotle's works are made to Immanuel Bekker's *Aristotelis Opera* (Berlin: 1831 [1970]), in the canonical form of page number, column letter, and line number, or occasionally in the form of book and chapter numbers. An † indicates a work whose authenticity has been seriously questioned; †† indicates a work attributed to Aristotle but generally agreed not to be by him (similarly in the case of Plato). The abbreviations used are as follows:

| | |
|---|---|
| *APo.* | *Posterior Analytics* |
| *APr.* | *Prior Analytics* |
| *Cael.* | *De Caelo* (Moraux) |
| *Cat.* | *Categories* |
| ††*Color.* | *De Coloribus* |
| *DA* | *De Anima* (Corcilius) |
| *Div. Somn.* | *On Divination in Sleep* (Ross) |
| *EE* | *Eudemian Ethics* |
| *GA* | *Generation of Animals* |
| *GC* | *On Coming to Be and Passing Away* (Rashed) |
| *HA* | *History of Animals* (Louis) |
| *IA* | *Progression of Animals* (Falcon and Stavrianeas) |
| *Int.* | *De Interpretatione* |
| *Juv.* | *On Youth and Old Age, Life and Death, and Respiration* (Ross) |
| *Long.* | *On Length and Shortness of Life* (Ross) |
| *MA* | *Movement of Animals* (Primavesi and Corcilius) |
| *Met.* | *Metaphysics* |
| *Mete.* | *Meteorology* (Fobes) |

| | |
|---|---|
| †*MM* | *Magna Moralia* (Susemihl) |
| ††*Mu.* | *On the Cosmos* |
| *NE* | *Nicomachean Ethics* |
| *PA* | *Parts of Animals* (Louis) |
| *Ph.* | *Physics* |
| *Po.* | *Poetics* |
| *Pol.* | *Politics* |
| †*Pr.* | *Problems* (Mayhew) |
| *Protr.* | *Protrepticus* (Düring) |
| ††*Resp.* | *On Respiration* |
| *Rh.* | *Rhetoric* |
| *SE* | *Sophistical Refutations* |
| *Sens.* | *Sense and Sensibilia* (Ross) |
| *Top.* | *Topics* (Brunschwig) |

I cite and translate the *Oxford Classical Texts* (OCT) editions of these works, where available, otherwise (with the exception of *GC* and *Mete.* themselves) Bekker or the editions noted:

Corcilius, K., *Aristoteles Über die Seele: De Anima* (Hamburg, 2017).

Brunschwig, B., *Aristote Topiques Livres I–IV, Livres V–VIII* (Paris, 1967, 2007).

Düring, I., *Aristotle's Protrepticus: An Attempt at Reconstruction* (Göteborg, 1961).

Falcon, A., and S. Stavrianeas, *Aristotle on How Animals Move* (Cambridge, 2021).

Fobes, F., *Aristotelis Meteorologicorum Libri Quattor* (Cambridge, MA, 1919).

Louis, P., *Aristote: Les Parties des Animaux* (Paris, 1956).

Louis, P., *Histoire des Animaux* (Paris, 1964–1969).

Mayhew, R., *Aristotle: Problems* (Cambridge, MA, 2011).

Moraux, P., *Aristote: Du Ciel* (Paris, 1965).

Primavesi, O., and K. Corcilius, *Aristoteles De Motu Animalium* (Hamburg, 2018).

Rashed, M., *Aristote: De la Génération et la Corruption* (Paris, 2005).

Ross, D., *Aristotle Parva Naturalia* (Oxford, 1955).

Susemihl, F., *Aristotelis Magna Moralia* (Leipzig, 1883).

# PLATO

| Chrm. | Charmides |
| --- | --- |
| Crat. | Cratylus |
| Epin. | Epinomis |
| Euthphr. | Euthyphro |
| Lg. | Laws |
| Phd. | Phaedo |
| Rep. | Republic |
| Ti. | Timaeus |

Translations of Plato in the notes are based on those in J. M. Cooper, ed., *Plato: Complete Works* (Indianapolis, 1997), and on my *The Trials of Socrates* (Indianapolis, 2002) and *Plato: Republic* (Indianapolis, 2004).

# OTHER ABBREVIATIONS AND SYMBOLS

Alex. = Alexander of Aphrodisias, *in Aristotelis Meteorologicorum Libros Commentaria* (Berlin, 1899).

Burnet = J. Burnet, *Plato's Phaedo* (Oxford, 1911).

Chantraine = P. Chantraine, *Dictionnaire Étymologique de la Langue Grecque* (Paris, 1968).

Coope = U. Coope, *Time for Aristotle: Physics 4.10–14* (Oxford, 2005).

De Haas & Mansfeld = F. de Haas and J. Mansfeld, *Aristotle's On Generation and Corruption 1* (Oxford, 2004).

DK = H. Diels and W. Kranz, eds., *Die Fragmente der Vorsokratiker*, 6th ed. (Berlin, 1951).

Düring = I. Düring, *Aristotle's Chemical Treatise: Meteorologica*, Book 4 (Göteborg, 1944).

Eichholz = D. Eichholz, *Theophrastus De Lapidibus* (Oxford, 1965).

Fobes = F. Fobes, *Aristotelis Meteorologicorum Libri Quattor* (Cambridge, MA, 1919).

Forster = E. Forster, *Aristotle: On Coming-to-Be and Passing-Away* (London, 1955).

Furley = D. Furley, *Cosmic Problems* (Cambridge, 1989).

Furth = M. Furth, *Substance, Form, and Psyche: An Aristotelian Metaphysics* (Cambridge, 1988).

## Abbreviations

Gill = M. Gill, *Aristotle on Substance: The Paradox of Unity* (Princeton, 1989).

Joachim-1 = H. Joachim, *Aristotle: On Coming-to-Be and Passing-Away: A Revised Text with Introduction and Commentary* (Oxford, 1926).

Joachim-2 = H. Joachim, *Aristotle: On Coming-to-Be and Passing-Away*, in D. Ross, ed., *The Works of Aristotle*, vol. 2 (Oxford, 1930).

Krizan = M. Krizan, "Elemental Structure and the Transformation of the Elements in *On Generation and Corruption* 2.4," *Oxford Studies in Ancient Philosophy* 45 (2013): 195–224.

Kupreeva = I. Kupreeva, *Philoponus: On Aristotle's On Coming-to-be and Perishing 1.6–2.4* (Ithaca, 2005).

Lee = H. Lee, *Aristotle Meteorologica* (London, 1952).

Lennox = J. Lennox, *Aristotle: On the Parts of Animals I–IV* (Oxford, 2001).

Lewis = E. Lewis, *Alexander of Aphrodisias: On Aristotle's Meteorology 4* (Ithaca, 1996).

Louis = P. Louis, *Aristote: Météorologiques* (Paris, 1982).

Melfos = V. Melfos, et al., "Raw Materials Used for the Millstones Production in Ancient Greece," IWA Regional Symposium on Water, Wastewater and Environment: Traditions and Culture. Patras, Greece, March 22–24, 2014, https://www.academia.edu/6973547/.

Migliori = M. Migliori, *Aristotele: La Generatione e la Corruzione* (Naples, 1976).

Mugler = C. Mugler, *Aristote: De la Génération et la Corruption* (Paris, 1966).

Philop. = Philoponus, *in Aristotelis Libros De Generatione et Corruptione Commentaria* (Berlin, 1887).

Ross = D. Ross, *Aristotle's Physics: A Revised Text with Introduction and Commentary* (Oxford, 1936).

Solmsen = F. Solmsen, *Aristotle's System of the Physical World* (Ithaca, 1960).

TEGP = D. Graham, *The Texts of Early Greek Philosophy: The Complete Fragments and Selected Testimonies of the Major Presocratics* (Cambridge, 2010).

Verdenius & Waszink = W. Verdenius and J. Waszink, *Aristotle On Coming-to-Be and Passing-Away: Some Comments* (Leiden, 1946).

Webster = E. Webster, *Meteorologica*, in D. Ross, ed., *The Works of Aristotle*, vol. 3 (Oxford, 1923).

Williams-1 = C. Williams, *Aristotle's De Generatione et Corruptione* (Oxford, 1982).

Williams-2 = C. Williams, *Philoponus: On Aristotle's On Coming-to-Be and Perishing 1.1–5, 1.6–2.4* (Ithaca, 1999).

Wilson = M. Wilson, *Structure and Method in Aristotle's Meteorologica* (Cambridge, 2013).

A = B = A is identical to, or equals, or is equivalent to B.

A ≈ B = A is roughly the same as B.

# Introduction

## *Life and Works*

Aristotle was born in 384 BC to a well-off family living in the small town of Stagira in northern Greece. His father, Nicomachus, who died while Aristotle was still quite young, was allegedly doctor to King Amyntas of Macedon. His mother, Phaestis, was wealthy in her own right. When Aristotle was seventeen, his guardian, Proxenus, sent him to study at Plato's Academy in Athens. He remained there for twenty years, initially as a student, eventually as a researcher and teacher.

When Plato died in 347, leaving the Academy in the hands of his nephew Speusippus, Aristotle left Athens for Assos in Asia Minor, where the ruler, Hermias, was a patron of philosophy. He married Hermias' niece (or ward) Pythias and had a daughter by her, also named Pythias. Three years later, in 345, after Hermias had been killed by the Persians, Aristotle moved to Mytilene on the island of Lesbos, where he met Theophrastus, who was to become his best student and closest colleague.

In 343, Aristotle seems to have been invited by Philip of Macedon to be tutor to the latter's thirteen-year-old son, Alexander, later called "the Great." In 335, Aristotle returned to Athens and founded his own institute, the Lyceum. While he was there his wife died and he established a relationship with Herpyllis, also a native of Stagira. Their son Nicomachus was named for Aristotle's father, and the *Nicomachean Ethics* may, in turn, have been named for him or transcribed by him. In 323, Alexander the Great died, with the result that anti-Macedonian feeling in Athens grew stronger. Perhaps threatened with a formal charge of impiety, Aristotle left for Chalcis in Euboea, where he died twelve months later, in 322, at the age of sixty-two.

Legend has it that Aristotle had slender calves and small eyes, spoke with a lisp, and was "conspicuous by his attire, his rings, and the cut of his hair." His will reveals that he had a sizable estate, a domestic partner, two children, a considerable library, and a large circle of friends. In it Aristotle asks his executors to take special care of Herpyllis. He directs that his slaves be freed "when they come of age," and that the bones of his wife, Pythias, be mixed with his "as she instructed."

*Introduction*

Although the surviving writings of Aristotle occupy almost 2,500 tightly printed pages in English, most of them are not works polished for publication but lecture notes and working papers. This accounts for some, though not all, of their legendary difficulty. It is unfair to complain, as a Platonist opponent did, that Aristotle "escapes refutation by clothing a perplexing subject in obscure language, using darkness like a squid to make himself hard to catch," but there is darkness and obscurity enough for anyone, even if none of it is intentional. There is also a staggering breadth and depth of intellect. Aristotle made fundamental contributions to a vast range of disciplines, including logic, metaphysics, epistemology, psychology, ethics, politics, rhetoric, aesthetics, zoology, biology, physics, and philosophical and political history. When Dante called him "the master of those who know," he was scarcely exaggerating.

## *What* GC *and* Mete. *Are*

One thing we might mean by *GC* is what we now find inscribed on the pages that make up Marwan Rashed's Budé edition of the Greek text (the *Thesaurus Linguae Graecae* has the older one of Mugler), first published in 2005, which is the basis of the present translation. This is the descendant of texts derived—via manuscripts copied in the Byzantine period (from the tenth to the fifteenth centuries AD)—from manuscripts that derive from the edition of Aristotle's works produced by Andronicus of Rhodes in the first century BC. Its more precise transmission is discussed in Rashed's introduction (pp. clxxvii–cclv). The same is true *mutatis mutandis* of *Mete.*, where the translation is based on F. H. Fobes' text (which is the one in the *Thesaurus Linguae Graecae*).

These editions, like most other modern editions, record in the textual apparatus at the bottom of the page various manuscript readings alternative to the one printed in the body of the text. In some cases, I have preferred one of these readings and, where required, have indicated so in the notes. Divisions of the text into books and chapters are the work of editors, not of Aristotle himself. Also present in Rashed's and Fobes' texts are the page numbers of Bekker's *Aristotelis Opera*. These appear here in the margins of the printed version and enclosed in vertical lines (| |) in the electronic one at the end of the line to which they apply. Occasional material in square brackets in the text is my addition.

The second thing we might mean, and are perhaps more likely to mean, by *GC* and *Mete.* are the works themselves—those more abstract things that are embodied in good Greek texts and (ideally) in any translation of them. The opening sentence of the former tells us that it deals with the causes and accounts of "the coming to be and passing away of the things that by nature come to be and pass away . . . alike with regard to all of them (*homoiôs kata pantôn*)," and with growth and withering (increase and decrease) and alteration, and how these differ, if they do, from coming to be and passing away (314$^a$1–6). A little later we learn that the focus includes "unconditional coming to be and passing away in general" (315$^a$26), and this is the subject assigned to the treatise in *Mete.*:

> Now, [1] the primary causes of nature, [2] all natural movement, [3] the stars arranged in the upper spatial movement, and [4] the elements of bodies, how many they are and of what sorts, their change into each other, and coming to be and passing away in general, have been spoken about previously. (338$^a$20–25)

[1] refers to *Physics* 1–2, [2] to *Physics* 3, 5–8, [3] to *De Caelo* 1–2, and [4] to *De Caelo* 3–4 and *GC*. Our first task is to determine what "in general" implies in these texts.

At the risk of trying to illuminate one difficulty by a yet greater one, let us look at a parallel issue raised as a puzzle in the *Metaphysics*:

> We might raise a puzzle as to whether the primary philosophy is universal or concerned with a particular genus and one particular nature (for it is not the same way even in the mathematical sciences, but rather geometry and astronomy are concerned with a particular nature, whereas universal mathematics is common to all). If, then, there is no other substance beyond those composed by nature, natural science will be the primary science. But if there is some immovable substance, this [that is, theological philosophy] will be prior and will be primary philosophy, and it will be universal in this way, namely, because it is primary. And it will belong to it to get a theoretical grasp on being qua being, both what it is and the things that belong to it qua being. (*Met.* 1026$^a$23–32)

The thought is that primary philosophy—which has just been identified with theological philosophy (*Met.* 1026$^a$19), or theological science (1064$^b$1–3)—is the universal science of being qua being, not because it deals with every sort of being, but because it deals with the primary being, namely, god, who as the immovable primary mover is the cause of all the others (see *GC* 2.10 and associated notes). Thus when we discover that this discussion focuses chiefly on the elements and their coming to be from each other and passing away into each other, affecting and being affected

*Introduction*

by each other, and mixing, we should see this as being general in the same way—not now in terms of top-down causation (theology), but of bottom-up. Thus we find *GC* 1.7 referred to as "our universal accounts concerning affecting and being affected," and evidence of its generality in the remark that "it is natural for a body to be affected by a body, flavor by flavor, color by color, and, in general, what is the same in genus by what is the same in genus" ($324^a33$–$324^a1$). By the same token, along with the transformation of water into air, and vice versa, we find a reference to blood coming to be "from the whole of the semen [changing]" ($319^b16$), as well as references to flesh and bone and their coming to be from the elements ($334^b25$–$30$).

What *GC* is, then, is an investigation of unconditional coming to be and passing away, and the rest, that is universal because—by being focused on elemental transformation—it is bottom-up. That is why it is useful to conjoin it with *Mete.* 4, to which 1.1–3 serve as a sort of introduction. For *Mete.* 4 also focuses on the transformation of the elements, deepening our understanding of them. Thus, Alexander of Aphrodisias, in his commentary on the *Meteorology* writes:

> The book entitled "the fourth" of Aristotle's *Meteorology* does belong to Aristotle, but not to the work on meteorology. For the things spoken about in it are not proper to meteorology. Rather, as far as the things spoken about are concerned, it would follow *On Coming to Be and Passing Away*. (179.3–6 = Lewis, p. 65)

So our next question must be to discover what sort of universal investigation we are talking about.

## *The Larger Picture*

It is clear from the beginning that the distinctive focus of *De Caelo*, to begin with *GC*'s immediate predecessor, is not primarily or exclusively on the world of sublunary nature (*phusis*), but on the superlunary or super-natural realm—*ho ouranos* ("the heaven"), as Aristotle calls it. The former consists canonically of matter-form compounds, whose material component involves the elements (earth, water, air, and fire); the latter of celestial spheres, composed of primary body or ether (*Cael.* $270^b21$), as well as the stars and planets affixed to them. Nonetheless, if its scope is more catholic than a strictly natural science, much of what it discusses (for example, the sublunary elements, heaviness and lightness, up and down) has obvious application in the sublunary realm. Some topics belonging to the superlunary one (to super-nature), indeed, are included in natural science's purview:

> The next thing is to get a theoretical grasp on . . . whether astronomy is distinct from natural science or a part of it; for if it belongs to the natural scientist to know what the sun or the moon is, for him not to know their intrinsic coincidents would be absurd—especially since it is evident that those who speak about nature discuss the shapes of the sun and the moon, and in particular whether the earth and the cosmos are spherical or not. (*Ph.* 193$^b$22–30)

Finally, and perhaps most revealingly, the evidentiary basis of the *De Caelo* science is that of natural science:

> The result [of making natural bodies be composed of planes] is that people speaking about what appears to be so say things that are not in agreement with what appears to be so. And the cause of this is not correctly grasping the primary starting-points, but instead wishing to lead everything back to certain previously determined beliefs. For presumably the starting-points of perceptible things must be perceptible, of eternal ones eternal, of things capable of passing away things capable of passing away, and, in general, each must be of the same genus as what falls under it. But out of love for these beliefs of theirs they seem to do the same thing as those defending their theses in [dialectical] arguments; for they submit to every consequence on the supposition that they possess true starting-points, as if starting-points must not sometimes be judged on the basis of what follows from them, and most of all on the basis of their ends. And the end in the case of productive science is the work, and in that of natural science what appears to be so to perception has the controlling vote in every case. (*Cael.* 306$^a$5–17)

That is why it is "experience in astronomy" that must provide the starting-points of astronomical science (*APr.* 46$^a$19–20). It could hardly be clearer that however we are to conceive of the super-natural it cannot be as a realm entirely different in kind from the natural one. Super-nature, to put it this way, is a sort of nature, not a sort of something else. Similarly, in *GC* we are reminded that the discussion must be conducted *phusikôs*—in a way appropriate to natural science (316$^a$11, 335$^b$25)—and that perception is not something theory should overstep or disregard (325$^a$13–14), but should be in agreement with the pertinent arguments (336$^b$15–17). The lab, to be anachronistic, not the armchair, has pride of place, even if there is also much that can be done in that more cozy place: "We consider that we have

*Introduction*

adequately demonstrated in accord with reason things unapparent to perception if we have led things back to what is possible" (*Mete.* 344ᵃ5–7).

Now, if the various bodies, natural and super-natural, were the only substances, the only primary beings, the science of them would be the science that the *Metaphysics* proposes to investigate, which it refers to as theoretical wisdom, the science of being qua being, and as primary science or primary philosophy:

> That natural science is a theoretical science, then, is evident from these considerations. Mathematics too is a theoretical one, but whether its objects are immovable and separable is not now clear; however, it is clear that some parts of mathematics get a theoretical grasp on their objects insofar as they are immovable and insofar as they are separable. But if there is something that is eternal and immovable and separable, it is evident that knowledge of it belongs to a theoretical science—not, however, to natural science (for natural science is concerned with certain moveable things) nor to mathematics, but to something prior to both. For natural science is concerned with things that are inseparable but not immovable, while certain parts of mathematics are concerned with things that are immovable and not separable but as in matter. The primary science, by contrast, is concerned with things that are both separable and immovable. Now, all causes are necessarily eternal, and these most of all; for they are the causes of the divine beings that are perceptible.\*
> There must, then, be three theoretical philosophies, mathematical, natural, and theological; for it is not unclear that if the divine belongs anywhere, it belongs in a nature of this sort.\*\* And of these, the most estimable must be concerned with the most estimable genus. Thus, the theoretical are the more choiceworthy of the various sciences, and this of the theoretical. . . . If, then, there is no other substance beyond those composed by nature, natural science will be the primary science. But if there is some immovable substance, this [that is, theological philosophy] will be prior and will be primary philosophy. (*Met.* 1026ᵃ6–30)

That there is a substance that is eternal and immovable is argued for in *Physics* 8, and presupposed in *GC* 2.10, and that the gods, including in

---

\*These divine beings are the stars and heavenly bodies (*Cael.* 285ᵃ29–30, *Met.* 1072ᵃ26–30, 1073ᵃ23–ᵇ1), whose causes are their immovable movers (*Met.* 12.8).
\*\*The three theoretical philosophies are referred to as theoretical sciences at *Met.* 1064ᵇ1–3.

particular *the* god, are among them is presupposed from quite early on in the *Metaphysics*. Thus in *Met*. 1.2 we hear that theoretical wisdom is the science of this god, both in having him as its subject matter and in being the science that is in some sense *his* science. When it is argued in 12.9 that he must be "the active understanding [that] is active understanding of active understanding" (1074$^b$34–35), we see how much his it in fact is. For actively understanding itself—contemplating itself in an exercise of theoretical wisdom—is just what Aristotle's god *is*.

With just this much on the table there is already a puzzle whose difficulty is increased by special doctrine. Aristotle usually divides the bodies of knowledge he refers to as *epistêmai* ("sciences") into three types: theoretical, practical, and productive (crafts). When he is being especially careful, he also distinguishes within the theoretical sciences between the "strictly theoretical" ones (astronomy, theology), as we may call them, and the "natural" ones, which are like the strictly theoretical ones in being neither practical nor productive but unlike them in consisting of propositions that—though necessary and universal in some sense—hold for the most part rather than without exception:

> If all thought is either practical or productive or theoretical, natural science would have to be some sort of theoretical science—but a theoretical science that is concerned with such being as is capable of being moved and with the substance that in accord with its account holds for the most part only, because it is not separable. (*Met*. 1025$^b$25–28; compare *Ph*. 200$^a$30–$^b$9)

Psychology, as a result, has an interestingly mixed status, part strictly theoretical (because it deals with understanding, which is something divine), part natural (because it deals with perception and memory and other capacities that require a body):

> It is clear that the affections of the soul are enmattered accounts. So their definitions will be of this sort, for example: "Being angry is a sort of movement of such-and-such a sort of body, or of a part or a capacity, as a result of something for the sake of something." And that is why it already belongs to the natural scientist to get a theoretical grasp on the soul, either all soul or this sort of soul. . . . And aren't those things that are not actually separable, but are considered insofar as they are not affections of this sort of body and in abstraction from it, the concern of the mathematician? And insofar as they are actually separable, that of the primary philosopher? (*DA* 403$^a$25–$^b$16)

*Introduction*

Psychology has a theological dimension, then, as well as a more naturalistic biological or psychological one.

We are now in a position to say something further about the science of *De Caelo*. That it is not a work of strictly natural science, but rather of super-natural science, we know. That it is theoretical rather than productive or practical is plain. But what sort of theoretical science is it exactly? Insofar as it is a work of astronomy (or what we would probably call "cosmology"), we at least know where Aristotle himself puts it, since he refers to it as "the mathematical science that is most akin to philosophy" (*Met.* 1073$^b$4–5). Yet it is not a branch of pure mathematics, but rather something closer to what we would call "applied mathematics":

> Odd and even, straight and curved, and furthermore number, line, and figure will be without movement, whereas flesh, bone, and human will not, but rather all of them are said of things just as snub nose is and not as curved is. This is also clear from the more natural-science-like parts of mathematics, such as optics, harmonics, and astronomy; for these are in a way the reverse of geometry. For whereas geometry investigates natural lines, but not insofar as they are natural, optics investigates mathematical lines, but not insofar as they are mathematical. (*Ph.* 194$^a$3–12)*

A mathematical science, then, but a more natural-science-like one than a pure or abstract one.

At the same time, Aristotle tells us too that while we think about "the stars as bodies only, that is, as units having a certain order, altogether inanimate," we should in fact "conceive of them as participating in action and life" (*Cael.* 292$^a$18–21) and of their action itself as being "like that of animals and plants" (292$^b$1–2). And the complexity does not end there. For he also includes the primary heaven (the sphere of the fixed stars) among things that are divine:

> The activity of a god is immortality, and this is eternal living. So it is necessary that eternal movement belong to the god. And since the heaven is such (for it is a certain divine body), because of this it has a circular body that by nature always moves in a circle. (*Cael.* 286$^a$9–12)

---

*Also, in the *Metaphysics*: "Mathematical beings are without movement, except for those with which astronomy is concerned" (989$^b$32–33).

*Introduction*

Apparently, then, the science to which *De Caelo* contributes is at once a natural-science-like branch of mathematics, a biological science, and a theological one.

When science receives its focused discussion in the *Nicomachean Ethics*, however, Aristotle is explicit that if we are "to speak in an exact way and not be guided by mere similarities" (1139$^b$19), we should not call anything a "science" unless it deals with eternal, entirely exceptionless facts about universals that are wholly necessary and do not at all admit of being otherwise (1139$^b$20–21). Since he is here explicitly epitomizing his more detailed discussion of science in the *Posterior Analytics* (as 1139$^b$27 tells us), we should take the latter too as primarily a discussion of science in the exact sense, which it calls *epistêmê haplôs*—"unconditional scientific knowledge." It follows that only the strictly theoretical sciences are sciences in this sense. It is on these that the others should be modeled to the extent that they can be: "it is the things that are always in the same state and never undergo change that we must make our basis when pursuing the truth, and this is the sort of thing that the heavenly bodies are" (*Met.* 1063$^a$13–15).

Having made the acknowledgment, though, we must also register the fact that Aristotle himself mostly does not speak in the exact way but instead persistently refers to bodies of knowledge other than the strictly theoretical sciences as *epistêmai*. His division of the *epistêmai* into theoretical, practical, and productive is a dramatic case in point. But so too is his use of the term *epistêmê*, which we first encounter in the *Metaphysics* as a near synonym of *technê* or craft knowledge, which is productive not theoretical (981$^a$3), and in *GC* as concerned with coming to be and alteration and whether or not they are different (315$^b$15–19).

An Aristotelian science, although a state of the soul rather than a set of propositions in a textbook, nonetheless does involve an affirmational grasp of a set of true propositions (*NE* 1139$^b$14–16). Some of these propositions are indemonstrable starting-points or first principles (*archai*), which are or are expressed in definitions, and others are theorems demonstrable from these starting-points. We can have scientific knowledge only of the theorems, since—exactly speaking—only what is demonstrable can be scientifically known (*NE* 6.6). Yet—in what is clearly another lapse from exact speaking—Aristotle characterizes "the most exact of the sciences," which is theoretical wisdom (*sophia*), as also involving a grasp by understanding (*nous*) of the truth where the starting-points themselves are concerned (1141$^a$16–18). He does the same thing in the *Metaphysics*, where theoretical wisdom is the *epistêmê* that provides "a theoretical grasp of the primary starting-points and causes"—among which are included "the good or the for-the-sake-of-which" (982$^b$7–10). It is for this reason that the god's grasp of himself through understanding is an exercise of scientific knowledge.

Now, each of these sciences, regardless of what group it falls into, must—for reasons having to do with the nature of definition and demonstration—be restricted in scope to a single genus of beings (*APo.* 75$^b$10–11, 84$^b$17–18, 87$^a$38–39). Since being is not itself a genus (*APo.* 92$^b$14), as Aristotle goes out of his way not just to acknowledge but to prove (*Met.* 4.2), it apparently follows that there should be no such science as the science of being qua being—as theoretical wisdom. To show that there is one thus takes some work. By the same token, there should be no such science as natural science, but only a collection of distinct sciences, each focused exclusively on its own distinct genus of natural beings.

It is a cliché of the history of philosophy that Aristotle is an empiricist and Plato a rationalist, and like all clichés there is some truth in it. In fact, Aristotle is not just an empiricist at the level of the sciences we call "empirical," he is an empiricist at all levels. To see what I mean, think of each of the special, genus-specific sciences—the *first-order* sciences—as giving us a picture of a piece of the universe, a region of being. Then ask, What is the universe like that these sciences collectively portray? What is the nature of reality as a whole—of being as a whole? If there is no answer besides the collection of special answers, the universe is, as Aristotle puts it, episodic—like a bad tragedy (*Met.* 1076$^a$1, 1090$^b$20). But if there is an answer, it should emerge from a meta-level empirical investigation of the special sciences themselves. As each of these looks for universals (natural kinds) that stand in demonstrable causal relations to each other, so this meta-level investigation looks for higher-level universals that reveal the presence of common structures of explanation in diverse sciences:

> The causes and starting-points of distinct things are distinct in a way, but in a way—if we are to speak universally and analogically—they are the same for all. . . . For example, perhaps the elements of perceptible bodies are, as form, the hot and, in another way, the cold, which is the privation; and, as matter, what is potentially these directly and intrinsically. And both these and the things composed of them are substances, of which these are the starting-points, that is, anything that comes to be from the hot and the cold that is one [something-or-other], such as flesh or bone; for what comes to be from these must be distinct from them. These things, then, have the same elements and starting-points (although distinct things have distinct ones). But that all things have the same ones is not something we can say just like that, although *by analogy*

they do.* That is, we might say that there are three starting-points—the form, the privation, and the matter. But each of these is distinct for each category (*genos*)—for example, in color they are white, black, and surface, or light, darkness, and air, out of which day and night come to be. (*Met.* 1070ª31–ᵇ21)

The first-order sciences show the presence in the universe of a variety of different explanatory structures. The trans-generic sciences, by finding commonalities between these structures, show the equally robust presence there of the *same* explanatory structure: form, privation of form, matter. The universe is thus a universe of stratified stabilities.

The science to which form, privation of form, and matter belong is, in the first instance, trans-generic or universal natural science. It is the one that would be the primary science, as we saw, were there no eternal immovable substances separable from the natural ones. But there is also a trans-generic—or universal—mathematical science:

> We might raise a puzzle indeed as to whether the primary philosophy is universal or concerned with a particular genus and one particular nature; for it is not the same way even in the mathematical sciences but rather geometry and astronomy are concerned with a particular nature, whereas universal mathematics is common to all. (*Met.* 1026ª23–27)**

---

*Which is no obstacle at all to their providing a robust subject of scientific knowledge: (1) "Another way is to select by analogy. For it is impossible to take one identical thing that cuttlefish bone, fish spine, and animal bone must be called; but there will be things that follow these too, just as if there were some single nature of this sort" (*APo.* 98ª20–24). (2) "As for the underlying nature, it is scientifically knowable by analogy" (*Ph.* 191ª8–9).

**Many theorems in mathematics are special to some branch of it, such as arithmetic or geometry, but there are also "certain mathematical theorems of a universal character" (*Met.* 1077ª9–10). Here is an example: "That proportionals alternate might seem to apply to numbers insofar as they are numbers, lines insofar as they are lines, solids insofar as they are solids, and times insofar as they are times, as used at one time to be demonstrated of these separately, although it is possible, at any rate, to prove it of all cases by a single demonstration. But because all these things—numbers, lengths, times, solids—do not constitute a single named [genus] and differ in species from one another, they used to be taken separately. But now it is proved universally; for it did not belong insofar as they are lines, or insofar as they are numbers, but insofar as they are this [unnamed thing], which is assumed to belong universally" (*APo.* 74ª17–25). Nonetheless, the universality of the demonstration is open to challenge on the grounds that lines and numbers differ in genus. For "the extreme and middle terms must be from the same genus" (75ᵇ10–11), so that trans-generic demonstrations are ruled out: "it is impossible that what is proved should cross from one genus to another" (84ᵇ17–18). Hence "the why [that is, why the theorem about proportionals holds in the case of lines and of numbers] is different" (99ª8–9), and

## Introduction

The introduction of intelligible matter (*Met.* 1036ᵃ11-12), as the matter of abstract mathematical objects, allows us to see a commonality in explanatory structure between the mathematical sciences and the natural ones. Between these two trans-generic sciences and the theological one (1026ᵃ19), on the other hand, the point of commonality lies not in matter, since the objects of theological science have no matter (1071ᵇ20-21), but rather in form. For what the objects of theology, namely, divine substances (which include human understanding or *nous*), have in common with those of mathematics and natural science is that they are forms, though— and this is the crucial point of difference—not forms in any sort of matter whatever. That form should be a focal topic of investigation for the science of being qua being, is thus the result of an inductive or empirical investigation of the various first-order sciences, and then of the various trans-generic ones, which shows form to be the explanatory feature common to all their objects—to all beings.

It is a nice question, but one now within reach of an answer, as to how the science of *De Caelo* is to be incorporated into this uniform explanatory structure. But it is perhaps enough to notice that its objects of study are matter-form compounds, like those of natural science, but with this one difference: their matter is primary body (ether) rather than earth, water, fire, and air in some combination or other. And because the difference this makes is that astronomical objects, though in many cases animate beings, are amenable to being studied by an applied mathematical science, it must be that primary body is relevantly similar to intelligible matter. It must be like it in not deforming geometrical shapes, unlike it in being concrete rather than abstract: a sphere made of earth (say) cannot be a perfect sphere; a sphere made of primary body can. Result: the heavenly bodies are perfect or exact models of geometrical theorems, while sublunary bodies are no better than imperfect ones. Hence the need to take account of the

---

so separate demonstrations seem to be needed in the case of each. Nonetheless, "insofar as admitting of a certain sort of increase in quantity" (99ᵃ9-10) the demonstration is the same, so that the theorem "holds in common of all quantities" (*Met.* 1061ᵇ19-21). For "the genera of the beings are distinct, and some things belong to quantities alone and others to qualities, and it is with the help of these that a proof is given through the common things" (*APo.* 88ᵇ1-3). But though the universal theorem holds of all quantities, it does so *by analogy*: "Of the things used in the demonstrative sciences, some are proper to each science while others are common, but common by analogy, since something is useful, in fact, [only] to the extent that it functions in the genus that falls under the science: proper ones—for example, that a line is such-and-such and straight such-and-such; common ones—for example, that if equals are subtracted from equals, the remainders are equal" (76ᵃ37-41). Thus the kind to which lines, numbers, and so on belong, which is the ontological correlate of a theorem of universal mathematics, is not a first-order genus, but an analogical unity—a quantity.

margin of error. Thus super-natural science of the *De Caelo* variety enters the uniform explanatory structure required for the existence of the science of being qua being, by doors already opened by natural and mathematical science.

It is all this that provides the science of being qua being with a genuine trans-generic object of study, thereby legitimating it as every bit as much a science as any first-order or universal one. The science of being qua being is accordingly a science of form. The question now is how can that science at the same time be theology, the science of divine substance? And to it, as we have seen more than once, Aristotle gives a succinct answer:

> If there is some immovable substance, this [that is, theological philosophy] will be prior and will be primary philosophy, and it will be universal in this way, namely, because it is primary. And it will belong to it to get a theoretical grasp on being qua being, both what it is and the things that belong to it qua being. (*Met.* 1026$^a$29–32)

So the primacy of theology, which is based on the fact that theology deals with substance that is eternal, immovable, and separable, is supposedly what justifies us in treating it as the universal science of being qua being.

To get a handle on what this primacy is, we need to turn to being and its structure. The first thing to grasp is that beings are divided into categories: substance, quality, quantity, relation, and so on (*Top.* 103$^b$7–25). But of these, only beings in the category of substance are separable, so that they alone enjoy a sort of ontological priority that is both existential and explanatory (316$^b$3n42). Other beings are affections of different sorts, which exist only by belonging to some substance. So if we want to explain what a quality is, for example, we have to say what sort of affection it is and ultimately what in a substance is receptive of it. It is this fact that gives one sort of unity to beings: they are all either substances or affections of substances. Hence the famous claim:

> Indeed, the question that was asked long ago, is now, and always will be asked, and is always raising puzzles—namely, What is being?—is just the question, What is substance? ... And that is why we too must most of all, primarily, and (one might almost say) exclusively get a theoretical grasp on what it is that is a being in this [substantial] way. (*Met.* 1028$^b$2–7)

The starting-points and causes of beings qua beings, then, must be substances. Thus while something is said to *be* in as many ways as there are

## Introduction

categories, they are all so said "with reference to one thing and one nature" (*Met.* 1003ᵃ33–34)—substance. It could still be the case, of course, that the universe is episodic like a bad tragedy, made up of lots of separate substances having little ontologically to do with each other, but the number of episodes has at least been systematically reduced.

Before turning to the next phase in being's unification, we need to look more closely at substance itself as it gets investigated and analyzed in *Met.* 7–9. The analysis begins with something quite widely accepted:

> Something is said to be (*legetai*) substance, if not in more ways, at any rate most of all in four; for the essence, the universal, and the genus seem to be the substance of each thing, and fourth of these, the underlying subject. (*Met.* 1028ᵇ33–36)

Since "the primary underlying subject seems most of all to be substance" (*Met.* 1029ᵃ1–2), because what is said or predicated of it depends on it, the investigation begins with this subject, quickly isolating three candidates: the matter, the compound of matter and form, and the form itself (1029ᵃ2–3), which is identical to the essence (1032ᵇ1–2). Almost as quickly (1029ᵃ7–32), the first two candidates are at least provisionally excluded, leaving form alone as the most promising candidate for being substance. But form is "most puzzling" (1029ᵃ33) and requires extraordinary ingenuity and resources to explore.

Aristotle begins the investigation into it with the most familiar and widely recognized case, which is the form or essence present in sublunary matter-form compounds. This investigation is announced in *Met.* 7.3 (1029ᵇ3–12), but not begun till some chapters later and not really completed till the end of 9.5. By then the various other candidates for being substance have been eliminated or reconceived, and actuality and potentiality have come to prominence. Hence in 9.6 it is with actuality or activity—*entelecheia* or *energeia* (*GC* 316ᵇ21n49)—that form, and so substance, is identified, and matter with potentiality.

Precisely because actuality and potentiality are the ultimate explanatory factors, however, they themselves cannot be given an explanatory definition in yet more basic terms. Instead we must grasp them by means of an analogy:

> What we wish to say is clear from the particular cases by induction, and we must not look for a definition of everything, but be able to comprehend the analogy, namely, that it is as what is building is in relation to what is capable of building, and what is awake is in relation to what is asleep, and what is seeing is in

> relation to what has its eyes closed but has sight, and what has been shaped out of the matter is in relation to the matter, and what has been finished off is to the unfinished. Of the difference exemplified in this analogy let the activity be marked off by the first part, the potentiality by the second. (*Met.* 1048ᵃ35–ᵇ6)

What is common to matter-form compounds, mathematical objects, and divine substances, then, is actuality. In the case of matter-form compounds and numbers, the actuality is accompanied by potentiality—perceptual sublunary matter in the first case, intelligible matter in the second. In the case of divine substances and other such unmoved movers, it is not. They are "pure" activities or actualities, wholly actual at each moment. Matter-form compounds, by contrast, are never wholly actual—they are always in some way potential. You are actually reading this now, not actually swimming, but you could be swimming, since you have the presently un-actualized capacity (or potential) to swim.

The science of being qua being, can legitimately focus on form, or actuality, as the factor common to divine substances, matter-form compounds, and mathematical objects. But unless it can be shown that there is some explanatory connection between the forms in these different beings, the non-episodic nature of being itself will still not have been established, and the pictures given to us by the natural, mathematical, and theological sciences will, so to speak, be separate pictures, and the being they collectively portray, divided. We notice fairly quickly how important actuality and potentiality are in *GC*, since these play a crucial role in explaining each of its focal topics: affecting and being affected (326ᵇ31), elemental transformation (334ᵇ9), growth (322ᵃ6), mixing (327ᵇ23), and unconditional coming to be and passing away (317ᵇ24).

The next stage in the unification of being, and the legitimation of the science dealing with it qua being, is effected by an argument that trades, unsurprisingly, on the identification of form and matter with actuality and potentiality. Part of the argument is given in *Met.* 9.8–9, where the various sorts of priority requisite in a substance are argued to belong to actuality rather than potentiality. But it is in *Met.* 12.6 that the pertinent consequences are most decisively drawn:

> If there is something that is capable of moving things or acting on them, but that is not actively doing so, there will not [necessarily] be movement, since it is possible for what has a capacity not to activate it. There is no benefit, therefore, in positing eternal substances, as those who accept the Forms do, unless there is to be present in them some starting-point that is capable of

> causing change. Moreover, even this is not enough, and neither is another substance beyond the Forms. For if it will not be active, there will not be movement. Further, even if it will be active, it is not enough, if the substance of it is a capacity; for then there will not be eternal movement; for what is potentially may possibly not be. There must, therefore, be such a starting-point, the very substance of which is activity. Further, accordingly, these substances must be without matter; for they must be eternal, if indeed anything else is eternal. Therefore, they must be activity. (*Met.* 1071$^b$12–22)

Matter-form compounds are, as such, capable of movement and change. The canonical examples of them—perhaps the only genuine or fully fledged ones—are living metabolizing beings (*Met.* 1041$^b$29–30). But if these beings are to be actual, there must be substances whose very essence is activity—substances that do not need to be activated by something else.

With matter-form compounds shown to be dependent on substantial activities for their actual being, a further element of vertical unification is introduced into beings, since layer-wise the two sorts of substances belong together. Laterally, though, disunity continues to threaten. For as yet nothing has been done to exclude the possibility that each compound substance has a distinct substantial activity as its own unique activator. Being, in that case, would be a set of ordered pairs, the first member of which was a substantial activity, the second a matter-form compound, with all its dependent affections.

In *Metaphysics* 12.8 Aristotle initially takes a step in the direction of such a bipartite picture. He asks how many substantial activities are required to explain astronomical phenomena, such as the movements of the stars and planets, and answers that there must be forty-nine of them (1074$^a$16). But these forty-nine are visibly coordinated with each other in such a way as to form a system. And what enables them to do so, and constitute a single heaven, is that there is a single prime mover of all of them:

> And that there is but one heaven is evident. For if there are many, as there are many humans, the starting-point for each will be one in form but in number many. But all things that are many in number have matter, for one and the same account applies to many, for example, humans, whereas Socrates is one. But the primary essence does not have matter; for it is an actuality. The primary immovable mover, therefore, is one both in account and in number. And so, therefore, is what is moved always and continuously. Therefore, there is only one heaven. (*Met.* 1074$^a$31–38; also *Cael.* 1.8)

The argument is puzzling, to be sure, since the immateriality that ensures the uniqueness of the prime mover would seem to threaten the multiplicity of the forty-nine movers, since they are also immaterial, nonetheless the point of it is clear enough: what accounts for the unity of the heaven is that the movements in it are traceable back to a single cause—the prime or primary mover.

Leaving aside the question of just how this primary mover moves what it moves directly, which is left unanswered (as not belonging to natural science) in the *Physics*, *De Caelo*, and *GC* but discussed in *Met.* 12.7, the next phase in the unification of beings is the one in which the sublunary world is integrated with the already unified superlunary one studied by astronomy. This takes place in *Met.* 12.10, although elements of it have emerged earlier. One obvious indication of this unification is the dependence of the reproductive cycles of plants and animals on the seasons, and their dependence, in turn, on the movements of the sun and moon:

> The cause of a human is both his elements, fire and earth as matter and the special form [as form], and furthermore some other external thing, such as the father, and beyond these the sun and its movement in an inclined circle. (*Met.* 1071$^a$13–16; also *GC* 2.10)

And beyond even that there is the unity of the natural world itself, which is manifested in the ways in which its inhabitants are adapted to each other:

> All things are jointly organized in a way, although not in the same way—even swimming creatures, flying creatures, and plants. And the organization is not such that one thing has no relation to another, but rather there is a relation. For all things are jointly organized in relation to one thing—but it is as in a household, where the free people least of all do things at random, but all or most of the things they do are organized, while the slaves and beasts can do a little for the common thing, but mostly do things at random; for this is the sort of starting-point that the nature is of each of them. I mean, for example, that all must at least come to be disaggregated [into their elements]; and similarly there are other things which they all share for the whole. (*Met.* 1075$^a$16–25)

Just how much unity all this results in—just what it means to speak of "the nature of the whole" (*Met.* 1075$^a$11) or of the universe as having "one ruler" (1076$^a$4)—is a matter of dispute. The fact remains, though, that the

### Introduction

sublunary realm is sufficiently integrated with the superlunary one that we can speak of them as jointly having a nature and a ruler, and as being analogous not to Heraclitus' "heap of random sweepings" (DK B24), but to an army (1075$^a$13) and a household (1075$^a$22). *Mete.* 1.1 begins, indeed, by describing how, at any rate, the natural sciences are integrated into a single body of knowledge.

We may agree, then, that the divine substances in the superlunary realm and the compound substances in the sublunary one have prima facie been vertically integrated into a single explanatory system. When we look at the form of a sublunary matter-form compound, then, we will find in it the mark of a superlunary activator, just as we do in the case of the various heavenly bodies, and, as in the line of its efficient causes, we find "the sun and its movement in an inclined circle" (*Met.* 1071$^a$15–16). Still awaiting integration, though, are the mathematical objects, and their next of kin, Platonic Forms.

That there is mathematical structure present in the universe can seem to be especially clear in the case of the superlunary realm, just as mathematics itself, with its rigorous proofs and necessary and certain truths, can seem the very paradigm of scientific knowledge. So it is hardly surprising that some of Aristotle's predecessors, especially Pythagoreans and Platonists, thought that the primary causes and starting-points of beings are to be found in the part of reality that is mathematics friendly, or in some way mathematizable. For example, some Platonists (Plato among them, in Aristotle's much disputed view) held that for each kind of sublunary (or perceptible) thing, there was an eternal intelligible Form or Idea to which it owed its being, and which owed its own being, in turn, to "the one," as its substance, and the so-called indefinite dyad of the great and the small, as its matter. So when we ask what makes a man a man, the answer will be, because it participates in the Form or Idea of a man, which owes its being to the way it is constructed or generated from the indefinite dyad and the one (*Ph.* 209$^b$7–16, 209$^b$33–210$^a$2). And because the Forms are so constructed, Aristotle says (anyway on one reading of the text) that "the Forms are the numbers" (*Met.* 987$^b$20–22). Between these so-called Form (or Ideal) numbers, in addition, are the numbers that are the objects of mathematics: the intermediates. This elaborate system of, as I put it, mathematics-friendly objects, then, are the substances—the ultimate starting-points and causes of beings qua beings.

Against these objects and the ontological role assigned to them, Aristotle launches a host of arguments (thirty-two or so in *Met.* 1.9, twenty-four in 13.8–9, and many others elsewhere), proposing in their place an entirely different account of mathematical objects, which treats them not as substantial starting-points and causes but as abstractions from perceptible sublunary beings—dependent entities, in other words, rather that self-subsistent or intrinsic ones:

> The mathematician too busies himself about these things [planes, solids, lines, and points], although not insofar as each of them is the limit of a natural body, nor does he get a theoretical grasp on the coincidents of natural bodies insofar as they are such. That is why he separates them; for they are separable in the understanding from movement, and so their being separated makes no difference, nor does any falsehood result from it. (*Ph.* 193$^{b}$31–35)

This completes the vertical and horizontal unification of being: affections depend on substances, substantial matter-form compounds depend on substantial forms, or activities, numbers depend on matter-form compounds.

Beings are not said to be "in accord with one thing," then, as they would be if they formed a single genus, but "with reference to one thing"—namely, a divine substance that is in essence an activity. And it is this more complex unity, compatible with generic diversity, and a genuine multiplicity of distinct first-order sciences, but just as robust and well-grounded as the simpler genus-based sort of unity, that grounds and legitimates the science of being qua being as a single science dealing with a genuine object of study (*Met.* 1003$^{b}$11–16). The long argument that leads to this conclusion is thus a sort of existence proof of the science on which the *Metaphysics* focuses.

It is the priority of a divine substance within that science that justifies the description, which we looked at on a few earlier occasions, of what the *Metaphysics* is about:

> If, then, there is no other substance beyond those composed by nature, natural science will be the primary science. But if there is some immovable substance, this [that is, theological philosophy] will be prior and will be primary philosophy, and it will be universal in this way, namely, because it is primary. And it will belong to it to get a theoretical grasp on being qua being, both what it is and the things that belong to it qua being. (*Met.* 1026$^{a}$27–32)

The science of being qua being is a sort of theology, as *Met.* 1.2 already told us it was, but it is a sort of theology only because of the special role of the primary god among beings.

*Introduction*

## Is the Investigation in GC and Mete. a Scientific One?

If we think of a science in the exact sense as consisting exclusively of what is demonstrable, as we saw Aristotle himself sometimes does, we will be right to conclude that a treatise without demonstrations cannot be scientific. But if, as he also does, we include knowledge of starting-points as part of science, we will not be right, since a treatise could contribute to a science not by demonstrating anything but by arguing to the starting-points themselves—an enterprise which could not without circularity consist of demonstrations from those starting-points. Arguments leading *from* starting-points and arguments leading *to* starting-points are different, we are invited not to forget (*NE* 1095ª30–32), just as we are told that because establishing starting-points is "more than half the whole" (1098ᵇ7), we should "make very serious efforts to define them correctly" (1098ᵇ5–6). We might reasonably infer, therefore, that *GC* and *Mete.* are contributions to natural science, at least in part by establishing the correct definition of some of its starting-points. And unconditional coming to be (*GC* 1.3), and its material, formal, final, and efficient causes (2.9–10), alteration (1.4), growth and withering (1.5), contact (1.6), affecting and being affected (1.7–9), mixing (1.10), the elements, their transformation and capacities (2.1–8), putrefaction (*Mete.* 4.1), and concoction (4.2), all certainly seem to be scientific starting-points of some sort.

Now, in our investigation of starting-points, "we must," Aristotle says, "start from things known to us" (*NE* 1095ᵇ3–4). For the sake of clarity, let us call these "raw" starting-points. These are the ones we start from when we are arguing to explanatory scientific starting-points. It is important not to confuse the two. In the case of the special sciences, the explanatory starting-points include, in particular, definitions that specify the genus and differentiae of the real (as opposed to nominal) universal essences of the beings with which the science deals (*APo.* 93ᵇ29–94ª19). Since scientific definitions must be apt starting-points of demonstrations, this implies, Aristotle thinks, that the "extremes and the middle terms must come from the same genus" (75ᵇ10–11). As a result a single canonical science must deal with a single genus (87ª38–39). To reach these definitions from raw starting-points, we first have to have the raw starting-points at hand. Aristotle is clear about this, as he is indeed about what is supposed to happen next:

> The method (*hodos*) is the same in all cases, in philosophy as well as in the crafts or any sort of learning whatever. For one must observe for both terms what belongs to them and what

> they belong to, and be supplied with as many of these terms as possible, and one must investigate them by means of the three terms [in a syllogism], in one way when refuting, in another way when establishing something. When it is in accord with truth, it must be from the terms that are cataloged as truly belonging, but in dialectical deductions it must be from premises that are in accord with [reputable] belief. . . . Most of the starting-points, however, are special to each science. That is why experience must provide us with the starting-points where each is concerned—I mean, for example, that experience in astronomy must do so in the case of astronomical science. For when the things that appear to be so had been adequately grasped, the demonstrations in astronomy were found in the way we described. And it is the same way where any other craft or science whatever is concerned. Hence if what belongs to each thing has been grasped, at that point we can readily exhibit the demonstrations. For if nothing that truly belongs to the relevant things has been omitted from the collection, then concerning everything, if a demonstration of it exists we will be able to find it and give the demonstration, and if it is by nature indemonstrable, we will be able to make that evident. (*APr.* 46$^a$3–27)

Once we have a catalog of the raw starting-points, then, the demonstrative explanation of them from explanatory scientific starting-points is supposedly fairly routine—at least, methodologically speaking. We should not, however, demand "the cause [or explanation] in all cases alike. Rather, in some it will be adequate if the fact that they are so has been correctly proved as it is indeed where starting-points are concerned" (*NE* 1098$^a$33–$^b$2). But what exactly is it to prove a starting-point correctly or adequately?

The science of *GC* and *Mete.*, as we saw, is a branch of theoretical natural science or natural philosophy, and to the explanatory scientific starting-points of philosophical sciences, he claims, there is a unique route:

> [Dialectic] is useful in the philosophical sciences because the capacity to go through the puzzles on both sides of a question will make it easier to judge what is true and what is false in each. Furthermore, dialectic is useful in relation to the primary [starting-points] in each science. For it is impossible to say anything about these based on the starting-points properly belonging to the science in question, since these starting-points are, of all of them, the primary ones, and it is through reputable

## Introduction

> beliefs (*endoxa*) about each that it is necessary to discuss them. And this is a task that is special to, or, at any rate, characteristic of, dialectic, which, because of its capacity to stand outside and examine, provides a route toward the starting-points of all methodical inquiries. (*Top.* 101$^a$34–$^b$4)

And this is repeated almost word for word in the *Physics* with reference to the concept of place, which is a natural scientific starting-point:

> We must try to make our investigation in such a way that the what-it-is is given an account of, so that the puzzles are resolved, the things that are believed to belong to place will in fact belong to it, and furthermore, so that the cause of the difficulty and of the puzzles concerning it will be evident, since this is the best way of proving each thing. (*Ph.* 211$^a$7–11)

Prima facie, then, *GC* and *Mete.* should correctly prove explanatory starting-points by going through puzzles and solving these by appeal to reputable beliefs and perceptual evidence. But before we rush off to see whether that is what we do find, we need to be clearer about what exactly we should be looking for.

Dialectic is recognizably a descendant of the Socratic elenchus, which famously begins with a question like this: *Ti esti to agathon?* What is the good? The respondent, sometimes after a bit of nudging, comes up with a universal definition, what is good is what the gods love, or whatever it might be (I adapt a well-known answer from Plato's *Euthyphro*). Socrates then puts this definition to the test by drawing attention to some things that seem true to the respondent himself but which conflict with his definition. The puzzle or *aporia* that results from this conflict then remains for the respondent to try to solve, usually by reformulating or rejecting his definition. Aristotle understood this process in terms that show its relationship to his own:

> Socrates, on the other hand, busied himself about the virtues of character, and in connection with them was the first to inquire about universal definition. . . . It was reasonable, though, that Socrates was inquiring about the what-it-is; for he was inquiring in order to deduce, and the what-it-is is a starting-point of deductions; for at that time there was not yet the strength in dialectic that enables people, and separately from the what-it-is, to investigate contraries, and whether the same science is a science of contraries; for there are two things

that may be fairly ascribed to Socrates—inductive arguments and universal definition, both of which are concerned with a starting-point of scientific knowledge. (*Met.* 1078$^b$17–30; also 987$^b$1–4)

In Plato too dialectic is primarily concerned with scientific starting-points, such as those of mathematics, and seems to consist in some sort of elenchus-like process of reformulating definitions in the face of conflicting evidence so as to render them puzzle-free (*Rep.* 532a–533d). Aristotle can reasonably be seen, then, as continuing a line of thought about dialectic, while contributing greatly to its exploration, systemization, and elaboration in works such as *Topics* and *Sophistical Refutations*.

Consider now the respondent's first answer, his first definition: what is good is what the gods love. Although it is soon shown to be incorrect, there is something quite remarkable about its very existence. Through experience shaped by acculturation and habituation involving the learning of a natural language the respondent is confident that he can say what goodness is. He has learned to apply the word "good" to particular people, actions, and so on correctly enough to pass muster as knowing its meaning, knowing how to use it. From these particular cases he has reached a putative universal, something the particular cases have in common. But when he tries to define that universal in words, he gets it wrong, as Socrates shows. Here is Aristotle registering the significance of this:

> The things that are known and primary for particular groups of people are often only slightly known and have little or nothing of the being in them. Nonetheless, beginning from things that are poorly knowable but knowable to ourselves, we must try to know the ones that are wholly knowable, proceeding, as has just been said, through the former. (*Met.* 1029$^b$8–12)

The route by which the respondent reaches the universal that he is unable to define correctly is what Aristotle calls "induction (*epagôgê*)." This begins with (1) perception of particulars, which leads to (2) retention of perceptual contents in memory, and, when many such contents have been retained, to (3) an experience, so that for the first time "there is a universal in the soul" (*APo.* 100$^a$3–16). The universal reached at stage (3), which is the one the respondent reaches, is described as "rather confused" and "better known by perception" (*Ph.* 184$^a$22–25). It is the sort of universal, often quite complex, that constitutes a nominal essence corresponding to the nominal definition or meaning of a general term. Finally, (4) from experience comes craft knowledge and scientific knowledge, when "from

*Introduction*

many intelligible objects arising from experience one universal supposition about similar objects is produced" (*Met.* 981ᵃ5–7).*

The nominal (or analytic, meaning-based) definition of the general term "thunder," for example, might pick out the universal *loud noise in the clouds*. When science investigates the things that have this nominal essence, it may find that they also have a real essence or nature in terms of which their other features can be scientifically explained:

> Since a definition is said to be an account of what something is, it is evident that one sort will be an account of what its name, or some other name-like account, signifies—for example, what triangle signifies. . . . One definition, then, of definition is the one just stated, but another is that a definition is an account that makes clear why the thing is. So the former one signifies, but does not prove, whereas it is evident that the latter will be like a demonstration of the what-it-is, differing from a demonstration in arrangement. For there is a difference between saying why it thunders and what thunder is. For in the first case one says "because the fire in the clouds is extinguished." But what is thunder? "The noise of fire in the clouds being extinguished." So the same account is said in another way, and in one way it is a continuous demonstration, while in the other way it is a definition. (The definition of thunder is also "noise in the clouds"; this is the conclusion of the demonstration of its what-it-is.) The definition of immediate things is the indemonstrable positing of their what-it-is. (*APo.* 93ᵇ29–94ᵃ10; compare *DA* 413ᵃ13–20)

A real (or synthetic, fact-based) definition, which analyzes this real essence into its "elements and starting-points" (*Ph.* 184ᵃ23), which will be definable but indemonstrable within the science, makes intrinsically clear what the nominal definition made clear only by enabling us to recognize instances of thunder in a fairly—but imperfectly—reliable way. As a result, thunder itself, now clearly a natural and not just a conventional kind, becomes

---

*Compare: "Unconditionally, what is prior is better known than what is posterior—for example, a point than a line, a line than a plane, and a plane than a solid, just as a unit is more so than a number, since it is prior to and a starting-point of all number. Similarly, a letter is more so than a syllable. To us, on the other hand, it sometimes happens that the reverse is the case; for the solid falls most under perception, the plane more than the line, line more than point; for ordinary people know things of the former sort earlier; for to learn them is a task for random thought, whereas to learn the others is a task for exact and extraordinary thought" (*Top.* 141ᵇ5–14).

better known not just to us but entirely or unconditionally. These analyzed universals, which are the sort reached at stage (4), are the ones suited to serve as starting-points of the sciences and crafts: "experienced people know the that but do not know the why, whereas craftsmen know the why, that is, the cause" (*Met.* 981ª28–30).

Socrates too, we see, wanted definitions that were not just empirically adequate but also explanatory: in telling Euthyphro what he wants in the case of piety, he says that he is seeking "the form itself *due to which* all the pieties are pieties" (*Euthphr.* 6d). That is why he rejects the definition of piety as being what all the gods love. This definition is in one way correct, presumably, in that if something is pious it must be loved by the gods and vice versa, but it is not explanatory, since it does not tell us what it is about pious things that makes all the gods love them, and so does not identify the form in virtue of which they are pious (9e–11b).

Let us go back. We wanted to know what was involved in proving a scientific starting-point. We were told how we could *not* do this, namely, by demonstrating it from scientific starting-points. Next we learned that dialectic had a route to it from reputable beliefs. At the same time, we were told that induction had a route to it as well—something the *Nicomachean Ethics* also tells us: "we get a theoretical grasp of some starting-points through induction, some through perception, some through some sort of habituation, and others through other means" (1098ᵇ3–4). This suggests that induction and dialectic are in some way or other related processes.

What shows a Socratic respondent to be wrong is an example that his definition does not fit. The presentation of the example might be quite indirect, however. It might take quite a bit of stage setting, elicited by the asking of many questions, to bring out a puzzle. But if it does succeed in doing so, it shows that the universal grasped by the respondent and the definition of it produced by him are not entirely or unconditionally known and that his state is not one of clear-eyed understanding:

> A puzzle in thought indicates the existence of a knot in the subject matter; for insofar as thought is puzzled it is like people who are tied up; for in both cases it is impossible to move forward. That is why we must get a theoretical grasp on all the difficulties beforehand, both for these reasons and because those who inquire without first going through the puzzles are like people who do not know where they have to go. And, in addition, a person [who has not already grasped the puzzles] does not even know whether he has found what he is inquiring about; for to someone like that the end is not clear, whereas to a person who has already grasped the puzzles it is clear. (*Met.* 995ª30–ᵇ2)

## Introduction

But lack of such clear-eyed understanding of a scientific starting-point has serious downstream consequences:

> Anyone who, on the other hand, is going to have scientific knowledge through demonstration must not only know the starting-points more and be more persuaded of them than of what is being proved, but also nothing else must be more persuasive or more known to him among the opposites of the starting-points from which there will be a deduction of the contrary error, if indeed someone who has unconditional scientific knowledge must be incapable of being persuaded out of it. (*APo.* 72$^a$37–$^b$4)

If dialectical examination brings to light a puzzle in a respondent's thought about a scientific starting-point, then, he cannot have any unconditional scientific knowledge even of what he may well be able to demonstrate correctly from it. Contrariwise, if dialectical examination brings to light no such puzzle, he apparently does have clear-eyed understanding, and his route to what he can demonstrate is free of obstacles.

At the heart of dialectic, as Aristotle understands it, is the dialectical deduction. This is the argument lying behind the questioner's questions, partly dictating their order and content and partly determining the strategy of his examination. In the following passage it is defined and contrasted with two relevant others:

> Dialectical [arguments] are those that deduce from reputable beliefs in a way that reaches a contradiction; examinational ones are those that do so from things that seem so to the answerer and that it is necessary for the one who pretends to possess the relevant science to know . . .; contentious ones (*eristikos*) are those that deduce or appear to deduce one from what appear to be reputable beliefs, but are not. (*SE* 165$^b$3–8)

If we think of dialectical deductions in this way, a dialectician, in contrast to a contender, is an honest questioner, appealing to genuinely reputable beliefs and employing valid deductions. "The arguments of disputatious people and sophists are the same," Aristotle says, "but are not for the sake of the same things: rather, if it is for apparent victory, it is contentious, if for apparent wisdom, it is sophistical; for in fact sophistry is a sort of appearance of wisdom without the reality" (*SE* 171$^b$29–34). Nonetheless, he does also use the term *dialektikê* as the name for the craft that honest dialecticians and sophists both use: "In dialectic a sophist is so called in virtue of his deliberate choice, and a dialectician is so called not in virtue of his deliberate choice, but in virtue of the capacity he has" (*Rh.* 1355ᵇ20–21). If dialectic is understood in this way, a dialectician who deliberately chooses to employ contentious arguments is a sophist (1355ᵃ24–ᵇ7).* We need to be careful, therefore, to distinguish honest dialectic from what we may call "plain" dialectic, which—like all crafts—can be used for good or ill (*NE* 1129ᵃ13–17).

The canonical occasion for the practice of the Socratic elenchus is, of course, the examination of someone else. But there is nothing to prevent a person from practicing it on himself: "How could you think," Socrates asks Critias, "that I would refute you for any reason other than the one for which I would refute myself, fearing lest I might inadvertently think I know something when I don't know it?" (*Chrm.* 166c–d). Dialectic is no different in this regard:

> But the philosopher, who is investigating by himself, does not care whether, though the things through which his deduction proceeds are true and known, the answerer does not concede them, because they are close to what was proposed at the start, and he foresees what is going to result, but rather is presumably eager for his claims to be as known and as close to it as possible; for it is from things of this sort that scientific deductions proceed. (*Top.* 155ᵇ10–16; compare *Ph.* 263ᵃ15–23)

> An investigation with another is through words, whereas one by oneself is no less through the thing at issue itself. (*SE* 169ᵃ38–40)

What we are to imagine, then, is that the philosopher surveys the raw scientific starting-points, constructing detailed catalogs of these. He then tries to formulate definitions of the various universals involved in them that seem to be candidate scientific starting-points, testing these against the raw scientific starting-points by trying to construct demonstrations from them. But these definitions will often be no more than partial: the philosopher is only on his way to complete definitional starting-points, just as the demonstrations will often be no more than proto- or nascent demonstrations. The often rudimentary demonstrations that we find in Aristotle's scientific treatises are surely parts of this process of arguing *to* not *from* starting-points.

---

*Compare: "There are some things that cannot be put in only one genus—for example, the cheat and the slanderer; for neither the one with the deliberate choice to do it but without the capacity, nor the one with the capacity but not the deliberate choice, is a slanderer or a cheat, but rather the one with both" (*Top.* 126ᵇ8–11).

*Introduction*

We argue to these in part by seeing whether or to what extent we could demonstrate from them. There are many such arguments in *GC* and *Mete.*: but they are typically arguments that prove, not arguments that demonstrate. (The verb *apodechesthai* occurs just once in *GC* at 333$^b$35, and just once in *Mete.* at 344$^a$6, in neither case referring to something accomplished in the work itself.) But it is clear that we must not overwork the distinction:

> It is no less possible to state a deduction or an enthymeme based on it about matters of justice than it is about matters of natural science, or about anything else whatever, even though these things differ in species. Special [topics], on the other hand, are the ones based on premises concerning a given species and genus. For example, there are premises concerning natural things on which neither an enthymeme nor a deduction can be based concerning ethical things, and about the latter there are others on which none can be based concerning natural ones. And the same holds in all cases. The common ones will not make someone wise about any genus, since they are not concerned with any underlying subject. But as to the special ones, the better someone is at selecting premises,* [the more] he will without noticing it produce a science that is distinct from dialectic and rhetoric; for if he hits upon starting-points, it will no longer be dialectic or rhetoric, but instead will be that science whose starting-points he possesses. (*Rh.* 1358$^a$14–26).

The two instances (and there are only two) in *De Caelo* where Aristotle refers to something he has proved (or takes himself to have proved) as something that has been demonstrated, namely, 269$^b$18 (*apodedeiktai*) and 273$^b$24 (*apodeixin*), are probably best seen in this light.

So: First, we have the important distinction between dialectic proper, which includes the use of what appear to be deductions from what appear to be reputable beliefs, and honest dialectic, which uses only genuine deductions from genuine reputable beliefs. Second, we have the equally

---

*Compare: "Unconditionally, then, it is better to try to make what is posterior known through what is prior. For proceeding in this way is more scientific. Nevertheless, in relation to those who cannot know through things of the latter sort, it is presumably necessary to produce the account through things known to them. . . . One must not fail to notice, however, that it is not possible for those who define in this way to make clear the essence of the thing defined, unless it so happens that the same thing is better known both to us and also unconditionally better known, if indeed a correct definition must define through the genus and the differentiae, and these are among the things that are unconditionally better known than the species and prior to it" (*Top.* 141$^b$15–28).

important distinction between the use of dialectic in examining a potentially hostile respondent and its use by the philosopher in a perhaps private pursuit of the truth. Third, we have an important contrast between honest dialectical premises and philosophical ones or scientific ones: honest dialectical premises are reputable beliefs, philosophical and scientific premises must be true and known. Fourth, we have two apparently equivalent routes to scientific starting-points, one inductive, which starts from raw starting-points, and the other dialectic, which starts from reputable beliefs.

According to the official definition, reputable beliefs are "things that are believed by everyone, by the majority, or by the wise—either by all of them, or by most, or by the most well known and most reputable" (*Top.* 100$^b$21–23). Just as the scientist should have a catalog of scientific (often perception-based) truths at hand from which to select the premises of his demonstrations, so a dialectician ought also to select premises "from arguments that have been written down and produce catalogs of them concerning each kind of subject, putting them under separate headings—for example, 'Concerned with good,' 'Concerned with life'" (105$^b$12–15). But for obvious reasons reputable beliefs in *outré* subjects like natural science (unlike in ethics and politics) are likely to have predominantly expert rather than non-expert sources. Thus the views that are reputable beliefs because they are those of other thinkers loom larger in *GC* and *Mete.* than beliefs reputable because they are held by ordinary people rather than the wise. By the same token, things that appear to be so on the basis of observation should figure along with these beliefs,\* since these, as we saw, have the controlling vote in natural science.

Clearly, then, there will be considerable overlap between the scientist's catalog of raw starting-points and the honest dialectician's catalog of reputable beliefs. For, first, things that are believed by reputably wise people are themselves reputable beliefs, and, second, any respondent would accept "the things believed by those who have investigated these crafts—for example, a doctor about issues in medicine, or a geometer about those in geometry, and similarly in other cases" (*Top.* 104$^a$34–37). The catalogs also differ, however, in that not all reputable beliefs need be true. If a proposition is a reputable belief, if it would be accepted by all or most people, it is everything an honest dialectician could ask for in a premise, since his goal is simply this: to show by honest deductions that a definition offered by any respondent whatever conflicts—if it does—with other beliefs the respondent has. That is why having a complete or fairly complete catalog

---

\*Notice *tôn endoxôn kai tôn phainomenôn* at *Cael.* 303$^a$22–23.

xlv

## Introduction

of reputable beliefs is such an important resource for a dialectician. It is because dialectic deals with things only "in relation to belief," then, and not as philosophy and science do, "in relation to truth" ($105^b30$–31), that it needs nothing more than reputable *beliefs*.

Nonetheless, the fact that all or most people believe something leads us "to trust it as something in accord with experience" (*Div. Somn.* $426^b14$–16), and—since human beings "are naturally adequate as regards the truth and for the most part hit upon it" (*Rh.* $1355^a15$–17)—as containing some truth. That is why having cataloged some of the things that people believe happiness to be, Aristotle writes:

> Some of these views are held by many and are of long standing, while others are held by a few reputable men. And it is not reasonable to suppose that either group is entirely wrong, but rather that they are right on one point at least or even on most of them. (*NE* $1098^b27$–29)

Later he generalizes the claim: "things that seem to be so to everyone, these, we say, are" ($1172^b36$–$1173^a1$). Raw starting-points are just that—raw. But when refined some shred of truth is likely to be found in them. So likely, indeed, that if none is found, this will itself be a surprising fact needing to be explained: "when a reasonable explanation is given of why an untrue view appears true, this makes us more convinced of the true view" ($1154^a24$–25).* It is the grain of truth enclosed in a reputable belief that a philosopher or scientist is interested in, then, not in the general acceptability of the surrounding husk, much of which he may discard.

The process of refinement in the case of a candidate explanatory starting-point is that of testing a definition of it against reputable beliefs and perceptual evidence. This may result in the definition being accepted as it stands or in its being altered or modified: when a definition is non-perspicuous, Aristotle tells us at *Top.* $151^b7$–8, it must be "corrected and reconfigured (*sundiorthôsanta kai suschêmatisanta*)," until it is made clear. The same process applies to the reputable beliefs and perceptual evidence themselves, since they may conflict not only with the definition but also with each other. Again, this may result in their being modified, often by uncovering ambiguities within them or in the argument supporting them, or by drawing distinctions that uncover complexities in these, or they may

---

*Compare: (1) "What we are about to say will also be more convincing to people who have previously heard the pleas of the arguments disputing them" (*Cael.* $279^b7$–9). (2) "Refutations of those who dispute [them] are demonstrations of the contrary arguments" (*EE* $1215^a6$–7).

*Introduction*

be rejected entirely, provided that their appearance of truth is explained away.

The canonical occasion for the use of honest dialectic, as of the Socratic elenchus and plain dialectic, is the examination of a respondent. The relevant premises for the questioner to use, therefore, are the reputable beliefs in his catalog that his respondent will accept. Just how wide this set of beliefs is in a given case depends naturally on how accessible to untrained respondents the subject matter is on which he is being examined. We may all have some beliefs about thunder and other phenomena readily perceptible to everyone and which are—for that very reason—reputable. But, as we mentioned earlier, about fundamental explanatory notions in an esoteric science we may have none at all.

When a scientist is investigating by himself, the class of premises he will select from is the catalog of *all* the raw starting-points of his science, despite a natural human inclination to do otherwise:

> [People] seem to inquire up to a certain point, but not as far as it is possible to take the puzzle. For it is customary for all of us to make our inquiry not with an eye to the thing at hand but with an eye to the person who says the contrary; for a person even inquires within himself up to the point at which he is no longer able to argue against himself. That is why a person who is going to inquire well must be capable of objecting by means of objections proper to the relevant genus, and this comes from having a theoretical grasp on all the differentiae. (*Cael.* 294$^b$6–13)

Hence a scientist will want to err on the side of excess, adding any reputable belief, any perceptual evidence, that appears to have any relevance whatever to his catalog. When he formulates definitions of candidate scientific starting-points from which he thinks he can demonstrate the raw ones, he must then examine himself to see whether he really does have the scientific knowledge of it that he thinks he does. If he is investigating together with fellow scientists, others may examine him: we all do better with the aid of co-workers (*NE* 1177$^a$34). What he is doing is using honest dialectic on himself or having it used on him. But this, we see, is little different from the final stage—stage (4)—of the induction we looked at earlier. Induction, as we might put it, is in its final stage (possibly self-directed) honest dialectic.

In a famous and much debated passage, Aristotle writes:

> We must, as in the other cases, set out the things that appear to be so, and first go through the puzzles, and, in that way, prove

> preferably all the reputable beliefs about these ways of being affected, or, if not all of them, then most of them and the ones with the most authority; for if the objections are refuted and the reputable beliefs are left standing, that would be an adequate proof. (*NE* 1145$^b$2–7)

The specific topic of the comment is "these ways of being affected," which are self-control and its lack as well as resilience and softness, as in the parallel passage in the *Physics* that we looked at, namely 211$^a$7–11, it is about place. Some people think that it applies only to this topic and should not be generalized, even though "as in the other cases" surely suggests a wider scope. And, as we can now see, that scope *is* in fact entirely general, since it describes the honest dialectical or inductive route to the starting-points of *all* the sciences and methods of inquiry, with *tithenai ta phainomena* ("setting out the things that appear to be so") describing the initial phase in which the raw starting-points are collected and cataloged.

Now that we know what it means for honest dialectic of the sort employed by the philosopher to provide a route to the explanatory starting-points of the philosophical sciences, we are in a position to see that it is just such a route that *GC* and *Mete.* take to those of natural science (a glance at the Index will show how often puzzles are in focus in them). Since this route is the sort any science must take to prove its explanatory starting-points, the investigation it undertakes is indeed a scientific one. It is not, to be sure, a demonstration from starting-points (the noun *apodeixis* occurs in neither), but rather a proof of the starting-points themselves, which, if successful, allows us to achieve the sort of puzzle-free grasp on them that comes with genuine understanding.*

## *The Place of* GC *in Aristotle's Account of the Universe*

The *Physics* ends with the following sentence: "the primary mover causes eternal movement for an unlimited time. It is evident, therefore, that it is indivisible and without parts, and has no magnitude" (267$^b$24–26). This mover, as we have seen, is the primary god, the immovable mover, which is "the sort of starting-point on which the heaven and nature depend" (*Met.*

---

*For argument bearing on the scientific status of *De Caelo*, which has application to our treatises, see A. Falcon and M. Leunissen, "The Scientific Role of *Eulogos* in Aristotle's *Cael* 2.12," in D. Ebrey (ed.), *Theory and Practice in Aristotle's Natural Science* (Cambridge, 2015), pp. 217–240. *Eulogos* and cognates occur nine times in *GC* and six in *Mete.* (though only twice in our selections).

$1072^b13-14$), and whose location (though not place: the primary god has no place) is outside the universe. Hence, as no part of the universe, he falls outside the ambit even of a science like astronomy (cosmology) that deals with the superlunary world, and with the sublunary, only as a part, so to speak, of it. It is this double fact that explains the odd structure of the *De Caelo*, with which we began the last section. For in Books 1-2 *De Caelo* deals with the universe as a whole, including the superlunary part, which the *Physics*, as natural science, left largely unexplored—although, of course, many of the concepts it analyzes, such as movement, place, time, and causation, have application there. But then in Book 3, as in *Mete.* 1.2, *De Caelo* explores the elements from that same general perspective: thus it discusses not just the superlunary element, ether or primary body, which, as such, is absent from the *Physics*, but also the sublunary ones—earth, water, air, fire. For the earth, after all, is as much a part of the universe as the various celestial spheres.

Moreover, the affections on which it focuses have to do with the sorts of movements used to determine the elements in the first place, whether upward (fire), downward (earth), or in a circle (ether). These are the lightness and heaviness discussed in *Cael.* 4, where "the unconditionally heavy is what sinks below everything else, and the unconditionally light, what rises above everything else" ($311^a17-18$). It is noteworthy—indeed Aristotle explicitly notes it—how ill-suited these affections are to explain how the elements are transformed into each other:

> Of these, heavy and light are neither capable of affecting nor of being affected; for they are not said of things in virtue of their affecting something else or being affected by something else. The elements, though, must be capable of affecting and being affected by each other; for they mix and change into each other. (*GC* $329^b20-24$)

*Cael.* 3.6-7 explains why such a transformation must occur, but without explaining how it happens, since the affections of bodies used to explain it in *GC* 2.4—hot, cold, wet, dry—lie outside its purview.

Three questions naturally arise at this point. The first concerns the definitions of the elements themselves. The first few chapters of *De Caelo* suggest that earth, water, fire, air, and ether are defined by their natural movements, and these by their proper places. Thus earth naturally moves down because its proper place is down at the center of the universe, while fire naturally moves up because its proper place is up at the universe's periphery. The following text makes it clear, however, that heaviness and lightness derive from the more primitive differentiae used in the explanation of elemental transformation:

> Because there are three compositions, one might put first the one from what some people call the "elements"—for example, earth, air, water, and fire. And yet perhaps it is better to speak of composition from the capacities, and not from all of them, but as stated previously in other works.* For wet, dry, hot, and cold are matter of the composite bodies, while the other differentiae—for example, heaviness and lightness, density and rarity, roughness and smoothness, and the other corporeal affections of this sort, follow along with these. (PA 646$^a$12–20)

So one problem is to explain just how heaviness and lightness do follow along with these others: is one lot basic and the others derived? A second problem, adverted to in the second sentence of this text, with its suggestion that composition is from capacities, not from what some people call "elements" (see GC 330$^b$21–25n219), is that of the status and identity of the elements as the basic building blocks from which "all the works of nature are composed" (Mete. 389$^b$27–28). The third problem, related to this one, is raised precisely by elemental transformation. For if elements can come to be from each other, so that what was earth is water, then air, then fire, it seems that there must be some underlying material substrate m that persists as one and the same through the change. But m, which obviously cannot be itself an element, now seems to be yet more primitive, more basic, than the supposedly most basic things. Since the traditional name for m is "prime matter," this problem may be put this way: Is Aristotle committed to the existence of prime matter?

## Elemental Transformation and Prime Matter

When Aristotle tells us that by matter he means "that which, intrinsically, is neither said to be a [this] something, nor some quantity, nor anything else by which being is determined" (Met. 1029$^a$20–21), the matter he is referring to is part of a thought experiment in which the ultimate subject of predication is isolated by a process of stripping away affections and dispositions from the substance to which they belong—a thought experiment alienated onto thinkers other than Aristotle himself by the phrase "for those who investigate in this way" (1029$^a$19) and later by the phrase "for those who

---

*The reference is to GC 2.2.

try to get a theoretical grasp on things in this way" (1029ᵃ26–27). Nonetheless, Aristotle seems to be committed, as we just saw, to an intrinsically featureless matter of this sort—thought, indeed, to be just what the term *prôtê hulê* refers to.

Let us start, then, with his use of that term. At *Ph.* 192ᵃ29 what *prôtê hulê* refers to is a thing's matter-based nature, which is not intrinsically featureless. At *GA* 729ᵃ32 the female menses, again not intrinsically featureless, are said to be like it because they provide the matter for the embryo not the form. At *Met.* 1015ᵃ7–10, it is once more a thing's matter-based nature, which would be water "if all meltable things are water." At *Met.* 1014ᵇ32 it is the matter, again not featureless, from which a thing is first made. At 1017ᵃ5–6, where it is contrasted with ultimate matter, it is "divisible in form," and so must have a form. At 1044ᵃ23, it is again contrasted with ultimate matter, and so cannot be featureless primary matter, which must be ultimate if it is to underlie the transformation of the elements. At 1049ᵃ24–27, fire (again not intrinsically featureless) would be *prôtê hulê* if other elements were composed of it, but not it of anything else (a similar story is told in greater detail at *Ph.* 193ᵃ9–28). From this complete survey it is clear that Aristotle does not use *prôtê hulê* to refer to intrinsically featureless prime matter.

Better evidence for a commitment to such matter, however, is provided by the following text, which uses the cognate term *prôton hupokeimenon*:

> In one way too the matter passes away and comes to be, and in another way it does not. For as that in which it does intrinsically pass away (for what passes away—the privation—is present in it); but as what is potentially it does not intrinsically pass away, but must be incapable of passing away and coming to be. For if it came to be, there must have been some first underlying subject (*proton hupokeimenon*) from which it came to be and is present in it. This, though, is the [material] nature itself, so that it will be before coming to be [which is impossible]. (For by "matter" I mean the first underlying subject of each thing from which it not coincidentally comes to be and which is present in it.) And if it passes away, it will come to this [material nature] at last, so that it will have passed away before it has passed away [which is also impossible]. (*Ph.* 192ᵃ25–34)

This text, with its focus on change and its conceptual requirements, provides a nice segue into the problem of elemental transformation.

The elements earth, water, air, and fire, which are by definition the most primitive of sublunary bodies, can nonetheless change into one another

## Introduction

in a way determined by their ultimate differentiae—hot, cold, wet, dry. If elements are adjacent, so that like earth and water, they share a differentia, transformation occurs when one of the differentiae masters its contrary (*GC* 331$^a$27–30). Suppose, then, that earth (E) is first transformed into water (W), then into air (A), then into fire (F), so that m (the underlying subject requisite for all change) is E at $t_1$, W at $t_2$, A at $t_3$, and F at $t_4$. Since m underlies all elemental transformation, it cannot have any of the ultimate differentiae as an intrinsic affection: if it did, it would not be able to lose them. But because these differentiae are the ultimate ones, there are no others m can possibly have (329$^a$10–13). So it must have these differentiae, but not in the same way as the elements themselves (329$^a$24–35). Thus while fire is essentially or intrinsically hot, m, while it may in fact be hot, must also be potentially cold, and so must be hot only coincidentally. For matter is "that which, primarily and intrinsically, is potentially" hot, cold, and the rest, without being any of them intrinsically or actually (*Met.* 1070$^b$12–13). It seems, then, that m must be intrinsically featureless matter.

However, if m is to underlie elemental transformation, a numerically identical portion or quantity of it must persist through the transformation: "The thing (whatever it is) by being which it underlies is the same, but its being is not the same" (*GC* 319$^b$3–4). But because it seems to possess none of the ultimate contrary differentiae intrinsically, such a portion of intrinsically featureless matter seems to impose no constraints whatever on elemental transformation. So, at the elemental level (and hence on up), anything could come from anything. But this Aristotle rules out:

> Let us first take it, then, that no being whatever is by nature such as to do or suffer any random thing due to any random thing, nor does anything come to be from just anything, except if one takes a coincidental case; for how could pale come to be from musical, unless musical were coincident with the not pale or with the dark?* Instead, pale comes from not pale—and not from any not pale but from dark, or something intermediate between the two. And musical comes to be from not musical— except not from any not musical but from unmusical, or something intermediate between the two, if there is such. Nor again do things pass away into the first random thing—for example, the pale does not pass away into the musical, except coincidentally, but into the not pale, and not into any random one

---

*That is, unless musical and pale or dark were coincidental affections of the same substantial subject.

but into the dark or the intermediate. Similarly too the musical passes away into the not musical, and not into any random one but into the unmusical or into some intermediate, if there is such. (*Ph.* 188ᵃ31–ᵇ8)

Since elemental transformation is not in fact indiscriminate, then, but is constrained by the causal relations holding between the ultimate differentiae, m's defining potentialities must themselves be constrained by these causal relations. That is why Aristotle can simultaneously think that the elements come to be from *prôtê hulê*, and that they come to be from each other: "Since the elements cannot come to be either from an incorporeal thing or from another body, it remains for them to come to be from each other" (*Cael.* 305ᵃ31–32). What an element comes from, then, is another element, but what underlies the transformation of one into the other is *prôtê hulê*, which is not a body separate from the elements, and has no essential or intrinsic affections besides the potentialities determined by the causal relations between the ultimate differentiae. Thus *Mete.* 378ᵇ34 and 379ᵇ19–20 actually identify matter with the affectable capacities, namely, dry and wet.

Normally, of course, a thing's potentialities or dispositional properties are based in its actual or categorical properties, as table salt's solubility in water is based in its molecular structure. But when we get down to ultimate components, there may be no base of this sort, as may be true, for example, in the case of mass or gravitational attraction. At that point, what we confront are dispositions or potentialities that are simply brute. All we can say is that m is something that (a) when coincidentally cold and dry (earth) has the potentiality to become cold and wet (water), and (b) when coincidentally cold and wet (water) has the potentiality to become hot and wet (air), and (c) when coincidentally hot and wet (air) has the potentiality to become hot and dry (fire), and (d) when coincidentally hot and dry (fire) has the potentiality to become cold and dry (earth). The higher-order disposition that m possesses to behave in these four ways but not in others shows that it is not a parcel of featureless matter, which is dispositionless as well as in all other ways indefinite. These causal continuities exhibited across the four ways explain why m is the same thing throughout them. After all, causal continuity (perhaps between their successive stages or so-called time slices) is what explains the diachronic identity of substances themselves.

Overall, then, there seems to be no compelling reason to think that the intrinsically featureless matter that is part of the thought experiment is something that Aristotle himself needs or uses. For how could something intrinsically featureless, and lacking an essence, a what-it-is, or a definition

*Introduction*

possibly be primary in knowledge, as substance is required to be (*Met.* 1028ª33)?

## What Are the Elements?

The textbook answer to this question is earth, water, fire, and air. The Aristotelian sublunary world, we all learn, is an EWAF one. It can be a bit of a shock, therefore, to come across passages that put the textbook answer in question. Here are some from our treatises:

> Fire, however, and air and each of the others that have been mentioned are not simple, but mixed. The simple ones are like these, but not the same as them—for example, if something is like fire, it is fire-form, not fire, and if like air, it is air-form, and likewise in the other cases. (*GC* 330ᵇ21–25)

> At the center and around the center what is heaviest and coldest is set apart, namely, earth and water. Around these, and continuous with them, are air and what due to custom we call "fire," but it is not fire; for fire is excess of hotness and a sort of boiling. But we must understand that, of what we call "air," the part surrounding the earth is wet and hot because it is vaporous and contains exhalations from the earth, whereas the part above this is at this point hot and dry. For vapor's nature is wet and cold, that of exhalation hot and dry. And vapor is potentially like water, exhalation potentially like fire. (*Mete.* 340ᵇ19–23)

And then we have the text we looked at earlier from *Parts of Animals*: "perhaps it is better to speak of composition from the capacities" (646ª14–15)—that is, from hot, cold, wet, dry. Notice how much in harmony with our account of the transformation of the elements that thought is. Notice too that in *GA* the elements are always referred to as "the *so-called* elements" (715ª11, 736ᵇ31)—not necessarily implying that they are not elements, but leaving open the possibility that they are not.*

Distinguishing, then, the fire-form, which is simple and genuinely elemental, from so-called fire, which is mixed, let us ask what each of them is. Happily in the case of so-called fire Aristotle gives a fairly explicit answer:

---

*For discussion of the meaning of the phrase τὰ καλούμενα στοιχεῖα, see T. Crowley, "Aristotle's 'So-Called Elements,'" *Phronesis* 53 (2008): 223–242.

> Cases in which the underlying subject is hot in virtue of being affected also make it apparent that cold is not a certain nature but a privation. Maybe even the nature of fire may turn out to be something of this sort; for perhaps the underlying subject is smoke or charcoal, smoke being always hot (for smoke is a vapor*), whereas charcoal, when extinguished is cold. (*PA* 649$^a$18–22; also *GC* 331$^b$25–26)

What, though, of elemental fire? In its case what is insisted on is that it is hot and dry. It also by nature moves upward to its proper place on the periphery of the universe, as we saw, just as earth moves downward toward its proper place at the center, but this follows along, as we also saw, with its hotness and dryness: "wet, dry, hot, and cold are matter of the composite bodies, while the other differentiae—for example, heaviness and lightness, density and rarity, roughness and smoothness, and the other corporeal affections of this sort, follow along with these" (*PA* 646$^a$16–20). Is it hotness and dryness, then, that hold the key to elemental fire, or is it its natural movement?

Let us start with hotness and dryness. About their nature, Aristotle is explicit:

> The elements, though, must be capable of affecting and being affected by each other; for they mix and change into each other. Hot and cold, by contrast, and wet and dry are said of things, the one lot being capable of affecting, the other capable of being affected; for hot is what aggregates things of the same kind (for the disaggregating, which is precisely what they say fire does, is the aggregating of things of the same kind; for this results in removing what is alien), and cold is what brings together and aggregates alike things of the same kind and things not of the same kind. Wet is what is not bounded by any defining mark proper to it, though it is easily bounded [by other things]; dry is what is easily bounded by a defining mark proper to it, though difficult [for other things] to bound. (*GC* 329$^b$22–33)

Moreover, the fact that the hot and the dry go together is itself explained by the "active" member of the pair: "the sort of thing heat accomplishes is to make things more compact, denser, and drier" (*Mete.* 380$^a$5–6). But though the hot aggregates and composes, so too, we see, does the cold. For "cold

---

*See *Mete.* 340$^b$2n334.

solidifies those things consisting of water only, while fire solidifies those things consisting of earth" (*PA* 649ª30–31). But since cold is just privation or deficiency of heat (*GC* 318ᵇ17, *Mete.* 380ª8), heat again emerges as the key player: "Drying is always due either to heating or cooling, but in both cases is by heat, whether internal heat or external heat" (*Mete.* 382ᵇ16–18).

Focusing on heat, then, we may renew our question: Are hotness and dryness the key to what heat is or is it its natural movement—most manifest in fire—upward?

## *Pneuma*

According to Aristotle we find in nature an apparently continuous scale of beings, in which, for example, animate beings—beings with souls—differ only very slightly from inanimate ones in their level of formation:

> Nature proceeds from the inanimate to the animals by such small steps that, because of the continuity, we fail to see to which the boundary and the middle between them belongs. For the first kind (*genos*) of thing after the inanimate is the plant kind, and, among these, one differs from another in seeming to have a greater share of life; but the whole kind, in comparison with the other inanimate bodies, appears almost as animate, while in comparison with the animal kind it appears inanimate. The change from plants to animals is continuous, as we said before. (*HA* 588ᵇ4–12)

The sublunary elements (earth, water, air, fire) aside, the simplest beings on this scale are homoeomerous or uniform stuffs, such as wood, olive oil, flesh, and bone, whose parts have the same account as the whole (*GC* 314ª20, 328ª10–12). These are constituted out of the elements in some ratio, when the active capacities (hot, cold) in the elements master the corresponding passive ones (dry, wet):

> Having determined these things, we must grasp the workings of these, namely, the workings of the ones capable of affecting, and the species of the affectable ones. In the first place, then, universally [speaking], unconditional coming to be and natural change is the function of these capacities, as is the opposite passing away that is in accord with nature. And these processes occur both in plants and in animals and their parts. Unconditional and natural coming to be is a change due to these capacities—when they stand in the right ratio—in the matter that

*Introduction*

underlies each nature, this being the capacities to be affected that we have just mentioned. And the hot and the cold produce [their effects] by mastering the matter. But when they fail partially to master it, the result is parboiling and non-concoction. (*Mete.* 378$^b$26–379$^a$1)

The fundamental form of such mastery is concoction (*pepsis*), which is responsible for producing a uniform stuff and for preserving its nature thereafter:

Concoction, then, is a completion due to the natural and proper heat and is [produced] from the opposing affectables, these being the matter proper to the given thing. For when it has been concocted, it is completed and has come to be. And the starting-point of the completion comes about due to the proper heat, even if certain external aids helped to accomplish it—for example, nourishment is helped in its concoctions even by baths and by other things of this sort. And the end in some cases is the nature—but nature, we say, as form and substance. . . . Concoction, in fact, is what everything is affected by when its matter—that is, its liquid—is mastered. For this is what is determined by the heat in its nature. For the thing has its nature as long as the ratio is in it. (*Mete.* 379$^b$18–35)

Natural heat is thus formative heat—the thing in nature partly responsible for the coming to be and preservation of matter-form compounds.

Uniform stuffs, as minimally formed, have a low level of such heat. As form is added, so that stuffs come to constitute the structural parts of animals (such as hands and eyes), and these to constitute whole animals of different degrees of complexity, natural heat increases: "the more complete animals are those that are hotter in nature and more fluid—that is, not earthy" (*GA* 732$^b$31–32). Such animals more completely pass on their form to offspring (733$^a$33–$^b$2). Since human beings are the most complete or most perfect animals (737$^b$26–27), they are also hottest and most estimable:

All animals with lungs breathe. . . . The reason some have this part, and why those having it need to breathe, is that the more estimable of the animals are hottest; for at the same time their soul must have been made more estimable, since they have a more estimable nature than the cold ones. Hence too . . . that animal in which the blood in the lungs is purest and most plentiful is the most upright, namely, the human being. And he

*Introduction*

> alone has his upper part directed to the upper part of the universe because he possesses such a part. (*Juv.* 477ª13–23)

Although male and female human beings both have formative heat, its level is not the same in each. This is revealed by the different roles played by their respective spermatic products—seed (*sperma*) or semen (*gonê*) in the case of males, menses (*katamênia*) in that of females—in reproduction: "what the male contributes to generation is the form and the efficient cause, while the female contributes the material" (*GA* 729ª9–11).

What seed does to menses to form them into a fetus is likened to what a carpenter does to wood to make it into a piece of furniture:

> Nothing comes away from the carpenter to the matter of the pieces of wood he works on, nor is there any part of the craft of carpentry in what is being produced, but the shape—that is, the form—is produced from the carpenter by means of the movement in the matter, that is, his soul, in which the form is present, and his scientific knowledge moves his hands or some other part with a certain sort of movement—distinct when what comes to be from it is distinct, the same when what comes to be from it is the same—and the hands move the instruments, and the instruments move the matter. Similarly, the nature present in the male, in those that emit seed, uses the seed as an instrument and as possessing active movement, just as in craft productions the tools are in movement; for the movement of the craft is in a way in them. (*GA* 730ᵇ11–23)

In the way that the movement of the carpenter's hands has its source in the form of the product present in his soul, the movement in the seed has its source in a form—namely, that of the male progenitor. Hence the very same formal constituents exemplified as potentialities in his form are exemplified as movements in his seed, guaranteeing that these movements are (at least to begin with) formally identical to the potentialities that transmit them: "When seed comes into the uterus it causes the female's menses to take shape and moves them in the same movement in which it itself is moving" (*GA* 737ª20–22). Were this not so, their transmission to seed could not result in the transmission of the male's form to the offspring.

What enables the transmission of such movements to seed is that they are present in the male's blood—where, encoded in formative heat, they are responsible for the preservation of his form—and that seed itself is a very concentrated or concocted blood product:

*Introduction*

> That blood is the last stage of the nourishment in blooded animals, and its analog in bloodless ones, has been said previously. And since semen too is a residue of nourishment, that is, from its last stage, it will be either blood, its analog, or something composed of these. And since each of the parts is generated from blood as it is being concocted and somehow divided into parts, and since—although quite different from blood when, having been concocted, it is secreted—the non-concocted seed that is forced out by too frequent indulgence in sexual intercourse is sometimes still bloodlike when it has come out, it is evident that the seed will be a residue of nourishment, namely, of the blood, the one that is finally distributed to the parts. And because of this it has great capacity (and in fact the discharge of the pure and healthy blood is apt to cause weakness) and that offspring should resemble their parents is reasonable; for what has gone to the parts resembles what is left over. So the seed of the hand, of the face, or of the whole animal is in an undifferentiated way a hand, a face, or a whole animal—that is, as each of the latter is actually, such the seed is potentially. (GA 726$^b$1–18)

When the male's formal movements are transmitted by concoction to menses, therefore, they first initiate the formation of the fetal heart. Once the heart is formed, the fetus then grows automatically, drawing its nourishment from its mother through the umbilicus, and in the process transmitting formative movements via the blood to the other developing parts (735$^a$12–26).

However, menses are (in part) also a type of seed—"seed that is not pure, but needs working on" (GA 728$^a$26–27). For a female's formative heat is cooler than a male's, and so cannot complete the final stage of forming or concocting menses into pure seed (728$^a$18–21). In species without "separated" males, however, this may not be so:

> If there is any genus of animal that, though the female exists, contains no separated male, it is possible that this generates an animal from itself. Though this has not been observed in a reliable way up to now at least—although a case in the fish genus does make one hesitate; for among the ones called "erythrinus" no male has so far been seen, whereas females full of embryos have been. But of this we have as yet no reliable experience. (GA 741$^a$32–38)

Nonetheless, even in species where males and females are clearly distinguished a female can concoct her menses (or the spermatic residue in it) to

*Introduction*

within that last stage of becoming pure seed, so that for each actual movement in seed, there is a corresponding potential movement stemming from the female form (*GA* 768ª11–14). While menses have the potential to move in such a way as to become a fetus, therefore, they cannot do so until they are set moving by seed, since "so far as things formed by nature or by human craft are concerned, the formation of what is potentially is brought about by what is actually" (734ª29–31). Equally well, of course, without menses to move, no new animal is generated either.

Just which movements will underlie the offspring's form—whether, for example, it will be male or female—depends on the interaction between the movements in the seed and the potential movements in the menses (*GA* 768ᵇ5–12). If a male movement is transmitted successfully to the menses, the offspring will have the corresponding component of the male form. If it fails to be transmitted, it may be wholly resisted, in which case it is replaced by the opposing movement in the menses, or resisted to a lesser degree, with different consequences in each case (768ª7–9, 768ᵇ7–8).

The difference, then, between male *gonê* or *sperma* and the seed (or spermatic residue) in female menses is in one way quite small: they both encode more or less the same genetic information, as we would say. But in another way it is quite large: only male semen contains that information as actual movements, making it "the first thing containing a starting-point of generation" (*GA* 724ᵇ12–14) (leaving aside possible species in which female seed also contains it). The question is, how does the semen encode this information?

Semen, as we now know, is made up of individual sperms, each viable one of which is in principle capable of fertilizing a female ovum. Aristotle's view is quite different. For him the quantity of semen ejaculated is the fertilizing agent, not its sub-parts, and its viability, to call it that, depends on the level of formative or soul-producing heat in it relative to the quantity of female menses that it must work up:

> In general, then, female and male are set apart from each other in relation to production of males and production of females due to the causes just mentioned. Nonetheless, there must also be a proportion in their relation to each other; for all things that come to be either in accord with craft or nature exist in virtue of a certain ratio. Now, the hot, if it too is mastering, dries up the wet things, whereas if it is very deficient it does not compose them, instead it must stand in the mean ratio in relation to what is being crafted. If it does not, just as in cooking where too much fire burns the food, while too little does not cook it, and either way the result is that what is being produced fails to be

completed, likewise too in the case of the mixing of what comes from the male and what comes from the female there must be a proportion. (*GA* 767ª13–23)

However, if the menses is not to be uniformly concocted, but rather differentially so, in the way requisite for stage-wise embryonic development, in which first the fetal heart is formed, then the parts around the head, and so on, the semen too, as Aristotle recognizes, must be "somehow divided into parts" (*GA* 726ᵇ5–6). Nothing is said explicitly about how this division actually takes place. But since semen is foamy, and foam contains bubbles, it is likely that the surrounding membranes of these are what mark the divisions and encapsulate the formative heat in them:

> The cause of the whiteness of seed is that the semen is a foam, and foam is white, and most so that composed of the smallest particles, and small in the way that each bubble is invisible, just as actually happens in the case when water and olive oil are mixed and beaten. (*GA* 736ª13–18)

It seems, then, that we should think of the male semen as somehow divided into bubbles, with different ones embodying the different movements needed to form the different parts of the embryo, and to endow them in turn with the formative heat needed for their growth and preservation.*
Thus it is that we hear about "the proper heat present in each part" (*GA* 784ª35–ᵇ1, 786ª20–21).

While seed, as a concocted blood product, is a very purified type of nourishment, its natural heat, in which its formative movements are encoded, is of a quite special sort:

> Now, the capacity of all soul seems to be associated with a body distinct from and more divine than the so-called elements. And as souls differ from each other in esteem and lack of esteem, so too this sort of nature differs. For within the seed of everything there is present that which makes the seeds be fertile, the so-called hot. This is not fire or that sort of capacity, but the pneuma enclosed within the seed and within the foamy

---

*For further discussion, to which my account is indebted, see Marwan Rashed's probing paper, "A Latent Difficulty in Aristotle's Theory of Semen: The Homogeneous Nature of Semen and the Role of the Frothy Bubble," in A. Falcon and D. Lefebvre (eds.), *Aristotle's Generation of Animals: A Critical Guide* (Cambridge, 2018), pp. 108–129.

*Introduction*

part—that is, the nature in the pneuma, which is an analog of the element belonging to the stars. (*GA* 736ᵇ29–737ᵃ1)

Characterized as "connate" (*sumphuton*), because it is not drawn in from outside but produced and maintained inside the body (*PA* 648ᵃ36–649ᵇ8), it is the sort of pneuma that plays a fundamental role in nourishment and reproduction (*GA* 741ᵇ37–742ᵃ16). It is distinguished from air and breath (also pneuma) in only one text included in the Aristotelian corpus:

> From the dry exhalation, when it is pushed by the cold so that it flows, wind is produced. For this is nothing except much air moving and gathered together. It is at the same time also said to be pneuma ["breath"]. But something is said to be pneuma in another way when it is the ensouled and fertile substance (*empsuchos te kai gonimos ousia*) in plants and animals and which pervades them totally. (††*Mu.* 394ᵇ9–11)*

The reproductive system, indeed, is in many ways simply a means of transmitting the form-preserving digestive system (of which blood and the heart are parts) into new matter, thereby initiating the formation of a new self-maintaining creature. That is why both functions are assigned to the *threptikon* or nutritive part of the soul (*DA* 416ᵃ19–20, 416ᵇ11–12).

Although many natural beings (for example, ones we think of as inanimate) do not preserve their form by means of nourishment, or transmit it by means of sexual reproduction, pneuma has a fundamental role to play in their existence too:

> Animals and plants come to be on earth and in liquid because in earth there is water present and in water pneuma, and in all pneuma there is soul-involving heat, so that in a certain way all things are full of soul. (*GA* 762ᵃ18–21)

> Democritus, however, omitting to mention the for-the-sake-of-which, reduces to necessity all that nature uses—but though they are such, they are nonetheless for the sake of something and in each case for the sake of what is better. So nothing prevents the teeth from being produced and being shed in the way

---

*On the authorship of *De Mundo*, see J. Thom, *Cosmic Order and Divine Power: Pseudo-Aristotle, On the Cosmos* (Tübingen, 2014), pp. 3–5, and M. Federspiel, *Pseudo-Aristote, Du Monde, Positions et Dénominations des Vents, Des Plantes, Introduits, Traduits et Commentés* (Paris, 2018), pp. 5–21.

he says, but it is not because of these things, but rather because of the end—although these are causes as movers, as instruments, and as matter, since it is reasonable, indeed, for nature to make most things using pneuma as instrument—for just as some things have many uses where the crafts are concerned, as in blacksmithing are the hammer and the anvil, so too does pneuma in those composed by nature. (*GA* 789$^b$2–12)

Yet despite its manifest importance, no focused discussion of pneuma occurs in Aristotle's extant works—unless we count ††*De Spiritu* among them.* This makes it difficult to determine his views with confidence—a difficulty exacerbated by the fact the pneuma may be more than one thing (as a glance at the Index will show). But by piecing together what he does say, a reasonably clear picture emerges.

From its role in embryology alone, for example, we can see that pneuma transmits movement by being itself in movement. The role accorded to it in animal movement confirms this fact:

[Pneuma] is evidently well disposed by nature to impart movement and supply strength. The functions of the movement, though, are pushing and pulling, so that its instrument must be capable of being expanded and being contracted. And this is just the nature of pneuma. For it is being both contracted [and expanded] without force, and is able to pull and push by force due to the same cause. (*MA* 703$^a$18–23)

Moreover, because the movements it imparts are formative, they must be complex and various—able, as geneticists now put it, to *code for* all of an animal's parts. Since movements are "either in a circle or in a straight line or in a combination of the two" (*Ph.* 261$^b$28–29), all the complex movements pneuma can produce must be some such combination. What makes this possible is that by actively expanding and contracting, and so pushing and pulling, it can cause not just rectilinear but also circular movements: "rotating is a compound of pulling and pushing; for what is rotating a thing is pulling one part of it and pushing another; for it leads one part away from itself and another part toward itself" (*Ph.* 244$^a$2–4). Hence all

---

*A. Bos and R. Ferwerda, *Aristotle on the Life-Bearing Spirit (De Spiritu)* (Leiden, 2008) argue that we should; P. Gregoric and O. Lewis, "Pseudo-Aristotelian *De Spiritu*: A New Case Against Authenticity," *Classical Philology* 110 (2015): 159–167, more convincingly, that we should not.

movements—rectilinear, circular, or a combination of the two—can be caused by pneuma (*DA* 433$^b$25–26).

Initially, pneuma is assigned a role in the transmission of form to non-controversially animate beings. However, its role gets expanded to explain other phenomena, such as transparency:

> For it is not insofar as something is water or insofar as it is air that it is visible, but because there is a certain nature in it that is the same in both of them and in the [eternal] body above. (*DA* 418$^b$7–9)

> What we call "transparent" is not something special to air, or water, or any other of the bodies usually called "transparent," but is a common nature or capacity present in these, and in all other bodies in a greater or lesser degree, and does not exist separately. (*Sens.* 439$^a$21–23)

Then, because pneuma is soul-transmitting, soul is to some extent itself attributed to anything in which pneuma is present. When "the capacity of all soul" is associated with "the nature in the pneuma, which is an analog of the element belonging to the stars," then, the point of analogy is that the nature in question is both transparent and—when combined with other elements, whose movements are rectilinear—an appropriate transmitter of soul, form, and life. For the element that belongs to the stars (ether or primary body) is a body "different from and additional to the elemental ones met with here, more divine than, and prior to, all of them" (*Cael.* 269$^a$30–32), and is both transparent and in eternal circular movement (270$^a$12–$^b$25). Hence pneuma is a "corporeal substance beyond the ones composed here, more divine and prior to all these," because it is an analog of ether, which is in fact more divine than they.

Focusing now on pneuma, let us see how best to understand it. One thing we know is that "it is being both contracted [and expanded] without force, and is able to pull and push by force due to the same cause" (*MA* 703$^a$21–22), but another is that it is "hot air" (*GA* 736$^a$1). Putting the two together we have air increasing in size and contracting due to heat. And this heat, we are within an inch of seeing, is primarily a factor to be understood in terms of its natural upward movement. For pneuma, we see, is not a new element, but rather a construction from old ones introduced to explain the existence in the sublunary world of the circular movements crucial for the transmission and preservation of forms, and so for the coming to be and passing away of the matter-form compounds whose forms they are. But it is equally central to the explanation of animal movement, perception, and thought:

Just as automata are set moving when a small movement occurs: when the strings are released and the pegs strike against one another . . . so too animals are set moving. For they have instrumental parts that are of the same sort as these, with the nature of sinews and of bones . . . when these are relaxed or loosened, they are set moving. . . . In an animal, however, [unlike in an automaton] the same thing can become both smaller and larger and change shapes, when the parts expand [and contract] because of heat, pneuma, and cold, and undergo alteration. These alterations, however, are caused by appearances, perceptions, and thoughts. For perceptions immediately have their being as alterations of a certain sort, and an appearance and a thought have the capacity of their objects. For in a way the form of something hot or cold or pleasant or frightening, when we think of it, is in being just like the thing itself. That is why we shudder and are frightened because of merely thinking of them. All these are affections and alterations; and of things in the body that are altered, some become larger and some smaller. And it is not hard to see that a small change occurring in a starting-point produces large and numerous changes at a distance from it—for example, by shifting the rudder a hair's breadth you get a large shift at the prow. Further, when under the influence of heat or cold or some other similar affection, an alteration is produced in the region of the heart, even in an imperceptibly small part of it, it makes a large difference to the body—causing instances of blushing, for example, or of turning white, as well as instances of shuddering, trembling, and their opposites. (*MA* 701$^b$1-32)

Form of every variety, one might almost say, just is a sort of movement.

## The Hot, the Cold, the Wet, and the Dry

Elemental fire, we saw, is a combination of what we will now, following Aristotle, call "the hot (*to thermon*)" and "the dry (*to xêron*)"—with the hot being the active or affecting factor and the dry being the passive one, the one capable of being affected. By the same token, elemental air is a combination of the hot and the wet (*to hugron*). But rather than seeing these elements as internally static things on a par with Democritean elements, we should see them as internally dynamic, as involving a struggle for "mastery," as Aristotle calls it, in which victory now goes to one factor, now to another. And this mastery, as our exploration of pneuma makes vivid, depends on internal (natural, formative) heat and on external heat: "boiled things do not draw liquid into themselves; the external heat masters the internal; whereas if a thing's internal heat did master, it would draw it into itself" (*Mete.* 380$^b$22–24). But the nature of this struggle, precisely because it is dynamic, must be understood in terms of movement—again our exploration of pneuma and its explanatory role shows us why. So within elemental air the internal dynamic struggle for mastery is between the hot's natural upward movement and the wet's natural movement in a contrary direction—it is, so to speak, the resultant of those two movements.

The discussion of cloud formation in *Mete.* 1.3 shows how resourcefully this struggle can be exploited for explanatory purposes. But so too does the account of perceived hotness:

> It is the differentiae of body insofar as it is body that are objects of touch. I mean the differentiae that determine the elements, namely, hot, cold, dry, and wet, of which we have spoken earlier in our account of the elements. The perceptual organ for these, in which the perceptual capacity called "touch" primarily belongs, is the part that is potentially such as they are; for perceiving is a sort of being affected, and so what does the affecting makes that part such as it is actually, the part being such potentially. That is why we do not perceive what is equally as hot, cold, hard, or soft [as the part], but only the excesses, the perceptual capacity being a sort of mean between the pairs of contraries in the perceptible objects. And that is why it judges the perceptible objects. For the mean is capable of judging; for in relation to each extreme it becomes the other. And just as what is to perceive white and black must be neither of them actively, although both potentially (and similarly too in the case of the other perceptual capacities), so in the case of touch it must be neither hot nor cold. (*DA* 423$^b$27–424$^a$10)

Thus when the perceptual mean that responds to and to some extent measures hotness is tipped one way, the touched thing feels hot, while if tipped the other way, cold. But this "tipping" is precisely a movement. As we see from the account of what happens when the thing is too hot to have its temperature measured by touch:

> It is evident from this why it is that excesses in perceptible objects destroy the perceptual organs (for if the movement is too strong for the perceptual organ, the ratio is dissolved—and this, as we saw, is the perceptual capacity—just as the consonance

and pitch [of a lyre] are if the strings are struck too forcefully).
(*DA* 424ᵃ28–32)

The answer to the question, then, as to which of elemental fire's capacities should be taken as basic or defining, its tendency to move upward or its hotness and dryness, is clearly that it is the former. The Aristotelian world is in this sense a world of different sorts of movements—which is just what the *Physics* and *De Caelo* should have led us to suspect.

But they do much more than lead us to suspect that the primary beings are substances, and in this they can hardly be thought to be alone: pretty much every work of Aristotle's from the *Categories* to the *Metaphysics* are at one in telling us that the world of beings is primarily a world of substantial beings—substances. This puts immediate pressure on the idea, which our discussion so far might mistakenly be thought to foster, that the hot, the cold, and the rest have emerged as the primary beings. For while hot exists in combination with the wet in air and with the dry in fire, it does not exist in separation from either of them. Yet being separable is the very mark of a substance (see *GC* 316ᵇ3n42). From a different perspective, in other words, we have reengaged with the problem of prime matter. As it cannot exist in separation from the hot, the cold, the wet, and the dry, so their active members (hot, cold) always go together with their passive ones (wet, dry). The dynamic tension at the heart of the elements that makes their natural movements their defining features requires as much.

Perhaps at this point no more is needed than a reminder that being for Aristotle is expressed by a verb, and that the god, the most substantial substance of all—the most substantial being—is an activity. For movement is "incomplete activity" (*Met.* 1066ᵃ20–21), and the elements "are always active; for they have their movement both intrinsically and within themselves," and imitate "the things that cannot pass away" (1050ᵇ28–30).

# *On Coming to Be and Passing Away*

# Book 1

## 1.1

314ᵃ1 But concerning the coming to be and passing away of the things that by nature come to be and pass away, we must determine—alike with regard to all of them—their causes and accounts.[1] Further, concerning growth and alteration, we must determine what each is, and also whether we must suppose that the nature of alteration and of coming to be are the same, or separate, just as there is a distinction regarding their names.[2]

Now, among the ancients, some say that what is called "unconditional coming to be" is an alteration, others that alteration and coming to be are distinct.[3] For those who say that the universe is some one thing and make everything come to be from one thing, must of necessity say that coming to be is alteration and that what, in the strict sense, comes to be, is altered.[4] On the other hand, for those who posit more than one [sort of] matter, like Empedocles, Anaxagoras, and Leucippus, they are two distinct things.[5] And yet Anaxagoras was ignorant of the proper sense of his utterance; for he says, at any rate, that coming to be and perishing are the same as altering, but says that the elements are many, just as others also do.[6] For Empedocles makes the corporeal elements four, but in all, together with those that move them, [they] are six in number, whereas for Anaxagoras they are unlimited, as they are for Leucippus and Democritus.[7] For he posits the homoeomerous things as elements—for example, flesh, bone, marrow, and each of the others where a part is synonymous with the whole.[8] Democritus and Leucippus, by contrast, posit indivisible bodies, unlimited in number and shape, from which all the others are composed, differing in relation to each other in the ones from which they are composed and in the position and order of these. For it is evident that the followers of Anaxagoras and those of Empedocles say contrary things. For the latter says that fire, water, air, and earth are the four elements, and that these—rather than flesh, bone, and the homoeomerous things of this sort—are simple; whereas for the former ones, the homoeomerous things are simple and elemental, while earth, fire, water, and air are composites; for they are a universal seedbed of the homoeomerous things.[9]

314ᵇ1 Those on the other hand who construct everything from one thing, must of necessity say that coming to be or passing away is an alteration; for the underlying subject always remains one and the same.[10] And this is the sort of thing that we say alters. Those, by contrast, who posit a plurality of kinds (*genos*) must distinguish alteration from coming to be; for, for them, coming to be and passing away occur when things come together and undergo dissolution.[11] That is why Empedocles in fact speaks in this way, saying that:

> Nothing that is has a nature . . .
> But rather there is only mixing and separating of things mixed.[12]

That the statement is properly in keeping with what they posit, then, is (one might almost say) clear; that is why they speak in this way.[13] But it is necessary for them too to say that alteration is something other than coming to be, yet this is impossible according to what they do say.

That we are speaking correctly in saying this is easy to see. For just as, while the substance remains at rest, we see in it a change with respect to magnitude, which is called "growth and withering," in the same way we see alteration occurring.[14] Nonetheless, on the basis of what is said by those who make the starting-points more than one, alteration is impossible.[15] For the affections with respect to which we say that this occurs are the differentiae of the elements—I mean, for example, hot cold, white black, dry wet, soft hard, and each of the others.[16] Just as Empedocles in fact says:

> Sun, white to see and everywhere hot . . .
> And rain everywhere dark and cold.[17]

And he determines the remaining ones in a similar way. So if it is not possible for water to have come to be from fire or earth from water, neither will it be possible for anything to have come to be black from white or hard from soft. And the same argument will also apply to the others. But it is this, as we said, that alteration consists in.

It is also evident from this that a single matter must always be supposed for contraries, whether the change is with respect to place, with respect to growth and withering, or with respect to alteration.[18] Further, it is equally necessary that this is [the case with matter] and that alteration is; for if there is alteration, the underlying subject is also one element and there is one matter for all the things that admit of change into each other, and if the underlying subject is one, there is alteration.

Empedocles, then, seems to contradict both the things that appear to be so and himself.[19] For while he says that none of the elements comes to be from another, but rather that all the other things come to be from them, at the same time, when he has made the whole of nature, except strife, come together into one, he says that from this one each thing again comes to be.[20] So it is clear that it was by being separated out from some one thing by certain differentiae and affections that something came to be water and something else fire, just as, he says, the sun is white and hot, earth heavy and hard. If, then, these differentiae are subtracted (for they can be subtracted; since they came to be, at any rate), it is clearly necessary both for earth to come to be from water and water from earth, and similarly for each of the others, not only *then* but also *now*, since they change, at any rate, with respect to their affections.[21] And, from what he has said, they can be added together as well as separated again, especially since strife and love are still fighting with each other. Which is precisely why even *at that time* they came to be from one thing; for the universe was certainly not fire *and* earth *and* water when it was one thing.

But it is also unclear whether he should posit as a starting-point the one or the many—I mean, fire, earth, and the co-ordinates of these.[22] For insofar as the one is like the underlying matter from whose changing due to movement earth and fire come to be, the one is elemental.[23] On the other hand, insofar as the one comes to be from composition by a coming together of the latter, and they through its dissolution, they are more elemental and prior in nature.[24]

## 1.2

It is about both unconditional coming to be and passing away in general, then, that we must speak, saying whether it exists or does not exist and in what way, and about the other sorts of movements—for example, growth and alteration. Plato, on the other hand, investigated only coming to be and passing away, in what way they belong to things, and not all coming to be but [only] that of the elements—he said nothing about the way flesh, bones, or anything else of that sort come to be.[25] Further, neither did he investigate alteration or growth, nor what way they belong to things. In general, no one seems to have paid anything besides superficial attention to these matters except for Democritus. By contrast, he seems to have given thought to all of them, in a way that was different from his times. For about growth none of them has determined anything, as we are saying, except what a random person might say, namely, that things grow by the addition of like to like (nothing, though, about the way this occurs).[26] Nothing either about mixture, nor about (one might almost say) any of the others—for example, affecting and being affected, or in what way one thing affects and another is affected in natural productions.[27] Democritus and Leucippus, however, having posited the shapes produce alteration and coming to be from these: coming to be and passing away by their aggregation and disaggregation, alteration by their order and position. But since they thought that the truth lies in what appears to be so, and the things that appear to be so are contraries and unlimited [in number], they made the shapes unlimited [in number], so that, due to changes in its composition, the same thing seems to be contrary ways to two different people and, due to the mixing in of something small, undergoes a transposition, and, one particle being shifted, appears wholly otherwise; for *tragô[i]dia* and *trugô[i]dia* come to be from the same letters.[28]

But since it seems to pretty much everyone that coming to be and alteration are distinct, and that while some things come to be and pass away by being aggregated and disaggregated, they alter by changing their affections, it is having turned one's attention to these that one must get one's theoretical grasp on the issues. For these involve puzzles that are at once many and reasonable.[29] For if coming to be is aggregation, many impossible things follow. Yet there are other opposing arguments on the other side, and ones not easy to resolve in a puzzle-free way, that it cannot possibly be anything else.[30] If, alternatively, coming to be is *not* aggregation, either there is no coming to be at all or it *is* alteration; or else this [puzzle] too, difficult though it is, it is necessary to try to resolve.[31]

A starting-point, however, of all these matters is whether the beings come to be, alter, grow, and undergo the contraries of these, the primary magnitudes being indivisible, or whether there is no indivisible magnitude; for this makes the greatest difference. And, again, if there are [indivisible] magnitudes, are they bodies, as Democritus and Leucippus say, or planes, as in the *Timaeus*?[32]

This, as we have also said elsewhere, is unreasonable in its own terms, namely, to resolve things no further than to planes.[33] That is why it is more reasonable for there to be indivisible bodies. Although this too involves many unreasonable things. Nonetheless, with indivisible bodies it is possible to produce alteration and coming to be, causing a transposition in what is the same by "turning" and by "contact" and by the differentiae of shapes, precisely in the way Democritus does.[34] (It is also why he says that color does not exist, for it is by turning that there is coloration.[35]) But for those who divide things into planes this is no longer possible; for, by putting together, nothing comes to be except solids. In fact they do not even attempt to generate any affection at all from them.

The cause of our being incapable of taking a comprehensive view of the agreed-upon facts is lack of experience. That is why those who are more at home among natural things are better able to posit the sort of starting-points that can string together a good many of these, whereas those who on the basis of their many [logico-linguistic] arguments do not get a theoretical grasp on the facts, but look at only a few, make their declarations too recklessly. One can see from this too how much difference there is between investigating in the way appropriate to natural science and in a logico-linguistic way; for concerning the existence of indivisible magnitudes, the latter lot say that the triangle-itself will [otherwise] be many, whereas Democritus would appear to have been convinced of this by arguments that are proper to and appropriate to natural science.[36] What we are saying will be clear as we go on.

For a puzzle would be involved if one were to posit that some body and magnitude is divisible at every point, and that this is possible. For what precisely will what escapes the division be?[37] For if it is divisible at every point, and this division is possible, it could also be in the state of being divided at every point at the same time, even if it had not been divided up at the same time (and even if this latter did happen, there would be nothing impossible involved).[38] Hence the same applies also at the mid-point and, in general, too, if it is naturally divisible at every point; then, if it is [in fact] divided up, nothing impossible will have happened, since not even if it is divided at a hundred million points is there any impossibility—although perhaps no one would so divide it.[39]

Since, therefore, the body is like this at every point, let it have been divided [at them]. What, then, will remain? For it cannot be any magnitude; for then there will be something undivided, but it was said to be divided at every point. But then, if there will be no body and no magnitude remaining, but there will be division, either the body will consist of points, and what it is composed of will be without magnitude, or there will be nothing remaining at all, so that it would come to be from, and be composed of, nothing, and the totality, then, would be nothing but an appearance. Similarly, even if it consists of points, there will be no quantity. For when the points were in contact and the magnitude was one and they were together, they did not make the totality any greater. For when it was divided into two or more, the totality was not greater or smaller than before, so that even if they are all put together, they will produce no magnitude.[40] But then even if, during division, something is produced like sawdust from the body, and in this way some body is removed from the magnitude, the argument is the same: it is divisible in some way.[41] But if what is removed is not a body but some separable form (*eidos*) or some affection, and the magnitude consists of points or contacts affected by this, it is absurd for a magnitude to be composed of components that are not magnitudes.[42]

Further, the points will be somewhere and they will be immovable or in movement; also, a single contact is always between two things, as there is always something beyond the contact, the division, and the point.[43]

6

If, then, someone posits that any body whatever of any magnitude whatever is divisible at every point, these are the things that follow.

Further, if I had divided and had put back together the piece of wood, or anything else, it would again be equal and one. Hence the same clearly applies if I cut the wood at any point whatever.[44] Therefore, it is at every point that it has been potentially divided.[45] What, then, is there beyond the division? For if there is also some affection, how is it dissolved into these and how does it come to be from these? And how are these separated?[46]

So, if indeed it is impossible for magnitudes to be composed of points or contacts, it is necessary for there to be bodies and magnitudes that are indivisible. Nonetheless, for those who posit these, no less impossible things follow. These, though, have been investigated elsewhere.[47] But an attempt must be made to resolve them.[48] That is why the puzzle must be stated again from the start.

That every perceptible body is divisible at every point and indivisible is no absurdity; for being divisible will belong to it potentially, whereas being indivisible will do so actually.[49] But that it should be potentially divisible at every point at the same time would seem to be impossible. For if it were possible, it could also come about (not so as to be at the same time both in actuality indivisible and divided, but so as to be divided at every point). Therefore, there will be nothing remaining, and the body will have passed away into something incorporeal, and could come to be again either from points or from something that is nothing at all. And how is this possible? Yet that it *does* get divided into magnitudes that are separable, and into ones that are always smaller and smaller, and into ones that are at a distance from each other and separated, is evident. Well, division part by part could not go on without limit and neither can a body be divided at every point at the same time (for that is not possible), but only up to some [limit]. Therefore, it is necessary for it to contain indivisible magnitudes that are invisible—especially if coming to be and passing away are going to be by aggregation and disaggregation.

This, then, is the argument that seems to make it necessary for there to be indivisible magnitudes. And that it contains a hidden fallacy, and where it is hidden, we now explain. For since no point is contiguous to another point, there is one way in which being divisible at every point does belong to magnitudes, and another in which it does not.[50] When this divisibility is posited, though, it seems that there is a point both anywhere and everywhere, so that it is necessary for the magnitude to be divided into nothing; for there is a point everywhere, so that the magnitude is composed of contacts or points. The way, however, in which divisibility does belong at every point is that anywhere at all there is one point in whichever direction, and that all points are like each; but there are not more than one [there]; for points are not successive, so that [it does not belong] at all points; for if a magnitude is divisible at the mid-point, will it also be divisible at a contiguous point?[51] For cut is not contiguous to cut or point to point.[52] And this cut serves as a division or a join.[53]

So there is both disaggregation and aggregation, but neither into indivisibles and from indivisibles (for the impossibilities involved are many) nor in such a way that division has occurred at every point (for [only] if point were contiguous to point, would this have been so). Instead, disaggregation is into small parts and then smaller ones, and aggregation is from smaller ones.

But it is not the case that unconditional and complete coming to be and passing away are defined by aggregation and disaggregation, as some say, whereas change in what is continuous is alteration.[54] On the contrary, this is where all the mistakes are made. For unconditional coming to be and passing away do not occur by means of aggregation and disaggregation, but are when a whole changes from a *this* to a *this*.[55] Others think that all this sort of change is alteration, but there is a difference; for within the underlying subject there is something corresponding to the account and something corresponding to the matter.[56] When, then, the change is in these, there will be coming to be or passing away. But when it is in the affections and is coincidental, there will be alteration.

By being disaggregated and aggregated, though, things do become more [or less] easily capable of passing away. For the smaller raindrops are divided, the faster they become air, whereas if they have been aggregated, they do so more slowly.[57] This will become clearer in what follows.[58] For now, however, let us take this much as determined, namely, that it is impossible for coming to be to be aggregation, as some people say it is.[59]

### 1.3

These things having been determined, we must first get a theoretical grasp on whether there is anything that comes to be and passes away unconditionally, or whether strictly speaking nothing does, but always it is something that comes to be and it comes to be from something [else]—I mean, for example, coming to be healthy from being sick, and sick from being healthy, or small from large and large from small, and all the others in the same way.[60]

For if there is going to be unconditional coming to be, something would come to be from not being unconditionally, so that it would be true to say that not being belongs to some things. For non-unconditional coming to be something is from not being something—for example, from not being white or not being nobly beautiful—whereas unconditional coming to be is from unconditional not being. But *unconditionally* signifies either what is primary in each category of being, or what is universal and encompasses everything.[61] If, then, it signifies the first, substance is going to come to be from not substance. But what neither substance nor thisness belongs to, clearly none of the other categories does either—for example, quality, quantity, or place; for otherwise affections would be separable from substance.[62] If, on the other hand, it signifies wholly not being, it will be the universal denial of everything, so that what comes to be will necessarily come to be from nothing.[63]

Well, the puzzles concerning these issues have been gone through and determined at greater length in other accounts.[64] But let us in a summary way now state again that in one way it is from what is not that a thing comes to be unconditionally, although in another way it is always from what is; for what potentially is but actually is not must of necessity preexist, and it is spoken of in both ways. But even when these distinctions have been drawn, a wondrous puzzle remains, which must be gone through again, as to how unconditional coming to be is possible, whether from what is potentially a substance or in some other way. For one might raise a puzzle as to whether there is a coming to be of substance—that is, of the this—which is not [a coming to be] of the thus qualified, the thus quantified, or the where placed. And it is the same way too where passing away is concerned. For if a [this] something comes to be, clearly there will be potentially, but not actually, some substance from which its coming to be will [proceed] and into which what passes away necessarily changes.[65] Will, then, any of the others actually belong to this?[66] I mean will what is only potentially a this and a being, but unconditionally is neither a this nor a being, have, for example, a quantity, a quality, or a somewhere? For if it has none, but all potentially, it follows that what in this way is not is separable, and further, what the first philosophers feared most of all has come to pass, namely, the coming to be of something from nothing preexisting. On the other hand, if being a this something or a substance is not going to belong to it, while some of the other things are going to, affections, as we said, will be separable from substance.[67]

It is necessary, then, to work on these issues as much as possible, and on what the cause is of there always being coming to be, both unconditional and partial.[68]

But since there is one cause that we say is the starting-point of movement, and another one that is the matter, it is the latter sort of cause that must be spoken about. For the former has already been spoken about in our accounts concerning movement, where we said that there is, on the one hand, what is immovable for all time and, on the other, what is always in movement.[69] The first of these—the immovable starting-point—it is the function of the other and prior philosophy to discuss.[70] Concerning the second, the one that moves the other things through being itself continuously moved, it must be determined later which of the things said to be particulars is a cause of this sort.[71] But for now let us speak about the cause posited as being in the material kind (*eidos*), due to which passing away and coming to be never fail to occur in nature; for at the same time as this becomes clear, we will perhaps also get clear about what is now puzzling us, as to how precisely one should in fact speak too about unconditional passing away and coming to be.

Enough of a puzzle is in fact involved in what the cause is of the unbroken continuity of coming to be, if indeed what passes away disappears into what is not, and what is not is nothing; for what is not is neither a something, nor a quality, nor a quantity, nor a somewhere. If indeed, then, some one of the beings is always disappearing, why precisely has not the universe been consumed long ago and vanished, if, at any rate, each of the things coming to be comes to be from something limited? For of course it is not because what each comes to be from is unlimited that it does not fail to occur; for this is impossible; for nothing is actively unlimited, but potentially so only in the direction of division, so that the only sort of coming to be that never fails to occur would be due to what comes to be always being smaller. But as things stand this is not what we see.

Is it, then, because the passing away of one thing is the coming to be of another, and the coming to be of one thing is the passing away of another, that change is necessarily unceasing? Well, where the existence of the coming to be and likewise of the passing away of each of the beings is concerned, this should be thought enough of a cause.

But why precisely some things are said to come to be and pass away unconditionally and others not unconditionally must be investigated again, if indeed the same thing is the coming to be of this and the passing away of that, and the passing away of this is the coming to be of that; for this seeks some account. For we say that passing away occurs now unconditionally, and not only that *this* passes away; also that this is a case of coming to be unconditionally, and this of passing away unconditionally.[72] On the other hand, if this comes to be something, it does not come to be unconditionally; for we say that a person who learns comes to be scientifically knowledgeable, not that he comes to be unconditionally.

Now, we often make a distinction by saying that some things signify a this something while others do not; what is being sought is a consequence of this.[73] For it makes a difference what the changing thing changes into—for example, perhaps the route that leads to fire is a coming to be unconditionally, but a passing away of something (of earth, for example), whereas the one to earth is a coming to be of something (but not an unconditional coming to be), but an unconditional passing away (of fire, for example).[74] Parmenides speaks of a pair like this, saying that what is and what is not are fire and earth.[75] Whether this pair or another of the same sort is posited makes no difference; for we are seeking the way it happens not what is being posited. And the route that leads to unconditional not being is unconditional passing away, while the one that leads to unconditional being is unconditional coming to be. Of the pair in terms of which the distinction is made, whether fire and earth or some other, one will be what is and the other what is not. This, then, is one way in which unconditional coming to be and passing away will differ from the one that is not unconditional.

Another way is by the sort of matter involved; for if the differentiae of the matter signify more of a this something, the matter is more of a substance, whereas if they signify a privation, it is more of a non-being.[76] For example hot is a certain [positive] predicate and a form, and cold is a privation, and earth and fire differ by these very differentiae.[77]

But it seems to ordinary people that the difference is more one of being perceptible and being imperceptible; for when the change is to perceptible matter, they say that it is a coming to be, when to matter that is unapparent, a passing away; for they distinguish being from non-being by what they perceive and do not perceive, just as, for example, what is scientifically knowable is [said to be] being, the unknowable [said to be] not being; for perception has the capacity of scientific knowledge.[78] Hence, just as they think themselves to live and be in virtue of their perceiving or being capable of perception, so it is too with things. And in a way they are tracking the truth, though what they say is not itself true. Indeed, unconditional coming to be and passing away turn out one way in accord with belief and another in accord with truth; for, in accord with perception, wind (*pneuma*) and air *are* less a this something and a form than earth is (that is why they say that what passes away unconditionally changes into these, while coming to be occurs when there is change into something tangible, that is, into earth), whereas, in accord with truth, they are more so.[79]

The cause, then, of there being unconditional coming to be that is the passing away of something, and of unconditional passing away that is the coming to be of something, has now been stated; for it is due to the matter differing, either in virtue of its being a substance or not, or of its being more a substance or not, or because of the matter from which or to which [it changes] being more perceptible in the one case and less so in the other.

But what is the cause due to which some things are said to come to be unconditionally, others only to come to be something, and not in virtue of the coming to be of one thing from another, in the way we have just now stated? For up to now we have determined only this much: why precisely, when every coming to be is the passing away of something else and every passing away the coming to be of a distinct thing, we do not in the same way attribute the coming to be and passing away to the changing things.[80] But the puzzle that was mentioned later was not the one gone through, but was precisely why what learns is not said to come to be unconditionally but to come to be scientifically knowledgeable, whereas what is born is said to come to be unconditionally.[81] This, then, is determined by their categories; for some things signify a this something, some a quality, some a quantity. Those that do not signify a substance are not said to come to be unconditionally, but to come to be something.

Nevertheless, in every case, coming to be is said in accord with one of the two columns [of contraries]—for example, in substance, if it is fire, but not if it is earth, in quality, if it is scientifically knowledgeable, but not if it is lacking in scientific knowledge.[82]

The unconditional coming to be of some things, then, but not of others, both in general and in the case of substances themselves, has now been spoken about; as has why the underlying subject is the cause, as matter, of the continuous occurrence of coming to be, namely, because it is capable of changing from contrary to contrary, and because in the case of substances the coming to be of one thing is always the passing away of another, and the passing away of one thing, the coming to be of another.

Moreover, there is no need to be puzzled either as to why there is coming to be when things are always being destroyed; for just as people speak of something unconditionally passing away when it passes into imperceptibility (that is, into what is not), similarly they say that something comes to be from what is not when it emerges from imperceptibility, whether the underlying subject is something or is not anything.[83] So in the same way as something comes to be from what is not, it also passes away into what is not. It makes perfect sense, then, that it does not fail to occur; for coming to be is the passing away of what is not and passing away the coming to be of what is not.[84]

But this *what unconditionally is not*, is it one of the two contraries—for example, is earth (that is, what is heavy) what is not, and fire (that is, what is light) what is—or not, but rather earth too is what is, while what is not is the matter of earth and fire alike?[85] Also, is the matter of each of these distinct? Or, in that case, is it that they would not come to be from each other, or from contraries (for it is to these that the contraries belong, namely, fire, earth, water, air)? Or is the matter in one way the same, and in another way distinct? For the thing (whatever it is) by being which it underlies is the same, but its being is not the same.[86]

About these issues, then, let this much be said.

## 1.4

Let us now say what the difference is between coming to be and alteration, since we say that these changes are distinct from each other. Since, then, the underlying subject is one thing and the affection that is naturally said of the underlying subject is another, and there is a change of each of them, there is alteration when the underlying subject, which is perceptible, while remaining [the same], changes in its own affections, which are either contraries or intermediates (for example, the body is healthy and again sick, while remaining, at any rate, the same [body], and the bronze is round and at another time angular, while being the same [bronze]).[87] But when a whole changes, while nothing perceptible remains as the same underlying subject, but rather is like when blood comes from the whole of the semen [changing], or air from water, or water from the whole of air, something of this sort is then a coming to be, and a passing away of the other thing, especially if the change is from something imperceptible to something perceptible, either to touch or to all the perceptual capacities—for example, when water comes to be from or passes away into air (for air is fairly imperceptible).[88]

In the latter cases, if some affection of a contrariety remains the same in what came to be and in what passed away (for example, when water comes to be from air, if both are transparent or cold), the other thing to which it changes must not be an affection of this former one.[89] Otherwise, the change will be an alteration.[90] For example, the musical human passed away, and the unmusical human came to be, but the human remains the same. If, then, musicality and unmusicality were not intrinsically affections of this latter, there would be a coming to be of the one and a passing away of the other.[91] That is why these are affections of the human, though of unmusical human there is a coming to be and of musical human a passing away. But as things stand this is an affection of the underlying subject.[92] That is why cases of this sort are alteration.

When, then, the change of a contrariety is with respect to quantity, there is growth and withering; when it is with respect to place, spatial movement; when with regard to an affection and a quality, alteration; but when nothing remains of which the other [resulting thing] is an affection, or, in general, a coincident, there is coming to be, and, on the other hand, passing away.

Matter in the most strict sense is the underlying subject receptive of coming to be and passing away, but in a certain way that of the other changes too, because all underlying subjects are receptive of certain contrarieties.[93]

Concerning coming to be—whether or not it exists, and in what way it exists—and alteration, let things be determined in this way.

## 1.5

It remains to speak about growth, in what respect it differs from coming to be and alteration, and how each of the things that grow grows and how any one of the things that wither withers.[94] It is necessary, then, to investigate first whether their difference from each other lies [only] in what they concern—for example, because the change is from a this to a this, that is to say, from a potential substance to an actual substance, it is coming to be; because it has to do with magnitude, growth; with affection, alteration (the latter two being a change from potential to actual of the things mentioned [namely, magnitude and affection])—or whether the mode of the change differs too; for it is evident that while what alters does not of necessity change with respect to place, and neither does what is coming to be, what grows and what withers does, but in another way than what spatially moves. For what spatially moves changes its place as a whole, whereas what grows does so like metal that is beaten out; for while it remains where it is, its parts change with respect to place, although not as the parts of a [revolving] sphere do; for these change within a place of the same magnitude, while the whole remains where it is, whereas the parts of what grows occupy an ever larger place, what withers always an ever smaller one. It is clear, then, that the change in the case of what is coming to be, what is altering, and what is growing differs not only in what it has to do with but also in its mode.

But what the change has to do with in the case of growth and in that of withering (granted that growth and withering seem to have to do with magnitude), how should it be supposed to be? [1] Is it from something potentially a body and a magnitude, but actually incorporeal and without magnitude, that a body and a magnitude come to be? But since this also admits of being said in two ways, in which of them does growth come to be? Is the matter from which it comes [1a] itself an intrinsically separated thing, or does it [1b] exist in another body? Or are both of these impossible? For, if it is separated, it will either [1a-i] occupy no space, like a point, or [1a-ii] it will be a void or an imperceptible body.[95] Of these, one [1a-ii] is impossible, while the other [1a-i] makes it necessary for it to be in something; for what comes to be from this matter is always going to be somewhere, so that the matter too must be somewhere, either intrinsically or coincidentally.[96] But then if [1b] it is going to be in something, if it is separated in such a way as not to belong to it either intrinsically or coincidentally, many impossibilities will follow. I mean, it would be as if water comes to be from air, not because the water is what changes, but because the matter of the air is present in the water like in a vessel. For then nothing would prevent there from being an unlimited number of matters [in it], so that they might actually come to be [from it]. Further, it is evident that air does not come to be from water in this way, as if coming out from something that persists. Therefore, [2] it is better in every case to make the matter inseparable, as being the same and one in number, though not one in account.[97] But then, points cannot be posited as the body's matter either, and neither can lines, due to the same cause.[98] The matter is what points and lines are limits of, and it is something that can never exist without affections and without shape.[99]

Now, one thing unconditionally comes to be from another, as has been determined elsewhere, and always as a result of something actually being, either the same in species or the same in genus (for example, fire as a result of fire, or human as a result of human), or else as a result of an actuality; for a hard thing does not come to be as a result of a hard thing.[100] But since there is also matter for corporeal substance, and this is already the matter for *this* sort [of body] (for there is no body that is common), the same one will also be matter for magnitude and affection—separable in account, but not separable in place, unless the affections too are separable.[101]

It is evident, then, from the puzzles gone through that growth is not a change from something that potentially has magnitude, but that actually has no magnitude; for then the void would be separable, and that this is impossible has been stated previously elsewhere.[102] Further, change of *this* sort would not be special to growth but would belong to coming to be generally. For growth is the increase of a preexisting magnitude, and withering its diminution. That is why, indeed, what is growing must have some magnitude. So growth must not be regarded as being from matter without magnitude to actual magnitude; for this would instead be the coming to be of a body, not growth.

We must, then, as if undertaking the investigation from the start, take up in greater detail the question of what sort of thing growth or withering is whose causes we are seeking. It is evident, then, that when a thing grows each and every part of it has grown, and similarly when a thing withers each and every part has become smaller, further, that a thing grows by something that is added, and withers by something that is subtracted.[103] Now, it is necessary that growth be either by something incorporeal or by a body. If, then, it is by something incorporeal, there will be a separable void (but it is impossible for the matter for magnitude to be separable, as was said previously), whereas if it is by a body, there will be two in the same place, the one that grows and the one that grows it; but this too is impossible.[104]

But then neither is it possible to say that growth or withering comes about just as when air comes from water; for in that case the mass has become greater, but this is not in fact growth but a coming to be of the thing the change will be to, and a passing away of its contrary, though not a growth of either.[105] Instead, either nothing grows or if [anything does] it is something that belongs jointly to both what passes away and what comes to be—for example, if body does. But the water has not grown, neither has the air, instead the one has been destroyed and the other has come to be, though the body involved has grown—if indeed anything has. But this too is impossible; for one must preserve in the account the things that belong to what is growing and what is withering. And these are three in number: one, each and every part of what is growing is larger (for example, if it is flesh, of flesh); second, something is added to it; and third, what grows is preserved and remains; for whereas in the case of something unconditionally coming to be or passing away the thing does not remain, in those of alteration and growth or withering, what grows or alters does remain the same, although in the first the affection and in the second the magnitude does not remain the same. If, then, the change just mentioned is to be growth, it would be possible for something to grow though *nothing* was added to it or remained (and to wither though nothing has been subtracted) and what grows did not remain.[106] But this must be preserved; for growth was posited to be like this.[107]

But someone might also raise a puzzle as to what it is that grows. Is it that to which something is added? For example, if someone's calf grows, it becomes larger, but that by which it grows, the nourishment, does not. Why is it, then, that not both have grown? For the thing that grows and the one by which it grows are both larger, just as when one mixes wine with water; for one has more of each of the two alike. Is it because the substance of the one remains, while that of the other—the nourishment—does not?[108] [No,] since in the other case too it is what masters in the mixture that it is said to be—for example, that it is wine; for the compound mixture performs the function of wine but not that of water.[109] Similarly too in the case of alteration, if being flesh remains and the what-it-is, but an intrinsic affection that did not belong to it previously [now] belongs to it, it has altered.¹¹⁰ [Response.] But that by which it is altered, though it is sometimes not affected at all, sometimes has also been altered. [Response.] But what alters it, that is, the starting-point of the movement, is within what grows and what is altered, because the mover is in these.¹¹¹ Since in fact what enters could sometimes become larger together with the body that has enjoyed it—for example, if having entered it became pneuma.¹¹² But it passes away, surely, having been thus affected, and the mover is not in it.

Since the puzzles about this have been sufficiently gone through, it is also necessary to try to find a resolution of the puzzle, while preserving the fact that [1] what grows remains and [2] grows by something added (and withers by something subtracted), and, further, [3] that each and every perceptible point [in it] has become larger (or smaller); and [4] that the [growing] body is not a void, nor [5] are two magnitudes in the same place, nor [6] does it grow by anything incorporeal.¹¹³ The cause, though, must be grasped by first making two distinctions: one is that non-homoeomerous things grow by the growth of homoeomerous things (for each one is composed of these); the next is that flesh, bone, and each part of this sort is twofold, just as are the other things that have an in-matter form; for both the matter and the form are said to be flesh and bone.¹¹⁴

Now, the growth of each and every part [and what is such by] something added is possible with respect to the form, but with respect to the matter it is not possible; for it must be understood as if someone were measuring out water by the same measure; for what comes to be is always one thing and then another.¹¹⁵ And this is how the matter for flesh grows, and not by each and every part being added to, but rather some flowing out and some added to each and every part of the figure and the form.¹¹⁶ This is more clear in the case of non-homoeomerous things—for example, a hand, because it grows proportionally; for in their case it is more clear that the form is distinct from the matter than in the case of flesh and homoeomerous things. That is also why a corpse would seem still to have flesh and bone more than a hand and an arm.¹¹⁷ So there is a way in which each and every part of flesh grows and a way in which it does not. For with respect to the form there has been addition to each and every part, but not with respect to the matter. The whole, however, has become larger by the addition of something called "nourishment," that is, of a contrary [to flesh] changing to the same form—for example, if wet were to be added to dry, and, having been added, were to be changed and become dry; for in one way like grows by like, in another way by unlike.¹¹⁸

One might raise a puzzle, though, as to what sort of thing that by which something grows must be.¹¹⁹ It is evident, then, that it must be potentially that thing—for example, if it is flesh, potentially flesh. Actually, therefore, it is something else. This having passed away, then, has become flesh.

Not, though, this thing intrinsically (for that would be coming to be, not growth), but rather what grows by this.[120] But what, then, is the affection of this thing by which the thing grows? Has it been mixed in it, as if one were to pour water into wine that was able to make what is mixed in it into wine, as fire takes hold of the combustible—is it in this way that the growth-producer, which is present in what grows (that is, in what is actually flesh), makes what is potentially flesh into actual flesh when added to it? In that case, then, [it is due to the two] being together; for if [it happens when they are] separate, it is coming to be. For one can make fire in this way, namely, by putting logs on a preexisting fire. In this way, then, it is growth, but when the logs themselves are set on fire, it is coming to be.

A quantity, taken universally, however, does not come to be any more than does an animal that is neither a human nor any other of the particular ones (as universal is here, quantity is there). Instead flesh or bone does, or hand (that is, the homoeomerous components of these). And what is added is in fact a certain quantity of something, but not a quantity of flesh. Insofar, then, as it is potentially both together—for example, so-and-so-much flesh—there will be growth by this; for it must have become both a certain quantity and flesh. But insofar as it is potentially flesh alone, it nourishes; for this is how nourishment and growth differ in account.

This, then, is why something is nourished for as long as it is preserved, even if it withers, but is not always growing. It is also why nourishment and that by which something will grow, though they are the same, are distinct in being; for insofar as what is added is potentially so-and-so-much flesh, it is a growth-producer of flesh, but insofar as it is potentially flesh alone, it is nourishment.[121] But this form without matter, like a pipe, is a certain in-matter capacity.[122] And if some matter were added that is potentially a pipe, and that also has the relevant quantity potentially, these [pipes to which it is added] will be bigger pipes. But if it is no longer capable of producing this [that is, the growth of pipes], but is like water continually mixed with wine, which ends up by making it watery, indeed water, then it will produce withering of the quantity. The form, though, remains.[123]

## 1.6

But since it is necessary first to speak about the matter and the so-called elements, saying whether there are any or not, and whether each is eternal or in some way they come to be, and if they do come to be, whether they all come to be from each other in the same way or whether one among them is primary—before this it is necessary to speak about things that are now said in an indefinite way.[124] For all the thinkers, both those for whom the elements come to be and those for whom things come to be from them, make use of both disaggregation and aggregation and affecting and being affected.

Now, aggregation is mixing. But what we mean by "mixing" has not been determined in a perspicuous way.[125] Moreover, neither alteration nor disaggregation and aggregation is possible without something affecting and something being affected; for in fact those who posit several elements make them come to be by affecting and being affected, and for those who make them come to be from one it is necessary to mention the affecting.[126] And in this regard Diogenes says correctly that if all things did not come from one, they would not be able to affect and be affected by each other, for example, for the hot to be cooled and for it in return to be heated; for heat and coldness do not change into each other, but rather it is clear that the underlying subject does.[127] So things in which there is affecting and being affected necessarily have a single underlying nature. But it is not true to say that everything is of this sort, but only the ones in which there is [affecting and being affected] by each other.[128]

But surely if we are to get a theoretical grasp on affecting and being affected and one on mixing, it is necessary to get one on contact as well; for affecting and being affected in the strict sense is not possible for things that are not in contact, and neither is mixing possible for those that are not first in a certain sort of contact.[129] So we must determine three things, what contact is, what mixing is, and what affecting is.

Let us take the following as a starting-point. For it is necessary for the beings for which there is mixing to be capable of contact with each other, and the same holds also for those things, where, in the strict sense, one affects and the other is affected. That is why we must first speak about contact. Now, just as pretty much each of the other names is said of things in many ways, some homonymously, others because one or other of the two derives from a distinct prior one, this is how it is with "contact."[130] Nonetheless, "contact" said in the strict way belongs to things that have position, and position belongs to the very ones that also have place; for even to mathematical objects contact and place are assigned equally, whether each of them exists in separation or in some other way.[131] If, then, as was determined previously, making contact is having the extremities together, those things make contact with each other which are definite magnitudes having size and position that have their extremities together.[132] And since whatever has a position also has a place, and the primary differentia of place is up and down, and other opposites of this sort, all things that make contact with each other will have heaviness or lightness, either both or one of the two.[133] And things of this sort are affectable and capable of affecting.[134] So it is evident that the sorts of things that naturally make contact with each other are definite magnitudes whose extremities are together that are capable of moving and being moved by each other.

But since the mover does not [always] move the moved in the same way, but one mover moves by being itself moved, and another while being immovable, it is clear that we must speak in the same way about the affecter; for the mover is said to affect something and the affecter to move something.[135]

Nonetheless, there is a *difference* and a distinction that must be made. For not every mover can affect something, if indeed we contrast the affecter with the affected, and apply this to those things whose movement is an affection—an affection being that with respect to which a thing alters, such as white and hot.[136] In other words, moving is wider in extension than affecting is.

But this point, at all events, is evident, namely, that there is a way in which the movers will make contact with the things they move and a way in which they will not.[137] Still, the universal definition of making contact applies to things having position, one of which is capable of causing movement and the other capable of being moved; whereas [that of making contact] with each other applies to things capable of being moved and capable of moving, between which there is affecting and being affected.[138] For the most part, to be sure, what makes contact makes contact with something that makes contact with it; for in fact pretty much all the movers we meet move by being moved, and in these cases it is necessary and evident that what makes contact makes contact with something that makes contact with it.[139] But it is possible, as we sometimes say, for the mover alone to make contact with the moved, and for what makes contact not to be made contact with by what it makes contact with (but because things of the same genus move by being moved, it seems necessary for what makes contact to be made contact with). So if something moves while being immovable, it will make contact with the thing moved, but nothing will make contact with it; for we sometimes say that a person who grieves us "touches" us, but we do not touch him.

Where contact among natural objects is concerned, then, let it be determined in this way.

## 1.7

The next thing that must be spoken about is affecting and being affected; for the accounts we have received from earlier thinkers are contrary to each other. For most are unanimous in saying this, namely, that like is in every case unaffectable by like, since one is no more capable of affecting or of being affected than the other (for all the same [affections] belong equally to like things), whereas it is unlike things and different ones that naturally affect and are affected by each other; for even when a smaller fire is caused to pass away by a much greater one, it is so affected, they say, because of the contrariety; for much is contrary to little. Democritus, on the other hand, stated a view contrary to the others and special to himself alone; for he says that the affecter and the affected are the same and like; for he does not allow things that are distinct and different to be affected by each other; on the contrary, even if things that are distinct do in some way affect each other, it is not insofar as they are distinct but insofar as they have the same something that this happens to them.[140]

The things said, then, are these.[141] And those who speak in this way seem to appear to be saying contrary things. And the cause of their speaking in contrary ways is that while it is necessary to get a theoretical grasp on the whole, each side succeeds in stating [only] a part of it. For that like—that is, what is entirely and in every respect undifferentiated—is not affected in any way by like is reasonable. (For why will one be more capable of affecting than the other? And if like is affectable by like, it is also affectable by itself; and if things are like that, there would be nothing incapable of passing away or immovable, if indeed like insofar as it is like is capable of affecting things; for everything will move itself.) And [that] what is entirely distinct and in no way the same [is not affected in any way] is likewise reasonable. (For whiteness could not be affected in any way by a line, or a line by whiteness, except coincidentally—for example, if the line were coincidentally white or black; for things that are neither contraries nor composed of contraries could not displace each other from their own nature.[142])

But since no random thing is naturally disposed to be affected and to affect, but rather things that have a contrariety or are contraries, it is necessary for the affecter and the affected to be like—in fact, the same—in genus, but unlike and contrary in species; for it is natural for a body to be affected by a body, flavor by flavor, color by color, and, in general, what is the same in genus by what is the same in genus. The cause of this is that all contraries are in the same genus, and it is contraries that affect and are affected by each other.[143] So it is necessary for the affecter and the affected to be in one way the same, and in another way distinct and unlike each other. And since the affected and the affecter are the same and alike in genus, but unlike in species, and contraries are things of this sort, it is evident that contraries and intermediates are affectable by and capable of affecting each other; for it is, in general, in these that passing away and coming to be reside.[144]

That is why it is reasonable too for fire to heat and for cold to cool, and why, in general, the thing capable of affecting makes the affected one like itself; for the affecter and the affected are contraries and coming to be is to the contrary thing. So it is necessary for the affected to change to the affecter; for this is the way coming to be will be to the contrary thing. And it is also in accord with reason, then, that both sides, though not saying the same things, touched on the nature [of the phenomenon] in a similar way.[145] For sometimes we say that the underlying subject is affected (for example, we say that a human being comes to be cured, heated, and cooled, and other things in the same way), but sometimes we say that what is cold comes to be heated and what is ill cured. And both are true. It is the same way in the case of the affecter; for sometimes we say that a human being heats, and sometimes that what is hot does; for there is a way in which matter is affected, and a way in which the contrary is. Those, then, who looked to the former thought that the affecter and the affected must possess the same something, whereas the others looked to the latter and thought the contrary.

The same account, though, must be assumed to apply to affecting and being affected, just as to being moved and moving; for something is also said to be a mover in two ways; for that in which the starting-point of movement is present seems to move things (for the starting-point is primary among the causes), and again the last in relation to the moved and the [thing's] coming to be. Likewise where the affecter is concerned; for we also say both that a doctor cures and that wine does. Now, in the case of movement nothing prevents the first mover from being immovable; in some cases this is even necessary; but the last is always a moved mover. And in the case of affection, while the first [affecter] is unaffectable, the last is also itself affected; for things that do not have the same matter affect while being unaffectable, for example, the craft of medicine; for this produces health but is not at all affected by what is being cured, whereas the food affects and is itself somehow affected; for it is heated, cooled, or affected in some other way at the same time as it affects. The craft of medicine, indeed, serves as starting-point, while the food serves as the last thing and the one making contact. So things capable of affecting that do not have their shape [or form] in matter are unaffectable, whereas those that do have it in matter are affectable.[146] For the matter, we say, is alike—(one might almost say) is the same—for either of the two opposites, being, as it were, the genus, and something capable of being hot is necessarily heated if what is capable of heating is present and comes near.[147] That is why, as has just been said, some things capable of affecting are unaffectable while others are affectable. And it is the same way in the case of things capable of affecting as in the case of movement; for there the first mover is unmoved, and in the case of the affecters, the first is unaffectable.

But the affecter is a cause as the starting-point from which the movement comes, whereas the for-the-sake-of-which is not capable of affecting.[148] That is why health is not capable of affecting, except by metaphorical transference; for when in fact the affecter is present what is affected comes to be something, but when states are present it is not any longer becoming something, but already *is*, and forms and ends are certain states, whereas matter, insofar as it is matter, is affectable.[149] To be sure, fire has the hot in its matter. But if hot were to exist separated, it would not be affected at all.[150] Now, presumably it is impossible for this to be separated.[151] But if there are such things, what was said would be true of them.

Let, then, what affecting and being affected is, to what things they belong, and why and how, be determined in this way.

## 1.8

But let us speak again about how it is possible for this to happen. Well, it seems to some people that each thing is affected when the last affecter—the affecter in the strictest way—enters in through some sort of "pores," and they say that it is in this way that we see and hear, and that all the other perceptual capacities perceive things. Further, they say that things are seen through air, water, and transparent bodies because they have ducts, invisible because of their smallness, but densely aligned in columns, and the more transparent the body, the more it has.[152]

Some people, then, determined certain cases in this way, just as Empedocles also did—not only cases of affecting and being affected, but also mixing, which they say occurs between bodies whose ducts match each other.[153] Leucippus and Democritus, however, made the most methodical determinations about all [these] things, having made a starting-point that is in accord with nature, as nature precisely is.[154] For some of the ancient philosophers believed that being is of necessity one and immovable; for the void is a non-being, and moving would be impossible if there is not a separated void; nor, again, would there be many things if there is nothing dividing them.[155] And to this point it makes no difference whether someone thinks that the totality is not continuous, but making contact while being divided, rather than claiming that there are many things, not one, and a void.[156] For if it is divisible at every contact point, there is no one, so that there is no many either, but rather the whole is a void. But if it is divisible at one point but not at another, it has come to seem like some sort of fabrication; for up to what quantity, and why, is one part of the whole this way—that is, a plenum—and another part divided? Further, it is equally necessary [on this view] for there not to be movement.[157] On the basis of these arguments, then, overstepping and disregarding perception, on the supposition that they must follow reason, they say that the totality is one and immovable, and some that it is unlimited; for the limit would be a limit next to the void. These people, then, in this way and due to these causes proclaimed their "truth."[158]

But since in view of the arguments these things do seem to follow, but in view of the facts to believe them without more ado is next door to mania (for no one suffering a manic attack degenerates to the extent of believing that fire and ice are one, instead it is only nobly beautiful things and those that appear so because of intimacy, that to some, because of their mania, seem not to differ); Leucippus, for his part, thought he had accounts that, saying things in agreement with perception, did not do away either with coming to be and passing away or movement or with the plurality of the beings.[159] Having agreed on these points with the things that appear to be so, and with those that establish the one in supposing that there would be no movement without a void, that the void is a non-being, and that no part of being is a non-being, he says that being, in the strictest sense, is being that is a total plenum, but that what is like this is not one, but unlimited in number, and invisible because of the smallness of the masses.[160] These things spatially move in the void (for there is void), and their coming together produces coming to be, their dissolution passing away. And they affect and are affected to the extent that they happen to be in contact (for, in that respect, they are not one), and when they are put together and interwoven there is coming to be. From what is truly one, on the other hand, a multiplicity could not have come to be, nor from what is truly many could one have; on the contrary, this is impossible. However, just as Empedocles and some of the others say that things are affected through ducts, so Leucippus says that all alteration and all being affected come about in this way: dissolution and passing away because of the void, and likewise growth, by other things slipping in.[161]

For Empedocles too it is pretty much necessary to speak just as Leucippus also does; for he must say that there are certain solids, which, however, are indivisible, unless there are continuous ducts at every point. But this is impossible; for then there will be nothing solid besides the ducts, but all of it will be void. It is necessary, therefore, for things that are making contact to be indivisible, while the intermediates between them are voids, and these he says are *poroi*.[162] This is the way Leucippus too speaks about affecting and being affected.

These, then, are pretty much the ways these [atomists] spoke about some things affecting and others being affected. And where they are concerned, it is clear what they say, and it is evident that it follows pretty much in agreement with the assumptions they employ. With the others, it is less so—for example, in the case of Empedocles it is not clear in what way there will be passing away and alteration. For to the others the primary bodies are indivisible, differing only in figure—from which primary ones [the other things] are composed and into which, as ultimate ones, they are dissolved. In the case of Empedocles, by contrast, it is clear that the other things have coming to be and passing away down to the elements, but about these elements themselves, heaping up a magnitude, it is neither clear how they come to be and pass away nor is it possible for him to tell us, unless he says that there is an element of fire as well, and likewise of all the others, as Plato wrote in the *Timaeus*.

For the latter is to this extent different from the way stated by Leucippus, namely, that while he says that the indivisibles are solids, Plato says that they are planes, and that while for him each of the indivisible solids is determined by [one of] an unlimited number of figures, for Plato they are limited, whereas both say that they are indivisible and are determined by figures.[163] From these indivisibles, then, we get comings to be and disaggregations. For Leucippus, though, there would be two ways, because of the void and because of contact (for it is with respect to this that each is divided), whereas for Plato it is by contact only; for he says that there is no void.[164]

Now, we have also spoken about the indivisible planes in previous accounts.[165] Where the indivisible solids are concerned, though getting a full theoretical grasp on what follows from them is something we must put aside for the moment, by way of a short digression we may say that it is necessary for each of the indivisibles to be unaffectable (for it is not possible to be affected except because of the void) and incapable of producing any affection [in anything else]; for it cannot be either cold or hard. And yet this, at any rate, is impossible, to assign hot only to the spherical figure; for then it is necessary for its contrary, cold, to belong to some other figure.[166] And it would also be absurd to suppose if they possess these—I mean hot and cold—that they will not possess heaviness and lightness and hardness and softness. And yet Democritus says that each of the indivisibles is heavier, at any rate, in accord with the excess [of size], so that it is clear that it is also hotter [in accord with the excess of size].[167] But if they are like this, it is impossible for them not to be affected by each other—for example, the slightly cold by the far exceeding hot.[168] Moreover, if hard and soft [belong], well, something is said to be soft because it is affected by something; for what is capable of being pressed in is soft.[169]

Moreover, it is absurd both if nothing belongs to them except shape alone, and, if something does belong, for it to be one thing only—for example, hard in one case, hot in another; for then there would not be some one nature belonging to these things.¹⁷⁰ It is equally impossible too if several belong to one; for since it is indivisible, it has its affections in the same place. So that if it is affected, where it is [, for example,] cooled, there it will affect or be affected in some other way as well.¹⁷¹ And it is the same way in the case of the other affections; for this consequence will follow in the same way both for those who say that the indivisibles are solids and for those who say that they are planes; for they cannot come to be either rarer or denser, because there is no void within the indivisibles.¹⁷²

Further, it is absurd too for small things to be indivisible, but not large ones; for as things stand it is reasonable for large ones to break up rather than small ones; for the former—namely, the large ones—more easily come apart, since they collide with many things. But why should indivisibility in general belong to small things rather than to large ones?¹⁷³

Further, is there one nature for all these solids, or do some differ from others, as would be so if some were fiery in their mass, others earthy? For if there is one nature for all, what separates them? Or else why, when they make contact, do they not become one, as a raindrop does when it makes contact with a raindrop? For the one behind is no different from the one in front.¹⁷⁴ On the other hand, if they are distinct, of what sorts are they? And it is clear that these must be posited as starting-points and causes of the things resulting from them, rather than the shapes.¹⁷⁵

Further, if they were different in nature, they would both affect and be affected on making contact with each other.

Further, what is their mover? For if it is a distinct thing, they will be affectable. On the other hand, if each moves itself, either it will be divisible (with respect to one part a mover, with respect to another a moved) or contraries will belong to it with respect to the same part, and its matter will be not only one in number but also potentially.¹⁷⁶

As for those who say that affections come about because of movement through ducts, even if the ducts are total plenums, the ducts are wasted work; for if this is how the totality is affected in some way, even if it had no ducts but were itself continuous, it would be affected in the same way.¹⁷⁷

Further, how is it possible for seeing through a medium to happen in the way they say?¹⁷⁸ For it is not possible to pass through the transparent medium either at the points of contact or through the ducts, if each of these ducts is a plenum. How will it differ, then, from what does not have ducts? For all of it will be similarly plenums. But even if these ducts are voids, though it is necessary for them to have [other] bodies in them, the same thing will again result. And if they are of such a magnitude as to receive no body, it is ridiculous to think that what is small is a void, but not what is large, whatever its size—that is, to think that "void" means something other than "space for body," so that it is clear that for every body there will be a void of equal mass.

In general, then, to posit ducts is wasted work; for if nothing can affect anything by making contact with it, neither will it affect it by passing through its ducts. On the other hand, if it can do so by making contact, then—even if there are no ducts—some things will be affected and others will affect them, provided they are naturally adapted in this way to each other.

That speaking in this way about ducts, as some have supposed they must, is either false or pointless, is evident from these considerations; for if bodies are divisible at every point, it is ridiculous to posit ducts; for where they are divisible, they are capable of being separated.

## 1.9

In what way being a cause of coming to be [such-and-such] and affecting and being affected belong to the beings, we state by taking for granted an often-mentioned starting-point; for if, on the one hand, there is what is potentially such-and-such and, on the other hand, what is actually such-and-such, it is natural for [what is affected] to be affected not at one point and not at another, but rather at all points, to the extent that it is such-and-such, though to a lesser or greater extent insofar as it is more or less such-and-such.[179] And one would more properly speak about ducts in this connection as veins of susceptibility to affection, just like [veins of ores] stretching continuously in mines.[180]

Certainly, when grown together and one, each thing is unaffectable.[181] Likewise too when things are making contact neither with each other nor with other things that are naturally affecting and affected. I mean, for example, that fire heats not only when making contact with things but also when at a distance from them; for the fire heats the air, and the air—being naturally affecting and affected—heats the body.

As for thinking that a thing is affected in some part but not in another, having drawn distinctions at the start, this is what must be said.[182] For if a magnitude is not divisible at every point, but there is a body or a plane that is indivisible, it would not be affectable at every point, but neither would any magnitude be continuous.[183] On the other hand, if this is false and all body is divisible, it makes no difference whether it was divided and is making contact or it is divisible; for if it is capable of being disaggregated at the contact points, as some people say, even if it is not yet divided, it will be divided; for it is possible for it to be divided; for nothing impossible results.[184]

In general, it is absurd for it to be only in this way, namely, by bodies being split, that anything comes to be [such-and-such]; for this account does away with alteration, whereas we see that the same body, while being continuous, is at one time liquid and at another time solidified, and being affected in this way not due to division and composition, or "turning" and "making contact," as Democritus says; for it has become solid from liquid without any change of order or position in its nature, nor does it now have hard and solidified particles, indivisible in mass—on the contrary, in the same way as it was liquid throughout, it is now hard and solidified throughout.[185]

Further, neither is it possible for there to be growth and withering; for not every part whatever will have become larger, if indeed [the change happening] is addition, and the totality will not have changed either by mixing with something or by having changed intrinsically.[186]

One must determine in this way, then, that there is a cause of coming to be [such-and-such] and affecting, coming to be [such-and-such] and being affected by each other, and in what way they are possible, and in what way some say they are, although it is not a possible one.

## 1.10

It remains to get a theoretical grasp on mixing in accord with the same mode of methodical inquiry; for this was the third of the things we proposed at the start.[187] We must investigate what mixing is, what it is to be mixable, and to which sort of beings it belongs, and in what way, and, further, whether mixing exists, or whether this is false; for some people say that it is impossible for one thing to be mixed with another; for if the things that have been mixed still exist and have not been altered, they are no more mixed now, they say, than previously, but are in a similar state; but if one of the two has passed away, they have not been mixed, but one exists and the other does not, whereas mixing is of two things in a similar state; and it is the same way even if when both of the things have come together, each of the things being mixed passes away; for things that have no being at all are not mixed. This argument, then, seems to be seeking to determine in what respect mixing differs from coming to be and passing away, and in what respect what is mixable differs from what can come to be and pass away; for clearly it must differ, if indeed it exists. So once these things are evident, the puzzles would be resolved.

Now, we do not say that wood has been mixed with fire, nor that it is being mixed when it burns, either itself with its very own parts or with the fire. On the contrary, we say that the fire comes to be and that the wood passes away. In the same way, we do not say that food is mixed with the body, or that the shape is mixed with the wax when it shapes its mass. Nor can the body and white—nor, in general, affections and states—be mixed in the things that have them; for they are seen to be preserved. But then neither can white and scientific knowledge be mixed, nor any other of the non-separables. Indeed this is what those who say that everything at one time was together and mixed say incorrectly; for not everything is mixable with everything; on the contrary, each of the things that have been mixed must preexist separately; but no affection is separable.[188]

But since some beings are potentially and others actually, it is possible for things that have been mixed in a certain way to be and not be, with what comes to be from them actually being distinct, and each of the very things that existed before being mixed still potentially being, and not having been destroyed; for this is the puzzle that the previous argument raised, and it is evident that things that are mixed come together from having been previously separate, and are capable of being separated again. So they neither actually remain, like the body and white, nor do they—either or both—pass away; for their capacity [or potential] is preserved. That is why this [puzzle] may be set aside.

However, a puzzle connected to this must be analyzed, as to whether mixing is something relative to perception.[189] For when the things that are mixed have been divided up so small and have been put next to each other in such a way that each is not clear to perception, have they, then, been mixed, or is it not so, but rather that any part whatever of one is next to some part of the other?[190] It is in the first way that it is said, for example, that grains of barley are mixed with grains of wheat, when any grain whatever of one is put next to some grain of the other. But if all body is divisible, if indeed a body that can be mixed with another is homoeomerous, any part whatever of one must come to be next to some part of the other.

But since it is impossible for a body to be divisible into smallest particles, and since composition is not the same as mixing but distinct from it, it is clear that one must not say *either* that the things are mixed, if they are preserved at the level of small particles—for this will be composition and not blending or mixing, nor will the part have the same account as the whole, whereas we say that, if indeed they have been mixed, the mixture is homoeomerous, and that just as a part of water is water, so it is too for what has been blended; however, if mixing were just composition at the level of small particles, none of these things will follow, but there will only be things that are mixed relative to perception, and the same thing will be mixed to one person whose sight is not sharp, while to Lynceus nothing will be mixed—*or*, if they are so divided, that any part whatever [of one] is next to some part [of the other], for it is impossible for them to be divided in this way.[191]

Either mixing does not exist, then, or it is necessary to state once again in what way it can possibly come about. There certainly are, we say, some beings that are capable of affecting and others affectable by them. Moreover, some—namely, those that have the same matter—convert, that is, are capable of affecting each other and of being affected by each other.[192] Other things, by contrast, though they affect, are unaffectable, namely, those that do not have the same matter. Of these, then, there is no mixing. That is why neither the craft of medicine nor health produces health by mixing with bodies.[193]

But among things that are capable of affecting and of being affected and are easy to divide, when many of these are put together with few, or large with small, this does not produce mixing, but rather growth of the mastering one; for the other changes into the mastering one, which is why a drop of wine does not mix with ten thousand *choes* of water; for its form dissolves and changes to the totality of the water.[194] But when the two are more or less equalized in capacity, then each of them changes from its own nature toward the mastering one, although it does not become the other, but something intermediate and common.[195] It is evident, then, that the mixable are the affecters that have a contrariety; for it is these indeed that are affectable by each other.[196]

Also, small particles put next to small ones are more mixable; for these more easily and more quickly change each other, whereas a large one, even under the influence of a large one, takes much time to accomplish this. That is why, of the things that are divisible and affectable, the easily bounded ones are mixable (for they divide easily into small particles; for this is what it is to be easily bounded). For example, the liquids are the most mixable of the bodies; for of the divisible things, what is liquid is most easily bounded, provided it is not viscous; for viscous ones, it is true, merely make the mass greater in volume and larger.[197]

But when only one of the two [things being mixed] is affectable—or is extremely so, while the other is altogether slightly so—the mixture of both is either not at all, or [only] a little, greater [in volume]—which is precisely what happens where tin and bronze are concerned. For some of the beings are hesitant with each other and play a double game; for they appear in a way as both slightly mixed and in a way as one of the two being recipient and the other form.[198] And this is precisely what happens in the case of these; for the tin, like some affection of the bronze that is without matter [of its own] pretty much vanishes after being all mixed, giving its color only.[199] And the same thing happens in other cases.

## 1.10

It is evident, therefore, from what has been said that mixing exists, what it is, and what causes it, and also what sorts of beings are mixable, since indeed they are the sorts of things that are affectable by each other, easily bounded, and easily divided; for it is neither necessary for these to pass away having been mixed, nor for them to be unconditionally still the same, nor for the mixing of them to be composition, nor to be in relation to perception. On the contrary, something is mixable that is easily bounded, and is capable of being affected and of affecting, and is mixable with a thing that is of this sort (for what is mixable is so in relation to a homonym), and mixing is the unification of mixable things when they have been altered.[200]

# Book 2

## 2.1

We have spoken about what way mixing, contact, affecting and being affected belong to things that in accord with nature are subject to change, and, further, about unconditional coming to be and passing away, in what way they happen, and to what, and due to what cause. Similarly, we have spoken about alteration, what alteration is, and how it differs from these. It remains to get a theoretical grasp on the so-called elements of bodies. For coming to be and passing away in the case of all substances that are by nature composite do not occur without the perceptible bodies.

Of these the underlying matter is said by some people to be one, supposing it to be air or fire or something intermediate between these that is a body and separable.[201] But others say that it is more than one, some saying fire and earth, others these and air as a third, others these and water as a fourth, as Empedocles did.[202] From the aggregation and disaggregation or alteration of these, the coming to be and passing away in things result.

Let it be agreed that the primary things are correctly said to be starting-points and elements, the ones from whose changing, whether by aggregation and disaggregation or another [sort of] change, coming to be and passing away result. But those, on the one hand, who posit a single matter beyond these, and it corporeal and separable, are making an error; for it is impossible for this perceptible body to exist without a contrariety; for it is necessary for this unlimited, which some say is the starting-point, to be either light or heavy or cold or hot.[203]

And the way things are written in the *Timaeus* has nothing definite about it; for [Plato] does not state perspicuously whether the all-receptive is separated from the elements, nor does he make any use of it when he says that it is a sort of underlying subject that is prior to the so-called elements, as gold is to works in gold (and yet this, said in this way, is not stated correctly: for the things of which there is alteration, it is this way, but for those of which there is coming to be and passing away, it is impossible to call something that from which it has come to be, and yet he says that by far the truest thing to say is that each of them is gold); on the other hand, he takes the resolution of the elements, which are solids, to extend as far as to planes, though it is impossible for planes to be the "wet nurse" and the primary matter.[204]

For our part, we say that although there is a sort of matter for the perceptible bodies, it is not separable but always goes along with a contrariety, and from this the so-called elements come to be. A more exact determination about these has been made elsewhere.[205] Nonetheless, since this is indeed the way that the primary bodies come from matter, we must make a determination about these also, thinking the matter, though inseparable, to be a primary starting-point, underlying the contraries; for neither is hot matter for cold, nor it for hot, but rather the underlying subject is matter for both. So first there is the starting-point for what is potentially a perceptible body; second, the contrarieties (I mean, for example, hot and cold); and only then, third, fire, water, and things of that sort; for these do change into each other, and it is not the way Empedocles and others say (for then there would be no alteration), whereas the contrarieties do not change. But nonetheless, even so we must state what sort and how many of them are the starting-points of body; for the others assume and make use of them, but say nothing about why they are these or this many.

## 2.2

Since what we are seeking are the starting-points of perceptible body, that is, of tangible body, and a tangible body is that for which touch is the perceptual capacity, it is evident that not all contrarieties produce forms and starting-points of body, but only those in accord with touch; for it is in accord with a contrariety that they differ, and [specifically] in accord with a tangible contrariety. That is why neither whiteness and blackness, sweetness and bitterness, nor (similarly) any of the other perceptible contrarieties [besides the tangible ones] produces an element. And yet sight is prior to touch, so that its subject matter too is prior; but it is not an affection of tangible body insofar as it is tangible, but rather is in accord with something else, even if it happens to be prior in nature.[206] It is among the tangible affections themselves, then, that one must distinguish which ones are primary differentiae and contrarieties.

The contrarieties that are in accord with touch are these: hot cold, dry wet, heavy light, hard soft, viscous brittle, rough smooth, coarse-grained fine-grained.[207] Of these, heavy and light are neither capable of affecting nor of being affected; for they are not said of things in virtue of their affecting something else or being affected by something else.[208] The elements, though, must be capable of affecting and being affected by each other; for they mix and change into each other.[209] Hot and cold, by contrast, and wet and dry are said of things, the one lot being capable of affecting, the other capable of being affected; for hot is what aggregates things of the same kind (for the disaggregating, which is precisely what they say fire does, is the aggregating of things of the same kind; for this results in removing what is alien) and cold is what brings together and aggregates alike things of the same kind and things not of the same kind.[210] Wet is what is not bounded by any defining mark proper to it, though it is easily bounded [by other things]; dry is what is easily bounded by a defining mark proper to it, though difficult [for other things] to bound.[211]

And the fine-grained and coarse-grained, viscous and brittle, hard and soft, and the other differentiae are derived from these; for since being capable of filling things belongs to the wet, because it does not have boundaries but is easily bounded, and follows along with what it makes contact with, and the fine-grained is capable of filling things (for its particles are fine, and what has small particles is capable of filling things; for whole makes contact with whole; and the fine-grained is most of all like this), it is evident that the fine-grained belongs to the wet, while the coarse-grained belongs to the dry. Again, the viscous belongs to the wet (because the viscous is the wet affected in some way, like olive oil), whereas the brittle belongs to the dry; for the completely dry is brittle—so that it has been solidified because of lack of liquid. Further, the soft belongs to the wet (for what can be pressed into itself and does not move to another place, which is precisely what the wet does, is soft; that is why it is also the case that the wet is not soft, but the soft does belong to the wet) and the hard to the dry; for what is solidified is hard and what is solidified is dry.

Things, though, are said to be dry and wet in many ways; for both wet and moist are opposed to dry, and, in turn, both dry and solid are opposed to wet; but all these belong to the wet and the dry said in the primary way.[212] For since dry is opposed to moist, and moist is what has alien liquid on its surface, whereas soaked is what has it to its depths, and dry is what is deprived of it, it is evident that moist will belong to the wet, and the dry that is opposed to it to what is dry in the primary way. Again, wet and solid are opposed in the same way; for wet is what has its own liquid down to its depths (whereas soaked is what has alien liquid down to its depths), and solid is what is deprived of this, so that these too belong, the one to the dry, the other to the wet.

It is clear, therefore, that all the other differentiae are led back to the primary four, whereas these can no longer be led back to fewer ones; for neither is the hot precisely wet or precisely dry, nor is the wet precisely hot or precisely cold, nor do the cold and the dry fall under each other or under the hot and the wet. So necessarily there are these four.

## 2.3

Since the elements are four in number, and of the four the pairings are six, and contraries do not naturally pair (for it is impossible for the same thing to be hot and cold, or, again, wet and dry), it is evident that the pairings of the elements will be four in number: hot and dry, hot and wet; and, again, cold and wet and cold and dry.[213] And these follow along, in accord with reason, with the apparently simple bodies: fire, air, water, and earth; for fire is hot and dry, air hot and wet (for air is like vapor), water cold and wet, and earth cold and dry, so that the differentiae are allocated to the primary bodies in a reasonable way, and the number of these is in accord with reason.

For of all those who make the simple bodies elements, some make them one, some two, some three, some four.[214] Now, the result for those who say that there is one only, and then generate the others by condensation and rarefaction, is to make the starting-points two: the rare and the dense, or the hot and the cold; for these are what play the role of handicraftsmen, while the one underlies them as matter.[215] Those who make them two right from the start, as Parmenides does with fire and earth, make the intermediates—for example, air and water—mixtures of these.[216] And it is the same way too for those who speak of three, as Plato does in the divisions; for he makes the middle a mixture.[217] And those who make them two and those who make them three are pretty much saying the same thing, except that the former divide the intermediate in two, whereas the latter make it one only. But some say there are four right from the start, as Empedocles does—but he in fact leads them back to two; for he opposes all the others to fire.[218]

Fire, however, and air and each of the others that have been mentioned are not simple, but mixed. The simple ones are like these, but not the same as them—for example, if something is like fire, it is fire-form, not fire, and if like air, it is air-form, and likewise in the other cases.[219] Fire is excess of hotness, just as ice is of coldness. And solidification and boiling are excesses of a sort, the one of coldness, the other of hotness. If, then, ice is the solidification of wet and cold, fire will be the boiling of dry and hot. That is why nothing comes to be either from ice or from fire.[220]

Since the simple bodies are four in number, two of each [pair] belong to each of the two places (fire and air belong to what spatially moves toward the limit, earth and water to what spatially moves toward the center).[221] And earth and fire are the extremes and the purest, whereas water and air are intermediates and more mixed. And two of them are contrary to the other two, for to fire water is contrary, and to air earth; for they are composed of the contrary affections. Nonetheless, being four in number, each is unconditionally one: earth is dry more than cold, water cold more than wet, air wet more than hot, and fire hot more than dry.[222]

## 2.4

But since it has been determined previously that coming to be for the simple bodies is from each other, and at the same time too it is evident from perception that they come to be (for otherwise there would be no alteration; for alteration is with respect to the affections of tangible things), we must speak about what way they change into each other, and whether every one can come to be from every one or whether some can but others cannot.[223]

Well, that all do naturally change into each other is evident; for coming to be is to contraries and from contraries, and the elements all have a contrariety in relation to each other due to their differentiae being contraries; for some both differentiae are contraries, for example, fire and water (for the one is dry and hot, the other wet and cold), for others only one is, for example, air and water (for the one is wet and hot, the other wet and cold). So universally, then, it is evident that all naturally come to be from all, and it is not difficult to see immediately with respect to each particular one in what way this occurs; for while all will come to be from all, they will differ with respect to faster and slower and with respect to easier and more difficult. For those that have tokens in relation to each other, the change is fast, for those that do not have them, slow, because it is easier for one thing to change than for many.[224] For example, from fire there will be air when one of the two [differentiae] changes (for the former was hot and dry, while the latter is hot and wet, so that if the dry is mastered by the wet, it will be air). Again, from air there will be water, if the hot is mastered by the cold (for the former was hot and wet, while the latter is cold and wet, so that if the hot changes, it will be water). And in the same way from water earth and from earth fire; for both have tokens in relation to each other; for water is wet and cold, while earth is cold and dry, so that when the wet is mastered, it will be earth. And again since fire is dry and hot, while earth is cold and dry, if the cold passes away, there will be fire from earth. So it is evident that the coming to be of the simple bodies will be in a circle, and this will be the easiest way of change, because there are tokens present in the successive ones.

It is possible, however, for water to come to be from fire, and from air earth, and again from water and earth for air and fire to do so, but it is more difficult, because there is change of more [affections]; for it is necessary, if there is going to be fire from water, that both the cold and the wet have passed away, and again if there is going to be air from earth, that both the cold and the dry have passed away. In the same way too if there is going to be water and earth from fire and air, it is necessary for both to change.

This sort of coming to be, then, takes more time. But if one [affection] of each of the two has changed, the change, though easier, is not into each other.[225] On the contrary, from fire and water there will be earth and air, and from air and earth there will be fire and water.[226] For when the cold of the water and the dry of the fire have passed away there will be air (for there remains the hot of the latter and the wet of the former). But when the hot of the fire and the wet of the water have passed away there will be earth, because of the remaining of the dry of the former and the cold of the latter. In the same way too from air and earth there will be fire or water; for when the hot of the air and the dry of the earth have passed away, there will be water (for there remains the cold of the latter and the wet of the former). But when the wet of the air and the cold of the earth have passed away there will be fire, because of the remaining of the hot of the former and the dry of the latter, and these, as we saw, are just what belong to fire.[227] And this coming to be of fire is also in agreement with perception; for flame is most of all fire, and flame is burning smoke, and smoke is composed of air and earth.[228]

In the case of successive bodies it is not possible for the passing away of one of the elements in each of them to have brought about a change into any of the bodies, because of the remaining in both either of the same ones or the contrary ones.[229] And from neither of these is it possible for a body to come to be—for example, if the dry of fire passed away, and the wetness of air; for in both cases the hot remains. Or if the hot passed away from both, contraries remain, namely, dry and wet. Similarly too in the other cases. For in all the successive ones there exists, on the one hand, the same [token] and, on the other, a contrary one. So at the same time it is clear that a change from one [body] to one [body] comes about through the passing away of one [token], whereas a change from two to one comes about through the passing away of more than one.

That all come about from all, and in what way their change into each other comes about, has now been stated.

## 2.5

Nonetheless let us also get a further theoretical grasp on these matters in the following way. For if the matter of natural bodies is, as it seems to some people to be, water, air, and things of that sort, it is necessary for there to be one, two, or more of these.[230] Well, they cannot all be one—for example, all air, or water, or fire, or earth—if indeed change is into the contraries. For if it were air, and if it remains, [the change] will be alteration, but it was [supposed to be] coming to be. At the same time, it does not seem to anyone that [it occurs] in such a way that water is at the same time also air (or whichever of the others). There will, then, be some contrariety (that is, a differentia) involved, of which something will have one of the two parts—for example, fire hotness.[231] Nonetheless, fire will not be hot air; for something of that sort is alteration, and is not what appears to happen. And at the same time, again, if there is to be air from fire, it will be due to the changing of the hot into its contrary. Therefore, this contrary will belong to the air, and the air will be something cold. So it is impossible for fire to be hot air; for then the same thing will be hot and cold. Therefore, both air and fire will be some same distinct thing, that is, some distinct sort of matter that is common to them.

The same argument applies to all of them, because it is not possible for there to be one of them from which all derive. But neither is there some other one beyond these—for example, a sort of intermediate between air and water or between air and fire (coarser-grained than air or fire, but finer-grained than the others); for air and fire will be that thing together with a contrariety. But one of the contraries is a privation.[232] So it is not possible for this thing ever to be alone, as certain people say the unlimited is and the encompassing.[233] Therefore, it is indifferently any of these whatever, or none of them. If, then, nothing—at any rate, nothing perceptible—is prior to these, it would be all these.[234] Therefore, it is necessary either for them to always remain and not change into each other or for all of them to change, or for some to do so but not others, as Plato wrote in the *Timaeus*.[235] Well, that it is necessary for them to change into each other was proved previously; and that they do not do so equally quickly one from another was stated previously, because those that have a token come to be from each other faster, those that do not have one, slower.[236]

If, accordingly, the contrariety with respect to which they change is one, it is necessary for there to be two [elements]; for the matter is the intermediate thing, being imperceptible and inseparable. But since there are seen to be more [elements], two would be the smallest number. And if there are two [contrarieties], there cannot be three [elements], but rather four, as is evident; for this is the number of pairings; for of the six, two cannot have come about because of being contraries to each other.

These matters have been spoken about previously.[237] But, since they change into each other, that it is impossible for there to be a starting-point of them either at the extremity or the middle will be clear from the following. In the case of the extremes, it will not be possible, because all will then be fire or earth, and the account is the same as the one saying that all come from fire or earth.[238] Nor is it possible that it is an intermediate, in the way that it seems to some that whereas air changes both into fire and into water, and water both into air and into earth, the extremes do not any longer change into each other; for the process must come to a stop and not go on without limit in a straight line in either direction.[239] For then there will be an unlimited number of contrarieties in the case of one [element].

Let E stand for earth, W for water, A for air, and F for fire. If, then, A changes to F and W, there will be a contrariety belonging to AF. Let these contraries be whiteness and blackness. Again, if A changes to W, there will be another contrariety (for W and F are not the same thing). Let these contraries be dryness and wetness: D for dryness, W for wetness. Well then, if white remains, wet and white will belong to water; if it does not, water will be black; for change is to the contrary. Therefore, it is necessary for water to be either black or white. Let it be the first. On similar grounds, accordingly, D (dryness) will belong to F. Therefore, there will also be a change of F (fire) into water; for contraries belong to them; for fire was first taken to be black, then dry, water wet, then white. It is evident, then, that there will be change from each other in every case, and, in the cases taken, that E (earth) will have the remaining two tokens, black and wet; for these have not yet been paired.

And that it is not possible to proceed without limit—which is precisely what we were going to prove, but we dealt with this issue before it—is clear from the following.[240] For if in turn fire (which F stands for) changes into something else, into X for example, and does not turn back, there will be some contrariety belonging to F (fire) and X other than the ones just mentioned; for it has been assumed that X is the same as none of E, W, A, or F.[241] Let K, then, belong to F, and Y to X. Then K will belong to all of E, W, A, and F, since they change into each other. But though in fact this has not yet been proved, at least it is clear that if in turn X changes into something else, another contrariety will belong to both X and F (fire).[242] And similarly, it is always the case that along with each additional [element] some [new] contrariety will belong to the previous ones, so that if it goes on without limit, the contrarieties that belong to a single [element] will also be unlimited.[243]

But if this is so, there will neither be a definition nor a coming to be of any [element]; for if one is to have come to be from another, it will have to go through so-and-so many contrarieties, and still more.[244] So there will be some things into which there will never be change—namely, if the intermediates are unlimited in number (which is necessary if indeed the elements are unlimited in number). Further, there will not even be a change from water to fire, if the contrarieties are unlimited in number. Further, all will come to be one; for it is necessary for all the contrarieties of those [elements] above F to belong to those below, and of those below F to those above, so that all will be one.²⁴⁵

## 2.6

One might well wonder at those who say that the elements of bodies are more than one—so that they do not change into each other, as Empedocles says—as to how it is open to them to say that the elements are comparable. And yet Empedocles does speak in this way: "For all these are equal."²⁴⁶ Now, if it is with respect to quantity, it is necessary for there to be some same thing belonging to all the comparable elements by which they are measured—for example, from one cotyle of water, ten cotyles of air might come.²⁴⁷ Therefore, there was some one thing that both are, if they are measured by the same thing. But if they are not in this way comparable in quantity, as quantity coming from quantity, but in capacity (for example, if a cotyle of water had the same capacity to cool as ten of air), in this way they are comparable in quantity, not insofar as it is quantity, but insofar as it has a certain capacity. And it would indeed be possible for these capacities to be compared not by a measure of quantity, but by analogy—for example, as this is white, that is hot. However, in quality the "as this" signifies likeness, but in quantity it signifies equality.²⁴⁸ It appears absurd, then, if bodies that are not capable of changing into each other are comparable not by analogy, but by a measure of their capacities, that is, that so-and-so much fire and many times that quantity of air be equal or similar in hotness; for the same thing in greater quantity, by being of the same kind, will have a ratio of this sort.²⁴⁹

But then there would not be growth either, according to Empedocles, except by addition; for fire will grow by fire, "earth makes its own kind grow; *aithêr* makes *aithêr* grow."²⁵⁰ These are additions. It seems, though, that growing things do not grow in this way.

It is much more difficult [for him] to give an account of the coming to be that is in accord with nature. For all the things that come to be by nature come to be either always or for the most part, whereas those that do so in a different way from always or for the most part come to be by chance or by luck.²⁵¹ What then is the cause of a human always or for the most part coming to be from a human, or wheat—and not an olive tree—from wheat? Or, again, if something is put together *this* way, [why] is it bone?²⁵² For when things come together by luck nothing comes to be, according to what he himself says, but only when they do so in a certain ratio. What, then, is the cause of this? For it certainly is not fire or earth. But then it is not love and strife either; for the former is the cause of aggregation only, the latter of disaggregation.²⁵³ In fact, it is the substance of each, not just "mixing and separation of what is mixed," as Empedocles says.²⁵⁴ And "luck" is "the name bestowed on them" and not "ratio"; for things can be mixed by luck.²⁵⁵ The cause, then, of things that are by nature is their being in a certain condition, and this is the nature of each, about which he says nothing. Therefore, he says nothing about nature.²⁵⁶ Moreover, this cause is the well-being and good, whereas he gives the praise to mixing alone.²⁵⁷ Yet, the elements, at any rate, are disaggregated not by strife but by love, and are by nature prior to the god—although they too are gods.²⁵⁸

Further, he speaks about movement in too simple a way; for it is not enough to say that love and strife move things, unless this was the being for love, namely, to move things in *this* way, whereas for strife it was to move them in *that* way.²⁵⁹ He should, then, either have defined, assumed, or demonstrated, either in an exact way, in a looser one, or in some other way.²⁶⁰ Further, since it is evident that the bodies move both by force—that is, contrary to nature—and in accord with nature (for example, while fire moves upward not by force, it moves downward by force), and what is by force is contrary to what is in accord with nature, and there is movement by force, there is also movement in accord with nature.²⁶¹ Is this, then, the movement that love moves things with?²⁶² Or not? For on the contrary the movement moving the earth downward is like disaggregation, and it is strife that is the cause of this movement in accord with nature rather than love. So, in general too, love would seem to be rather contrary to nature. But unless either love or strife moves them, there is simply no movement of the bodies themselves, nor is there rest.²⁶³ But that is absurd.

Further, it is evident that bodies do move. [Let it be,] then, that strife disaggregated them; *aithêr*, however, was spatially moved upward, not by strife, but, so he sometimes says, as if by luck, "it happened to run in this way then, but often in another way," while at other times he says that it is in the nature of fire to spatially move upward, whereas *aithêr*, he says, "sank under the earth with long roots."²⁶⁴

At the same time, though, he also says that the cosmos is in the same state now under strife as it was previously under love.²⁶⁵ What, then, was the primary mover and cause of movement? For it cannot then be love and strife. But of which of these movements are these the causes, if the primary mover is the starting-point?²⁶⁶

It is also absurd if the soul is composed of the elements, or is one of them; for how will the alterations characteristic of the soul—such as being musical and then again unmusical, or memory or forgetting—take place? For it is clear that if the soul is fire, the affections it will have will be those of fire insofar as it is fire, and if it is a mixture, the corporeal ones. But none of these alterations of the soul is corporeal. But discussing these issues is the function of another branch of theoretical knowledge.[267]

## 2.7

As for the elements of which the bodies are composed: for those people who think that these elements have something in common or change into each other, if one of these views holds, the other necessarily follows.[268] For those, on the other hand, who do not make the elements come to be from each other, nor in such a way as to come from each (except as bricks come to be from a wall), it will be absurd how fleshes and bones, or anything else of this sort, will come from them.[269] And what was said also involves a puzzle for those who make the elements come to be from each other, as to what way something else beyond them comes to be from them. I mean, for example, that water comes to be from fire and fire from it, for they have something in common, namely, the underlying subject. But, of course, flesh and marrow also come to be from them. In what way, then, do these come to be?

And for those who speak as Empedocles does, what will the way be? Necessarily, in fact, it is composition, just the way a wall comes to be from bricks and stones. And this mixture will come from the elements that are preserved but put together next to each other in the form of small particles. This, then, will be the way it is with flesh and each of the others. It follows, then, that it is not from any particle of flesh whatever that fire and water will come to be—in the way that from *this* bit of wax a sphere might come to be, and from some other bit a pyramid, but it would also be possible the other way around. This, then, is the way coming to be occurs when from any particle of flesh whatever both fire and water come to be. But for those who speak in the way under discussion it is not possible; on the contrary, it occurs in the way that from a wall a stone and a brick come to be, one from one place and part, and another from another.

Similarly, a certain puzzle is also involved for those who posit a single matter [for the elements], as to how something is to come from two of them—for example, from hot and cold or fire and earth. For if flesh comes from both and is neither, nor again is it a composite in which they are preserved, what remains except for the matter to be what comes to be from both? For the passing away of one produces either the other or the matter.

Or, since more and less applies to hot and cold, is it that when one of the two is fully actual, the other will be potential, but when it is not fully so, but in the way it is hot, it is [somewhat] cold, or [in the way that it is] cold [it is somewhat] hot, because when mixed they destroy each other's excesses, at that time neither the matter nor either of the contraries will be fully actual, but rather something intermediate, which, insofar as it is more potentially hot than cold, or the contrary, is in accord with the relevant ratio potentially twice as hot as cold, or three times, or related in some other such way?[270] The other things, then, will result from the contraries having been mixed, or rather from the elements, and the elements from the contraries, which in a certain way potentially are, not in the way the matter is, but in the way just mentioned. And in this way what comes to be is a mixture, whereas in the other way it is matter.[271]

But since the contraries are also affected in the way determined in our first investigations (for the actually hot is potentially cold and the actually cold is potentially hot, so that unless they are equal, they change into each other, and similarly in the case of the other contraries), in fact it is in this way that first the elements change [into each other].[272] And from these come flesh, bones, and things of this sort, the hot becoming cold, and the cold hot, when they approach the mean (for there they are neither), and the mean is of considerable extent and not indivisible.[273] Similarly, dry, wet, and things of this sort, in the region of the mean, produce flesh, bone, and the others.[274]

## 2.8

All the mixed bodies, the ones around the place at the center, are composed of all the simple bodies. For earth is present in all of them, because each simple body is most of all and in greatest quantity in its proper place.[275] And water is, because the composite must be bounded, and water alone of the simple bodies is easily bounded, and, further, because earth is incapable of holding together without the wet, this being what keeps it together; for if the wet were completely removed from it, it would fall apart. It is due to these causes, then, that earth and water are present in them, but also fire and air, because they are the contraries of earth and water; for earth is contrary to air, and water to fire, to the extent that substance admits of being contrary to substance.[276] Since, then, comings to be are from contraries, and one of the two [pairs of] extreme contraries is present, it is necessary for the other one to be present too, so that all the simple bodies are present in every composite one.[277]

The nourishment of each thing seems to attest to this; for everything is nourished by the very same things it is composed of, and everything is nourished by several things. For even precisely the things that might seem to be nourished by only one thing, like plants by water, are in fact nourished by several; for earth is mixed with the water; that is why farmers try to mix in something when watering.[278]

But since nourishment belongs with the matter, whereas what is nourished is the shape (that is, the form) taken together with the matter, it is immediately reasonable that fire alone of the simple bodies is nourished (though all of them come to be from each other), as previous thinkers also say; for fire alone and most of all belongs with form because its nature is to spatially move toward the defining mark.[279] And each thing naturally spatially moves toward its own place.[280] And the shape and form of all things lies in their defining marks.

It has been stated, then, that all the [mixed] bodies are composed of all the simple bodies.

## 2.9

But since there are some things that come to be and pass away, and coming to be does occur in the place around the center, we must state about all coming to be alike how many starting-points there are of it and what they are; for this way we shall more easily get a theoretical grasp on the particular ones, namely, when we first get hold of the universal ones.[281]

Now, the starting-points are equal in number and [the same] in genus to those in the province of the eternal and the primary things; for one is so as matter, the other as form.[282] But in addition, the third starting-point must also exist; for the two are not sufficient for coming to be, any more than in the case of the primary things.[283]

The cause as matter for things that come to be is what is capable of being and of not being; for some things of necessity are (for example, the eternal ones), while others of necessity are not—of these, it is impossible for the first lot not to be, and impossible for the second lot to be, because it is not open to them, contrary to necessity, to be otherwise. Some things, however, are capable of being and of not being—which is precisely what the capable of coming to be and of passing away is; for it at one time is and at another is not. So it is necessary for coming to be and passing away to have to do with what is capable of being and of not being. That is also why this is the cause as matter for the things that come to be. The cause as the for-the-sake-of-which is the shape—that is, the form—and this is the account of the substance of each thing.[284]

But one must also add a third, which all [philosophers] dream about, but none has stated.[285] On the contrary, some thought that the nature of the Forms was sufficient cause for coming to be, as Socrates says in the *Phaedo*; for he, in fact, after blaming others for having said nothing, supposes that some of the beings are Forms, others things that participate in the Forms, and that everything is said to be in accord with the Form, and to come to be in accord with partaking of it and to pass away in accord with losing it, so that if these things are true, the Forms, he thinks, are of necessity the causes of both coming to be and passing away.[286] Others, however, thought it was the matter itself; for [, in their view,] it is from this that the movement comes.[287] But neither lot speaks correctly. For if the Forms are causes, why do they not always cause coming to be continuously rather than sometimes doing so and sometimes not, since there are always both Forms and things that participate in them? Further, in some cases we see something else being the cause; for it is the doctor who produces health in things and the scientific knower who produces scientific knowledge, despite there being health-itself, scientific knowledge-itself, and the things that participate in them.[288] And it is the same way in the case of other things accomplished in accord with a capacity.

On the other hand, if someone were to say that it was the matter that caused coming to be due to its movement, he would speak in a way more appropriate to natural science than those who speak in the way just mentioned; for what alters and changes [something's] shape is more a cause of coming to be, and in all cases we are accustomed to say that the producer, both in the case of what is by nature and what is from craft, is whatever it is that is capable of causing movement. Nonetheless, these people too do not speak correctly; for it is characteristic of matter to be affected and to be moved, whereas causing movement and producing are characteristic of another capacity. This is clear both in the case of things that come to be by craft and of those that come to be by nature; for the water itself does not produce an animal from itself, nor does the wood produce a bed, but rather craft does. So these people too, because of this, speak incorrectly, and because they omit the more controlling cause; for they take away the essence and the shape [or form].[289]

Further, the capacities they assign to the bodies, due to which they cause coming to be, are too instrumental, since they do away with the cause that is in accord with the form.[290] For since, as they say, it is natural for the hot to disaggregate and for the cold to cause coming together, and for each of the others, either to affect or be affected, they say that from these, and because of these, all the others come to be and pass away. It is evident, however, that even fire itself is moved and affected.²⁹¹ Further, what they do is somewhat as if someone were to assign a saw and each of the instruments as the cause of things' coming to be; for it is necessary for the wood to be divided when someone saws it, and to be smoothed when someone planes it, and similarly in the other cases. So however much fire affects and moves something, in what way it moves it these thinkers do not go on to consider, [nor] that [it is] worse than the instruments.²⁹²

We have spoken in universal terms about the causes previously, and have now made determinations about matter and shape [or form].²⁹³

## 2.10

Further, since it has been proved that spatial movement is eternal, it is necessary, these things being so, for coming to be to occur continuously as well; for the spatial movement will produce coming to be perpetually through bringing to and bringing away what is capable of causing coming to be.²⁹⁴ At the same time, though, it is clear that what was said previously was correct, namely, saying that spatial movement, and not coming to be, was the primary [sort of] movement; for it is much more reasonable for what is to be the cause of the coming to be for what is not than for what is not to be the cause of being for what is.²⁹⁵ Well, what is spatially moving is, but what is coming to be is not. That is why indeed spatial movement is prior to coming to be.

But since we have posited and proved that things are subject to continuous coming to be and passing away, and since we say that spatial movement is the cause of coming to be, it is evident that if the spatial movement is one, it will not be possible for both processes to occur, because they are contraries (for what is the same, and remains in the same state, by its nature always produces the same thing, so that either coming to be will always occur or passing away will), so the spatial movements must be more than one and must be contraries, either because of the direction [of their movement] or because of its irregularity; for contraries have contraries as their causes.²⁹⁶

That is why it is not the primary spatial movement that is the cause of coming to be and passing away, but the one in the inclined circle; for in this there is both continuity and being moved with two movements; for it is necessary, if coming to be and passing away are always to be continuous, for there to be, on the one hand, something that is always moved, so that these changes do not fail, and, on the other hand, for there to be two movements, in order that not only one of the two processes will occur.²⁹⁷ The spatial movement of the whole, then, is the cause of the continuity, whereas the inclination is the cause of the approach and retreat; for this results in its becoming further away at one time and closer at another, and, since the distance is unequal, the movement will be irregular.[298] So, if it causes coming to be by approaching and being close, this same thing causes passing away by retreating and becoming further away; and if it causes coming to be by repeatedly approaching, it also causes passing away by repeatedly retreating; for contraries have contraries as their causes, and passing away and coming to be in accord with nature occur in equal periods of time.

That is why the times—that is, the lives—of each [sort of] thing have a number that determines them; for there is an order of all things, and every time—that is, every life—is measured by a period, except that it is not the same for all, but shorter for some and longer for others; for, for some things, this period, which is their measure, is one year, while for some it is longer, for others shorter. And it is evident that things we perceive are also in agreement with our arguments; for we see that when the sun is approaching there is coming to be, but when it is retreating there is withering, and each of these in equal time; for the time of withering and of coming to be in accord with nature are equal. But it often happens that things pass away in a shorter time because of the co-blending with each other; for because the matter is irregular, and not everywhere the same, it is necessary for the comings to be of things to be irregular too, some faster, some slower, with the result that, because of the comings to be of these things, others come to pass away.[299] But, as we said, coming to be and passing away will always be continuous, and will never fail to occur, due to the cause we have mentioned.[300]

And it is reasonable that this happens; for we say that in all cases nature always desires what is better, and that being is better than not being (in how many ways things are said to *be* has been stated elsewhere), but this cannot belong to all things, because of their being too far removed from the starting-point, although in the remaining way, the god has completed the whole, and made coming to be perpetual; for in this way being would most of all be connected together, because the closest things to being in the fullest sense are perpetual coming to be and coming to be.[301]

The cause of this, as has often been said, is circular spatial movement; for it alone is continuous.[302] That is also why the other things that change into each other in virtue of their affections and their capacities—for example, the simple bodies—imitate the circular spatial movement; for when from water air comes to be, from air fire, and from fire water again, we say that coming to be has gone around in a circle, because it turns back again. So even the rectilinear spatial movement is continuous by imitating the circular one.

At the same time, something certain people are puzzled about—as to why it is that, when each of the bodies is spatially moving to its own proper space, the bodies have not become separated out in the unlimited time that has elapsed—is clear from these. For the cause of it is their transition into each other; for if each remained in its own place and was not changed by its neighbor, they would already have been separated out. They change, then, because of the spatial movement's being double; and because of changing it is not possible for any of them to remain in any of the places assigned in the order.³⁰³

That there is coming to be and passing away, then, and due to what cause, and what the capable of coming to be is and the capable of passing away, is evident from what has been said.

But since [1] it is necessary for there to *be* something if there is to be movement ([1a] as was said previously elsewhere); and [1b] if movement is always to be, for there always to be something; and if continuous, for it to be one, the same, immovable, incapable of coming to be, and unalterable; and [1c] if the movements in a circle are several, for there to be several, but for all of them to be somehow under a single starting-point; and [2] because for time to be continuous, it is necessary for the movement to be continuous, if indeed it is impossible for there to be time without movement (therefore time is the number of a certain continuous movement, therefore of the one in a circle—as [2a] was determined in our starting accounts); but [3] is the movement continuous because of the continuity of what is moved or because of the continuity of that in which it is moved (I mean, for example, the place or the affection)?—it is clear surely that it is because of what is moved (for how could an affection be continuous except because of the continuity of the thing to which it belongs—if, though, it is also continuous because of that in which it is moved, this holds only of the place, since it has a certain magnitude); but [4] of it only the movement in a circle is continuous, in such a way that it is always continuous with itself; therefore [5] that is what produces continuous movement, namely, the body spatially moving in a circle, and its movement produces time.³⁰⁴

## 2.11

But since in the case of things that are in continuous movement in virtue of coming to be, or alteration, or change in general, we see that what is successive (that is, *this* coming to be after *that* in such a way as not to leave intervals), it must be investigated whether there is something, or nothing, which of necessity will be, but everything admits of not having come to be. For that some do is clear, and the fact that *will be* and *is going to be* are distinct is directly due to this; for of a thing of which it is true to say that it will be, it must at some time be true to say that it is.[305] On the other hand, of that of which it is now true to say that it is going to be, there is nothing to prevent its not having come to be; for someone who is going to take a walk may not take a walk. And, in general, since some beings admit also of not being, it is clear that the same will hold also of things coming to be—that is, their coming to be will not occur of necessity. Are, then, all of them of this sort? Or not so, but rather it is unconditionally necessary for some of them to come to be, and just as in the case of being some are incapable of not being while others are capable, is it that way too where coming to be is concerned? For example, is it necessary for solstices to have come to be—that is, is it impossible for them not to admit of not doing so?

Now, if it is necessary for what is earlier to have come to be, if what is later is to do so (for example, if a house, a foundation, and if a foundation, clay), does it also follow, then, that if a foundation has come to be, it is necessary for a house to have come to be? Or is this no longer so, unless it is unconditionally necessary for the latter to have come to be? In this case, though, if a foundation has come to be, it is also necessary for a house to have come to be; for the relation that the earlier has to the later was [assumed to be] such that if the latter is to be, it is necessary for the former to be earlier. If, therefore, it is necessary for the later one to have come to be, it is also necessary for the earlier one, and if for the earlier one, it is therefore necessary for the later one—not, though, because of the earlier one, but because it was assumed that of necessity it will be. Therefore, in those cases where it is necessary for the later to be, it converts—that is, always, if the earlier has come to be, it is necessary for the later to have come to be.

If, then, it goes on without limit downward, it will not be unconditionally necessary for *this* one of the later ones to have come to be, but hypothetically so; for always it will be necessary for there to be another before it, because of which it is necessary for it to have come to be.[306] So if there is no starting-point of what is unlimited, there will be no first thing because of which it will be necessary for it to have come to be. But then even in the case of the ones that have a limit it will not be true to say that it is unconditionally necessary for it to have come to be (for example, a house when a foundation has come to be; for when a foundation has come to be, if it is not always necessary for the house to have come to be), the result will be that something always is, although it admits of not always being. But if something's coming to be is of necessity, it must always be by coming to be; for *"necessary"* and *"always"* go together (for what it is necessary for there to be cannot not be), so that if it is of necessity, it is eternal, and if it is eternal, it is of necessity.[307] And if coming to be is therefore of necessity, the coming to be of this is eternal, and if eternal, of necessity.

If, therefore, the coming to be of something is of unconditional necessity, it is necessary for it to close the circle and turn back again. For it is necessary for coming to be to have a limit or not, and if not, for it to be rectilinear or in a circle. But of these, if indeed it is to be eternal, it cannot be rectilinear, because of there being no starting-point of any sort, whether taken going downward (going toward the future) or upward (going toward the past).[308] But it is necessary for coming to be to have a starting-point, and—not being limited—to be eternal.[309] That is why it is necessary for it to be in a circle.

It is necessary, therefore, for it to convert—that is, if of necessity *this*, therefore also the earlier; moreover, if the earlier, it is also necessary for the later to have come to be. And this goes on always continuously; for it makes no difference whether we say it is because of two things or of more.[310] It is in movement and coming to be in a circle, therefore, that there is unconditional necessity. And if it is in a circle, it is necessary for each thing to come to be and to have come to be, and if this is necessary, the coming to be of these things is in a circle.

This is certainly reasonable, since it was also evident on other grounds that movement in a circle—that is, that of the heaven—is eternal, because those things of necessity come to be and will be that are movements belonging to it and movements due to it; for if what is moved in a circle moves something always, it is necessary for the movements of these things to be in a circle as well—for example, since the highest spatial movement is produced in a circle, the sun moves in this circular way, and since it moves in this way, the seasons come to be in a circle because of it and turn back again, and since these come to be in this way, so in turn do the things due to them.[311]

Why, then, is it that some things evidently come to be in this way (for example, rain and air come to be in a circle, and if there is to be cloud, it must rain, and if rain, there must also be cloud), whereas human beings and animals do not turn back on themselves, so that the same one comes to be again? For it is not necessary, if your father has come to be, that you have come to be; but if you did, he did. And it seems that this coming to be is rectilinear. The starting-point of the investigation, for its part, is to ask again whether all [such processes] turn back on themselves or not, but rather some do so in number, others only in form.[312] It is evident, then, that the things whose substance (the thing moved) is incapable of passing away will be the same in number (for the movement follows along with the thing moved), whereas those whose substance is not so, but rather is capable of passing away, necessarily turn back again in form, but not in number.[313] That is why the water that comes from air and the air that comes from water are the same in form, not in number. If, though, these too are the same in number, still it is not by being things whose substance comes to be—that is, being [substance] of the sort that admits of not being.[314]

# *Meteorology*

# Book 1

### 1.1

Now, [1] the primary causes of nature, [2] all natural movement, [3] the stars arranged in the upper spatial movement, and [4] the elements of bodies, how many they are and of what sorts, their change into each other, and coming to be and passing away in general, have been spoken about previously.[315] It remains, then, to get a theoretical grasp on a part of this methodical inquiry, which all our predecessors have called "meteorology." It is concerned with whatever things happen in accord with nature, but a nature more disorderly, certainly, than that of the primary element of the bodies, and which occur in the place nearest to the spatial movement of the stars—for example, the Milky Way, comets, shooting stars, and moving and burning phenomena in the heavens.[316] It is also concerned with whatever affections may be regarded as common to air and water, and further the parts and forms (*eidos*) of earth and the affections of the parts, on the basis of which we may get a theoretical grasp on the causes of winds, earthquakes, and all the consequences that are in accord with their movements. Some of these we puzzle over, while others in a certain way we grasp. Further, it is concerned with the fall of lightning bolts, tornadoes and fire-tornadoes, and whatever other recurrent affections of these same bodies as are due to solidification.

After we have discussed these things, let us then get a theoretical grasp on whether we can give some account, in the way we have laid down, of animals and plants, both universally and separately; for when we have stated it, all of what we deliberately chose for ourselves at the start would pretty much have achieved its end.[317]

Having made a start in this way, let us speak about the following things first.

### 1.2

We previously determined that there is one starting-point of bodies, from which the nature of the bodies in circular spatial movement is composed, but four other bodies that are due to four starting-points, the movement of which, we say, is twofold, either away from or toward the center.[318] These four are fire and air, water and earth, and fire always rises to the top of them, whereas earth sinks down, while the other two stand to each other in an analogous relation; for air is nearest of all to fire, water to earth.[319] The whole cosmos around the earth, then, is composed of these bodies, the affections belonging to which, we say, must be grasped. It is of necessity continuous with the upper spatial movements, so that all its capacity [for movement] is governed from there; for the starting-point of all movement is from there, and *it* must be considered the primary cause.[320] In addition to this, it is eternal and it has no end as regards the place of its movement, but is always at its end, whereas these other bodies all have limited places that are separate from each other.[321] So fire, earth, and what is of the same kind as these must be regarded as the kinds (*eidos*) of in-matter cause of the things that come to be (for the underlying affected subject is what we refer to in this way), whereas in the sense of the cause from which, that is, the starting-point of movement, one must assign causality to the capacity of the things that are always moving.

## 1.3

Let us take up again our initial posits and the distinctions stated previously and then discuss the appearance of the Milky Way and comets, and whatever other things happen to be of the same kind as these.

We say, then, that fire, air, water, and earth come to be from each other, and that each is potentially present in the other, just as in the case of other things in which one and the same something underlies, into which they are at last resolved.[322]

First, though, someone might raise a puzzle about so-called air, as to what we must take its nature to be in the cosmos encompassing the earth, and what its position in the order might be in relation to the other so-called elements of bodies. (For how great the mass of the earth is in relation to the encompassing magnitudes is certainly not unclear; for astronomical observations have already shown us that the earth is far smaller even than some of the stars.[323] By contrast, we never see the nature of water collectively and marked off by boundaries, nor does it admit of being separated from the body of it settled around the earth—for example, the evident cases of the sea and rivers, and any that there may be below the earth and unclear to us.) But must we consider there to be one body of one nature or several intermediate between the earth and the outermost stars? And if several, how many, and as far as where do their places extend?

Now, we have spoken previously about the primary element, of what sort it is in virtue of its capacity, and why all of the cosmos around the upper spatial movements is filled with that body.[324] And we do not happen to be the only ones to hold this belief: it appears to be an ancient supposition and one held previously by human beings; for so-called *aithêr* [ether] was given this name in antiquity. Anaxagoras, though, seems to me to think that it signifies the same thing as *fire*; for he thought that the upper regions are full of fire, and that the ancients called the capacity there *aithêr*.[325] And on this latter point he believed correctly; for people seem to have supposed that the body that is always running (*aei theon*) is at the same time in a way divine (*theion*) in nature, and decided to name something of this sort *aithêr*, as not being the same as any of the things around us; for we say that the same beliefs come about in cycles among human beings, not once or twice or a few times, but an unlimited number of times.[326]

On the other hand, those who say that not only the bodies in spatial movement but also what encompasses them are pure fire, and that what is intermediate between the earth and the stars is air, would perhaps have ceased to hold this childish belief if they had got a theoretical grasp on what mathematics has now adequately proved; for it is too simple to consider each of the spatially moving things to be small in magnitude, because it appears so to us when we look at it from here.[327] We have also spoken about these matters previously in our speculations about the upper place.[328] But let us state the same account again now.

If the intervals were full of fire and the bodies were composed of fire, each of the other elements would long ago have vanished.[329] But then neither are they full of air alone; for then air would far exceed the equality of its common proportion in relation to the co-ordinate bodies, even if two elements filled the place intermediate between earth and the place of heaven; for the mass of the earth, in which the whole quantity of water is comprised, is (one might almost say) a mere nothing in comparison to the encompassing magnitude.[330] However, we see the excess between their masses not to be of such a magnitude when air comes to be disaggregated from water or fire from air. But it is necessary for the same ratio to hold between however small a quantity of water and the air coming to be from it as holds between the totality of air and the totality of water. And it makes no difference if someone will deny that these come to be from each other, yet allows that they are equal in capacity; for on this way of proceeding it is necessary for the equality in capacity to belong to quantities of these, just as it would have belonged if these came to be from each other.[331] It is evident, then, that neither fire nor air alone fills the intermediate place.

It remains, after having gone through the puzzles, to say in what way the two—I mean air and fire—are ordered in relation to the position of the primary body, and due to what cause the heat from the stars above reaches the places around the earth. Let us speak about air first, then, as we proposed, and in turn speak in this way also about these [other things].

If water comes to be from air and air from water, why are no clouds composed in the upper place?[332] For it would be more fitting for them to be composed the further the place is from the earth and the colder it is, due to its not being that close to the heat of the stars nor to the rays reflected from the earth, which prevents clouds from being composed near the earth, by disaggregating their composition because of the heat; for cloud gatherings come to be where the rays already abate because of their dispersal into the vastness.[333]

Either, then, water does not naturally come to be from all air, or, if it comes from all of it alike, the air surrounding the earth is not air alone, but rather a sort of vapor, which is why it gets composed into water again. But then if however much air there is, is all vapor, the nature of air and the nature of water would seem to be too excessive [in quantity], if indeed the intervals between the things above must be filled with some body; and if this cannot be fire because all the others would have been dried up if it were, it remains for it to be air and all the water surrounding the earth; for vapor is disaggregated water.[334]

About these things, then, let the puzzles be gone through in this way; for our part, though, let us speak at once with a view to the determinations that have already been stated and with a view to the ones we are now to state. For we say that what is upper and as far as the moon is a body distinct from fire or air, but varying in itself in purity and freedom from admixture, and admitting of differences, especially toward its limit on the side of the air, and the cosmos surrounding the earth.[335] Now, the circular spatial movement of the primary element and the bodies set in it disaggregate and ignite by their movement the part of the lower cosmos that is nearest to it, and so produce heat. And we must also understand it in this way starting as follows. In fact, the body below the upper circular movement is like a sort of matter, and is potentially hot, cold, dry, wet, and whatever other affections follow along with these.[336] But it becomes these and [actually] is them due to movement and immobility, the cause and starting-point of which we spoke about previously.[337] At the center and around the center, what is heaviest and coldest is set apart, namely, earth and water. Around these, and continuous with them, are air and what due to custom we call "fire," but it is not fire; for fire is excess of hotness and a sort of boiling.[338] But we must understand that of what we call "air," the part surrounding the earth is wet and hot because it is vaporous and contains exhalations from the earth, whereas the part above this is at this point hot and dry. For vapor's nature is wet and cold, that of exhalation hot and dry.[339] And vapor is potentially like water, exhalation potentially like fire. We must suppose, then, that the cause of clouds not being composed in the upper place is that air alone is not present in it, but rather a sort of fire.[340]

However, there is nothing to prevent the fact that clouds are not composed in the upper place from also being due to its circular spatial movement; for the totality of air encircling the earth is necessarily flowing, except that part of it caught within the circumference that evens it out, so that the earth is entirely spherical; for it is evident as things stand that the winds come to be in marshy places of the earth, and do not seem to blow excessively above the highest peaks.[341] This air flows in a circle because it is drawn along by the circular spatial movement of the whole. For the fire is continuous with the upper element and the air is continuous with the fire. So their movement prevents them from being composed into water. Instead, whenever any part becomes heavy the heat in it is squeezed out into the upper place and it spatially moves downward, but other particles in turn spatially move upward together with the fiery exhalation, and in this way it is continually the case that while one layer is always full of air and the other of fire, each of them is always coming to be one from the other.[342]

About why clouds do not come to be, why the air [there] is not aggregated into water, what way one must conceive of the place intermediate between the stars and the earth, and what sort of body it is filled with, let this much be said.

As for the generation of heat that is provided by the sun, it is more fitting to speak about it intrinsically and exactly in the works on perception (for heat is a sort of affection of perception), but due to what sort of cause it comes to be, though the nature of the things there [where the sun is] is not of this sort, must be stated now.[343]

We see, then, that movement is capable of disaggregating and igniting air, so that even things in spatial movement often appear to melt. The sun's spatial movement alone, then, is sufficient by itself to produce warmth and provide heat; for to do so it must be fast and not too far away. Now, the spatial movement of the [fixed] stars, though fast, is far off, while that of the moon, though close by, is slow. But that of the sun has enough of both characteristics. That more heat should be generated when the sun itself is there is reasonable, if we take the similarity from what comes about where we are; for here too it is the air that is closest to what is spatially moving by force that becomes most hot. And this happens quite reasonably; for the movement of a solid object disaggregates it most. This, then, is one cause due to which heat reaches this place here. Another is that the fire encompassing the air is often dispersed by the [sun's] movement and by force carried downward.

An adequate sign that the upper place is not hot or fiery is also provided by shooting stars. For they do not come about there but below; and yet the more and the faster things move, the faster they ignite. In addition to this, the sun, which is the precise thing that seems to be the most hot of all, is evidently bright but not fiery.

# Book 4[344]

## 4.1

Four causes have been distinguished for the elements, and in virtue of the combinations of these, it results that the elements are also four, of which two are capable of affecting, namely, the hot and the cold, and two of being affectable, namely, the dry and the wet.[345] Conviction on these matters is based on induction; for in every case we see hotness and coldness determining, naturally unifying, and changing both things of the same kind, and things not of the same kind, and wetting, drying, hardening, and softening them. Things dry and wet, by contrast, both intrinsically and when jointly present in bodies composed of both, are determined, and are affected, by the other affections just mentioned.

Further, it is clear from the accounts by which we define the natures of these; for we speak of the hot and cold as capable of affecting (for the capacity to aggregate is a sort of capacity to affect), but the wet and dry as affectable (for things are said to be easily bounded, and difficult [for other things] to bound, in virtue of their nature being affected in a certain way). [Since all this is so,] it is evident that some things are capable of affecting, others affectable. Having determined these things, we must grasp the workings of these, namely, the workings of the ones capable of affecting, and the species of the affectable ones.[346]

In the first place, then, universally [speaking], unconditional coming to be and natural change is the function of these capacities, as is the opposite passing away that is in accord with nature. And these processes occur both in plants and in animals and their parts. Unconditional and natural coming to be is a change due to these capacities (when they stand in the right ratio) in the matter that underlies each nature—this being the affectable capacities we have just mentioned.[347] And the hot and the cold produce [their effects] by mastering the matter. But when they fail partially to master it, the result is parboiling and non-concoction.

But the most common contrary to unconditional coming to be is putrefaction; for all passing away that is in accord with nature is *en route* to it—for example, old age and drying up. Putrescence is the end of all these things, that is, of the ones put together by nature, unless something passes away by force; for it is indeed possible to burn flesh, bone, and whatever, but the end of their passing away in accord with nature is putrefaction.[348] That is why putrefying things become first wet and then, in the end, dry; for they came to be from these, the wet being determined by the dry through the workings of the ones capable of affecting.

Passing away comes about when what is being determined masters what is determining it because of the environment (although in a special sense putrefying is said of things that partially pass away, when they have been separated from their nature).³⁴⁹ That is why, indeed, all the others except fire putrefy; for earth, water, and air indeed putrefy; for all these are matter for fire.³⁵⁰

Putrefaction is the passing away of the proper and natural heat within a given wet thing caused by an alien heat, that is, the heat from its environment.³⁵¹ So, since a thing is affected in this way because of a deficiency of heat, and since everything deficient in this sort of capacity is cold, both would be a cause, and putrefaction would be the common affection of proper coldness and alien heat.³⁵² For this is also why everything that putrefies becomes dry, and in the end becomes earth or dung; for as its proper heat leaves it, its natural liquid evaporates with it, and there is nothing to suck in liquid; for its proper heat is what attracts it and draws it in.

Also, a thing putrefies less in cold spells than in warm ones; for in winter the environmental air and water contain little heat, so that they have no strength, whereas in the summer they have more. Also, what is frozen does not putrefy (for its cold is greater than the air's heat, and hence is not mastered by it, whereas the mover does master), nor does what is boiling or hot putrefy (for the heat in the air is less than in the thing, so that it does not master it or produce any change whatever).³⁵³ Similarly too anything that is moving or flowing putrefies less easily than what is immobile; for the movement due to the heat in the air is weaker than the one preexisting in the thing, so that it does not make it change at all.

And due to the same cause, a large quantity of a thing putrefies less easily than a small one; for in the larger quantity there is too much proper fire and cold for the capacities in what surrounds it to master. That is why the sea putrefies quickly when segregated out into parts, but when all together it does not, and all other waters likewise. Also, living things come to be in putrefying things, because the heat being segregated out from them, being natural, causes the composition of the things segregated out with it.³⁵⁴

What coming to be is, then, and passing away, has been stated.

## 4.2

It remains to state the subsequent species, namely, the ones that the aforementioned capacities produce from things that are already composed by nature as underlying subjects.³⁵⁵

Of heat, then, this is concoction (*pepsis*), and of concoction [the species are] ripening (*pepansis*), boiling (*hepsêsis*), and, further, broiling (*optêsis*). Of cold, on the other hand, it is non-concoction (*apepsia*), and of it [the species are] rawness (*ômotês*), parboiling (*molunsis*), and parbroiling (*stateusis*). We must take it, however, that these names are not said strictly of the things. On the contrary, there are no names established universally for similar things. So we must consider the species just mentioned as not the same as these things but as of the same sort. However, let us say of each of them what it is.

Concoction, then, is a completion due to the natural and proper heat and is [produced] from the opposing affectables, these being the matter proper to the given thing.[356] For when it has been concocted, it is completed and has come to be. And the starting-point of the completion comes about due to the proper heat, even if certain of the external aids contributed to its accomplishment—for example, nourishment is helped in its concoctions even by baths and by other things of this sort. But the starting-point, at any rate, is the heat within the body itself. And the end in some cases is the nature—but nature, we say, as form and substance. In others the end of concoction lies in a certain underlying shape [or form], as when the wet has come to be of such-and-such quality, or of such-and-such quantity, when broiled or boiled or putrefied, or heated in some other way; for at that time it is useful and we say it has been concocted, like wine must, what gets composed in boils, when pus arises, and tears when they become rheum, and likewise in other cases.[357]

Concoction, in fact, is what everything is affected by when its matter—that is, its liquid—is mastered. For this is what is determined by the heat in its nature. For the thing has its nature as long as the ratio is in it.[358] So things of this sort are signs of health, namely, urine and stool and residues in general.[359] And we say that they have been concocted, because they make clear that the proper heat is mastering the indefinite [matter]. And it is necessary for concocted things to be denser and hotter; for the sort of thing heat accomplishes is to make things more compact, denser, and drier.

This, then, is what concoction is, whereas non-concoction is non-completion due to a deficiency of proper heat (and deficiency of heat is coldness). And the non-completion is of the opposed affectables, which is for each thing the natural matter.

Let concoction and non-concoction, then, be defined in this way.

## 4.3

Ripening is a sort of concoction; for the concoction of the nourishment in fruit is said to be ripening. And since concoction is a completion, ripening is complete when the seeds in the fruit are capable of producing another of the same sort as the fruit itself; for this is also what we mean by "complete" in other cases. In the case of fruit, then, this is ripening, but many other things that have been concocted are said to be *ripe*, with reference to the same species [of ripeness], but by transference, because, as we said previously, no names have been established for each particular sort of completion having to do with the determinations [of the matter] due to natural heat and cold.[360] In the case of boils, phlegm, and things of this sort, ripening is the concoction of the liquid within them by their natural heat; for it is impossible for what does not master to determine. Everything that ripens, then, if it comes from pneumatized things, is watery; and from things of the latter sort earthy ones are composed; and always from fine-grained things more coarse-grained ones come to be.[361] And in accord with this the nature draws some of these into itself, while others it rejects.[362]

It has been stated, then, what ripening is. Rawness is its contrary; for its contrary is non-concoction of the nourishment in the fruit; and this is the indefinite liquid. That is why rawness is either pneumatized, watery, or both. And since ripening is a completion, rawness will be an incompletion. Incompletion, though, comes about because of a deficiency of natural heat and a lack of proportion in relation to the liquid that is being ripened. (But nothing wet ripens intrinsically without something dry; for water alone of the liquids does not become coarse-grained.[363]) This lack of proportion results either due to the quantity of the hot being small or because the quantity being determined is large. That is also why the humors of raw things are fine-grained, and cold rather than hot, and they are inedible and undrinkable.[364]

But rawness, in fact, just like ripening too, is said of things in many ways. Thus urine, excreta, and catarrhs are all said to be raw due to the same cause; for raw things are all so called due to the [matter] not having been mastered or composed by the heat. And if we go further, potter's clay is said to be raw and milk and many other things are said to be raw if they are capable of changing and being composed by the heat but have remained unaffected. That is why water is said to be boiled, but not raw, because it does not become coarse-grained.

It has now been stated what ripening is, and rawness, and what causes each of them is due to.

Boiling in general is concoction by wet heat of the indefinite [matter] present in the liquid [in the thing being boiled], but the name is said in the strict sense only of things being cooked by boiling. This, as was stated, is either pneumatized or watery.[365] The concoction comes about due to the fire in the liquid; for what is cooked on griddles is broiled; for it is affected by the external heat and, as for the liquid [that is, the fat] in which it is contained, it dries this up, taking it into itself.³⁶⁶ But what is boiled produces the contrary effect; for its water is segregated out of it due to the heat in the water outside it. That is why boiled things are drier than broiled ones; for boiled things do not draw liquid into themselves; the external heat masters the internal; whereas if a thing's internal heat did master, it would draw liquid into itself.

Not every body, though, can be boiled; for neither can something—for example, stones—in which there is no liquid to be boiled, nor can things in which there is liquid, but which are too dense for it to be mastered—for example, wood. But those bodies that contain liquid that is affectable by the fire burning in the liquid outside them can be boiled. Again, gold, wood, and many other things are said to be boiled, with reference not to this same species (*idea*), but by transference; for no names have been established for the differentiae. We also speak of liquids such as milk and grape must as being boiled when the humor in the liquid changes to a certain form (*eidos*) due to the heat of the external fire that surrounds them, so that it produces an effect quite like the boiling just mentioned.

But the end for which things are boiled or concocted is not the same in all cases. In some, it is with a view to eating, in others, with a view to drinking, in others, with a view to some other use, since we speak of drugs too as being boiled.

So all things can be boiled that are capable of becoming more coarse-grained, smaller, heavier; as can those of which some parts are of these sorts, while other parts are of the contrary sorts, because when these things disaggregate some parts become coarse-grained and other parts fine-grained (as milk disaggregates into whey and curd). Olive oil by itself, on the other hand, does not boil, because it is affected in none of these ways.³⁶⁷

This, then, is what concoction by boiling is said to be. And it makes no difference whether it occurs in craft-produced instruments or in natural ones, because the cause will be the same in all cases.

Parboiling is the [species of] non-concoction contrary to boiling. And so the contrary of boiling, and what is called "parboiling" in the primary sense, would be non-concoction of the indefinite [matter] in the body due to a deficiency of heat in the surrounding liquid (that deficiency of heat is presence of cold has already been stated).³⁶⁸ This comes about because of another sort of movement; for the heat doing the concocting is expelled, and the deficiency of heat is due either to the quantity of cold in the liquid or due to the quantity of it in the thing being boiled; for then the result is that the heat in the liquid is too great to cause no movement at all, but too small to make it even and concoct throughout. That is why things are harder when they are parboiled than when they are boiled, and the liquid parts more distinguished.

It has now been stated what boiling is, and what parboiling is, and what cause each is due to.

Broiling is concoction by dry and alien heat. That is why even if someone were to produce a change and a concoction by boiling, but not due to the heat of the liquid but rather that of the fire, when the process is complete, the thing is broiled, not boiled, and if excessively it is said to be burned as well.[369] And it is due to dry heat when the thing ends up becoming drier. That is also why the outside is drier than the inside, whereas with boiled things it is the contrary. Also, when the work is artificial, broiling is more difficult than boiling; for it is difficult to heat the outside and the inside evenly. For the parts nearer the fire dry faster and so dry more as well. When, then, the outer ducts contract, the liquid contained in the thing cannot get segregated out, but is trapped inside when the ducts shut.

Broiling and boiling are, of course, due to craft, but, as we said, the same universal species are also due to nature; for the affections that come about are similar, although they are nameless; for craft imitates nature, since in fact the concoction of nourishment in the body is similar to boiling; for it too comes about in a liquid and hot [place] due to the heat in the body.[370] And non-concoction is sometimes like parboiling. Also, it is not in the process of concoction that living things come to be, as some people say, but rather they come to be in the excreta that putrefy in the lower intestines, and then ascend; for concoction takes place in the upper intestines, whereas the excreta decay in the lower ones.[371] The cause of this has been spoken about elsewhere.[372]

Parboiling, then, is contrary to boiling. And to the concoction we have called "broiling," there is a similarly opposed one, but it is harder to find a name for it. It is the sort of thing that would happen if there were par-broiling but not broiling [proper] because of a deficiency of heat that would take place either because of too little external fire or because of the quantity of water in the thing being broiled; for then the heat is too great to cause no movement at all, but too small to concoct [properly].

What concoction is and non-concoction, ripeness and rawness, boiling and broiling and their contraries, has now been stated.

## 4.4

We must now speak about the species of the affectables, namely, the wet and the dry.

The starting-points of the [elementary] bodies, the affectable starting-points, are wet and dry, and the others are mixtures composed of these, and whichever of them there is more of, of it the nature of the thing is more—for example, some are more dry, others more wet. All of them, though, will, on the one hand, be actual, and, on the other, the opposite—for example, this is how melting stands in relation to meltable.[373]

But since the wet is easily bounded, whereas the dry is difficult to bound, they are affected by each other somewhat as a gourmet dish is by its seasonings; for the wet is a cause of the dry's being bounded, and each becomes a sort of glue to the other—just as Empedocles puts it in *On Nature*, "gluing meal together with water."[374] And because of this the definite body is composed of both. And of the elements earth is said to have the most special affections of dry, water of wet.[375] That is why all the definite bodies here are not without earth and water (and whichever it is more of, this capacity is the one each appears to be in accord with), and it is only in earth and in water that there are animals, and not in air or fire, because these are the matter for their bodies.[376]

Of the affections of bodies, the primary ones that of necessity belong to a definite thing are hardness and softness; for it is necessary for what is composed of the wet and dry to be either hard or soft. Hard is that whose surface cannot be pressed into itself; soft is that whose surface can be pressed in, but not by being replaced; for water is not soft; for its surface is not pressed downward by pressure, but is replaced.[377] Something is unconditionally hard or unconditionally soft if it is unconditionally like that, whereas it is so in relation to something else if it is like that in relation to it. Now, in relation to each other they are undetermined by more or less, but since we judge all perceptibles in relation to perception, it is clear that we determine both the hard and the soft in relation to touch, and touch is what we use as a mean.[378] That is why we say that what exceeds it is hard and what is deficient is soft.

### 4.5

It is necessary for a body that is determined by its own proper defining marks to be hard or soft; for either it can be pressed or it cannot. Further, it must be solidified; for it is determined by this. So since everything determined and composed is either soft or hard, and softness and hardness are due to solidification, no composed and definite thing could exist without solidification. Solidification, then, must be spoken about.

There are, then, two causes that have to do with the matter, namely, the affecter and the affection—the affecter as starting-point of the movement, the affection as form.[379] So solidification and diffusion, drying and wetting, also [involve these]. And the affecter affects due to two capacities and the thing is affected due to two affections, as has been stated.[380] It affects due to heat and cold, and the affection is due either to the absence or presence of heat or cold.

But since solidification is a sort of drying, we must speak about drying first. What is affected, then, is either wet or dry or composed of both. And we suppose that water is the body of what is wet, and earth of what is dry; for of things that are wet and dry these are the affectable ones. That is also why the cold is more characteristic of the affectable ones; for it is present in them; for in fact we take both to be cold. And the cold is capable of affecting [only] as destructive or coincidentally, as was said previously; for sometimes the cold is said to burn and heat, not in the way the hot does, but by bringing together and compressing the hot.[381]

Drying affects whatever is water, or is a form (*eidos*) of water, or contains water, whether brought in or connate (by "brought in" I mean like the water in wool, by "connate" like the water in milk). Forms of water are things such as the following: wine, urine, whey, and, in general, whatever contains—not due to viscosity—no, or very little, sediment; for sometimes the cause of having no sediment is viscosity, as with olive oil and pitch. Drying is always due either to heating or cooling, but in both cases is by heat, whether internal heat or external heat; for even things that are dried by cooling, like a cloak, in which the water is intrinsically separated, are dried by their internal heat, which makes the liquid evaporate together with it, if their liquid content is small, when, in the form of evaporation, the liquid comes out together with the heat due to the surrounding cold.

All things become dry, then, as was said, either by being heated or cooled, and always because of heat, whether internal or external, evaporating the liquid content together with it (by "external" I mean, for example, when things are boiled; "internal," when the heat exhales, subtracts, and consumes [the liquid content]).[382]

Drying has now been spoken about.

## 4.6

Liquefaction is in one case water coming to be by composition, in the other the melting of a solid. Of these, composition occurs when the pneuma is cooled, whereas melting will be clear at the same time as solidification.

Things that solidify either solidify because they are watery or a mixture of earth and water, and do so due to either dry heat or cold. That is also why all bodies solidified by heat or cold when they dissolve, dissolve due to their contraries; for those that solidify due to dry heat dissolve due to water, which is wet cold, while bodies that solidify due to cold dissolve due to fire, which is hot.[383] Some things, though, would seem to solidify due to water—for example, boiled honey. But it does not solidify due to the water, but due to the cold within it.

Watery things do not solidify due to fire. For they dissolve due to fire, and the same thing in relation to the same thing will not be the cause of the contrary effect in the same thing.[384] Further, it is by the exiting of heat that they are solidified, so it is clear that it is by its entry that they will be dissolved. So its being solidified is a product of the cold. That is also why when watery things solidify they do not become coarse-grained; for coarse-grainedness comes about because of the exiting of water, and of the composing of the dry. And water alone of the liquids does not become coarse-grained.[385]

Compounds of earth and water are solidified both by fire and by cold, and become coarse-grained due to both, in some respects in the same way, in others in distinct ways, namely, due to heat drawing out the liquid (for when the liquid evaporates, the dry becomes coarse-grained and composed), or due to cold squeezing out the heat along with which the vaporizing liquid also departs. Things, then, that are soft but not liquid do not become coarse-grained, but rather solidify when water exits them—for example, clay when baked. But mixtures that are liquid become coarse-grained as well—for example, milk. And those that were previously coarse-grained and hard due to the cold often become wet at first, as again clay on first being baked gives off steam and becomes softer (which is why indeed it [sometimes] gets distorted in the kilns).

Now, of the things solidified due to the cold that are compounds of earth and water, but contain more earth, those that solidify because of the exiting of heat melt when the heat enters them again—for example, mud when it has frozen. But those that solidify due to cold, and because of the evaporation of all their heat at the same time, are indissoluble except by excessive heat, although they can be softened—for example, iron and horn. Wrought iron, though, will indeed melt, so that it becomes pliant and then solidifies again.[386] Steel too is produced in this way; for the dross sinks down to the bottom and is cleared away below.[387] And when it has been affected often in this way and becomes pure, steel results, but they do not do this often because the clearing away involves much waste and loss of weight.[388] But the better the iron, the less the waste. Pyrimachus stone also melts, so that it forms drops and becomes molten, and when it solidifies after it has run, it becomes hard again; and millstones melt, so that they become molten, and when they solidify again, though they are black in color, they become like lime [in consistency].³⁸⁹ Mud and earth both melt as well.³⁹⁰

Of things solidified by dry heat, some are non-dissolvable, others dissolvable by a liquid. Pottery and some kinds (*genos*) of stone that are made of earth calcined by fire, such as millstones, are non-dissolvable.³⁹¹ But soda and salt are dissolvable in liquid, not in all liquid though, but [only] in cold.³⁹² That is why they melt in water and in things watery in kind (*eidos*), but not in olive oil.³⁹³ For wet cold is contrary to dry heat. If one solidifies, then, the other will dissolve; for in this way contraries will be causes of contraries.

## 4.7

Things that are composed more of water than of earth only become coarse-grained due to fire, whereas those that are composed more of earth become solidified. That is why soda and salt are composed more of earth, as are stone and clay.

The nature of olive oil, however, is most puzzling. For if it is composed [more] of water, it should be solidified due to cold, but if more of earth, due to fire. But as things stand it is solidified due to neither, but becomes coarse-grained due to both. The cause is that it is full of air. That is also why it rises to the surface of water; for in fact air spatially moves upward.³⁹⁴ Cold makes it coarse-grained by producing water from the pneuma within it. For always, when water and olive oil are mixed, the two together become more coarse-grained. And due to fire and time olive oil becomes coarse-grained and whitens. It whitens, though, due to the evaporation of any water there was within it, whereas it becomes coarse-grained because, as its heat dies out, water comes to be from the air.³⁹⁵ In both ways, then, the same affection comes about, and due to the same thing, but not in the same way. It certainly becomes coarse-grained due to both [heat and cold], but it does not become dry due to either (for neither the sun nor cold dries it), not only because it is viscous, but also because it is composed of air. But the water does not get dried out or boiled off due to the fire, because, due to the viscosity, it does not evaporate.

Things that are mixtures of water and earth are fittingly said [to be what they are] in accord with the quantity of each; for a sort of wine becomes both solid and coarse-grained when it is boiled—for example, wine must. In the case of all things of this sort, it is the water that departs when they are drying. A sign that it is the water is that the vapor gets composed into water, if one wishes to collect it. So in those in which something remains, that something is composed of earth. Some of these things, as was said, also become coarse-grained and dried due to cold; for cold not only solidifies, but also dries water, and makes things coarse-grained by making air into water.[396] And solidification, as was said, is a sort of drying.[397]

Things, then, that do not become coarse-grained due to cold, but solidified, are composed more of water—for example, wine, urine, vinegar, lye, and whey.[398] But things that become coarse-grained [due to cold] (not by evaporation due to fire) are either composed more of earth or are compounds of water and air—for example, honey more of earth, olive oil more of air. And milk and blood are compounds of both earth and water, but more so of earth in most cases, as too are the liquids from which soda and salt come to be (and stones are also composed of certain ones of this sort).[399] That is why whey, if it has not been separated out, burns off when it is boiled by fire.

But what is earthy [in milk] also becomes composed due to fig juice, if one boils it in the way doctors do when they curdle it.[400] This is the way the whey and the cheese are separated. But when whey is separated, it no longer becomes coarse-grained but boils off like water. And if milk contains little or no cheese, it is composed more of water and is without nourishment. And blood is similar; for it becomes coarse-grained when dried by cooling. But the sorts of blood that do not become coarse-grained, like that of the deer, are composed more of water, and are cold. Hence they do not contain fibers; for fibers are composed of earth and are solid.[401] So when they are removed, the blood does not become coarse-grained. This is because it does not become dry; for what remains is water, as with milk when the cheese has been removed. A sign of this is that diseased blood tends not to solidify; for it is serous, [that is,] it is phlegm and water, because of being incapable of being concocted and mastered by the nature.[402]

Further, some of these [compounds of water and earth] are dissolvable—for example, soda; others are indissoluble—for example, pottery. And of these latter, some can be softened—for example, horn; others cannot be softened—for example, pottery and stone. The cause of this is that contraries are a cause of contraries, so that if solidification is due to two, namely, cold and dry, it is necessary for dissolution to be due to hot and wet. That is why dissolution is due to fire and water (for these are contraries): to water, of what is solidified by fire alone, and to fire, of what is solidified by cold alone. So if any things happen to be solidified by both, these are most indissoluble of all. And things are of this sort when they have been heated and then solidified by the cold; for the result is that when the exiting heat has evaporated most of their liquid, they are squeezed together again by the cold, so that they provide no entry route even for liquid. And because of this they are dissolved neither by heat (for it dissolves only things solidified by cold) nor by water (for it does not dissolve things solidified by cold but only things solidified by dry heat). But iron is melted by heat and solidifies when cooled.

Woods are composed of earth and air. That is why they are combustible, not meltable or softenable, and float on water—except for ebony, which does not; for while the other woods contain much air, in black ebony the air has evaporated out and there is more earth in it.

Potter's clay is composed of earth alone because while drying it solidifies by small degrees; for water has no ways in even where pneuma alone had escaped just by itself, nor has fire; for it solidified the clay.[403]

What solidification is, and melting, and the number of causes they are due to and of things in which they occur, have now been stated.

## 4.8

From the preceding it is evident that bodies are composed by heat and cold, and are made coarse-grained and solid by the workings of these. And because of being handicrafted by these, there is heat in all of them, while in some there is also cold, insofar as heat is wanting. So, since these belong [to bodies] due to being capable of affecting, wet and dry due to being capable of being affected, compound bodies have a share of all of them.

The homoeomerous bodies, then, are composed of water and earth, both in plants and in animals, and metals, such as gold, silver, and others of this sort are composed of them and from their exhalations when they are enclosed [under the earth], as has been stated elsewhere.[404]

All these things differ from each other with regard to the special objects of the perceptual capacities, in virtue of their being capable of affecting [the capacities] in a certain way (for a thing is white, fragrant, resonant, sweet, hot, or cold, in virtue of being capable of affecting the perceptual capacity in a certain way), and also with regard to other affections more proper to themselves, which are called what they are in virtue of being affectable—I mean, for example, being dissolvable, solidifiable, bendable, and whatever others are of this sort; for all things of this sort are affectables, like wet and dry.[405] It is in virtue of these that bone, flesh, sinew, wood, bark, stone, and each of the other homoeomerous natural bodies differ.

Let us state first the number of these that there are, namely, the ones that are said of things as capacities and as incapacities. They are as follows:

| | |
|---|---|
| solidifiable (*pêkton*) | non-solidifiable |
| meltable (*têkton*) | non-meltable |
| softenable by heat (*malakton*) | non-softenable by heat |
| drenchable (*tegkton*) | non-drenchable[406] |
| bendable (*kampton*) | non-bendable |
| breakable (*katakton*) | non-breakable |
| shatterable (*thrauston*) | non-shatterable |
| receptive of impressions (*thlaston*) | non-receptive of impressions |
| plastic (*plaston*) | non-plastic |
| compressible (*pieston*) | non-compressible |
| pullable (*helkton*) | non-pullable |
| malleable (*elaton*) | non-malleable |
| splittable (*schiston*) | non-splittable |
| cuttable (*tmêton*) | non-cuttable |
| viscous (*glischron*) | crumbly (*psathuron*)[407] |
| kneadable (*pilêton*) | non-kneadable |
| combustible (*kauston*) | non-combustible |
| capable of giving off fumes (*thumiaton*) | incapable of giving off fumes |

The majority of bodies, pretty much, differ in virtue of these affections. What sort of capacity each of them has, let us now state.

Well, about solidifiable and non-solidifiable, meltable and non-meltable, we have spoken in universal terms previously, but let us return to them again now.[408] Of bodies that solidify and harden, some are affected in this way due to heat, others due to cold—the one lot due to heat drying liquid, the other lot due to cold squeezing out heat. So one lot is thus affected in virtue of absence of liquid, the other lot in virtue of absence of heat, the watery ones in virtue of absence of heat, the earthy ones in virtue of absence of liquid. The ones affected in this way in virtue of absence of liquid are melted by liquid, unless they are composed in such a way that their ducts are rendered too small for the masses of the water to enter—for example, pottery. Those, though, that are not composed this way are all melted by liquid—for example, soda, salt, and dried mud. On the other hand, those solidified by privation of heat are melted by heat—for example, ice, lead, and bronze.

The sorts of bodies, then, that are solidifiable and meltable, and the sorts that are non-meltable, have now been stated.

The non-solidifiable ones are the ones that do not contain watery liquid nor are watery, and are composed of more heat and earth—for example, honey and wine must (for they are as if fermenting); also those in which, though they contain water, there is more air—for example, olive oil, quicksilver, and any that are viscous, such as pitch and birdlime.

## 4.9

Bodies softenable by heat are those solid ones that are not composed of water (as ice is composed of water), but are more earthy, and whose water is neither all evaporated (as in soda or salt) nor possessed irregularly (as in pottery), but are pullable (without admitting water) or malleable (without consisting of water), and softenable by fire—for example, iron, horn, and woods.[409]

Of bodies that are meltable and of those that are non-meltable, some are drenchable, others non-drenchable—for example, bronze, which is non-drenchable, is meltable, whereas wool and earth are drenchable; for they become wet through. And bronze, though it is meltable, is not meltable due to water. But some things too, though meltable due to water, are non-drenchable—for example, soda and salt; for nothing is drenchable either that does not become softer when soaked through. Some things, on the other hand, that are drenchable do not melt—for example, wool and grains. And the drenchable ones are the ones that are earthy and have ducts larger than the masses of water, though they are harder than the [masses of] water.[410] And bodies that have ducts throughout are meltable by water. Why is it, though, that earth is both melted and drenched due to water, whereas soda is melted but not drenched? Because in soda the ducts are throughout, so that its parts are divided immediately by the water, whereas in earth, though there are also ducts, they lie so as not to meet, so that the affection differs, depending on which of the two ways it enters.[411]

Some bodies are bendable or straightenable (for example, reed and withy), whereas other bodies are not (for example, stone and pottery). The ones that are non-bendable and non-straightenable are those bodies whose length is incapable of being changed from being bent to being straight and from being straight to being bent, and bending and straightening consist in the change or movement to being straight or to being curved; for whether a thing is being bent convexly or bent concavely it is being bent. Bending, then, is movement to the convex or to the concave that preserves a thing's length; for if we were to add "or to the straight," a thing would be simultaneously bent and straight—which is precisely what is impossible, namely, for the straight to be bent. And if everything that is bent is either bent convexly or bent concavely, and of these the one is a change to the convex, the other to the concave, there would again not be a bending to the straight, but bending and straightening would be different things. These, then, are the bendable and straightenable things, and the non-bendable and non-straightenable ones.

Some things are both breakable and shatterable, either both at once or separately—for example, wood is breakable but not shatterable, ice and stone are shatterable but not breakable, while pottery is both shatterable and breakable. The difference is that breaking is division and separation into large parts, shattering into more than two parts of random size. Things, then, that solidify so that they have many ducts lying so as not to meet, are shatterable (for up to this number they can be divided), and things with ones that stretch a long way, are breakable, while things that have ducts of both sorts, are both.[412]

Some things are receptive of impressions, like bronze and wax, whereas others are non-receptive of impressions, like pottery and water. An impression is a shifting downward of part of a thing's surface by a pushing or a blow, or, in general, by contact. And such things are either soft, like wax, part of whose surface is shifted while the rest remains the same, or hard, like bronze.[413] Things that are non-receptive of impressions are either hard, like pottery (for its surface cannot be pressed in downward), or wet, like water (for water can be pressed in, but not by a part's being so, but by replacement).[414]

Of things receptive of impressions, the ones that retain the impression and are easily impressible by hand are plastic, whereas those not easily impressible, like stone or wood, or that, though easily impressible, do not retain the impression, like wool or sponge, are non-plastic but are compressible.

Compressible things are ones that are capable of contracting into themselves on being pushed, their surface deviating downward without dividing and without one part changing places with another, as happens with water; for it does involve exchange of places. Pushing is a movement due to the mover which comes about due to [continuous] contact.[415] A blow is when [the movement is] due to a spatial movement.[416] And things are compressible that have ducts empty of body of the same kind as themselves, and are capable—under compression—of compacting into the empty places within them, or rather into their own ducts; for sometimes the ones they contract into are not empty—for example, in a wet sponge (for its ducts are full).[417] But then what the ducts are full of is softer than the thing itself that is naturally such as to compact into itself. Compressible things, then, are ones like sponge, wax, and flesh. Non-compressible ones are ones that are not naturally such as to contract under compression into their own ducts, either because they do not have any or because they have ones filled with things that are harder; for iron is non-compressible, as are stone, water, and every liquid.

Pullable things are ones whose surface is capable of shifting in the same plane, since for a thing to be pulled is for its surface to be shifted, while being continuous, in the direction of the mover.[418] And some things are pullable (for example, hair, a leather thong, sinew, dough, and birdlime), others non-pullable (for example, water and stone). Some things indeed are themselves pullable and compressible (for example, wool), others not (for example, phlegm, which is non-compressible but pullable, or sponge, which is compressible but not pullable).

Some things are malleable too (for example, bronze), others non-malleable (for example, stone and wood). The malleable ones are the ones part of whose surface is capable of simultaneously shifting both sideways and downward due to the same blow; things incapable of this are non-malleable. All malleable things are receptive of impressions, but not all things receptive of impressions are malleable (for example, wood). But generally speaking the two convert. And of things that are compressible, some are malleable, others not (wax and mud are malleable, wool not).

Some things are splittable (for example, wood), others non-splittable (for example, pottery). To be splittable is to be capable of being divided beyond the point to which the divider divides; for a thing is split when it divides beyond the point to which the divider divides and in advance of the process of division, whereas in cutting this is not so. Non-splittable things are the ones that are not capable of being affected in this way. Nothing soft is splittable either (I mean unconditionally soft, not soft in relation to something else; for in the latter way even iron will be soft), nor are all hard things, but only those that are neither liquid, nor receptive of impressions, nor shatterable. And things of this sort are those in which the ducts along which they cohere run lengthwise and not breadthwise.

Cuttable things are hard or soft compositions that are capable, when being divided, of not necessarily splitting in advance of the process of division nor of shattering. And the ones that are not wet are non-cuttable. Some things, though, are both cuttable and splittable—for example, wood. But for the most part things are splittable lengthwise and cuttable breadthwise; for since each is divided into many parts, insofar as the unit is composed of many running lengthwise, it is splittable, and insofar as its unity is composed of many running breadthwise, it is cuttable.

A thing is viscous when, being wet or soft, it is pullable. And those among bodies which, because of the linking of their parts, are composed like chains are of this sort; for these are capable of much stretching and contracting. And those that are not of this sort are crumbly.

Kneadable things are those compressible ones that retain the compression; non-kneadable ones are either those that are wholly non-compressible or that do not retain the compression.

Some things are combustible, others non-combustible—for example, wood is combustible, as are wool and bone, whereas stone and ice are non-combustible. Combustible things are the ones that have ducts receptive of fire and have liquid in their longitudinal ducts that is weaker than fire. But things that have no ducts or have liquid stronger than fire—for example, ice and very green woods—are non-combustible.

Capable of giving off fumes are those bodies that, though they contain liquid, do so in such a way that it does not evaporate separately when they are treated with burning heat; for vapor is a disaggregation due to burning heat, from liquid into air and wind, capable of wetting things.[419] But fumes can be disaggregated into air due to the passing of time, some drying out as they vanish, others becoming earth.[420] But this disaggregation is different [from vapor] because it does not wet things nor does it become wind. Wind is a continuous flow of air in a given direction, whereas fuming is the disaggregation all at once of a compound exhalation of dry and wet due to burning heat. That is why it does not wet things, but rather colors them.

The fuming of a woody body is smoke. For I mean to include bones, hair, and all such things in this same class; for a name common to them has not been established. By analogy, however, they are all in the same class.[421] As Empedocles said:

Hair, leaves, and birds' thick feathers
And scales on stout limbs are all the same.[422]

The fumes from fat are a sooty smoke, those from oily material a greasy steam. That is why olive oil does not boil or become coarse-grained, namely, because it is capable of giving off fumes but does not evaporate, whereas water is incapable of giving off fumes but does evaporate. Sweet wine, though, is capable of giving off fumes, because it is fat, and this produces the same effects as olive oil does; for cold does not solidify it, and it does burn.[423] And though it is named "wine," it does not function like wine; for its flavor is not winey. This is also why it does not intoxicate in the way a random wine does. But it does give off a few fumes, which is why it makes the flames go up.

Combustible bodies seem to be the ones that dissolve into ashes. And all the ones that are solidified due to heat, or by both heat and cold, are so affected; for it is evident that all these are mastered by fire. But of stones, the gemstone called *anthrax* is the least so.[424]

Of the combustible things, some are flammable, others non-flammable, and of the former some can be carbonized. The flammable ones are the ones capable of producing flames, while those that are incapable are non-flammable. The flammable ones are the ones that, while not liquid, are capable of giving off fumes. And pitch, olive oil, and wax are more flammable when mixed with other things than by themselves. Most flammable of all are the ones that make smoke go up. Of the ones of this sort, those that contain more earth than smoke can be carbonized.

Further, some meltable things are non-flammable (for example, bronze), some flammable bodies are non-meltable (for example, wood), while some are both meltable and flammable (for example, frankincense). The cause is that the liquid contained in wood is collected together, and it is continuous throughout the whole, so that it burns out, whereas in bronze, though it has it in each part, it is not continuous, and is too little to produce flame.[425] Frankincense, on the other hand, has it both ways.

Of things capable of giving off fumes, the flammable ones are the ones that are non-meltable because they are composed more of earth; for the dry is something they have in common with fire. And when this—the dry—becomes hot, fire is generated. That is why flame is wind or burning smoke. The fumes of wood, then, are smoke, those of wax, frankincense, and things of this sort, those of pitch, and of things containing pitch or the like, are a sooty smoke, while those of olive oil and oily things are a greasy steam. Those of things that burn very badly on their own are also [greasy smoke], because they contain little that is dry, and the change [to fire] is due to this, but do burn quickly together with something else.[426] For the fat is [just] this: the dry oily. Liquids that give off fumes, then, are more wet, like olive oil and pitch, while those that burn are more dry.

## 4.10

It is by these affections and by these differentiae, as we have said, that the homoeomerous bodies are distinguished from each other by touch, and further by taste, smell, and color.[427]

By homoeomerous bodies, I mean, for example, metals (bronze, gold, silver, tin, iron, stone, and others of this sort, and those that come to be segregated out of these) and the ones in animals and plants (for example, flesh, bone, sinew, skin, visceral body, hair, fiber, veins), from which the non-homoeomerous parts (for example, face, hand, foot, and others of this sort) are forthwith composed (and in plants, wood, bark, leaf, root, and things of this sort).[428]

But since these are composed by another cause, but the matter of the things of which they are composed is the wet and the dry, that is, water and earth (for each most clearly has each of the capacities), whereas the affecting ones are the hot and the cold (for these latter produce composition and solidification from the former), let us get hold of which species (*eidos*) of homoeomerous bodies are [composed of] earth, which of water, and which of a compound of them.[429]

Of bodies that have been handicrafted, some are liquid, some soft, some hard.[430] And of these, the hard ones and the soft ones are due to solidification, as was stated previously.[431]

Liquids that evaporate are composed of water. Those that do not are composed of earth, or of a compound of earth and water (for example, milk), of earth and air (for example, wood), or of water and air (for example, olive oil).[432] And those that become coarse-grained due to heat are compounds. (But of the liquids, wine raises a puzzle. For it both evaporates and becomes coarse-grained, as new wine does. The cause is that wine is not said of only one kind (*eidos*) of thing, and each kind behaves differently; for new wine contains more earth than old, and so becomes most coarse-grained due to heat, but solidifies less due to cold; for it also contains much heat and earth. Thus the wine in Arcadia gets so dried up in its skins due to the smoke that it is scraped off for drinking.[433] If, then, all wine has sediment, it will be composed of earth or of water, depending on the quantity of it that it contains.) Liquids that become coarse-grained due to cold are composed of earth. Those that become so due to both cold and heat are compounds of several things—for example, olive oil, honey, and sweet wine.

Of composed things those solidified due to cold are composed of water (for example, ice, snow, hail, and frost), those solidified due to heat are composed of earth (for example, pottery, cheese, soda, salt), those solidified due to both—and those solidified by cooling, that is, by both a privation of heat and liquid departing with the heat, are of this sort (for salt is solidified by the privation of liquid alone, as are things composed of pure earth, whereas ice is solidified by the privation of heat alone)—are composed of both water and earth. That is why in fact it is due to both, namely, they contained both.

All those from which all liquid has been evaporated (for example, pottery or amber) are composed of earth; for both amber and the bodies said to be like tears are due to cooling (for example, myrrh, frankincense, and gum; and [river] amber seems to be in this genus, and it solidifies—at any rate, it is evident that insects are enclosed in it, and the heat expelled due to the cold of the river, as with boiled honey when it is dropped into water, evaporates the liquid [in it]). And some of these are non-meltable and non-softenable by heat—for example, amber and certain stones, such as stalactites in caves; for these too come about in the same way, not due to fire but due to the cold expelling the heat, and the liquid coming out along with it due to the heat exiting from the thing, whereas in the case of the others, it is due to external fire.[434] Those from which the liquid has not wholly evaporated, are composed more of earth, but are softenable by heat—for example, iron and horn. Frankincense and other things of this sort give off vapor in a quite similar way to wood.[435]

Now, since things meltable by fire, at any rate, must be put down as meltable, these are mostly composed of water, though some are in fact a compound of water and earth—for example, wax. The ones meltable due to water are composed of earth, the ones not meltable due to either fire or water are composed either of earth or of both earth and water.

If, then, all [homoeomerous] things are either liquid or solid, and the ones with the affections just mentioned belong among these, and there is nothing intermediate, all the ones we have mentioned would serve to determine whether a thing is composed of earth, water, or a compound of more than one of them, and whether it is composed due to fire, due to cold, or due to both.

Gold, then, and silver, bronze, tin, lead, glass, and many nameless stones are composed of water; for all these are melted by heat. Further, some wines, urine, vinegar, lye, whey, and serum are composed of water; for all of these are solidified by cold.[436] Iron, on the other hand, and horn, nail, bone, sinew, wood, hair, leaves, and bark are composed more of wood. As, further, are amber, myrrh, frankincense, all the ones said to be tears, stalactites, and crops, such as pulse and corn; for things of this sort are to a greater or lesser extent composed of earth; for some are softenable by fire, whereas others are capable of giving off fumes and come about by cooling. As, further, are soda, salt, and the genera of stone that are neither due to cooling nor are meltable. Blood, on the other hand, and semen, are compounds of earth, water, and air. But blood that contains fibers is composed more of earth (which is why it is solidified by cooling and melted by liquid), blood that contains no fibers is composed of water (that is why indeed it does not solidify), and semen is solidified by cooling when its liquid exits along with its heat.

## 4.11

What sorts of solids and liquids are hot and cold must now be investigated on the basis of what has just been said.

Bodies composed of water are for the most part cold, unless they contain alien heat—as, for example, do lye, urine, and wine. Those composed of earth are for the most part hot, because they are handicrafted by heat—for example, lime and ashes.

And it must be grasped that the matter is a sort of coldness; for since the dry and the wet are matter (for they are affectable), and of these earth and water are most of all the bodies (for they are determined by cold), it is clear that all bodies composed simply of one of these two elements are more cold, unless they contain alien heat—as, for example, do boiling water and water strained through ashes; for it too contains the heat from the ashes; for in everything that has been burned there is heat, either more or less. That is also why animals come to be in rotten things; for the presence of [alien] heat has destroyed the heat proper to the given thing.[437]

Compound bodies contain heat; for most of them have been composed due to concocting heat, although some are products of putrefaction—for example, the colliquescences.[438] So blood, semen, marrow, fig juice, and all things of this sort are hot as long as they possess their nature, but when they pass away and depart from their nature they are no longer so; for [only] the matter remains, this being earth or water. That is why they seem two ways to people, and some say they are cold, others that they are hot, seeing that when they are in their natural state they are warm, but when they are separated from it, they solidify. But though this is the case, nonetheless, as we determined, things in which the matter is mostly water are cold (for water is most of all opposed to fire), whereas those in which it is mostly earth or air are hotter.

It sometimes happens, however, that the same things become extremely cold and hot due to alien heat; for the solidest and hardest ones are coldest if they are deprived of heat, and most of all cause burning if exposed to fire—for example, water then causes burning more than smoke and stone more so than water.

## 4.12

Since these things have been determined, let us speak in particular about what flesh is, or bone, or the other homoeomerous things; for we grasp what the nature of the homoeomerous things is composed of, the genera of them, and which genus each belongs to, through their coming to be; for the homoeomerous things are composed from the elements, and of these as matter all the works of nature are composed.

But while all are composed as from matter from the things just mentioned, as regards substance it is by the account.[439] This, though, is always more clear in the case of the later ones and, in general, of the ones that are instrumental and for the sake of something. For it is more clear that a corpse is a human being homonymously.[440] In the same way, therefore, the hand of a dead man is homonymously a hand, just as stone flutes too might be called "flutes"; for these [bodily parts] also seem to be instruments of sorts.

But the cases of flesh and bone are less clearly of this sort, and the cases of fire and water are less clear still; for the for-the-sake-of-which is less clear in those cases where the matter has the greatest extent; for just as, if one wished to take the extreme cases, matter is nothing beyond itself, and substance nothing other than an account, each intermediate thing is in proportion to the closer extreme, since any one of these is also for the sake of something, and is not entirely water or fire or flesh or viscera. And this is still more so in the case of a face and a hand. They are all defined by their function; for the capacity to perform its function is what each of them truly is—for example, an eye if it sees, but when it is incapable of doing so, it is homonymously an eye, like one that is dead or made of stone; for a wooden saw is not truly a saw either, but like one in a picture. It is the same way, therefore, with flesh as well; but the function of it is less clear than that of the tongue.

Similarly with fire too, although presumably its function is yet less clear from a natural scientific point of view than the function of flesh.[441] And similarly also with the [parts] in plants and inanimate things—for example, bronze and silver; for they all are [what they are] in virtue of a certain capacity to affect or to be affected, just like flesh and sinew. But the accounts of these are not exact, so that it is not easy to see clearly when they are [what they are] and when they are not, unless they have lost their capacity so exceedingly that only their shapes remain—for example, the bodies of ancient corpses suddenly become ashes in their graves, and fruits, when they are exceedingly old, retain only their shape, though their perceptible [taste] is not apparent. So too with the solids that come from milk.

Parts of this sort, then, can come to be by virtue of heat and cold and the movements due to these, since they are solidified by hot and by cold—I mean the homoeomerous ones, such as flesh, bone, hair, sinew, and the like; for these are all distinguished by the differentiae previously mentioned, namely, tension, ductility, fragmentability, hardness, softness, and the others of this sort, all of which come about due to heat and cold and the mixing of their movements.[442] But of the non-homoeomerous parts composed of these—for example, a head, a hand, or a foot—no one could any longer believe this. On the contrary, although cold and heat and movement cause the coming to be of bronze and silver, of a saw, bowl, or box they are no longer the cause. Instead, in their case craft is the cause and in the previous one nature or some other cause.

Now, if we grasp what genus each of the homoeomerous parts is in, we must now get hold of what each of them is—for example, what blood is, or flesh, or seed, as well as each of the others; for we know why each thing is and what it is when we grasp either the matter or the account of their coming to be and passing away, but especially when we grasp both, and also know where its starting-point of movement comes from. And when these parts have been made clear, we must get a theoretical grasp on the non-homoeomerous ones, and in the end the things composed of these—for example, human being, plant, and the others of that sort.[443]

# Appendix

Plato, *Timaeus* 48b–57d*

We shall of course have to study the intrinsic nature of fire, water, air, and earth prior to the heaven's coming to be, as well as the affections they had then. So far no one has as yet revealed how these four came to be. We tend to posit them as the elemental letters of the universe and tell people they are its starting-points, on the assumption that they know what fire and the other three are. In fact, however, they shouldn't even be compared to syllables. Only a very unenlightened person might be expected to make such a comparison. So let me now proceed with my treatment in the following way: for the present I cannot state the starting-point or starting-points of all things, or however else I think about them, for the simple reason that it is difficult to show clearly what my view is if I follow my present manner of exposition. Please do not expect me to do so then. I couldn't convince even myself that I could be right to commit myself to undertaking a task of such magnitude. I shall keep to what I stated at the start, the virtue of likely accounts, and so shall try right from the start to say about things, both individually and collectively, what is no less likely than any—more likely, in fact, than what I have said before.[1] Let us therefore at the start of this discourse call upon the god to be our savior this time, too, to give us safe passage through a strange and unusual exposition, and lead us to a view of what is likely. And so let me start my speech again.

The new starting-point in my account of the universe needs to be more complex than the earlier one. Then we distinguished two kinds (*eidos*), but now we must specify a third, one of a different sort. The earlier two sufficed for our previous account: one was proposed as a model, intelligible and always changeless, a second as an imitation of the model, something that possesses becoming and is visible. We did not distinguish a third kind at

---

*The translation is that of Donald J. Zeyl, *Plato: Timaeus* (Indianapolis, 2000), lightly edited for consistency.
1. Accepting the insertion of <*tôn*> after *mallon de* in 48d3.

the time, because we thought that we could make do with the two of them. Now, however, it appears that our account compels us to attempt to illuminate in words a kind (*eidos*) that is difficult and vague. What must we suppose it to do and to be? This above all: it is a *receptacle* of all becoming—its wet nurse, as it were.

However true that statement may be, we must nevertheless describe it more clearly. This is a difficult task, particularly because it requires us to raise a preliminary puzzle about fire and the other three:

It is difficult to say of each of them—in a way that employs a reliable and stable account—which one is the sort of thing one should really call "water" rather than "fire," or which one should call some one of these rather than just any and every one of them. What puzzle, then, do they present for us to work through in likely fashion? And then how and in what manner are we to go on to speak about this third kind?

First, we see (or think we see) the thing that we have just now been calling "water" condensing and turning to stones and earth. Next, we see this same thing dissolving and disaggregating, turning to wind and air, and air, when ignited, turning to fire. And then we see fire being aggregated and extinguished and turning back to the form of air, and air coalescing and thickening and turning back into cloud and mist. When these are compressed still more we see them turning into flowing water, which we see turning to earth and stones once again. In this way, then, they transmit their coming to be one to the other in a cycle, or so it seems. Now then, since none of these appears ever to remain the same, which one of them can one categorically assert, without embarrassment, to be some particular thing, *this* one, and not something else? One can't. Rather, the safest course by far is to propose that we speak about these things in the following way: what we invariably observe becoming different at different times—fire for example—to characterize that, that is, fire, not as "this," but each time as "what is such," and speak of water not as "this," but always as "what is such." And never to speak of anything else as "this," as though it has some stability, of all the things at which we point and use the expressions "that" and "this" and so think we are designating something. For it gets away without abiding the charge of "that" and "this," or any other expression that indicts them of being stable. It is in fact safest not to refer to it by any of these expressions. Rather, "what is such"—coming around like what it was, again and again—*that's* the thing to call it in each and every case. So fire—and generally everything that has becoming—it is safest to call "what is altogether such." But that in which they each appear to keep coming into being and *from* which they subsequently pass out of being, *that's* the only thing to refer to by means of the names "that" and "this." A thing that is some "such" or other, however,—hot or white, say, or any one of the opposites, and all things constituted by these—should be called none of these things [that is, "this" or "that"].

I must make one more effort to describe it, more clearly still. Suppose you were molding gold into every shape there is, going on non-stop remolding one shape into the next. If someone then were to point at one of them and ask you, "What is it?," your safest answer by far, with respect to truth, would be to say "gold," but never "triangle" or any of the other shapes that come to be in the gold, as though it is these, because they change even while you're making the statement. However, that answer, too, should be satisfactory, as long as the shapes are willing to accept "what is such" as someone's designation. This has a degree of safety.

We must always refer to [that nature which receives all the bodies] by the same term, since it does not depart from its own capacity in any way. Not only does it always receive all things, it has never in any way whatever taken on any shape similar to any of the things that enter it. Its nature is to be available for anything to make its impression upon, and it is modified, shaped, and reshaped by the things that enter it. These are the things that make it appear different at different times. The things that enter and leave it are imitations of those things that always are, imprinted after their likeness in a marvelous way that is hard to describe. This is something we shall pursue at another time. For the moment, we need to keep in mind three kinds of things: that which comes to be, that in which it comes to be, and that after which the thing coming to be is modeled, and which is the source of its coming to be. It is in fact appropriate to compare the receiving thing to a mother, the source to a father, and the nature between them to their offspring. We also must understand that if the imprints are to be varied, with all the varieties there to see, this thing upon which the imprints are to be formed could not be well prepared for that role if it were not itself devoid of any of those characters that it is to receive from elsewhere. For if it resembled any of the things that enter it, it could not successfully copy their contraries or things of a totally different nature whenever it were to receive them. It would be showing its own face as well. That is why the thing that is to receive in itself all the elemental kinds (*genê*) must be totally devoid of any characteristics. Think of people who make fragrant ointments. They expend skill and ingenuity to come up with something just like this [that is, a neutral base] to have on hand to start with. The liquids that are to receive the fragrances they make as odorless as possible. Or think of people who work at impressing shapes upon soft materials. They emphatically refuse to allow any such material to already have some definite shape. Instead, they'll even it out and make it as smooth as it can be. In the same way, then, if the thing that is to receive repeatedly throughout its whole self the likenesses of the intelligible objects, the things which always are—if it is to do so successfully, then it ought to be devoid of any inherent characteristics of its own.[2] This, of course, is why we shouldn't call the mother or receptacle of what has come to be, of what is visible or perceivable in every other way, either "earth" or "air," "fire" or "water," or any of their compounds or their constituents. But if we speak of it as an invisible and characterless sort of thing, one that receives all things and shares in a most perplexing way in what is intelligible, a thing extremely difficult to comprehend, we shall not be misled. And insofar as it is possible to arrive at its nature on the basis of what we've said so far, the most correct way to speak of it may well be this: the part of it that gets ignited appears on each occasion as fire, the dampened part as water, and parts as earth or air in so far as it receives the imitations of these. . . .

Since these things are so, we must agree that that which keeps its own form unchangingly, which has not been brought into being and is not destroyed, which neither receives into itself anything else from anywhere else, nor itself enters into anything else anywhere, is one thing. It is invisible—it cannot be perceived by the senses at all—and it is the role of understanding to study it. The second thing is that which shares the other's name and resembles it. This thing can be perceived by the senses, and it has been begotten. It is constantly borne along, now coming to be in a certain place and then perishing out of it. It is apprehended by belief, which involves sense perception. And the third type is place, which exists always and cannot be destroyed. It provides a fixed state for all things that come to be. It is itself apprehended by a kind of bastard reasoning that does not involve sense perception, and it is hardly even an object of conviction. We look at it as in a dream when we say that everything that exists must of necessity be somewhere, in some place and occupying some space, and that that which doesn't exist somewhere, whether on earth or in heaven, doesn't exist at all.

We prove unable to draw all these distinctions and others related to them—even in the case of that unsleeping, truly existing reality—because our dreaming state renders us incapable of waking up and stating the truth, which is this: Since that for which an image has come to be is not at all intrinsic to the image, which is invariably borne along to picture something else, it stands to reason that the image should therefore come to be in something else, somehow clinging to being, or else be nothing at all. But that which really is receives support from the accurate, true account—that as long as the one is distinct from the other, neither of them ever comes to be in the other in such a way that they at the same time become one and the same, and also two.

---

2. Accepting the insertion of *noêtôn* before *pantôn* in 50a1.

Let this, then, be a summary of the account I would offer, as computed by my "vote." There are being, space, and becoming, three distinct things which existed even before heaven (*ouranon*) came to be.

Now, as the wet nurse of becoming turns watery and fiery and receives the shape of earth and air, and as it acquires all the affections that come with these characters, it takes on a variety of visible aspects, but because it is filled with capacities that are neither similar nor evenly balanced, no part of it is in balance. It sways irregularly in every direction as it is shaken by those things, and being set in movement it in turn shakes them. And as they are moved, they drift continually, some in one direction and others in others, separating from each other. They are winnowed out, as it were, like grain that is sifted by winnowing sieves or other such instruments. They are carried off and settle down, the dense and heavy ones in one direction, and the rare and light ones to another place.

That is how at that time the four kinds (*genê*) were being shaken by the receiver, which was itself agitating like a shaking machine, separating the kinds most unlike each other furthest apart and pushing those most like each other closest together into the same region. This, of course, explains how these different kinds came to occupy different regions of space, even before the universe (*to pan*) was set in order and constituted from them at its coming to be. Indeed, it is a fact that before this took place the four kinds all lacked proportion and measure, and at the time the ordering of the universe was undertaken, fire, water, earth, and air initially possessed certain traces of what they are now. They were indeed in the condition one would expect thoroughly godforsaken things to be in. So, finding them in this natural condition, the first thing the god then did was to give them their distinctive shapes, using forms and numbers.

Here is a proposition we shall always affirm above all else: The god fashioned these four kinds to be as nobly beautiful and excellent as possible, when they were not so before. It will now be my task to show you what structure each of them acquired, and how each came to be. My account will be an unusual one, but since you are well schooled in the fields of learning in terms of which I must of necessity proceed with my exposition, I'm sure you'll follow me.

First of all, it is clear to everyone, I'm sure, that fire, earth, water, and air are bodies. Now, everything that has bodily form also has depth. Depth, moreover, is of necessity comprehended within plane, and any plane bounded by straight lines is composed of triangles. Every triangle, moreover, derives from two triangles, each of which has one right angle and two acute angles. Of these two triangles, one [the isosceles right-angled triangle] has at each of the other two vertices an equal part of a right angle, determined by its division by equal sides; while the other [the scalene right-angled triangle] has unequal parts of a right angle at its other two vertices, determined by the division of the right angle by unequal sides. This, then, we presume to be the starting-point of fire and of the other bodies, as we pursue our likely account in terms of Necessity. Starting-points yet more ultimate than these are known only to the god, and to any man he may hold dear.

We should now say which are the most nobly beautiful four bodies that can come to be. They are quite unlike each other, though some of them are capable of breaking up and turning into others and vice-versa. If our account is on the mark, we shall have the truth about how earth and fire and their proportional intermediates [water and air] came to be. For we shall never concede to anyone that there are any visible bodies more nobly beautiful than these, each conforming to a single kind (*genos*). So we must wholeheartedly proceed to fit together the four kinds of bodies of surpassing noble beauty, and to declare that we have come to grasp their natures well enough.

Of the two [right-angled] triangles, the isosceles has but one nature, while the scalene has unlimitedly many. Now, we have to select the most nobly beautiful one from among the unlimitedly many, if we are to get a proper start. So if anyone can say that he has picked out another one that is more nobly beautiful for the construction of these bodies, his victory will be that of a friend, not an enemy. Of the many [scalene right-angled] triangles, then, we posit as the one most nobly beautiful, surpassing the others, that one from [a pair of] which the equilateral triangle is constructed as a third figure. Why this is so is too long a story to tell now. But if anyone puts this claim to the test and discovers that it isn't so, his be the prize, with our congratulations. So much, then, for the selection of the two triangles from which the bodies of fire and the other bodies are constructed—the [right-angled] isosceles, and [the right-angled] scalene whose longer side squared is always triple its shorter side squared [i.e., the half-equilateral].

At this point we need to determine more perspicuously something that was not stated perspicuously earlier. For then it appeared that all four kinds of bodies could come to be from each other by successive stages.* But the appearance is wrong. While there are indeed four kinds of bodies that come to be from the [right-angled] triangles we have selected, three of them come from triangles that have unequal sides, whereas the fourth alone is fashioned from isosceles triangles. Thus not all of them have the capacity of breaking up and turning into each other, with a large number

---

*See 49b–c.

*Appendix*  54c–55c

of small bodies turning into a small number of large ones and vice-versa. There are three that can do this. For all three are made up of a single sort of triangle, so that when once the larger bodies are broken up, the same triangles can go to make up a large number of small bodies, assuming shapes appropriate to them. And likewise, when numerous small bodies are fragmented into their triangles, these triangles may well combine to make up some single massive body belonging to another kind.   54d

So much, then, for our account of how these bodies come to be from each other. Let us next discuss the form that each of them has come to have, and the various numbers that have combined to make them up.

Leading the way will be the primary form [the tetrahedron], the tiniest structure, whose elementary triangle is the one whose hypotenuse is twice the length of its shorter side. Now, when a pair of such triangles are juxtaposed along the diagonal [i.e., their hypotenuses] and this is done three times, and their diagonals and short sides converge upon a single   54e point as center, the result is a single equilateral triangle, composed of six such triangles. When four of these equilateral triangles are combined, a single solid angle is produced at the junction of three plane angles. This, it turns out, is the angle which comes right after the most obtuse of the plane angles.* And once four such solid angles have been completed, we get the   55a primary solid form, which is one that divides the entire circumference [of the sphere in which it is inscribed] into equal and similar parts.

The second solid form [the octahedron] is constructed from the same triangles which, however, are now arranged in eight equilateral triangles and produce a single solid angle from four plane angles. And when six such solid angles have been produced, the second body has reached its completion.

Now, the third body [the icosahedron] is made up of a combination of one hundred and twenty of the elementary triangles, and of twelve solid angles, each enclosed by five plane equilateral triangles. This body turns   55b out to have twenty equilateral triangular faces. And let us take our leave of this one of the elementary triangles, the one that has begotten the above three kinds of bodies and turn to the other one, the isosceles [right-angled] triangle, which has begotten the fourth [the cube]. Arranged in sets of four whose right angles come together at the center, the isosceles triangle produced a single equilateral quadrangle [i.e., a square]. And when six of these quadrangles were combined together, they produced eight solid angles, each of which was constituted by three plane right angles. The shape of   55c

---

*The solid angle is the conjunction of three 60° plane angles, totaling 180°.

the resulting body so constructed is a cube, and it has six quadrangular equilateral faces.

One other construction, a fifth, still remained, and this one the god used for the universe, embroidering figures on it.*

Anyone following this whole line of reasoning might very well be puzzled about whether we should say that there are unlimitedly many cosmoses or a limited number of them. If so, he would have to conclude that to answer "infinitely many" is to take the view of one who is really "unfinished" in things he ought to be "finished" in. He would do better to stop with the question whether we should say that there's really just one or five and be puzzled about that. Well, our "probable account" answer declares there to be but one, a god—though someone else, taking other things into consideration, will come to a different belief. We must set him aside, however.

Let us now assign to fire, earth, water, and air the structures which have just been given their formations in our speech. To earth let us give the form of a cube, because of the four kinds of bodies earth is the most immobile and the most pliable—which is what the solid whose faces are the most secure must of necessity turn out to be, more so than the others. Now, of the [right-angled] triangles we postulated at the start, the face belonging to those that have equal sides has a greater natural stability than that belonging to triangles that have unequal sides, and the plane that is composed of the two triangles, the equilateral quadrangle [the square], holds its position with greater stability than does the equilateral triangle, both in their parts and as wholes. Hence, if we assign this solid figure to earth, we are preserving our "likely account." And of the solid figures that are left, we shall next assign the least mobile of them to water, to fire the most mobile, and to air the one in between. This means that the tiniest body belongs to fire, the largest to water, and the intermediate one to air—and also that the body with the sharpest edges belongs to fire, the next sharpest to air, and the third sharpest to water. Now, in all these cases the body that has the fewest faces is of necessity the most mobile, in that it, more than any other, has edges that are the sharpest and best fit for cutting in every direction. It is also the lightest, in that it is made up of the least number of identical parts. The second body ranks second in having these same features, and the third ranks third. So let us follow our account, which is not only likely but also correct, and take the solid form of the pyramid that we saw constructed as the element or the seed of fire. And let us say that the second form in order of coming to be is that of air, and the third that of water.

---

*The remaining one of the regular solids is the dodecahedron. It approaches most nearly a sphere in volume, which is the shape of the universe, according to Timaeus.

Now, we must understand all these bodies as being so small that due to their small size none of them, whatever their kind, is visible to us individually. When, however, a large number of them are clustered together, we do see them *en masse*. And in particular, as to the proportions among their numbers, their movements and their other capacities, we must understand that when the god had brought them to complete and exact perfection (to the degree that Necessity was willing to comply obediently), he arranged them together proportionally.

Given all we have said so far about the kinds of elemental bodies, the following account [of their transformations] is the most likely: When earth encounters fire and is dissolved by fire's sharpness, it will drift about— whether the dissolution occurred within fire itself, or within a mass of air or water—until its parts meet again somewhere, refit themselves together and become earth again. The reason is that the parts of earth will never pass into another form. But when water is broken up into parts by fire or even by air, it could happen that the parts recombine to form one corpuscle of fire and two of air. And the fragments of air could produce, from any single particle that is dissolved, two fire corpuscles. And conversely, whenever a small quantity of fire is enveloped by a large quantity of air or water or perhaps earth and is agitated inside them as they move, and in spite of its resistance is beaten and shattered to bits, then any two fire corpuscles may combine to constitute a single form of air. And when air is overpowered and broken down, then two and one half entire forms of air will be consolidated into a single, entire form of water.

Let us recapitulate and formulate our account of these transformations as follows: Whenever one of the other kinds is caught inside fire and gets cut up by the sharpness of fire's angles and edges, then if it is reconstituted as fire, it will stop getting cut. The reason is that a thing of any kind that is alike and uniform is incapable of producing any change in, or being affected by, anything that is similar to it. But as long as something involved in a transformation has something stronger than it to contend with, the process of its dissolution will continue non-stop. And likewise, when a few of the smaller corpuscles are surrounded by a greater number of bigger ones, they will be shattered and quenched. The quenching will stop when these smaller bodies are willing to be reconstituted into the form of the kind that prevailed over them, and so from fire will come air, and from air, water. But if these smaller corpuscles are in process of turning into these and one of the other kinds encounters them and engages them in battle, their dissolution will go on non-stop until they are either completely squeezed and broken apart and escape to their own likes, or else are defeated, and, melding from many into one, they are assimilated to the kind that prevailed over them, and come to share its abode from then on.

And, what is more, as they undergo these processes, they all exchange their regions of space: for as a result of the Receptacle's agitation the quantities of each of the kinds are separated from each other, with each occupying its own place, but because some parts of a particular kind do from time to time become unlike their former selves and like the other kinds, they are carried by the shaking toward the place occupied by whatever masses they are becoming like to.

These, then, are the sorts of causes by which the unalloyed primary bodies have come to be. Now, the fact that different varieties are found within their respective forms is to be attributed to the constructions of each of the elementary triangles. Each of these two constructions did not at the start yield a triangle that had just one size, but triangles that were both smaller and larger, numerically as many as there are varieties within a given form. That is why when they are mixed with themselves and with each other they display an infinite variety, which those who are to employ a likely account in their study of nature must take note of.

# Notes

## ON COMING TO BE AND PASSING AWAY, BOOK 1

**Note 1**
**But:** *De* ("but") answers the solitary *men* in the final sentence of *Cael.* 313$^ب$22, indicating that *GC* comes next in a series. See Introduction, pp. xvii–xix; De Haas & Mansfeld (Brunschwig), pp. 28–31.
**By nature:** Things that are "by nature (*phusei*) are the ones whose cause is within themselves and are orderly" (*Rh.* 1369$^a$35–$^b$1). This cause is an internal starting-point of "moving and being at rest—some with respect to place, some with respect to increase and decrease, others with respect to alteration" (*Ph.* 192$^b$13–15). And each such thing is a substance: "for a substance is a sort of underlying subject, and a nature is always in an underlying subject" (192$^b$33–34). Examples are "animals and their parts, plants, and simple bodies—for example, earth, fire, air, and water" (192$^b$9–11), as well as "the whole heaven and its parts" (*Cael.* 298$^a$31). Nonsubstantial phenomena, like the upward movement of fire, by contrast, though they occur by or in accord with nature, do not themselves have a nature: "And these things [that are by nature and have a nature] are also in accord with nature, as too is whatever belongs intrinsically to them, as spatial movement upward belongs to fire—for this neither is nor has a nature but is by nature and in accord with nature" (*Ph.* 192$^b$35–193$^a$1).

When substantial things do have a nature, moreover, it derives not from their matter but from their distinctive manner of composition, or form: "That is why, as regards the things that are or come to be by nature, although that from which they naturally come to be or are is already present [namely, the matter], we still do not say that they have their nature if they do not have their form or shape" (*Met.* 1015$^a$3–5). Thus, for example, a feline embryo has within it a starting-point that explains why it grows into a cat, why that cat moves and alters in the ways it does, and why it eventually decays and dies. A house or any other artifact, by contrast, has no such source within it; instead the starting-point is "in something else and external" (*Ph.* 192$^b$29), namely, the understanding of the craftsman who produces it. See *Met.* 1032$^a$32–$^b$10 (quoted in 324$^b$4–6n146).
**Their causes:** The four causes Aristotle recognizes (final, formal, material, efficient) are discussed in *Ph.* 2.3.
**Accounts:** (1) A *logos* in ordinary Greek is a word or organized string of words constituting an account, argument, explanation, definition, principle, reason, or piece of reasoning, discussion, conversation, speech, or statement. (2) What such words or their utterances mean, express, or refer to, such as, the ratio between

*Notes 2–4*

quantities (*NE* 1131ᵃ31–32). (3) The capacity that enables someone to argue, give reasons, and so on (*Pol.* 1332ᵇ5).

### Note 2
**Growth:** In non-biological contexts *auxêsis* and *phthisis* are probably best translated as "increase" and "decrease." But in *GC*, as in *DA* and biological contexts generally, they have a more specific meaning best captured by "growth" and—though somewhat less happily—"withering." This is especially clear in *GC* 1.5, where this process is focally discussed.
**Alteration:** (1) "There is alteration (*alloiôsis*) when the underlying subject, which is perceptible, while remaining [the same], changes in its own affections, which are either contraries or intermediates" (*GC* 319ᵇ10–12). (2) "Everything that is altered is altered due to perceptibles, and . . . there is alteration only of those things that are said to be intrinsically affected by these" (*Ph.* 245ᵇ3–5).
**Names:** An *onoma* is not always what we call a "name," but a word more generally, or—when contrasted with a verb—a noun: "A name is a composite significant voiced sound, without a reference to time, the parts of which are not significant by themselves. . . . A verb is a composite significant voiced sound, involving a reference to time, the parts of which are not significant by themselves" (*Po.* 1457ᵃ10–15). A *name*, however, often signifies an account or (in some cases) a definition (*Met.* 1012ᵃ22–24, 1045ᵃ26) of the form (1035ᵃ21) or essence (1029ᵇ20) of the thing named.

### Note 3
**Unconditional:** The adjective *haplous* means "simple" or "single." The adverb *haplôs* thus points in two somewhat opposed directions. (1) To speak *haplôs* sometimes means to put things simply or in general terms, so that qualifications and conditions will need to be added later. (2) Sometimes, as here, to be F *haplôs* means to be F unconditionally, or in a way that allows for no ifs, ands, or buts (*Top.* 115ᵇ29–35). In this sense, some things that are F *haplôs* are F in the strictest, most absolute, and most unqualified way (*Met.* 1015ᵇ11–12), so that what is unconditionally F is what is intrinsically F (*NE* 1151ᵇ2–3).
**Unconditional coming to be:** "A change from what is not an underlying subject to an underlying subject, the relation being that of contradiction, is a coming to be—an unconditional coming to be when the change is unconditional, in a certain respect when the change is in a certain respect. For example, a change from not pale to pale is a coming to be in this respect, pale, whereas a change from unconditionally not being to substance is unconditional coming to be, with respect to which we say that a thing comes to be unconditionally, not that it comes to be something" (*Ph.* 225ᵃ12–17).

### Note 4
**The universe:** Literally: the all. However, at *Met.* 982ᵇ17 *to pan* is something that comes to be; at 984ᵇ2 it is nature as a whole; and at 988ᵇ22 it is material and corporeal. That is why, for example, Aristotle can claim that everything (that is,

everything that is a part of the universe) has matter and a moving cause ($1071^a33$–34)—something that is manifestly false of all the substances he recognizes, which include the immaterial primary (or prime) mover ($1071^b20$–21). Thus here, as at *GC* $318^a18$, *to pan* is the totality of things that come to be and pass away.

**In the strict sense:** What is *kurios* is what has executive power or authority or the power to compel, so that a general is *kurios* over his army (*NE* $1116^a29$–$^b2$) and a political ruler is *kurios* over a city and its inhabitants. Since what is *kurios* in a sphere determines or partly determines what happens within it, it is one of the most estimable or important elements in the sphere, so that what is inferior or less important is not *kurios* over it ($1143^b33$–35, $1145^a6$–7). The *kurios* meaning of a term is thus its "prevailing" meaning (*Rh.* $1405^a1$–2). When Aristotle contrasts natural virtue of character with the *kurios* variety (*NE* $1144^b1$–32), the control exerted by the latter seems to be teleological: the natural variety is a sort of virtue because it is an early stage in the development of mature virtue. Hence *kuria aretê* is "full virtue" or virtue in the strict sense of the term. It is in this sense that the life of those who are active and awake is a more *kurios* life—life in a fuller or stricter sense—than that of the inactive or asleep ($1098^a5$–8). *Kuriôs* and *haplôs* are, as a result, sometimes nearly equivalent in meaning, as they are here.

## Note 5

**Empedocles:** See DK 31 = TEGP pp. 326–433.
**Anaxagoras:** See DK 59 = TEGP pp. 271–325.
**Leucippus:** See DK 67 = TEGP pp. 516–685.

## Note 6

**Anaxagoras . . . :** "Anaxagoras seems to think that these [the elements] are unlimited in this way because he accepted as true the common belief of the physicists that nothing comes to be from not being (for it is because of this that they say that 'all things were together' and that he makes a thing's coming to be such-and-such sort of thing an alteration, while they make it aggregation and disaggregation)" (*Ph.* $187^a26$–31). The thought is that Anaxagoras too should have employed aggregation and disaggregation. The assumption being, apparently, that he was ignorant of the proper sense of *alloiousthai*. If Aristotle is reporting something Anaxagoras said in so many words, the text is not one we possess. In support of this translation of *tên oikeian phônên êgnoêsen*, as opposed to "Anaxagoras failed to understand his own utterance," and variants, see Rashed, pp. 86–87n9.

## Note 7

**Empedocles . . . :** "Empedocles, however, posits four things, positing earth along with those already mentioned [air, water, fire] as a fourth (for these, he says, always persist and do not come to be, except in quantity or smallness, aggregating into one and disaggregating from one)" (*Met.* $984^a8$–11 = DK A28 = TEGP 28). The other two (non-corporeal) elements, for a total of six, are his aggregating agent, love, and his disaggregating agent, strife. See TEGP 41 F20 and *Met.* $985^a21$–$^b4$ for some discussion and criticism.

**For Anaxagoras . . . :** "Anaxagoras of Clazomenae . . . says that the starting-points are unlimited; for he says that pretty much all the homoeomerous things (like water and fire) come to be and are destroyed in this way, namely, through aggregation and disaggregation alone. Otherwise, they neither come to be nor are destroyed but persist and are eternal" (*Met.* 984$^a$11–16).

**Leucippus and Democritus:** "Leucippus, however, and his associate Democritus say that the plenum and the void are the elements, calling the one 'being,' and the other 'not being,' and, of these, the plenum or the solid is being, while the void is not being (that is why they also say that being no more *is* than not being, because the body no more *is* than the void), and that these, as matter, are the causes of beings. And just as those who make the underlying substance one generate the other things by means of its affections, positing the rare and the dense as starting-points of these affections, in the same way, these people too say that the differentiae are the causes of the other things. And these differentiae, they say, are three—shape, order, and position. For they say that being is differentiated by rhythm, contact, and turning alone. And of these rhythm is shape (*schêma*), contact is order, and turning is position" (*Met.* 985$^b$4–17). The beings that constitute the plenum are the atoms. On Democritus, see DK 68 = TEGP pp. 516–685.

## Note 8

**Where a part is synonymous with the whole:** Although Aristotle here employs this understanding of homoeomerous, which he repeats at *PA* 655$^b$5–6, he recognizes that, for example, the heart is "in one way homoeomerous and in another non-homoeomerous" (647$^b$8–9; also 647$^b$17–20). It is homoeomerous at the level of the "chemical" formula of heart stuff, but because of "the shape of its configuration, it is non-homoeomerous" (647$^a$33). "It may sound odd to us; but it seems we are being told that certain 'parts' are *proto*-structural, of an intermediate nature or at an interface between uniform and non-uniform: the same nature somehow doubling as stuff and as structure" (Furth, p. 81). "Things are said to be *synonymous* when they have both a name in common and the same account of their substance corresponds to the name—for example, both a human and an ox are animals; for each of them is called by the same name, "animal"; moreover, the account of what they are is the same" (*Cat.* 1$^a$6–12).

## Note 9

**Universal seedbed:** See DK 59 B4a = TEGP 13 F4: "There are many things of all sorts in all composites, namely, seeds of all things having all sorts of forms, colors, and tastes."

## Note 10

**The underlying subject:** In addition to being (1) a subject of predication and, as here, (2) what underlies or remains through every change whether in affections or in the coming to be or passing away (*Ph.* 191$^a$13–$^b$10, *Met.* 1042$^a$32–$^b$6), a *hupokeimenon* can be (3) the subject matter of a science or body of knowledge (*NE* 1094$^b$12).

## Note 11
**A plurality of kinds:** Aristotle uses the term *genos* (here "kind") to refer to a race or bloodline and to a genuine genus, which is studied by a single science (*Met.* 1024$^a$29–$^b$5). Similarly, he uses *eidos* to refer to the species of a genus, but also to form (as opposed to matter) and to a separate Platonic Form. But he also uses both terms in a more general sense to mean "kind." Transliterations are added for precision when needed.

## Note 12
**In fact:** On the translation of *kai* (untranslated by Rashed; translated as "too" by Joachim-2 and taken to couple Empedocles with Anaxagoras), see Verdenius & Waszink, p. 2.
**Nothing that is has a nature:** Empedocles, DK B8 = TEGP 32 F11 = *Met.* 1015$^a$1–3. If nothing has a nature, there is no unconditional coming to be, since unconditional coming to be involves the coming into existence of a substance that has a nature. Thus *phusis* here, as explicitly at *Met.* 1014$^b$16–17, is pretty much equivalent to "coming to be."
**Separating:** The precise meaning of *diallaxis* is disputed: it can mean "separation," but also "exchange" or "interchange." But it seems reasonably certain that it is what Aristotle takes Empedocles to be saying that passing away consists in, since he cites it to show that "for them coming to be and passing away occur when things come together and undergo dissolution" (*Cael.* 314$^b$5–6).

## Note 13
**One might almost say:** Here οὕτω φάναι = ὡς οὕτως εἰπεῖν. See Rashed, p. 3n3.

## Note 14
**Substance:** *Ousia* is a noun perhaps formed from the present participle *ousa* of the verb *einai* ("to be"). "Substance" is the traditional translation. (1) The substance *of* something is its essence (335$^b$35n289), whereas (2) *a* substance, on the other hand, which is the sense relevant here, is something that has the fundamental sort of being possessed by an ultimate subject of predication—a *tode ti* ("this something")—which is not itself ever predicated of anything else (*Met.* 1017$^b$23–26). It is usually, but not always, clear which of (1) or (2) is intended.
**Growth and withering:** "Movement with respect to quantity, as regards its common feature, has no name, but with regard to each of its two varieties it is called 'increase and decrease'—that to the complete magnitude being increase, that away from it being decrease" (*Ph.* 226$^a$29–32). Growth and withering are more specific cases of this more general phenomenon, see 314$^a$5n2 and 1.5.

## Note 15
**Starting-points:** An *archê* ("starting-point," "first principle") is a primary cause: "This is what it is for something to be a starting-point, that it is itself the cause of many things, with nothing above it being a cause of it" (*GA* 788$^a$14–16).

## Note 16

**Affections:** What X *paschei* is what happens to him or affects him, so that he is passive with respect to it, as opposed to what he *poiei* ("affects," "does," "produces"). When Y does something to X, X is affected by it, so his *pathê* as a result are, in one sense, his affections and in another his passions or feelings. Here, as often elsewhere, however, while a thing's *pathê* include its affections, they encompass its attributes more generally.

**We say:** Aristotle's own view is in fact more refined. See GC $329^b7$–$330^a29$, also *Sens.* $445^b23$–$446^a20$.

**Differentiae:** *Diaphorai* are sometimes, as here, the differentiae that divide a genus into species, and so figure in their essential definitions: "species are composed of the genus and the differentiae" (*Met.* $1057^b7$). But sometimes they are simply the different features that distinguish one kind of thing from another, without necessarily suggesting that the kinds are genera or species in the strict sense or that the differences are differentiae.

**Hot cold ... dry wet:** See $329^b26$–32.
**Soft hard:** See *Mete.* $382^a11$–14.

## Note 17

**"Sun, white...":** Empedocles, DK B21 (lns. 3, 5) = TEGP 45 F22 (lns. 3, 5). Thus, as Aristotle understands it, Empedocles makes white (or bright; *leukon* can mean either) and hot differentiae of sun (fire), which, as definitive of fire's essence, ensures that fire cannot lose them, as it would if it became rain (dark, cold).

## Note 18

**A single matter . . . :** "Some matter is [1] perceptible, however, while [2] some is intelligible—perceptible matter being, for example, bronze, wood, and any matter that is movable, and intelligible matter being the sort that is in the perceptible things but not insofar as they are perceptible, such as the objects of mathematics" (*Met.* $1036^a9$–12). Perceptible (as opposed to intelligible) matter comes in a variety of different sorts. [1a] Movable matter (*kinêtê hulê*), mentioned at *Met.* $1036^a10$, is the sort something needs if it is to be capable of moving from place to place. Hence it is also referred as *hulê topikê* ($1042^b6$). [1b] Matter for alteration (*alloiôtê*) is the sort that things need if they are to change in quality ($1050^b16$–18). [1c] Then there is matter needed for movement with respect to magnitude, or growth and withering (*Ph.* $260^a27$). [1d] And finally the matter needed for coming to be and passing away (*gennêtê kai phthartê*), which is matter most of all and in the full sense (*GC* $320^a2$). Things that have [1a] but not [1d] include the various heavenly bodies (*Met.* $1050^b22$–28, $1069^b24$–26). Intelligible matter (*hulê noêtê*) is mentioned by name only in [2] and at *Met.* $1037^a5$ and $1045^a33$–35: "Some matter is intelligible, and some perceptible, and of the account always one part is the matter and the other the actuality [= the form]—for example, the circle is shape plus plane (*ho kuklos schêma epipedon*)." But "the matter of the objects of mathematics (*hê tôn mathêmatikôn hulê*)" ($1059^b15$–16) is fairly certainly a reference to the same sort of thing. On contraries, see $324^a2$n143.

## Note 19
**Things that appear to be so:** *Phainomena* are things that appear (often to perception) to be so, but that may or may not be so. The corresponding verb *phainesthai* ("appear"), when used with a participle endorses what appears to be so and is translated as "it is evident that," or "it is seen to be that," or the like, and when used with an infinitive neither endorses nor rejects what appears to be so and is translated as "appears." When it occurs without a participle or an infinitive, it may either endorse or reject.

## Note 20
**He says that . . .:** Compare: "Love often disaggregates things for him, while strife aggregates them. For whenever the universe is divided up into its elements because of strife, the fire is aggregated into one, and so is each of the other elements, and whenever things come together into one again under the influence of love, it is necessary that the parts from each get disaggregated again" (*Met.* 985$^a$24–29).

## Note 21
**These differentiae are subtracted:** "Assuming that in the 'Sphere' all things are fused into a unity, Aristotle urges that, when Love begins to go out and Strife to come in, the elements come into being as distinct things. For an 'addition' and 'subtraction' of the πάθη [affections] which distinctively characterize the elements then occur: so that, whereas, e.g., Moist and Hot were originally distributed uniformly over the 'Sphere', Hot is *now* added *here* and subtracted *there*, Moist subtracted *here* and added *there*. Hence *this* portion becomes separated from *that*, *this* being distinctively Moist (i.e. Water) and *that* distinctively Hot (i.e. Fire)" (Joachim-1, pp. 68–69).

## Note 22
**Co-ordinates:** A *sustoichia* is a column, like the two columns of contraries in which the Pythagoreans arranged their basic starting-points (listed at *Met.* 983$^a$23–26). Co-ordinates (*sustoicha*) here are thus items in the same column as earth and fire, namely, water and air.

## Note 23
**Insofar as the one is like the underlying matter . . . :** See 335$^b$16n286.

## Note 24
**Prior in nature:** "Others, however, are said to be prior in nature and substance, when it is possible for them to be without other things, but not the others without them" (*Met.* 1019$^a$2–4).

## Note 25
**Plato investigated only . . . :** See 315$^b$30n32.

**He said nothing about . . . :** "If there is going to be flesh, bone, or any of the others whatever, we must not just say that they are potentially present [in the element], but rather we must get a further theoretical grasp on what their mode of coming to be is" (*Cael.* 302$^a$26–28).

## Note 26
**Things grow by the addition of like to like:** See 322$^a$3–16.

## Note 27
**Mixture:** Aristotle often distinguishes between a mere combination (*sunthesis*) or mechanical mixture and a chemical one (*mixis*), which involves the formation of a new homogeneous stuff with new emergent affections: "mixture (*mixis*) is unification of the mixables, resulting from their alteration" (*GC* 328$^b$22).

## Note 28
***Tragô[i]dia* and *trugô[i]dia* come to be from the same letters:** *Trugô[i]dia* is a rare word meaning "comedy." The idea is not that the two words are composed of the same letters, which they obviously aren't, but that they come from the same letters, and then one particle, namely, "a," gets "shifted" when "u" gets mixed in and replaces it.

## Note 29
**Puzzles:** A puzzle (*aporia*) exists when "there are persuasive arguments concerning both sides" of an issue (*Top.* 104$^b$13–14).

## Note 30
**A puzzle-free way:** See Introduction, pp. xli–xliii.

## Note 31
**It is necessary to try to resolve:** Aristotle's own proposed resolution appears in 1.2–4.

## Note 32
**In the *Timaeus*:** The reference is to Plato's account of the generation of the elements from triangles at *Ti.* 52d–57d.

## Note 33
**As we have also said elsewhere:** For example, *Cael.* 299$^a$6–11: "It is clear, then, that on the same account on which a solid is composed of planes, a plane is composed of lines, and these of points. But if so, it is not necessary for a part of a line to be a line. These, though, are matters we have previously investigated in the discussions concerning movement [in *Ph.* 5, 6, 8], proving that there are no indivisible lengths."
**In its own terms:** The terms are mathematical. Since mathematical planes are further resolvable into lines and points, there is no good mathematical reason to stop with them.

## Note 34
**By "turning"** ... : "Democritus for his part seems to think that there were three differentiae; for he thinks that the underlying body and the matter are one and the same, but that it is differentiated either by rhythm (that is, shape), or by turning (that is, position), or by contact (that is, order). It is evident, however, that there are many differentiae" (*Met.* 1042$^b$11–15).

## Note 35
**He says** ... : = DK A123 = TEGP 128. See also DK A125 = TEGP 129.

## Note 36
**Logico-linguistic way:** (1) The adjective *logikos* is used to distinguish a set of propositions and problems from a set belonging to natural science or ethics: "Propositions such as this are ethical—for example, whether one should obey our parents or the laws, if they disagree. *Logikos*, whether contraries belong to the same science or not. Natural scientific, whether the cosmos is eternal or not. And similarly for the problems" (*Top.* 105$^b$21–25). Since the question about a science of contraries is a philosophical one (*Met.* 996$^a$18–21), *logikos* problems overlap with philosophical ones. At the same time, "if an argument depends on false but reputable beliefs, it is *logikos*" (*Top.* 162$^b$27), suggesting that *logikos* arguments overlap with dialectical ones, since both may rely on reputable beliefs (*endoxa*) or—more or less equivalently—on things said (*legomena*) about the topic (*Ph.* 185$^a$2–3). Indeed, the question about a science of contraries is itself identified as one for dialectic (*Met.* 1078$^b$25–27).

(2) When Plato, unlike previous thinkers, is accorded a share of dialectic it is due to his investigation of *logoi* or accounts (*Met.* 987$^b$31–33), which he almost always undertook through staged Socratic conversations, whose aim was to discover the correct definition (1078$^b$23–25) of what something essentially or intrinsically is, or is itself-by-itself (*auto kath' hauto*)—the "itself" in the name of a Form probably stems from its being the ontological correlate of such a definition (*Met.* 997$^b$8–9). One core meaning of *logikos*, in fact, relates it to conversation and speaking, while another relates it to reason—the *logikai aretai* are the virtues of reason or thought (*NE* 1108$^b$9–10). When we ask *logikôs* (adverb) why it is that these bricks and stones are a house, what we are asking for is a formal cause or an essence (*Met.* 1041$^a$26–28), which is presumably why a deduction of the essence is a *logikos sullogismos* (*APo.* 93$^a$15).

(3) When dialecticians are contrasted with natural scientists, it is on the grounds that "the scientist gives the matter, whereas the dialectician gives the form and the account" (*DA* 403$^b$1–2)—again associating dialectic with proceeding *logikôs*. The dialectician proceeds *logikôs*, the natural scientist *phusikôs*—looking to matter but also to form, when the relevant essence requires it (*Met.* 1026$^a$5–6). So to proceed in a strictly *logikôs* way, when there is empirical evidence bearing on the subject, is bad scientific practice: "It seems that the knowledge of the what-it-is is not only useful for getting a theoretical grasp on the

causes of the coincidents connected to the essences [= intrinsic coincidents] ... but also, conversely, knowing these coincidents contributes in great part to knowing the what-it-is; for when we can give an account of the way either all or most of these coincidents appear to be, we will then be able to speak best about the essence; for the starting-point of all demonstration is [the definition of] the what-it-is, so that insofar as definitions do not lead us to know the coincidents, or fail even to facilitate a likely conjecture about [how to demonstrate] them, it is clear that they have all been stated in a dialectical and empty way" (*DA* 402$^b$16–403$^a$2).

**Indivisible magnitudes:** The author of ††*LI* gives the argument: "If there is an Idea of line, and if the first of the things is called by the same name, then, since the parts are prior to the whole, line-itself must be indivisible (*adiairetos*). And in the same way so must the [Idea of] the square, the triangle, the other [Ideas of] figures, and in general plane-itself and body-itself, since otherwise there will be things prior to each of them" (968$^a$9–14). See also Philop. 27.2–13 = Williams-2, pp. 47–48.

## Note 37
**Precisely:** "Terms that signify substance signify precisely (*hoper*) that thing of which they are predicated, or precisely that sort of thing. Those, on the other hand, that do not signify substance, but are said of some underlying subject that is neither precisely what that thing is nor precisely what sort of thing that thing is, are coincidents—for example, white is a coincident of the human. For the human is neither precisely white nor precisely a sort of white, but rather an animal, presumably; for the human is precisely an animal. But terms that do not signify substance must be predicated of some underlying subject, and there cannot be anything white that is not some other thing that is white" (*APo.* 83$^a$24–32).

## Note 38
**This division is possible:** That is, possible to actually carry out by cutting the thing up into pieces, like the sawdust mentioned at 316$^a$34–$^b$1.

## Note 39
**The same applies also at the mid-point ... :** In other words, it does not matter whether the division proceeds by bisection, and so is made at the mid-point, or in some other way, so that it is made at any random point whatever.

## Note 40
**When it was divided into two or more ... :** Think of points as points of contact, as 316$^b$6–8 suggests. Division increases the number of contact points, since what was one point is now two: the end-point of one of the new segments, the starting-point of the other. Reconnection, by contrast, reduces the number of contact points. See De Haas & Mansfeld (Sedley), p. 70.

## Note 41

**It (*ekeino*) is divisible in some way:** Reading πως with Rashed for Mugler and mss. πῶς ("in what way is this divisible?"). *Ekeino* refers to the sawdust, which the argument shows to have no magnitude, once it too is submitted to division.

## Note 42

**Separable:** Verbals ending in *-ton*—of which *chôriston* is an example—sometimes have the meaning of a perfect passive participle ("separated") and sometimes express possibility ("separable"). When *chôriston* is applied to substances "separable" often seems to better capture its sense, especially that of its negation (see *Met.* 1028ᵃ23–24). For things, such as the form and matter of a matter-form compound, are not just not separated, in that they are always found together (1036ᵇ3–4)—they cannot be separated. Moreover, things that are separable, such as the understanding and the other parts of the soul, do not become actually separated until, for example, death: "this [productive] understanding is separable (*chôristos*), impassive, and unmixed, being in substance an activity, [that is,] not sometimes understanding and at other times not. But, when separated (*chôristheis*), this alone is just what it is" (*DA* 430ᵃ17–23). Just what the separability of substance amounts to is another matter.

(1) Walking and being healthy are characterized as "incapable of being separated," on the grounds that there is some particular substantial underlying subject of which they are predicated (*Met.* 1028ᵃ20–31). Often, separability is associated with being such a subject: "If we do not posit substances to be separated, and in the way in which particular things are said to be separated, we will do away with the sort of substance we wish to maintain" (1086ᵇ16–19). Similarly, not being separable is associated with being predicated of such a subject. Being predicated of a substance—being an affection—seems, then, to be a sufficient condition of not being separable. Moreover, not being separable seems itself to be a sufficient condition of being ontologically dependent: (1a) "All the other things are either said of the primary substances as subjects or in them as subjects. So if the primary substances were not, it would be impossible for any of the other things to be" (*Cat.* 2ᵇ3–6).

(2) Couched in terms of priority, what is attributed to primary substances in (1a) is *substantial* priority, or priority in nature, which Aristotle defines in two ways: (2a) "Things are said to be prior in nature and substance, when it is possible for them to be (*einai*) without other things, but not the others without them" (*Met.* 1019ᵃ3–4); (2b) "Those things are prior in substance [to others] which, when separated, surpass [them] in being (*tô[i] einai huperballei*)" (1077ᵇ2–3). Moreover, in a text apparently expressing an idea similar to (2b), the form of a matter-form compound is said to be "prior to the matter and more (*mallon*) of a being" (1029ᵃ5–6). Since existence, like identity, does not come in degrees, the use of the verb *huperballein* and the adverb *mallon* makes it difficult to understand *einai* ("being," "to be") as having an exclusively existential sense. At the same time, *einai* does seem

*Note 42*

to have some existential import, as it surely does in (2c): "if everyone were well, health would be (*estai* = exist) but not sickness, and if everything were white, whiteness would be (*estai*) but not blackness" (*Cat.* 14$^a$7–10).

It seems reasonable, therefore, to think that to be is to be a being of some sort, and that to be a being entails existing. To be a being, however, is to be either a coincidental being (the pale human) or an intrinsic being, something with an essence (the human). To be an intrinsic being, in turn, is to be either an intrinsic coincident, a matter-form compound, or simply a substantial form (*Met.* 1025$^b$28–1026$^a$15). As identical to its tightly unified essence (1037$^b$10–27), a substantial form, is an intrinsic being of the highest order—a primary substance (1037$^a$33–$^b$4). A matter-form compound, by contrast, since it is never identical to its essence (1037$^b$4–7), is an intrinsic being of a lower order (1072$^a$30–32), since it is always a complex thing—a this in this (1030$^b$18)—whose essence is complex in a structurally parallel way (1035$^b$27–30). Similarly, an intrinsically coincidental being, while it follows from an essence, is still a complex of two intrinsic beings, one a substance with an essence, the other an affection. For X to be more of a being than Y, or to exceed Y in being, we might reasonably conclude, is for it to be closer to a substantial form on this scale. It is, as we might put it, for X to be more intrinsic a being than Y. Degrees of being are degrees of intrinsicality, then, not degrees of existence.

(3) Affections depend for their existence on substance, but not on that of some particular substance, any substance that has them will do: white exists if something is white, but the something does not have to be Bucephalus. Hence the parallel claim about substances should not be that a substance can exist without any affections, suggesting that substances are bare particulars, but that substances in general can exist whether or not affections do. On an *ante rem* (or Platonist) theory, affections can exist uninstantiated by particulars. On an *in re* theory, like Aristotle's, they cannot. That is the message of (2c). Hence the ontological dependence of affections—and the cognate ontological independence of substances—must be formulated differently by these theories. It seems, then, that if *in re* affections were ontologically independent of substances, it could only be because *they were instantiated by something else*, since they cannot exist uninstantiated by particulars of some sort. This is the way we see Aristotle thinking in the following text: "Heat and straightness [and whiteness] can be present in every part of a thing, but it is impossible for all of it to be hot, white, or straight [and nothing else]. For then the affections would be separated" (*Long.* 465$^b$12–14). White would be separate from substance, notice, not if it existed entirely uninstantiated, but if it were instantiated by a being that was wholly and exclusively white. Such a being is obviously not an Aristotelian substance, but something more like the Platonic Form of white, which does seem to be white and nothing else (Plato, *Phd.* 78d). Aristotelian substances can exist, then, whether or not their affections exist by being instantiated by something else. Affections, on the other hand, cannot exist unless they are instantiated by Aristotelian substances, since such substances are (in Aristotle's view) the only ultimate subjects of predication. The separability of substance from affections, on this way of looking at it, is entirely of a piece with their inseparability from it.

Note 42

(4) The verb *chôrizein* derives from *chôra* ("place"), and means "to separate, part, sever, or divide" things by causing them (roughly speaking) to be in separate (or disjoint) places (*Met.* 998$^a$17–19, 1068$^b$26–27). Thus when Aristotle describes Plato as separating the Forms from perceptible particulars (1078$^b$30–34), a view he adverts to in our text, the primary connotation is that of putting them in separate places: perceptible particulars are "here (*entautha*)," Forms are "over there (*kakei*)" (990$^b$34–991$^a$1). For a Form is "a particular, they say, and separable" (1040$^a$8–9) and "place is special to particular things, which is why they are separable by place" (1092$^a$18–19). Moreover, the fundamental objection Aristotle makes to such separable Forms is that they are an incoherent mixture of universals and of the particulars needed for their instantiation and existence: (4a) "they say that there is man-itself and horse-itself and health-itself, and nothing else—like those who introduce gods, but say that they are human in form; for those people were making the gods nothing but eternal human beings, and these are making the Forms nothing but eternal perceptibles" (997$^b$9–12). (4b) "They at the same time make the Forms universal and contrariwise treat them as separable and as particulars . . . that this is not possible is a puzzle that has been gone through before" (1086$^a$32–35; also 1003$^a$5–17). We might expect, therefore, as (4) implies, that the separability Aristotle accords to his own substances, but denies to affections, would be the separability he denies to Platonic Forms: affections are in substances around here not in substances (= Forms) that are elsewhere.

(5) Though separability is often characterized in terms of existential independence, in some cases this seems not to be required: "Even where there is a converse implication of existence, what is somehow the cause of the other's existence might reasonably be called prior by nature. That there are such cases is clear; for there is a converse implication of existence between there being a human and a true statement about him; for if there is a human, the statement in which we say that there is a human is true; and the converse certainly holds; for if the statement in which we say that there is a human is true, there is a human. But the true statement is in no way the cause of there being the thing, while the thing seems somehow to be the cause of the statement's being true; for it is in virtue of whether or not the thing exists that the statement is said to be true or false" (*Cat.* 14$^b$11–22). What lies at the bottom of separability, then, seems rather to be a sort of ontological independence that is causal or explanatory in nature. In any case, this is clearly what we find in the following texts: (5a) "This [vegetative soul] can be separated from the others, but the others cannot be separated from it, in the case of the mortal ones. This is evident in the case of plants, since they have no other capacity of soul" (*DA* 413$^a$31–$^b$1; also 403$^a$10–16, $^b$17–19). (5b) "Bodily parts . . . cannot even exist when they are separated. For it is not a finger in any and every state that is the finger of an animal; instead, a dead finger is only homonymously a finger" (*Met.* 1035$^b$23–25). For what makes perceptual soul inseparable from nutritive soul, or a finger inseparable from an animal, are the causal relations that make the former dependent on the latter. Again, this makes the separability accorded to substances, but denied to affections, the same as the separability denied to Platonic Forms. For the latter too were intended to play an explanatory role: "the Forms are the causes

of the what-it-is of other things, as *the one* is of the Forms" (988ᵃ10–11). Thus what all the gods love does not pick out the Form of piety, even though something is pious if and only if all the gods love it, because being loved by the gods is not what makes something pious (Plato, *Euthphr.* 10d–e).

(6) The separability of substance and the inseparability of affections, while obviously essential to the account of both, is a special case of a more general phenomenon. For substance as form is not just separable from affections but from matter as well. But if this is the sort of separability characterized in (1)–(5), it must be antisymmetrical, so that form can exist apart from matter but not matter apart from form. In the case of the forms of form-matter compounds, whether their matter is perceptible or intelligible, this is clearly not the case: like snub, but unlike concavity, they cannot exist apart from matter (*Met.* 1025ᵇ28–1026ᵃ15). But in the case of other forms, those that are like concavity, it is possible (1026ᵃ15–16, 1071ᵇ20). These are the primary intelligible substances, on which all others—including matter-form compounds—causally depend for their existence (1050ᵇ19) and order (1060ᵃ26–27). Matter, by contrast, cannot exist apart from form of some sort (1089ᵇ27–28), since without form it is not intrinsically anything at all (1029ᵃ20–21).

(7) In (1) separability is tied to being a particular subject of predication, and so seems to be somehow logical or logico-linguistic in nature. (6), on the other hand, seems to tell a different sort of story, in which separability has more to do with causation and explanation than with logic proper. To bring the two together we need only reflect that Aristotle's logic is primarily a logic of science, and that whenever we have a subject-predicate proposition there is always a question as to why the predicate holds of the subject. The target of scientific explanation, indeed, is always just that: Why does predicate P hold of subject S (*Met.* 1041ᵃ10–11)? If P holds of S coincidentally, or by luck or chance, science has nothing to say about it (1026ᵇ3–5). There is no explanation. What this implies is that the primary explanatory entities cannot themselves have a subject-predicate structure (*Met.* 1051ᵃ34–ᵇ5). They cannot be expressed as one thing said of another—they are not thises-in-thises. Instead, in comparison to things with such a structure, they are simple—forms, not form-matter compounds. The problem is—and it is one of the deepest—how separable forms, which, like all forms, are universals (1036ᵃ28–29), can indeed be primary subjects and this somethings—separable "in the way in which *particular things* are said to be separated." For Aristotle's answer, see 1087ᵃ10–25.

**Form or some affection:** *Eidos ê pathos* is probably purposely vague, and means simply "some non-bodily thing of some sort." Nonetheless, it has to be capable of existing apart from whatever body is affected by it if it can be removed from body, so as no longer to inhere in it.

## Note 43

**The points will be somewhere:** Reading που with Rashed for Mugler, Joachim-1, ποῦ ἔσονται ("where will the points be, and will they be immovable or in movement?"). But this "somewhere" may be either a place in the strict sense (which it must be if the points are in movement), or in a looser sense (if the points are immovable limits, or points of contact): "Place too is somewhere, although not as in a place, but in the way that a limit is in what is limited. For not every being is in a place, but [only] movable body" (*Ph.* 212$^b$27–29).

**There is always something beyond the contact . . . :** "Every contact is a limit; but not every limit is therefore also a contact. So if you call cuts (*sêmeia*) and points 'limits,' it is impossible for there to be a limit without there being something that is limited; and if you call them 'contacts,' they will be contacts of things that are in contact. The fact that the things that are in contact are distinct from and beyond the *contact, point,* or *division* (for these all signify the same thing) is made clear by the contacts being one while the things that are in contact are two. The argument, then, can be understood in this way as making clear that it is impossible to dissolve a body into points. But it is also possible to understand the argument as directed against the possibility of putting together points to produce something possessed of magnitude. For how is it at all possible for them to be put together, since they are unable to make contact with each other? For things that are in contact make contact with each other at some part of themselves, so that there are parts of them that are beyond [the one] making contact, but points cannot make contact with each other at [such a part]" (Philop. 32.6–16 = Williams-2, p. 54).

## Note 44
**Point:** On the relationship between *stigmê* (also "point") and *sêmeion* (used here and at 316$^b$31), see 317$^a$11–12n52.

## Note 45
**It has been potentially divided:** The perfect *diê[i]rêtai* comes from the thought experiment. The piece of wood $W_1$ was in fact divided and reassembled at point $p_1$, resulting in getting a unified piece $W_2$ that is equal in quantity to $W_1$. Since the same would be true if it had been divided at any point $p_x$ in $W_1$, $W_1$ has been potentially divided at every point.

## Note 46
**Further, if I had divided . . . separated?:** With Rashed, Mugler, and Joachim-1, I read this passage here; De Haas & Mansfeld (Sedley), p. 72, with some justification, reads it post 316$^b$27.

## Note 47
**Investigated elsewhere:** *Ph.* 231$^a$21–$^b$18, *Cael.* 303$^a$3–$^b$8.

## Note 48
**An attempt must be made to resolve (*luein*) them:** "It must be noted that his [Aristotle's] purpose now is not directly to prove that there are no indivisible things possessed of magnitude (for the possibility of this theory is refuted in the books just mentioned [see previous note]), but to resolve the arguments by which indivisible things possessed of magnitude are introduced" (Philop. 34.5–8 = Williams-2, p. 56). To *luein* an argument is to untie (also, *luein*) the aporia or

puzzle that it produces when it conflicts with another argument (*Met.* 995ᵃ27–31). But *luein* can also mean "refute," though it sometimes differs from *elegchein* (also "refute") by involving a diagnosis of what is wrong with the target argument: "The person, then, who does away with the thing through which the falsehood comes about has entirely resolved the argument, but it is the person who knows that the argument proceeds through it who knows the resolution" (*Top.* 160ᵇ33–35). But in the *Rhetoric*, for example, this is not so: "It is possible to refute (*luein*) either by stating a counter-deduction or by bringing an objection" (1402ᵃ31–32). Indeed, the two seem to be used more or less interchangeably (for example, *elegktikous* at 1397ᵃ1, *luseôn* at ᵃ5).

## Note 49

**Every perceptible body:** That is every natural or physical body, even if, like a Democritean atom, it is too small to perceive. See 316ᵇ32–33.

**Potentially ... actually:** The term *energeia*, which is used only a few times in *GC* (318ᵃ20, 327ᵇ23), is an Aristotelian coinage, translated as "activity," with the dative or adverbial form *energeia[i]* translated as "active" or "actively," in order to signal its relation to *energeia*. The etymology of the coinage is unclear, but Aristotle is explicit that it has been extended from movement to other things (*Met.* 1046ᵃ1–2, 1047ᵃ30–32), and that it is related to another term with an *erg*- root, namely, *ergon*: "The *ergon* ('function,' 'work') is the *telos* ('end'), and the *energeia* is the *ergon*, and that is why the name *energeia* is said [of things] with reference to the *ergon* and extends to the *entelecheian* ('actuality')" (1050ᵃ21–23). *Entelecheia*, which is used here, is mostly used as a synonym of *energeia*, but with a slightly different connotation, and is also an Aristotelian coinage: *energeia* is action, activity, and movement oriented; *entelecheia*—as the *tel*- suggests—is end or *telos* or completion (*enteles*) oriented (*Met.* 1021ᵇ24–30). The dative or adverbial form *entelecheia[i]*, used here, is translated as "actual" or "actually." The *entelecheia* of something is thus "the actualization" of it. Putting all this together: the activation or actualization of X is an activity, which is X active or actual, which is X achieving its end, which—since "the for-the-sake-of-which is the function" (996ᵇ7)—is X fulfilling its function, and being actively or actually X, and so being complete.

## Note 50

**Contiguous** (*echomenê*): "What are contiguous are what are successive and making contact" (*Ph.* 227ᵃ6).

## Note 51

**There are not more than one [there]; for points are not successive:** Reading οὐκ εἰσίν· ἐφεξῆς γὰρ οὐκ εἰσίν with Rashed, Mugler, and the mss. De Haas & Mansfeld (Sedley), p. 78, reads οὐκ εἰσίν ἐφεξῆς (<ἐφεξῆς> γὰρ οὐκ εἰσίν), which gives the meaning, "but there are not more than one in succession (for points are not successive)." The presupposition, which the clarificatory addition of [there] makes unnecessary, is that "there obviously are more points than one" (p. 78n25). There are indeed more points than one in the magnitude, but not exactly where the one at issue is.

**Successive:** "What is successive (*ephexês*) is what is after the starting-point (the order being determined by position or form or in some other way) and has nothing of the same kind (*genos*) between it and what it succeeds—for example, lines in the case of line, units in that of unit, or houses in that of house (but there is nothing to prevent something of some other kind from being in between)" (*Met.* 1068$^b$31-35).

## Note 52

**[1] The way, however, in which divisibility does belong at every point is that anywhere at all there is one point in whichever direction, and that all points are like each; [2] but there are not more than one [there]; for points are not successive, so that [it does not belong] at all points; [3] for if a magnitude is divisible at the mid-point, will it also be divisible at a contiguous point? [4] For cut is not contiguous to cut or point to point:** [1] Pick any arbitrary minimal region (read: point-sized region) $r_1$ in a magnitude M and there is a point $p_1$ at $r_1$ that is exactly like any $p_x$ at $r_x$ in M. Ask: How many points are there at $r_1$? [2] answers that because points are not successive, there can only be one there; for since $r_1$ is minimal or point-sized, the only way there could be more than one is if $p_1$ could be divided into $p_{1a}$ and $p_{1b}$ that are successive. But [3] suppose $p_1$ was divided into $p_{1a}$ and $p_{1b}$ at its mid-point $p_m$. Then will it also be divisible at a point contiguous to $p_m$, as the successiveness of $p_{1a}$ and $p_{1b}$ requires? Of course not, because [4] cut is not contiguous to cut or point to point. In effect Joachim-1's reading of [3] εἰ γὰρ κατὰ μέσον διαιρετόν, καὶ κατ' ἐχομένην στιγμὴν ἔσται διαιρετόν· <οὐκ ἔστιν δέ,>, which gives the meaning "for if it is divisible in the middle, it will also be divisible at a contiguous point. But it is not,..." spells out what the transmitted text leaves implicit.

**Cut...point:** A *sêmeion* (neuter) is a mark, trace, track, sign, indication, but also a mathematical point, and so a near synonym of *stigmê* (feminine)—Aristotle has already used it in this sense at 316$^b$11, 31, where it is the place a cut is made. The modern mathematical notion of a cut, indeed, is closely approximate in meaning, so I have used it here instead of "point." In Greek mathematics it eventually replaced *stigmê*. It has the additional advantage of providing a more intuitive segue into the next sentence, where the neuter *touto* refers back more specifically to *sêmeion*.

## Note 53

**A division or a join:** When our magnitude M is cut at point $p_1$, $p_1$ is at once the end-point of one segment of M and the starting-point of the other segment. If $p_1$ were itself cut into $p_{1a}$ and $p_{1b}$, we would have the problem that Aristotle has already diagnosed and solved. Thus $p_1$ at once divides and joins the segments.

## Note 54

**Change in what is continuous is alteration:** See 319$^b$10-12.

## Note 55

**When a whole changes from a *this* to a *this*:** "A change from what is not an underlying subject to an underlying subject, the relation being that of contradiction, is a coming to be—an unconditional coming to be when the change is unconditional, in a particular respect when the change is in a particular respect. For example, a change from not pale to pale is a coming to be in this respect, pale, whereas a change from unconditionally not being to substance is unconditional coming to be, with respect to which we say that a thing comes to be unconditionally, not that it comes to be something. A change from an underlying subject to what is not an underlying subject is a passing away—an unconditional one when the change is from substance to not being, in a particular respect when the change is to the opposite contradictory, as was said in the case of coming to be" (*Ph.* 225ᵃ12–20). See 319ᵇ14–20n88. A this (*tode*) is a *tode ti*. See 317ᵇ31–32n67.

## Note 56
**Something corresponding to the account and something corresponding to the matter:** What corresponds to the account is the form, while what corresponds to the matter just is the matter: (1) "In one way, then, something is said to be *nature* when it is the first underlying matter for each of the things that have within themselves a starting-point of movement and change. In another way, though, what is said to be *nature* is the shape—that is, the form—that is in accord with the account" (*Ph.* 193ᵃ28–31). (2) "Even what is contrary to nature is in a way in accord with nature, whenever, that is, the nature corresponding to the form does not master the one corresponding to the matter" (*GA* 770ᵇ15–17).

## Note 57
**The smaller raindrops are divided:** That is, the more mist-like rain becomes. Reading ὕδατα with Rashed for Mugler and Joachim-1 ὑδάτια.

## Note 58
**In what follows:** See 328ᵃ23–ᵇ22.

## Note 59
**As some people say it is:** "At least not the kind of 'association' some philosophers assert it to be" (Joachim-2). That is, "(as Philoponus [42.26 = Williams-2, p. 66]) rightly explains) γένεσις cannot be identified with σύγκρισις ἐξ ἀτόμων ['aggregation from atoms']" (Joachim-1, p. 88). "This forestalls the objection that the information of matter, which is what Aristotle himself asserts generation [= coming to be] to be, could also be called aggregation of a kind" (Williams-1, p. 80). But Aristotle is hardly likely to be worried about that. See 327ᵇ10–19 and Rashed, pp. 111–112n5.

## Note 60
**We must first:** For what comes second, see 317ᵇ34–35.

## Note 61
**What is primary in each category of being:** Ask with regard to each category what is primary in it, bearing in mind that, though "things are said to be primary in many ways. Nonetheless, substance is primary in all of them—in account, in

knowledge, and in time. For of the various things that are predicated none is separable, but only this" (*Met.* 1028ª31–34). The answer is that what is primary in the category of substance is substance, what is primary in that of quality is substance, since qualities are not separable from substance, what is primary in that of quantity is again substance, and likewise for all the other categories. On separability, see 316ᵇ3n42.

**What is universal and encompasses everything:** In this case unconditional not being is the universal that encompasses whatever is not F, whether F is in the category of substance, quality, quantity, or whatever. That is why, in this sense, what is not will not be anything at all (317ᵇ12).

## Note 62
**Thisness:** *To tode* is what by belonging to X makes X a *tode ti* and a substance. See 317ᵇ31–32n67.

## Note 63
**Wholly not being:** That is, again, not being F for any value of F, regardless of what category F is in.

## Note 64
**Other accounts:** The reference is usually taken to be to *Ph.* 1.6–9, or some part thereof, and this is probably correct. For though there the distinction between potentially and actually does little explicit work (as Williams-1, pp. 83–85 notes), whereas in the summary here it has pride of place, matter does have a major role to play there, and matter in its broadest sense just is potentiality: "by 'the matter' I mean what though not actively a this something is potentially a this something" (*Met.* 1042ª27–28). That is why in the following text Aristotle can move so seamlessly from speaking in terms of one to speaking in terms of the other: "If, then, changes are of four sorts, either with respect to the [this] something, or with respect to the quality, quantity, or place, and if unconditional coming to be and passing away are with respect to the this, growth and withering with respect to quantity, alteration with respect to an affection, spatial movement with respect to place, then changes would in each case be to the corresponding contrary states. It must, then, be the matter, since it is capable of both states, that changes. But since being is twofold, everything changes from what is potentially to what is actively—for example, from what is potentially white to what is actively white, and similarly in the case of growth and withering. So not only is it possible, coincidentally, for something to come to be from what is not, but also for all things to come to be from what is—from what is potentially, however, but from what actually is not" (1069ᵇ9–20).

## Note 65
**Some substance [1] from which its coming to be will [proceed] and [2] into which what passes away necessarily changes:** Reading ἐξ ἧς ἡ γένεσις ἔσται καὶ εἰς ἣν ἀνάγκη μεταβάλλειν τὸ φθειρόμενον with Mugler and Joachim-1; Rashed

secludes ἐξ ἧς ἡ γένεσις καὶ. [1] holds because unconditional coming to be is when "a whole changes from a *this* to a *this*" (317ᵃ21–22); [2], which is introduced by the preceding sentence—"And it is the same way too where passing away is concerned" (317ᵇ22–23)—holds for the same reason.

## Note 66
**Any of the others:** That is, any of the beings in the categories other than substance.

## Note 67
**A this something or a substance:** *Tode ti* involves a particularizing element and a generalizing element. I take the demonstrative pronoun *tode* as particularizing (as suggested by *Met.* 1030ᵃ5–6) and the indefinite pronoun *ti* as generalizing, but since *tode* need not be particularizing (as it may not be in 1032ᵇ6–21) and *ti* may be, it is possible to go the other way and translate as "thing of a certain sort." Often *tode ti* appears in translations simply as "a this," and in at least one place Aristotle himself suggests that *tode* and *ti* are interchangeable (1069ᵇ9, 11).

(1) In very many cases, as in the present one, being a *tode ti* is a distinctive mark of *ousia* ("substance"), and so has some share in the ambiguity of the latter, as between (1a) an ultimate subject of predication and (2a) the substance or essence of something (314ᵇ14n14). This is reflected in the fact that (1b) a particular man and a particular horse are primary substances (*Cat.* 2ᵃ11–14), so that "it is indisputably true that each of them signifies a *tode ti*" (3ᵇ10–12), while at the same time (2b) what is separable and a *tode ti* is "the shape or form of each thing" (*Met.* 1017ᵇ24–26; also 1042ᵃ27–29, 1049ᵃ35, 1070ᵃ11). Some things, to be sure, are one and the same as their forms or essences—which would remove the ambiguity at least in their cases—but it is not true that all are (1037ᵃ33–ᵇ7).

(3) As strong as the connection between substance and being a *tode ti* is the disconnection between being a *tode ti* and being a universal—"no common thing signifies a this something, but rather a such-and-such sort of thing" (*Met.* 1003ᵃ8–9; also 1039ᵃ15–16)—and the connection between being substance and being a *kath' hekaston*: "If we do not posit substances to be separated, and in the way in which the *kath' hekasta* are said to be separated, we will do away with the sort of substance we wish to maintain" (1086ᵇ16–19). Apparently, then, a form that is (2b) a primary substance—as some are explicitly said to be (1032ᵇ1–2)—must be a *kath' hekaston*.

(4) A *kath' hekaston*, in turn, is "what is numerically one" (*Met.* 999ᵇ34–1000ᵃ1), and so, (4a) taking "numerically one" to mean that no two things can be one and the same *kath' hekaston*, as no two things can be you or Socrates (1039ᵃ34), it is translated as "particular." But it is also possible to take "numerically one" to mean (4b) "indivisible" or "individual," so that like an ultimate differentia—identified with form and substance at 1038ᵃ25–26—something is *kath' hekaston* because it cannot be further divided or differentiated.

(5) As we try to disambiguate *tode ti*, then, we run into ambiguities that parallel the initial one in substance itself, or that are related to it. That this may be no accident but rather the heart of the issue is suggested by *Met.* 1087ᵃ19–21.

(6) Finally, a point about matter. What *Ph.* 190$^b$24–26 refers to as "countable matter (*hulê arithmêtikê*)," and treats as a generalization of such things as the human and the bronze, is "more of a this something," as, no doubt, is the "this wood (*todi to xulon*) of this [box]" at *Met.* 1049$^a$24 and the "this (*toudi*), which is bronze" at 1033$^b$2, from (some or all of) which the smith makes this brazen sphere. But these are particular identifiable and countable parcels of matter—minimally shaped up by form, perhaps, but enough to count as (anyway low-grade) *tade tina*. Matter taken more generally, however, is "what not being actually a this something, is potentially a this something" (1042$^a$27–28).
**As we said:** At 317$^b$10–11.

## Note 68

**Both unconditional and partial:** Partial coming to be is the non-unconditional one we met at 317$^b$3. The distinction is explained in the following texts: (1) "I mean by 'partially,' is the moon eclipsed or is it increasing? For in such cases we are inquiring about whether it is or is not something. By 'unconditionally,' I mean whether the moon or night exists or does not exist" (*APo.* 90$^a$2–5). (2) "[Fallacious arguments] depending on what is said to be unconditionally this, or this in some respect and not strictly, come about when what is said of things in part is taken as if it applied unconditionally—for example, 'If what is not is believable, then what is not is'; for 'to be something' and 'to be' unconditionally are not the same. Or, again, 'What is, is not' (if it is not one of the things that is—for example, a human); for it is not the same thing not to be something and not to be unconditionally. But it appears, because of the closeness of the modes of expression, that 'to be something' differs little from 'to be,' and 'to not be something' from 'to not be'" (*SE* 166$^b$37–167$^a$6).

## Note 69

**Our accounts concerning movement:** *Ph.* 5, 6, and 8 form a unified discussion, parts of which are often referred to as—or as included in—*ta peri kinêseôs*. *Ph.* 6 is referred to in this way at 263$^a$11–12, *APo.* 95$^b$11, *Sens.* 445$^b$20, *Met.* 1049$^b$36; *Ph.* 8 at *Cael.* 272$^a$30. *Ph.* 7 interrupts this sequence, suggesting that it may have been incorporated at a later date. See Ross, pp. 11–19.

**There is, on the one hand, [1] what is immovable for all time and, on the other, [2] what is always in movement:** "If indeed there must be continuous movement, there must be a primary mover that is not moved even coincidentally, if there is to be, as we have said, an unceasing and undying movement among the beings, and if being itself is to remain in itself and in the same [limits]. . . . Moreover, if there is in fact something that is always of this sort, namely, moving something while itself remaining immovable and eternal, then the first thing that is moved by it must be eternal as well" (*Ph.* 259$^b$22–260$^a$1). [1] is the immovable (traditionally, "unmoved") mover, identified in *Met.* 12.7, 12.9 with the primary god; [2] is the primary or outermost heaven, which is the sphere of the fixed stars.

## Note 70
**The other and prior philosophy:** Aristotle sometimes applies the term *philosophia* (or sometimes just *sophia*) to any science aiming at truth rather than action (*Met.* 993$^b$19–21). In this sense of the term, all the broadly theoretical sciences count as branches of philosophy, and *philosophia* is more or less equivalent in meaning to *epistêmê* in its most exact sense. *Philosophia* also has a narrower sense, however, in which it applies exclusively to sciences providing knowledge of starting-points (1059$^a$18, *NE* 1141$^a$16–18). In addition to these, Aristotle occasionally mentions practical philosophies, such as "the philosophy of human affairs" (*NE* 1181$^b$15). It is among these that his own ethical writings belong (*Pol.* 1282$^b$18–23). It is the narrower sense that is pertinent here. The "other and prior philosophy" mentioned is the science of being qua being, developed in the *Metaphysics*, and the philosophy or science that it is other than and prior to is the natural science pertinent to the sorts of beings that come to be and pass away, which are the particular focus of *GC*. See Introduction, pp. xix–xxxv.

## Note 71
**It must be determined later:** At *GC* 336$^a$23–$^b$12.

## Note 72
**[1] For we say that passing away occurs now unconditionally** (*phtheiretai nun haplôs*), **and [2] not only that *this* passes away:** The contrast is between [1] a substance passing away, which is unconditional passing away, and [2] the passing away of an affection—here referred to with the deictic "this"—where the substance loses this feature. *Phtheiretai* should not therefore be translated as "something is passing away," but as "it is passing away," understood on the model of "it is raining," that is, as feature placing ("rain is occurring"), not as subject-predicate, "something is raining."

## Note 73
**What is being sought:** Namely, an account of the difference between coming to be unconditionally and coming to be this (notice *zêtei* at 318$^a$31).

## Note 74
**But not an unconditional coming to be:** Reading γένεσις δ'οὐχ ἁπλῶς with Mugler and Joachim-1; Rashed secludes as a gloss.

## Note 75
**Parmenides (of Elea):** See DK 28 = TEGP pp. 203–244.
**Saying that what is and what is not are fire and earth:** "Parmenides, however, seems perhaps to speak with more insight; for claiming that beyond being there is no such thing as not being, he thinks that being is necessarily one and that nothing else exists (about this we have spoken more perspicuously in our works on nature). But finding himself compelled to follow the things that appear to be so, he takes it that there is one thing according to reason but more than one according to

perception, and now posits two causes and two starting-points, hot and cold—in other words, fire and earth. And of these he ranges the first with being and the second with not being" (*Met.* 986$^b$27–987$^a$2).

**What is and what is not:** Or "being and not being." We think of the word "being" as having four different senses or meanings: (1) Existential "is"—where to say that something is means that it exists. This is the sense captured by the existential quantifier. (2) "Is" of identity—where to say that A is B means that A is identical to B, or A is one and the same thing as B. (3) "Is" of predication—where to say that A is B means that B belongs to A. (4) Veridical "is"—where to say that something is means that it is the case or that it is true. In his account of being in *Met.* 5.7, Aristotle mentions a sort of being that corresponds to (2), and in 5.9 and 10.3 (1054$^a$32–$^b$3) he has much to say about identity and sameness, including that "everything that is a being is either distinct or the same" (1054$^b$25). (1), however, is absent from his discussion, although it does seem to play some role in explaining what the separability distinctive of substance consists in (see 316$^b$3n42). One reason for this absence is that a demonstrative science posits the existence of the genus it investigates, and proceeds to investigate it (1064$^a$2–4, *APo.* 76$^b$11–22), so that existence itself escapes the focus of the science—even of the science of being qua being. (This does not mean, however, that there may not be puzzles to solve before the existence of the posited genus can be taken as established.)

## Note 76

**If the differentiae of the matter signify more of a this something:** "What is special and what is particular is always stronger in relation to generation. For Coriscus is both human and animal, but human is closer to what is special than animal is. Both the particular and the genus generate, but the particular more so; for this is the substance. For though what comes to be comes to be this sort of thing too, it also becomes a this something—and this is the substance. That is why the movements existing in the seed are from capacities such as all these" (*GA* 767$^b$29–36).

**Privation:** "The positive is prior to the privation" (*Cael.* 286$^a$25–26), because to say, for example, what cold is we refer to the positive notion heat, of which cold is the privation, so that cold is what is *not* hot. That is why "the same account makes clear both the positive thing and its privation, except not in the same way—that is, in a way it is of both, but in a way it is rather of the positive thing" (*Met.* 1046$^b$8–9). Privation (*sterēsis*), however, may be a matter of degree, so that what is colder is deprived of more of the hot than what is less cold. Privation is focally discussed at *Met.* 1022$^b$22–32.

## Note 77

**A certain [positive] predicate and a form:** The idea is that if hot is the (substantial) form of fire, then the matter of fire, when that form is predicated of it, is more a substance (since it is a matter-form compound), more a this something, than if cold (the privation of form) is predicated of it.

**Cold is a privation:** See also, *Mete.* 380$^a$7–8, *PA* 649$^a$18–19 (on which, see Lennox, pp. 194–195), *GA* 743$^a$36, 784$^a$33, *Met.* 1070$^b$11–12.

## Note 78
**Ordinary people:** Sometimes Aristotle uses *hoi polloi* (literally, "the many," "the multitude") to refer simply to a majority of people of whatever sort—to most people. But quite often he uses it to refer to the unrefined masses (*NE* 1095$^b$16) in contrast to cultivated, sophisticated, or wise people (1095$^a$21). "Ordinary people" often seems to convey the correct sense.
**Perceptible matter . . . :** See 314$^b$27n18.
**Just as . . . :** I take the train of thought to be this: ordinary people think that beings are perceptible and non-beings imperceptible, and in this regard they are just like those (namely, Protagoras and his followers) who think that beings are scientifically knowable, non-beings unknowable, because they think the perceptible and the scientifically knowable are the same: (1) "We say that scientific knowledge is a measure of things, as is perception, because of the same thing, namely, that we come to know something by them, since really they are measured more than they measure. It is as if someone else measured us and we came to know how big we are by seeing that he applied the cubit-measure to such-and-such a fraction of us. But Protagoras says that 'man is the measure of all things,' as if he had said 'the man who has scientific knowledge' or 'the man who perceives,' and that these are the measure because they have in the one case perception and in the other case scientific knowledge, which we say are measures of the underlying objects. People who say what Protagoras says, then, are saying nothing, though they appear to be saying an extraordinary thing" (*Met.* 1053$^a$31–$^b$3). Both groups wrongly exclude the possibility of intelligible beings: (2) "If, then, someone posits that scientific knowledge is just perception, the scientifically knowable must also be just the perceptible. But this is not so; for not everything that is scientifically knowable is perceptible; for some scientifically knowable things are intelligible. So the perceptible is not the genus of the scientifically knowable. And, if this is so, perception is not the genus of scientific knowledge either" (*Top.* 125$^a$28–32). (3) "If nothing exists beyond the particular things, there will be nothing intelligible, but all will be perceptible, and there will be no scientific knowledge of anything, unless someone says that perception is scientific knowledge" (*Met.* 999$^b$1–4).
**Capacity:** See 322$^a$29n122.

## Note 79
**They are more so:** Presumably, because earth is cold (privation) and dry (privation), whereas air is hot (positive) and wet (positive). See 330$^a$30–$^b$7. A wind (*pneuma*), which is analogized to a river or spring, is even more a this something, since it is not just air in movement, but has a specific starting-point and a distinctive cause (*Mete.* 360$^a$31–33). Thus, like an animal, "a wind too has a sort of life and a coming to be and passing away" (*GA* 778$^a$2–3).

## Note 80
**To the changing things:** Secluding εἰς ἄλληλα with Rashed; Mugler and Joachim-1 retain ("to the things changing into each other").

## Note 81
**The puzzle that was mentioned later:** See 318ᵃ27–35.

## Note 82
**Coming to be is said in accord with one of the two columns** (*sustoichia[i]*) **[of contraries]:** At *Met.* 996ᵃ22–26, Aristotle speaks of the Pythagoreans as arranging their ten starting-points in two columns of contraries:

| | |
|---|---|
| limited | unlimited |
| odd | even |
| one | plurality |
| right | left |
| male | female |
| being at rest | moving |
| straight | curved |
| light | darkness |
| good | bad |
| square | rectangular |

At 1093ᵇ12–13, he refers to the first column as being that of good things (*NE* 1096ᵇ6) or nobly beautiful ones, the second that of bad or evil ones. At *Met.* 1004ᵇ27 he refers to a column of contraries, one column consisting of "positive" notions, the other of privations; 1066ᵃ15 and 1072ᵃ31 also refer to this, suggesting that it is a device or way of thinking that Aristotle himself accepts. The point made in our text is that the column in accord with which coming to be is said is that of the *positive* notions.

## Note 83
**Whether the underlying subject is something or is not anything:** Secluding γίνεται ἐκ μὴ ὄντος with Rashed; Mugler and Joachim-1 read Εἴτ' οὖν ὄντος τινὸς τοῦ ὑποκειμένου εἴτε μή, γίνεται ἐκ μὴ ὄντος ("Whether, then, the underlying subject is or is not something, what comes to be emerges from not being"). If the underlying subject is not anything, it is a (supposed) case of unconditional coming to be or passing away; if it is something, it is a coming to be or a passing away corresponding to a change of a different sort, such as a qualitative or quantitative change.

## Note 84
**Moreover, there is no need . . . :** If what is not is what is not *anything*, it is false that what passes away passes into what is not; whereas if what is not is what is not *perceptible*, then, while it is true that passing away is into what is not, it is equally true that coming to be is from what is not. Thus a passing away is just as much a coming to be as it is a passing away. So the fact that it is always going on is no threat to the eternal continuity of coming to be.

## Note 85
**But this *what unconditionally is not*:** Secluding ἀπορήσειε τις with Rashed and Joachim-1; Mugler and Williams-1, following Bekker, read ἀπορήσειεν ἄν τις ("a puzzle might be raised as to whether this *what unconditionally is not* is one of two contraries").

## Note 86
**[1] The thing (whatever it is) by being which it underlies** (*ho men gar pote on hupokeitai*) **is the same:** Compare: "That thing (whatever it is) by being which movement is (*ho men pote on kinêsis estin*) [what it is], but the being for it is distinct and not a movement" (*Ph.* 219$^a$20–21). Phrases with similar constructions are found again at 219$^b$14–15, 18–19, 26, 220$^a$7–8, 223$^a$26–28, and without the participle *on* at 219$^b$10–11. See the discussion of such phrases in Coope, pp. 173–177, and, on its significance in our text, De Haas & Mansfeld (Charles), pp. 151–169.
**But [2] its being** (*einai*) **is not the same:** [1] X is the thing, whatever it is, by being which Y underlies the change of one element into another. Since nothing is more basic than an element, that is one reason to doubt that X is something—some being with an essence of its own—that persists through elemental change. [2] The being for X = what X is intrinsically = the essence of X (*Met.* 1029$^b$13–1030$^b$13). Since nothing can survive a change in its essence, that is another reason to think that X cannot be a being with an essence that persists through elemental change. On what, then, it means to say that X *is* the same, see Introduction, pp. l–liv.

## Note 87
**Naturally said of the underlying subject:** That is, that is said of it intrinsically, as opposed to coincidentally. See 319$^b$27n91, 321$^b$3–4.
**There is a change of each of them:** That is, a change in the underlying subject (as in coming to be and passing away) and in the affection (as in alteration).
**Changes in its own affections:** In contrast to a case where, for example, X becomes shorter than Y because Y grows while X remains the same height.

## Note 88
**When a whole changes:** Consider one of Aristotle's examples of genuine or unconditional coming to be: water becoming air. If we model this as follows, (∃x)(water (x) at $t_1$ & air (x) at $t_2$), it will prompt the question, what is the x that was water at $t_1$ and is air at $t_2$? Since water and air are both elements, it seems that nothing can persist through the change of water into air (or of any element, indeed, into any other element), since it would have to have a sub-elemental nature—which seems impossible. Nonetheless, tradition has found such a thing in the notion of prime matter (*prôtê hulê*), taken to be the underlying subject of elemental change. So suppose there is such a subject. Notice the results. First, nothing changes *as a whole* from water to air. Why? Because the prime matter that underlies the change, and is there in the water and in the air, remains the same, persisting as the same underlying subject through the change. Yet 319$^a$33–$^b$1 tells us that "nothing remains" in such a change, as does 321$^a$22–23. Second, we will wonder why water becoming

air is really all that different from water being hot, since in both cases there is a persisting underlying subject.
**If nothing perceptible remains as the same underlying subject:** Not, notice, "unless something imperceptible (such as prime matter) does remain as the same underlying subject." See Gill, p. 51.
**Semen:** In Aristotle's view male semen, or seed, is a very concentrated or "concocted" blood product (*GA* 726$^b$1–11).

## Note 89
**Affection of a contrariety:** Where F is such an affection if and only if it is one of a pair of contraries, F, G (like musical and unmusical in the forthcoming example).

## Note 90
**The change will be an alteration:** If Y came to be from X, and an affection F remains the same through the change, then F must not be an affection of X. If F is an affection of X, the change is an alteration, not a coming to be. But when water comes to be from air, it is a coming to be because the affection (transparent, cold) that remains the same through the change is an affection of air (mutatis mutandis if air comes to be from water).

## Note 91
**If, then, musicality . . . :** Musicality and unmusicality are intrinsically affections of the human being—the substance—that remains through the change, because they are qualities and so are inseparable from that substance.
**There would be a coming to be of the one . . . :** That is, a coming to be of the unmusical human and a passing away of the musical one. See De Haas & Mansfeld (Broadie), pp. 134–135.

## Note 92
**That is why . . . :** Namely, because musical and unmusical are in fact intrinsically affections of the human being that remains through the change.
**But as things stand (*nun*) this (*touto*) is an affection of the underlying subject:** Reading νῦν δὲ πάθος τοῦτο τοῦ ὑπομένοντος here with Rashed, Mugler, and Gill (p. 47); Joachim-1, following Philop. 68.30–69.3, transposes it to follow "and a passing away of the other" at 319$^b$28. *Touto* refers to musicality. Since it is an affection, so too is its privation.

## Note 93
**[1] Matter in the most strict sense is the underlying subject receptive of coming to be and passing away, [2] but in a certain way that of the other changes too:** If the matter referred to in [1] is intrinsically featureless prime matter, the contrast with [2] is mistaken, because a qualitative change in a substance, as when Socrates changes from pale to dark, is not any sort of change in prime matter. It is better, therefore, as De Haas & Mansfeld (Broadie), pp. 135–136, notes, to take the claim in [1–2] as cognate with this one: "the definition is the account of the essence,

and ... the essence is either of the substances alone, or of them most of all and primarily and unconditionally" (*Met.* 1031ª12–14). For of the various sorts of matter (on which, see 314ᵇ27n18), the one that is the matter for coming to be and passing away, since it is the matter of substances, which are beings in the strictest sense, inherits its status from theirs. *Kuriôs* and *haplôs* are often used interchangeably.

## Note 94
**Grows ... withers:** Aristotle seems to have particularly in mind natural growth and withering.

## Note 95
**It will be a void or an imperceptible body:** Reading κενὸν ἔσται ἢ σῶμα with De Haas & Mansfeld (Code), p. 176n16; Rashed, Mugler, and Joachim-1 read κενὸν ἔσται καὶ σῶμα. "What people mean by 'void' is an extended space in which there is no perceptible body" (*Ph.* 213ª27–29).

## Note 96
**One [1a-ii] is impossible, while the other [1a-i] makes it necessary for it to be in something:** This chiastic reading of the clause is defended in De Haas & Mansfeld (Code), p. 176: "It is usually assumed that he [Aristotle] is claiming that option [1a-i] is impossible, and that option [1a-ii] leads to the requirement that the matter is in something. On this interpretation the reason that [1a-ii] has this consequence must be that a void or an imperceptible body must have a location coincidentally, and hence must be in something else that has a location per se [= intrinsically]. This assumes that only an actual body could have a place in its own right [= intrinsically], and so a matter that is merely potentially corporeal would have to occupy a location coincidentally by being in something that has a location in its own right. There is, however, in the context of this argument no justification for the assumption that only actual corporeal bodies have places of their own. After all, option [1a-i] was that the separate matter has no place, but option [1a-ii] is that it *does* have a place." On the impossibility of [1a-ii], see *Cael.* 301ᵇ33–302ª9.

## Note 97
**Not one in account:** A and B, which are two numerically distinct things, are one in account, if and only if the account of A = the account of B.

## Note 98
**Points cannot be posited ... :** This follows from the previous sentence. The matter of a growing (withering) body is one and the same as the body (though differing from it in account). Hence, unlike points and lines, it must be a bulky mass and have magnitude.

## Note 99
**Shape:** *Morphê* is often used as a substitute for *eidos* ("form").

## Note 100

**One thing unconditionally comes to be from another . . . :** Since substances alone unconditionally come to be, this is the doctrine of the following text: "What we grasp from these cases as special to the substance is that it is necessary for there always to preexist another substance, which is actual, to produce it (for example, an animal if an animal is what comes to be), whereas for quality or the quantity this is not necessary, except potentially" (*Met.* 1034$^b$17–19). But Aristotle's reference is probably to *Met.* 7.7–9 as a whole.

**Always . . . :** Reading ἀεὶ with Rashed; Mugler and Joachim-1 read ἐντελεχείᾳ ὄντος ("as a result of something actually being").

**For a hard thing . . . :** Reading σκληρὸν γὰρ οὐχ ὑπὸ σκληροῦ γίνεται here with Rashed and Mugler; Williams-1 secludes; Joachim-1 reads with "same in genus," and "for example, fire as a result of fire, human as a result of human" with "same in species." I take the point to be the one made in the following texts: (1) "Heavy and light, soft and hard, hot and cold, seem to be sorts of density or rarity. And condensation and rarefaction are aggregation and disaggregation, in virtue of which substances are said to come to be and pass away" (*Ph.* 260$^b$8–12). (2) "It is necessary for a body determined by its own boundary to be either hard or soft (for it either takes an impression or does not). Further, it must be cohesive (for it is by this that it is determined). Since, then, everything that is determined and composite is either hard or soft, and these are due to cohesion, no composite and determined bodies would exist without cohesion. Cohesion, then, must be spoken about. The causes beyond matter are two in number: the producer and the affection, the producer as the starting-point from which the movement comes [= efficient cause], the affection as form [= formal cause]. So these are also the causes of cohesion and diffusion (*diachuseôs*), and of drying and wetting" (*Mete.* 382$^a$23–31). Thus it is aggregation (itself caused by cold, or dry heat) that causes hard things to come to be, not things that are already actually hard: (3) "Things that solidify either solidify because they are water or a mixture of earth and water, and do so due to either dry heat or cold" (382$^b$31–33).

## Note 101

**There is also matter for corporeal substance:** That is, matter for unconditional (substantial) coming to be and passing away rather than for qualitative change or spatial movement. See 314$^b$27n18.

**No body that is common:** (1) "Each of those [who say that the elements are four] says not that what is common—for example, body—is an element, but rather fire and earth" (*Met.* 992$^a$4–5). (2) "The thinkers of olden days . . . [posit] the particulars, such as fire and earth, [as substances to a higher degree] but not what is common to both, namely, body" (1069$^a$28–30). What Aristotle is denying, then, is that there is a particular body common to the elements (earth, water, air, fire), and so, of course, to all the bodies composed of them. He thus appears to be denying by implication that prime matter is such a body.

**Matter for . . . affection:** See 319$^b$31–32. The affection referred to is the one involved when one thing unconditionally comes to be from another as a result of

an actuality, referred to as "the affection as form" in *Mete.* 382ª29 (quoted in the previous note).
**Separable in account, but not separable in place:** The matter for body or corporeal substance $M_b$ = the matter for magnitude and affection $M_m$, but the account of $M_b$ ≠ the account of $M_m$.
**Unless the affections too are separable:** Which they are not. See 316ᵇ3n42.

## Note 102
**Stated previously elsewhere:** *Ph.* 4.6–9.

## Note 103
**It is evident, then, that when a thing grows . . . :** At 321ª21–22 a third condition is added.

## Note 104
**If, then . . . :** Compare *Cael.* 305ª14–22: "The account saying that the elements come from an incorporeal thing produces a separated void. For everything that comes to be will have its coming to be either in something incorporeal or in one that has a body. And if it is one that has a body, there will be two bodies in the same place, the one that comes to be and also the preexisting one [which is impossible (see *Ph.* 213ᵇ20)]. On the other hand, if it is incorporeal, it is necessary for there to be a definite void. But that this is impossible was proved previously [at *Cael.* 301ᵇ33–302ª9]."
**As was said previously:** At 320ª27–ᵇ25.

## Note 105
**Just as when air comes from water:** (1) "It is possible for things . . . to increase not only by the entry of something else, but also by undergoing alteration—for example, when air comes to be from water" (*Ph.* 214ª32–ᵇ3). (2) "When air comes to be from water, the same matter, not by acquiring something in addition, becomes another thing—although what it was potentially it becomes actively—and, again, water comes to be from air in the same way, the change being sometimes to greatness from smallness, sometimes to smallness from greatness" (217ª27–31).
**Mass:** An *ogkos* is generally a bulky body or mass.

## Note 106
**Though *nothing* was added to it or remained:** That is, entered what is growing and remained within it—not to be confused with the remaining the same of the growing thing itself.

## Note 107
**Was posited:** At 321ª17–22.

## Note 108
**The substance of:** Substance of X = essence of X. See 314ᵇ14n14.

## Note 109

**Function:** A function (*ergon*) is (1) an activity that is the use or actualization of a state, capacity, or disposition; (2) a work or product that is the further result of such an activity (*NE* 1094$^a$5–6). It is intimately related to its possessor's end or final cause: (2a) "The function is the end, and the activity is the function" (*Met.* 1050$^a$21–22). (2b) "Each thing of which there is a function is for the sake of the function" (*Cael.* 286$^a$8–9). Moreover, a thing's good or doing well "seems to lie in its function" (1097$^b$26–27). But this holds only when the thing itself is not already something bad (*Met.* 1051$^a$15–16). Finally, a thing's function is intimately related to its nature, form, and essence. For a thing's nature is "its for-the-sake-of-which" (*Ph.* 194$^a$27–28), its form is more its nature than its matter (193$^b$6–7), and its essence and form are the same (*Met.* 1032$^b$1–2). Hence "all things are defined by their function" (*Mete.* 390$^a$10), with the result that if something cannot function, it has no more than a name in common with its functional self (*Met.* 1035$^b$14–25, *Pol.* 1253$^a$20–25, *PA* 640$^b$33–641$^a$6). Functions are thus attributed to a wide variety of things, whether living or non-living. These include plants (*GA* 731$^a$24–26) and animals generally (*NE* 1176$^a$3–5), including divine celestial ones (*Cael.* 286$^a$8–11), parts of their bodies and souls (*PA* 652$^b$6–14, 686$^a$26–29), instruments or tools of various sorts (*EE* 1242$^a$15–19), crafts, sciences (1219$^a$17), philosophies (*GC* 318$^a$6) and their practitioners (*NE* 1141$^b$10), cities (*Pol.* 1326$^a$13–14), and nature itself (1258$^a$35).

**It is what masters . . . :** Start with the account of a function just essayed. Because the compound mixture performs the function of wine, its essence or substance is that of wine, so that it satisfies the definition of wine, and is correctly called "wine," not "water." And the reason for this is that wine "masters" or "prevails" over water in such a way as to make the compound wine. As a result, the mixing example seems to be like the calf example at 321$^a$31 in the respect that was supposed to distinguish them, namely, that the substance (= essence, function) of one of the ingredients—the one said to grow—remains, while that of the other does not.

## Note 110

**The what-it-is:** When we ask, *Ti esti A?* we ask, What is A? The correct answer defines or makes clear the what-it-is (*to ti esti*) of A, or—a related notion—the being for A, or—another related notion—the essence or what-it-was-to-be of A. Any intrinsic being, regardless of its category, has a what-it-is, although not all in the same unconditional way (*Met.* 1030$^a$17–27).

## Note 111

**But what alters it . . . :** The reference to flesh at 321$^b$3 takes us back to the growth of a person's calf at 321$^a$31, indicating that the alteration in focus is in particular the sort involved in it. It is this that justifies the present claim that *to alloioun*—here, as at 335$^b$26, something active—is within what grows and is altered. For in other sorts of alteration, this is obviously not so: the sun that bleaches the paint is not in the paint. What this inner starting-point of movement is, is explained in the following text: "As the things that come to be due to craft come to be because of its instruments—or to put it more truly, because of the movements of these—and this is the activation of the craft, and the craft is the shape [or form] of the things that come to be present in something else, so it is with the capacity of nutritive soul. Just as it also does in the animals and plants themselves later on, it produces growth from nourishment, using heat and cold as its instruments (for in these its movements are present and a certain account of each [part of the animal]), in the same way at the outset as well it composes what is by nature coming to be. For the matter by which the thing grows is the same as that of which it is first composed, so that the productive capacity [of growth] is the same as the starting-point of [the animal]; although it is greater. If, then, it is the nutritive soul, it is also the generative one. And it is the nature of each thing, present in all plants and animals, whereas the other parts of the soul are present in some living things, not present in others" (*GA* 740$^b$25–741$^a$3). On the central role of the heart and blood in this process, see *Juv.* 469$^a$2–10.

### Note 112
**Pneuma:** See Introduction, pp. lvi–lxv.

### Note 113
[1]: Also at 321$^a$21–22.
[2]: Said to be evident at 321$^a$2–4.
[3]: That is, each and every part (321$^a$3, 321$^a$19); geometrical points have no magnitude, and are abstract and imperceptible.
[4], [5], [6]: We have seen [5] and [6] before at 321$^a$7–8 and 320$^a$26–34, with [4] mentioned at 320$^a$27–28. If the growing body were a void, or contained voids, addition of material could fill these, without making the body grow. Similarly too if two bodies could be in the same place, or if what was added was itself incorporeal.

### Note 114
**The other things that have an in-matter (*en hulê[i]*) form:** (1) "It is clear that the affections of the soul are enmattered accounts (*logoi enuloi*)" (*DA* 403$^a$24–25). (2) "But we must not neglect to consider the *way* the essence or its account is, because, without this, inquiry produces no result. Of things defined, however, that is, of the whats that things are, some are the way the snub is, others the way the concave is. And these differ because the snub is grasped in combination with the matter (for the snub is a concave *nose*), whereas the concavity is without perceptible matter" (*Met.* 1025$^b$28–34).
**Both the matter and the form are said to be flesh and bone:** (1) "For the homoeomerous things are composed of the elements, and of these as matter all the works of nature are composed. But while all are composed as matter from the things just mentioned, as regards substance it is by the ratio [= the form]" (*Mete.* 389$^b$26–29). (2) "The second sort of composition is that of the nature of the homoeomerous parts in animals—for example, bone, flesh, and other things of this sort—from the primary things (= the elements)" (*PA* 646$^a$20–22). Thus flesh as matter—or "the

matter for flesh" (*GC* 321$^{b}$26)—is the elements that are potentially flesh, while the form is what they take on when they become actually flesh.

## Note 115

**The same measure:** Suppose we take the measure (*metron*) as being the analog of form, and the water as that of matter. Then we seem to have the problem that though new water enters it, the measure does not increase in size, since if it did it would be a bad, because non-invariant, measure. Despite this, both Philoponus (113.21–23 = Williams-2, p. 146) and Joachim-1 (p. 130) imagine the measure itself to be expanding. One way to solve this problem is to follow De Haas & Mansfeld (Code), p. 190, and "take the measuring example as illustrating no more than the sense in which the water that comes to constitute the cup (or bag) [= the measure] changes on each occasion." But this makes it difficult to explain why *metron* is used rather than *aggeion* ("vessel"), as at 320$^{b}$9. An alternative solution is to take the analogy as illustrating not growth but the nourishment requisite for it (notice the reference to sameness of quantity in (1) below), its point being that every different part of water takes on the form (shape) of the measure. For growth a further condition is required, namely, "some flowing out and some added to each and every part of the figure and the form" (*GC* 321$^{b}$27–28).

**One thing and then another:** (1) "But there is a puzzle it is necessary to talk about first, as to whether the sea always remains one in number and composed of the same parts, or one in form and quantity while its parts are always changing, like air, river water, and fire. For each of these is always one thing changing and then another (*allo kai allo*), while their form and quantity remains, just as in the case of a flow of water or a burning flame. And it is evident and persuasive that it is quite possible for the same account to apply to all of these, and, though they differ in the fastness and slowness of the change, for each case to involve coming to be and passing away, which yet happens to all of them in an orderly way" (*Mete.* 357$^{b}$26–358$^{a}$3). (2) "In general the unlimited exists in the following way: in virtue of one thing always being taken after another, and each thing taken is always limited, but is always one thing and then another (*allo kai allo*)" (*Ph.* 206$^{a}$27–29). (3) "We say that time has passed when we get a perception of the before and after in movement. And we define it by grasping one [now] and then another (*allo kai allo*), and something else in between them" (219$^{b}$23–26).

## Note 116

**The matter for flesh:** The matter for flesh is the elements that are potentially flesh. Adding more such matter to each part of that does not result in more actual flesh, only more potential flesh. To result in more actual flesh, the matter must take on the form of flesh, which it does by taking on the movements that "code for" that form. This is particularly clear in the case of the transmission in embryogenesis of the male progenitor's form to the matter (the menses, in Aristotle's view) that will compose the embryo: (1) "The male's nature, in those that emit seed, uses the seed as an instrument containing actual movements, just as in craft productions the instruments are in movement; for the movement of the craft is in a way in them.

(*GA* 730$^b$19–23). (2) "When seed comes into the uterus it causes the female's menses to take shape and moves them in the same movement in which it itself is moving" (737$^a$20–22). In the present example of flesh, such movements are the metabolic flowing out of some parts (for example, parts that are dead, and so no longer functional flesh) and addition of other ones (those that, as properly informed, can function as flesh). When more are added than flow out, the actual flesh (the matter-form compound) grows as a whole, that is, in each and every part.

**Figure:** *Schêma* ("figure") and *morphê* ("shape") amount to pretty much the same thing (*Cat.* 10$^a$11–12), and the latter especially is often used as an equivalent of *eidos* ("form").

## Note 117
**That is also why a corpse . . . :** Because the form (= function) of the arm and hand are more clearly missing in the case of a dead hand or arm than in that of dead flesh or bone. See 321$^b$1n109.

## Note 118
**By like . . . by unlike:** (1) "What increases is in one way increased by what is like itself, but in another way by what is unlike itself; for contrary is said to nourish contrary. But everything gets added by becoming like to like" (*Ph.* 260$^a$30–32). (2) "But a puzzle arises; for while some people say that like is nourished by like, just as with growth, others think the reverse, as we said, that it is contrary by contrary—the supposition being that like is unaffectable by like, whereas nourishment changes and gets concocted, and in every case change is into the opposite or into the intermediate. Further, the nourishment is affected by the thing being nourished, but not it by the nourishment, just as the carpenter is not affected by his material, but it by him; the carpenter, for his part, merely changes from inactivity to activity. But whether the nourishment is the final state of the thing added or the first makes a difference here. And if it is both, but one is non-concocted and the other concocted, it would be possible to speak of it as nourishment in both ways; for insofar as the nourishment is non-concocted, contrary is nourished by contrary, whereas insofar as it is concocted, like is nourished by like. So it is evident that both parties speak in a way correctly and in a way incorrectly" (*DA* 416$^a$29–$^b$9). Thus once the non-concocted nourishment—or nourishment in its first state—has been concocted by nutritive soul, and turned into nourishment in its final state, it has taken on the form of the living thing whose soul it is, and so can be absorbed by that thing: (3) "The final matter is that of what is most of all the substance" (*Met.* 1070$^a$20).

## Note 119
**That by which something grows:** Namely, the nourishment.

## Note 120
**Not, though, this thing intrinsically:** Suppose some nourishment N becomes flesh $F_1$. N cannot do this intrinsically, since it can only do it by being digested

Notes 121–123

and transformed into $F_1$ by an animal already possessed of flesh $F_2$, which thereby grows by the addition of $F_1$.

## Note 121

**Growth-producer ... nourishment:** "The being for nourishment, however, is distinct from the being for a growth-producer; for it is insofar as the animate thing has some quantity that a growth-producer exists for it, whereas it is insofar as it is a this something and a substance that nourishment does; for the animate thing preserves its substance and lasts just as long as it is nourished, and it is generative not of what is being nourished, but of something of the same sort as what is being nourished; for its own substance already exists, and nothing generates itself, but rather preserves itself. So this sort of starting-point of the soul is a capacity of the sort that preserves what has it, insofar as it has it, whereas nourishment equips it to be active. That is why, if deprived of food, it cannot exist. And since there are three things, what is nourished, what it is nourished by, and what nourishes, what nourishes is the primary soul, what is nourished is the body that has it, and what it is nourished by is the nourishment. And since it is right to call everything after its end, and the end is to generate something of the same sort as itself, the primary soul will be one that can generate something of the same sort as itself" ($DA$ 416$^b$11–25).

## Note 122

**Capacity:** The term *dunamis* (plural: *dunameis*) is used by Aristotle to capture two different but related things. (1) As in ordinary Greek, it signifies a power or capacity something has, especially to cause movement in something else (productive *dunamis*) or to be caused to move by something else (passive *dunamis*). (2) It signifies a way of being, namely, potential (*dunamei*) being as opposed to actual (*entelecheia[i]*) or active (*energeia[i]*) being. See also *Met.* 5.12.

## Note 123

**[1] But this (*touto*) form without matter, like a pipe, is [2] a certain in-matter capacity. And [3] if some matter were added that is potentially a pipe, and that also has the relevant quantity potentially, these [pipes to which it is added] will be bigger pipes. But [4] if it is no longer capable of producing this [that is, the growth of pipes], but is like water continually mixed with wine, which ends up by making it watery, indeed water, then it will produce withering of the quantity. [5] The form, though, remains:** Reading with Mugler, Τοῦτο δὲ τὸ εἶδος ἄνευ ὕλης, οἷον αὐλός, δύναμίς τις ἐν ὕλῃ ἐστίν. Ἐὰν δέ τις προσίῃ ὕλη, οὖσα δυνάμει αὐλός, ἔχουσα καὶ τὸ ποσὸν δυνάμει, οὗτοι ἔσονται μείζους αὐλοί. Ἐὰν δὲ μηκέτι ποιεῖν δύνηται, ἀλλ' οἷον ὕδωρ οἴνῳ ἀεὶ πλεῖον μιγνύμενον τέλος ὑδαρῆ ποιεῖ καὶ ὕδωρ, τότε φθίσιν ποιεῖται τοῦ ποσοῦ, τὸ δ' εἶδος μένει; Joachim-1, followed by Forster and De Haas & Mansfeld (Code), p. 191n58, secludes ἄνευ ὕλης; Williams-1 obelizes the entire text. Rashed reads τὸ δ' εἶδος μένει at the beginning and οὗτοι for οὗτοι ("The form, though, remains. And this form, without matter, like a pipe, is in matter a certain capacity. If, then, some matter were added that

Note 123

is potentially a pipe, and that also has the relevant quantity potentially, *there will not indeed* be bigger pipes. But if it is no longer capable, but is like water continually mixed with wine, which ends up by making it watery, indeed water, then it will produce withering of the quantity"). It will be useful to proceed by looking at interpretative options.

*Option 1:* Aristotle uses the term *aulos* ("pipe") elsewhere for certain parts of animals, such as the blowhole of whales (*HA* 589$^b$19), the funnel of a cuttlefish (524$^a$10), the *conus arteriosus* in fish (507$^b$10), and the part in birds analogous to the umbilical cord in mammals (*GA* 752$^b$2). If he were using it that way here, the *aulos* would be a living part of an animal, and what is said of it in [3] would be like what is said of flesh, with the addition in [4] of an account of withering. This is the standard account. Thus De Haas & Mansfeld (Code), p. 192: "he does seem to be using it [*aulos*] to stand for some kind of non-uniform part of a growing thing." One thing it is difficult to explain on this account is why Aristotle would choose so ambiguous and easily misunderstood a term to make his point. Another, much weightier, one is that it positively requires the seclusion of ἄνευ ὕλης ("without matter") in [1], though it is present in all the mss., since the entire text is about what happens to the forms present in matter-form compounds.

*Option 2:* Another option, favored by Rashed, is that *aulos* means "flute," as it most commonly does in Aristotle. The point of the passage then becomes one of *contrasting* what happens in the case of animal parts to what happens in the case of artifacts: even if you add matter that is potentially a flute and potentially of the relevant quantity, you will not get bigger flutes. Why? Because flutes are not living things that can grow in that way. We can see now why Rashed reads οὔτοι for οὗτοι. What this option makes difficult is a plausible explanation of [4]. For it refers to a capacity that is no longer possessed, and this seems to be precisely the capacity to produce bigger flutes. Since what was never had cannot be lost, this option seems hard to sustain.

*Option 3:* Nonetheless, Rashed does seem right that here an *aulos* is an artifact of some sort. But the sort of artifact it is, is not a flute, as he thinks, but the tube of a clepsydra, as at †*Pr.* 914$^b$14 (or the *aulos* through which a person looks to see things at a distance at *GA* 780$^b$19). Now, a clepsydra is often a water clock in which time is measured by water dripping slowly from a small opening at the bottom when the top is opened. But when water is instead allowed to enter and then the top is closed, it also functions as a pipette or syphon, which is how it is functioning at *Ph.* 213$^a$26 and *Cael.* 294$^b$21, and in our text. In other words, Aristotle is returning to the analogy of the *metron* ("measure") used for similar purposes at 321$^b$24–25, with *aulos* now playing the role of the measure. This being so, it is most natural to understand the *aulos* (though it is in fact an artifact) as serving as a stand-in for a non-homoeomerous part of a living animal in the way that Option 1 suggested, though for the wrong reasons. And this in turn being so, it is most natural to treat [4] as a return to the water-wine analogy of 322$^a$9–13, and so to treat [3] as a sort of counterfactual, functioning within the scope of the analogy between clepsydra tubes (*auloi*) and functioning animal parts.

Now turn to [1] and [2] and [5]. What *touto* refers to is *auxêtikon* ("growth-producer") in the previous sentence (322ª27). And an *auxêtikon* is "a starting-point of the soul" that is "a capacity of the sort that preserves what has it, insofar as it has it, whereas nourishment equips it to be active" (*DA* 416ᵇ17–19). Hence, as a sort of soul, it is precisely something without matter that, in matter, is a certain capacity. Thus while the matter-form compound is what grows and withers, what preserves it as what it is, its soul or formal element, remains the same.

## Note 124
**The matter and (*kai*) the so-called elements:** The matter is presumably what the form mentioned in the final sentence of the previous chapter is contrasted with. If the *kai* is epexegetic or explicative, it is here identified with the elements; if not, it is contrasted with them, and is perhaps prime matter.
**Whether each is eternal . . . :** Discussed in 2.4.
**And if they do come to be . . . :** Discussed in 2.5.
**Things that are now (*nun*) said in an indefinite way:** The indeterminacy Aristotle discusses is in earlier thinkers, but *nun* suggests that it has been inherited by later ones.

## Note 125
**In a perspicuous way:** *Saphêneia* ("perspicuousness") is associated with explanation, which is ultimately from starting-points: "On the basis of what is truly but not perspicuously stated, we shall make progress toward perspicuousness, always substituting what is more knowable for what is usually expressed in a confused way. . . . That is why even politicians should not regard as peripheral to their work the sort of theoretical knowledge that makes evident not only the that but also the why. For such is the philosophical way in each methodical inquiry" (*EE* 1216ᵇ32–40).

## Note 126
**By affecting and being affected:** Secluding ὑπ' ἀλλήλων with Rashed and Migliori; Mugler, Joachim-1, Forster, and Williams-1 retain, reading τῷ ποιεῖν καὶ πάσχειν ὑπ' ἀλλήλων ("those who posit several elements make them come to be by affecting and being affected by each other").

## Note 127
**Diogenes (of Apollonia):** See DK 64 = TEGP pp. 434–461.
**If all things . . . :** A paraphrase of DK B2 = TEGP 4 F2.

## Note 128
**Only the ones . . . :** See 324ª24–ᵇ13.

## Note 129
**Not first in a certain sort of contact:** Verdenius & Waszink read πρῶτον with the next sentence: "So, first, we must determine. . . ."

## Note 130

**Homonymously** (*homônumôs*): "Things are said to be *homonymous* when they have only a name in common but a different account of their substance corresponds to the name—for example, both a human and a drawing are animals; for only the name of these is common to them both, whereas a different account of their substance corresponds to the name; for if one gives what it is for each of them to be an animal, one will give a distinctive account for each" (*Cat.* 1ª1–6). Though in our text it is names, not as more usually things, that are homonymous, the relationship between the two is a close one because of Aristotle's views about names themselves. On which, see 314ª6n2.

## Note 131

**Place:** "Place (*topos*) is . . . the limit of what encompasses something at which it is in contact with what is encompassed" (*Ph.* 212ª5–6a).

**Mathematical objects:** "And aren't those things that are not separable, but are considered insofar as they are not affections of this sort of [material] body and in abstraction from it, the concern of the mathematician?" (*DA* 403ᵇ14–15). But though mathematical objects are in this way abstract and do not exist in separation from perceptible matter, they have an analog of perceptible matter, namely, intelligible matter (see 314ᵇ27n18). Thus as material objects make natural contact in a natural place or space, mathematical objects make the abstract analogs of these in intelligible space.

## Note 132

**Make contact . . . :** "Things are making contact when the extremities are together in place" (*Ph.* 227ª7; also *Met.* 1068ᵇ27). Since, though, this definition applies to both natural objects and mathematical ones, Aristotle proceeds to add conditions so as to pick out the sort of contact that can only hold between the natural ones.

## Note 133

**The primary differentia:** See 329ᵇ7–330ª24.

**Other opposites of this sort:** "The contrarieties of place are up and down, front and back, right and left" (*Cael.* 271ª26–27).

**All things that make contact with each other . . . :** Each of the elements has not just a place but a proper place, which is the one to which it naturally moves if unimpeded: "it is necessary for things to move either in accord with nature or contrary to nature, and these are determined by their proper places" (*Cael.* 276ª10–12). Heavy and light, in turn, are defined in terms of such natural movements: "Heavy is what naturally moves spatially toward the center, light, away from the center; heaviest, what sinks below all the downward-moving bodies, lightest, what rises to the top of all the upward-moving ones" (269ᵇ23–27). Thus earth, which naturally moves down toward the center of the universe, has heaviness but no lightness, whereas fire, which naturally moves upward toward the innermost surface of the primary heaven, which encompasses the universe, has lightness but no heaviness. "The body, though, that spatially moves in a circle [= the primary heaven] cannot possibly have heaviness or lightness. For neither in accord with nature nor contrary to nature does it admit of moving toward the center or away from the center" ($269^{b}29$–32). This body, however, precisely because it circumscribes everything while nothing circumscribes it, has no place. It cannot, then, make contact with another body.

## Note 134
**Things of this sort . . . :** If the claim is (1) things that have heaviness or lightness are, in virtue of having it, affectable and capable of affecting, it is in tension (to put it mildly) with $329^{b}21$: "heavy and light are neither affectable nor capable of affecting." But the claim might instead be (2) things that are heavy and light are, in virtue of being X or Y (things entailed or presupposed by heaviness or lightness), affectable and capable of affecting. And here the plausible values of X and Y are the natural movements of the things that possess them, which, in the first instance, are earth and fire (see previous note). By having these natural movements, these elements become (moved) movers and so capable of affecting things. (This explains why in the next paragraph ($323^{a}16$–22) distinctions need to be drawn between moving and affecting: the two are already covertly in play.) Of course, this raises a question as to why heaviness and lightness are mentioned at all. And the reason for that, I think, is to distinguish the things in question from the mathematical objects mentioned at $323^{a}1$. For movement alone might be thought not to do this, since "the more natural-science-like parts of mathematics, such as optics, harmonics, and astronomy" (*Ph.* $194^{a}7$–9) include sciences that deal with moving objects: "Mathematical beings are without movement, except for those with which astronomy is concerned" (*Met.* $989^{b}32$–33).

## Note 135
**It is clear that . . . :** So, just as there are immovable movers, there are unaffectable affecters: (1) "It is reasonable, not to say necessary, to suppose that there is also a third thing that causes movement while being immovable. That is why Anaxagoras speaks correctly when he says that the [divine] understanding is unaffectable and unmixed, since, at any rate, he makes it the starting-point of movement" (*Ph.* $256^{b}23$–26). (2) "Things [such as the divine understanding or primary god] that are there [outside the heaven] are naturally such as not to be in place, nor does time age them, nor is there any change for any of the things that are stationed above the outermost spatial movement; instead, unalterable and unaffectable, having the best and most self-sufficient life, they are attaining their end throughout all eternity" (*Cael.* $279^{a}18$–22).

## Note 136
**Not every mover can affect something:** "The primary body [= the primary or outermost heaven] is eternal and not subject to increase or decrease, but rather [is] incapable of aging, incapable of alteration, and unaffectable" (*Cael.* $270^{b}1$–3). Thus the immovable mover or divine understanding (see previous note) that moves the primary heaven does so without affecting it.

## Note 137

**The movers:** Reading κινοῦντα with Mugler and De Haas & Mansfeld (Natali), p. 208n60; Rashed and Joachim-1 read κινητικὰ ("the things capable of causing movement").

**There is a way in which the movers . . . :** (1) "The sorts of things that naturally make contact with each other are definite magnitudes whose extremities are together that are capable of moving and being moved by each other" (323$^a$10–12); (2) there are (2a) immovable movers and (2b) movers that move by being themselves moved (322$^a$12–14); therefore (3) there is (2b) a way in which the movers make contact with the things they move and (2a) a way in which they do not. See also 324$^a$24–$^b$13.

## Note 138

**The universal definition of making contact . . . :** Go back to 323$^a$4–6: "making contact is having the extremities together." Call that $D_1$ (definition$_1$). It applies to abstract mathematical objects and to natural (physical) ones. Notice that the relation it defines is symmetrical: if an extremity of A is together with an extremity of B, an extremity of B is together with an extremity of A. Thus if A is making contact with B, B is making contact with A. What happens to $D_1$ in the subsequent discussion has two phases. *Phase-1* (323$^a$6–12): $D_1$ is applied to natural magnitudes and is shown to apply only to certain ones: "the sorts of things that naturally make contact with each other are definite magnitudes whose extremities are together that are capable of moving and being moved by each other" (323$^a$10–12). Call this definition, which is the definition of natural contact, $D_n$. *Phase-2* (323$^a$12–22): a division in the notion of a mover, and so in that of an affecter, shows that some movers make natural contact with what they move, while others do not. In other words, not all natural contact is symmetrical, some cases are antisymmetrical. This conclusion then leads to the formulation of a new definition of natural contact that applies both to the symmetrical and the antisymmetrical cases, and for that reason is universal. This is $UD_n$—notice *en tois phusikois* at 323$^a$34.

**Between which there is affecting and being affected:** The point of this clause is to show us $D_n$ in a new light, as not a universal definition of natural (physical) contact but a special case of $UD_n$.

## Note 139

**All the movers we meet:** Or: "pretty much all the movers move that are in front of them." But compare: "All these thinkers seem to have supposed that movement is what most properly belongs to the soul, and that other things are moved because of the soul, whereas it is moved by itself. This is because they never see a mover that is not itself moving" (*DA* 404$^a$20–25).

## Note 140

**Democritus . . . :** A fragment from Theophrastus' *Phusikai Doxai*, preserved by Simplicius in his commentary on the *Physics*, suggests that Aristotle is reporting Democritus' views accurately: "Democritus of Abdera . . . posited atoms as the

matter of the beings like things are naturally disposed to be moved by like and generated the others in virtue of their differentia. . . . For like is naturally disposed to be moved by like and bodies of the same genus to spatially move together" (in *Ph.* 28.15–20). He held it, presumably, because all atoms are "essentially alike" (De Haas & Mansfeld (Wildberg), p. 226).
**Special to himself alone:** "It is strange that Aristotle should attribute this view to Democritus alone" (Joachim-1, p. 150). For, referring to this chapter of *GC*, *DA* includes perceptibles among the movers and affecters and perceptual organs or capacities among the things moved and affected by them: "Perception comes about in being moved and affected, as has been said, since it seems to be a sort of alteration. And some people say indeed that like is affected by like" (*DA* 416$^b$33–35). And earlier a group of thinkers is mentioned who "posit that knowing is of like by like, as if positing that the soul is the things [it knows]," perhaps including Empedocles among them (409$^b$26–410$^a$10).
**He does not allow:** Reading ἐγχωρεῖ with Rashed for Mugler, Joachim-1, ἐγχωρεῖν ("it is impossible for things that are distinct and different to be affected by each other").

## Note 141
**The things said:** *Legomena* ("things said") and *phainomena* ("things that appear to be so") are often pretty much the same things. So what we have had up to now in 1.7 is probably best seen as that phase in a dialectical inquiry in which we "set out the things that appear to be so," so as to then "go through the puzzles," and in that way "prove preferably all the reputable beliefs . . . or, if not all of them, then most of them and the ones with the most authority" (*NE* 1145$^b$2–6). See De Haas & Mansfeld (Wildberg), pp. 227–231; Introduction pp. xxviii–xlviii.

## Note 142
**Each other:** Reading ἄλληλα with Mugler, Joachim-1; Rashed reads ἑαυτά, which has the sense of ἄλληλα here. See De Haas & Mansfeld (Wildberg), p. 227n11.

## Note 143
**Contraries:** "Said to be contraries are: [1] Those things differing in genus that cannot belong to the same thing at the same time. [2] The most different of the things in the same genus. [3] The most different of the things in the same recipient. [4] The most different of the things falling under the same capacity. [5] The things whose difference is greatest either unconditionally or in genus or in species" (*Met.* 1018$^a$25–31; also 1055$^b$13–17). Here [2] picks out what is meant.
**All contraries are in the same genus:** "Since contraries admit of an intermediate and in some cases there is one, intermediates must be composed of the contraries. For all intermediates are in the same genus as what they are intermediates of. For we say that those things are intermediates into which what changes must change earlier—for example, if we proceed from the highest string to the lowest by the smallest intervals, we will come earlier to the intermediate notes, and, in colors, if we proceed from white to black we will come earlier to purple or gray than to

black, and similarly in the other cases. But to change from one genus to another genus is not possible except coincidentally, as from a color to a shape. Therefore, it is necessary that the intermediates be in the same genus both as each other and as what they are intermediates of" (*Met.* 1057ᵃ18–30).

## Note 144
**It is evident that . . . :** Because contraries are capable of affecting each other and intermediates are composed of contraries.

## Note 145
**In a similar way:** Reading ὁμοίως with Rashed and De Haas & Mansfeld (Wildberg), p. 232n19; Mugler and Joachim-1, followed by Williams-1, read ὅμως ("it is also in accord with reason that both sides alike grasped the nature [of the phenomenon]").

## Note 146
**The craft of medicine . . . :** "From craft, though, the things whose form is in the soul come to be (and by 'form' I mean the essence of each thing and the primary substance); for even contraries in a way have the same form; for the opposing substance is the substance of the privation—for example, health is the substance of disease; for it is by its absence that disease is made clear, while health is the account in the soul and the scientific knowledge. So what is healthy comes to be when one has understood as follows: Since this is what health is, necessarily if the thing is to be healthy, this must be present—for example, a uniform state—and if the latter is to be present, there must be heat, and the doctor goes on, always understanding in this way, until he is led to a final this that he himself is able to produce. Then the movement from this point onward is called a 'production'—the one that leads to being healthy. And so it turns out that in a way health is produced from health, and a house from a house, the one that has matter from one without matter; for the craft of medicine and the craft of house-building are the form of health and of a house (by 'the substance without matter' I mean the essence)" (*Met.* 1032ᵃ32–ᵇ14). Thus the form in the soul of the doctor, being without matter, is unaffected, whereas the form or shape of the food, since it is present in matter, is affected when it affects the body and produces health in it.

## Note 147
**For [1] the matter, we say, is alike—(one might almost say) the same—for either of the two opposites, [2] being, as it were, the genus, and [3] something capable of being hot is necessarily heated if what is capable of heating is present and comes near:** "There is a way in which [a] matter is affected, and [b] a way in which the contrary is" (324ᵃ21–22). What makes [a] true is that the affected and affecter have their genus in common, while what makes [b] true is that they differ in species. And things like that are contraries (324ᵃ24), which, as [2] makes clear, are the sorts of opposites at issue here. For "all contraries are in the same genus, and it is contraries that affect and are affected by each other" (324ᵃ2–3). Thus [2], which is

licensed by [a] and [b], in turn licenses the claim about matter, which, in turn again, licenses the claim that unaffectable affecters are forms without matter, while those affectable are forms in matter (see previous note). What, then, about [2] itself? Why is it true? Since we are looking in [1] at affecters and affected that are contraries, the way in which they differ is as species of the same genus. That is what makes [b] true. Now look at the following text: "Something is said to be the genus . . . as matter, since that to which the differentia or quality belongs is the underlying subject, which we call the 'matter'" (*Met.* $1024^{b}8-9$; also $1058^{a}37-^{b}3$). [3] makes clear its relevance for us. For it is the matter $m_1$ that is capable of being—or is potentially—hot, though actually not hot (cold or cool), that is of necessity made hot by the matter $m_2$ that, though not actually heating anything, is capable of heating what is capable of being made hot by it, when the two are in contact (*GC* $322^{b}13-21$). But when $m_1$ is made actually hot(ter) by $m_2$, $m_2$ is made actually cold(er) by $m_1$, since interaction of contraries is always reciprocal ($324^{a}2-3$). Therefore, $m_1$ and $m_2$ are the same, that is, they are the same [2] in the way things are the same in genus.

## Note 148
**The for-the-sake-of-which:** The so-called final cause, or end.

## Note 149
**States:** A state (*hexis*), in contrast with an affection (*pathos*), which may be possessed quite fleetingly, is a relatively stable condition (*Cat.* $8^{b}25-9^{a}13$), ensuring that a thing is "either well or badly disposed, whether intrinsically or relative to something—for example, health is a state, since it is a disposition of this sort" (*Met.* $1022^{b}10-12$). Here the state is the for-the-sake-of-which—the final cause.
**Forms and ends are certain states:** The forms referred to are like that of health as present in the doctor's soul, and the ends like health as present in the patient as a result of what the doctor does ($324^{b}2-6$n146). The following account of carpentry tells the same story in somewhat simpler terms: "Nothing comes away from the carpenter to the matter of the timbers, nor is there any part of the craft of carpentry in the product, but the shape and the form are produced from the carpenter through the movement in the matter. And his soul, in which the form is and his scientific knowledge, moves his hands or some other part in a movement of a particular sort, different when the product is different, the same when it is the same, and the hands move the instruments, and the instruments move the matter" (*GA* $730^{b}11-19$). When the hands and instruments stop moving, then, the form has been transferred to the matter, the end has been achieved, and the movement stops: "Whenever a continuous movement has a certain end of its movement, this is a last thing and the for-the-sake-of-which" (*Ph.* $194^{a}29-30$). And just as the movement stops when it reaches its end, so the affecting stops when the affection is possessed by the thing.

## Note 150
**If hot were to exist . . . :** Hot separated from matter would be a form, like that of health as it exists in the understanding of the doctor, and like it would be an immovable mover, or unaffectable affecter ($324^{b}2-6$n146).

## Note 151
**It is impossible . . . :** For if it were possible for hot to be separated from matter, it would be possible for it to be unaffected by its contrary.

## Note 152
**Ducts:** Or, "pores," "passageways."

## Note 153
**Empedocles:** See DK A86–89, 92–93 = TEGP 168, 169, 172, 117, 155, 170.
**Bodies whose ducts match (*summetroi*) each other:** "The word *summetroi* must mean, not 'proportionate' nor just 'of the same size' but 'of the same dimensions'; that is, 'of the same size and shape': so as to fit something else exactly. Next, 'the pores [or ducts] are of the same size and shape, in relation to one another' implies not that, for mixture to occur, the pores have to fit *into* one another (which would naturally be absurd), but just that they have to fit *on to* one another. Given that their adjacent pores *match* one another in shape and size, two adjacent bodies will possess continuous passageways, each of the same cross-section throughout, by means of which they can exchange materials in some minute form ('effluences')" (De Haas & Mansfeld (Hussey), p. 245).

## Note 154
**The most methodical (*hodô[i]*) determinations:** *Hodos* means "route" or "road," but here, as at *APr.* 46$^a$3 and elsewhere, it stands in for *methodos*, which is a route of inquiry (*APo.* 46$^a$32, $^b$36).
**About all [these] things:** Mugler and Joachim-1 read ἐνὶ λόγῳ διωρίκασι ("in a single account"); with Rashed, I seclude ἐνὶ λόγῳ.
**As nature precisely is:** Understanding *hêper* (feminine) *estin* like *hoper estin* at 316$^a$16. See Rashed, p. 138n1. Leucippus and Democritus are being praised for doing what Parmenides and Melissus (referred to as "some of the ancient philosophers" in the next sentence) are criticized for not doing: "even if they speak correctly about other things, they do not do so in a way appropriate to natural science" (*Cael.* 298$^b$17–18). In denying that natural beings move, they deny a starting-point of natural science. See 316$^a$11n36.

## Note 155
**The void is a non-being . . . :** "The Pythagoreans too said that a void exists, and that it enters the heaven itself from the unlimited breath, as the heaven is also inhaling the void, which distinguished the natures of things, since it is what separates and distinguishes the successive things in the series. This happens first in the case of the numbers, since the void distinguishes their nature" (*Ph.* 213$^b$23–27). For "numbers were primary in the whole of nature," and so "they took the elements of numbers to be the elements of all beings" (*Met.* 986$^a$1–2).

## Note 156
**Continuous:** (1) "The continuous (*suneches*) is what is divisible into things that are themselves always divisible" (*Cael.* 268ᵃ6–7). (2) "Continuity is just a sort of contiguity. I mean that two things are continuous when the limits of each, by which they make contact and by which they are kept together, become one and the same, and—as the name signifies—contained in each other" (*Ph.* 227ᵃ10–12).

## Note 157
**It is equally necessary . . . :** Both exclude spatial movement from one place to another, but not circular movement in a place, or alteration (*Ph.* 214ᵃ26–32).

## Note 158
**Proclaimed their "truth":** Parmenides refers to part of his poem as the "unshaken heart of persuasive Truth," contrasting it with the "opinions of mortals in which there is no true trust" (DK B1 = TEGP 10 F1).

## Note 159
**But since:** Reading ἐπεὶ δὲ with Mugler, Rashed, and De Haas & Mansfeld (Hussey), p. 263; Joachim-1 reads ἔτι δὲ ("But, further").
**[1] In view of the facts to believe them without more ado is next door to mania (*mania[i]*)** ([2] **for no one suffering a manic attack degenerates to the extent of believing** [3] **that fire and ice are one,** [4] **instead it is only nobly beautiful things and those that appear so because of intimacy (*sunêtheian*), that to some (*eniois*), because of their mania, seem (*dokei*) not to differ (*diapherein*)):** The first thing to settle is what *mania* is. And of the relatively few passages in which it is mentioned, the following are perhaps the most illuminating: (1) "Naturally clever stock degenerates into rather manic characters (for example, the offspring of Alcibiades and of Dionysius), whereas steady stock degenerates into stupidity and sluggishness (for example, the offspring of Cimon, of Pericles, and of Socrates)" (*Rh.* 1390ᵇ27–31). (2) "The craft of poetry is for the naturally clever rather than the manic person (*manikou*)" (*Po.* 1455ᵃ32–33). (3) "Why does wine make people both stupefied and manic?" (†*Pr.* 873ᵃ23–24). (4) "Those in whom black bile is copious and cold become sluggish and dull, whereas those in whom it is exceedingly copious and hot become manic, naturally clever, prone to sexual desire, and easily moved by their spirits and appetites, while some become more garrulous. But many too, because of this heat being near to the location of the understanding, are affected by manic diseases or those related to inspiration (*enthousiastikois*), from which come Sibyls and Bakides [inspired seers], and all divinely inspired people, when it does not come about because of disease but because of a natural blending" (†*Pr.* 954ᵃ31–38). We are not, then, dealing with literal madness but with something more like an overly excited, frenzied condition—a state of "possession"—that may be episodic.

The next thing to focus on is *sunêtheia*. It can mean "habit," or "custom," but it can also mean "intimacy" or "sexual intercourse." If it means "habit" or "custom," however, it is difficult to see why noble beauty is selected as the only thing that *mania* distorts the perception of. Indeed, it is difficult to see why "habit" or "custom" should come into the picture at all: Why should mania need the assistance of habit to produce distortion? What is far more plausible is to think that the *mania* in question is actually induced by (sexual?) intimacy, leading a person to think nobly beautiful what simply appears that way to him—a familiar human experience.

The point of [1] is to establish a similarity between philosophers and manic people: the former get carried away from the facts by the arguments; the latter get carried away by sexual desire, wine, or whatever it is that causes their manic enthusiasm. The point of [2] is to establish a difference between them and [3] to do so in terms of a contrast between the objects of their beliefs: philosophers, in believing that all things are one are committed to believing that fire and ice are one, which no one suffering a manic attack would be far enough gone to do. [4] is syntactically ambiguous, since *eniois* could be governed by *dokei* or by *diapherein* (see De Haas & Mansfeld (Hussey), pp. 250–251), so I have preserved the Greek word order. But once we are clear about *mania* and *sunêtheia*, its meaning becomes clear as well. Its point is to contrast what *mania* cannot get one to think to be the same (fire and ice) with what it can get one to think to be the same (what is nobly beautiful and what one's intercourse with it makes one think to be nobly beautiful).

## Note 160
**He says that being . . . :** Omitting γὰρ—read by Mugler and Joachim-1—with Rashed, but reading κυρίως ὄν with Mugler, Joachim-1, and De Haas & Mansfeld (Hussey), p. 264; Rashed reads κυρίως ἕν ("the one, in the strictest sense . . .").

## Note 161
**Other things slipping in:** Reading εἰσδυομένων ἑτερῶν with Rashed for Mugler and Joachim-1 ὑπεισδυομένων στερεῶν ("solids creeping in").

## Note 162
**These he says are *poroi*:** Empedocles does not use the term *poros* ("duct") in the extant fragments, but other equivalent terms such as *alox* ("furrow"), *surigx* ("tube"), and *porthmos* ("channel") (in DK B100.2, 3, 17 = TEGP 127.2, 3, 17 F27).

## Note 163
**Each of the indivisible solids:** Reading τῶν ἀδιαιρέτων στερεῶν ἕκαστον with Rashed and Mugler; Joachim-1, followed by Forster, secludes on the grounds that it is not *each* solid that is determined by an unlimited number of shapes. The addition of "one of," proposed by Williams-1, provides an easy fix for Aristotle's less than careful formulation.

**For Plato . . . :** Again Aristotle's formulation is less than careful: the solids themselves are not indivisible for Plato (notice Aristotle's own contrast a few lines later at 325$^b$33–35), but rather the planes into which they can be decomposed. See *Ti.* 52d–57d (Appendix).

## Note 164

**There would be two ways:** Reading δύο τρόποι ἂν εἶεν with Rashed and Mugler; Joachim-1, followed by Forster, secludes. The alleged problem is that both void and contact are involved in coming to be and disaggregation (passing away), since coming to be destroys a void, while disaggregation produces one. Apparently, then, there are not two "ways" in which these processes occur, but one. See Verdenius & Waszink, p. 49, De Haas & Mansfeld (Hussey), p. 264. Earlier, however, contact and void are assigned different causal roles in Leucippus' account: void causes passing away ($325^b3-4$), while contact causes affection and alteration ($325^a33$). So the point here should be understood as being about which of two things, void or contact, is functioning as a cause, not about their non-causal involvement. Since one functions as a cause in passing away, the other in coming to be, Leucippus is committed to these occurring in two ways, not just in one.

**Plato . . . says that there is no void:** See *Ti.* 58a: "Once the circumference of the universe has encompassed the [four] kinds, then, because it is round and has a natural tendency to gather in upon itself, it constricts them all and allows no void space."

## Note 165

**In previous accounts:** See *Cael.* $298^b33-300^a19$, $305^b36-306^b2$; see also *GC* $315^b28-316^a14$.

## Note 166

**This, at any rate, is impossible . . . :** "If fire heats and burns because of its angles, all the elements will be capable of heating, though one perhaps more than another; for all have angles—for example, the octahedron and the dodecahedron. (For Democritus indeed even the sphere is a sort of angle, which cuts because it is most capable of movement.)" (*Cael.* $307^a13-17$ = DK 68 B155a = TEGP 157 F42). To grasp Democritus' idea, start with a straight line. As soon as you bend it you have a sort of (blunt or curved tip) angle; bend it sharply and you have an angle proper: "Bending is the change from what is straight to what is curved or angled; straightening is the change from either of these to what is straight" (*IA* $708^b22-24$). A sphere, on this showing, is a solid (curved) angle.

**For then it is necessary . . . :** "Since hot and cold are contrary in capacity, it is impossible to assign any shape to cold; for the shape assigned to it must be contrary to [the one assigned to hot], but no shape is contrary to a shape. That is why all these thinkers omit this [namely, assigning a shape to cold]. Yet it is fitting to have defined all by shape or none" (*Cael.* $307^b5-10$).

## Note 167

**Democritus says . . . :** "While for those who say that planes are the primary and indivisible things of which bodies having heaviness are composed, it is absurd to say this; for those who say that they are solids it is more open to say that the greater of them is the heavier" (*Cael.* $308^b35-309^a2$). See Furley, pp. 93–94.

**So that it is clear that it is also hotter:** For why would this be true of heaviness but not of heat?

## Note 168
**The slightly cold:** Reading τὸ ἠρέμα ψυχρόν with Rashed and most mss. for Mugler, Joachim-1, Forster, Migliori, Williams-1 τὸ ἠρέμα θερμόν. There is little need to prefer θερμόν to ψυχρόν. For, since coldness is the privation of heat (*Cael.* 286ª25–26), what is slightly cold is what is deprived of a little heat, and so may be quite hot.

## Note 169
**What is capable of being pressed in is soft:** See 330ª8–9, *Mete.* 382ª11–14.

## Note 170
**Shape alone:** For if they have shape alone, they will have none of the things that make them capable of affecting and being affected by each other.
**One thing only:** Suppose that an indivisible atom $A_1$ is round, hot, and nothing else, while another, $A_2$, is square, hard, and nothing else. Then the nature of $A_1$ (round and hot) ≠ the nature of $A_2$ (square and hard). But Leucippus and Democritus say that "the nature of each of them [the indivisibles] is one nature, as if each one were a separate piece of gold" (*Cael.* 275ᵇ31–32). Also: "Democritus says that none of the primary things [= atoms] comes to be from another. Nonetheless, the common body is for him a starting-point of all, differing from part to part in magnitude and shape" (*Ph.* 203ª33–ᵇ2). For because atoms differ only in size and shape, they are modifications of something common to all of them, namely, body. See *Met.* 1069ᵇ20–24.
**Hard in one case:** Reading τὸ μὲν σκληρὸν with Rashed and Migliori for Mugler, Joachim-1, Forster, τὸ μὲν ψυχρὸν ("cold in one case").

## Note 171
**Where it is [, for example,] cooled:** Reading ἧπερ ψύχεται with Mugler and Joachim-1; Rashed reads εἴπερ ψύχεται ("if indeed it is cooled").
**In some other way as well:** Since it has several affections at that point, not just one.

## Note 172
**[1] For this consequence will follow in the same way both for [2] those who say that the indivisibles are solids and for [3] those who say that they are planes; [4] for (*gar*) they cannot come to be either rarer or denser, because [5] there is no void within the indivisibles:** The consequence referred to in [1] is presumably that of having a plurality of affections in the same place. Those referred to in [2] are atomists, like Leucippus and Democritus; those referred to in [3] are Platonists. The latter deny that there is a void at all (325ᵇ32–33); the former that there is one within the full atoms. [1–3] is not—despite *gar*—entailed or justified by [4]. Instead [4] provides an illustration and a response to a possible objection to what has gone before. For suppose someone had the somewhat natural thought that an indivisible thing could have weight or mass (= heaviness or lightness) in addition to having a shape and an affection of some other sort. Then he would be open to the following objection: "If what is heavy is a sort of dense, and what is light a sort

of rare, and dense differs from rare in containing a greater quantity in an equal mass, then, if a point is heavy or light, it is also dense or rare. But what is dense is divisible, whereas a point is indivisible" (*Cael.* 299ᵇ7–11).

## Note 173
**Indivisibility:** One sense of "immovable" is "difficult to move" (*Ph.* 226ᵇ12). "Indivisibility" has a parallel sense (notice "more easily come apart" at 326ᵃ27). Perhaps in that sense small things are more difficult to divide. But why should we think that indivisibility in general is caused by smallness of size?

## Note 174
**The one behind ... the one in front:** "'The one in front' and 'the one behind' are puzzling expressions, but may refer to atoms drawn diagrammatically. ... To take τὸ ὕστερον as 'the latter example [of raindrops]' and πρότερον as 'the former case [of atoms]' is not in accord with Aristotelian usage" (De Haas & Mansfeld (Hussey), p. 264).

## Note 175
**These must be posited ... :** Whatever the affections are that define and distinguish the sorts, they will be what explain how and why the indivisible atoms affect and are affected by each other. Therefore, they, not the shapes, will be starting-points and causes. For the shapes themselves cannot explain this. See 326ᵃ15n170.

## Note 176
**It will be divisible ... :** "It is necessary, of course, for everything that is in movement to be divisible into parts that are always divisible; for it was proved previously in our universal discussions about nature [at *Ph.* 234ᵇ10–20] that everything that is intrinsically moved is continuous. It is impossible, then, for what moves itself to move itself in its entirety; for it would be spatially moved as a whole, and it would spatially move itself with the same spatial movement, while being one and indivisible in species, and it would be altered and alter itself, so that it would be teaching and learning at the same time, and making healthy and being made healthy with the same health. Further, it was determined that it is the movable that is moved [at *Ph.* 251ᵃ9–16]; but it is in movement potentially, though, not actually. But what is potentially proceeds to actuality, and movement is the incomplete actualization of what is moveable. The mover, on the other hand, is already in activity—for example, what is hot heats, and in general what has the form begets [something that has] it. So [if a thing can move itself as a whole] the same thing will be hot and not hot at the same time in the same respect, and likewise in each of the other cases in which the mover and the moved must be synonymous. Therefore, one part of what moves itself is the mover and another part is the moved" (*Ph.* 257ᵃ33–ᵇ13).

## Note 177
**Because of movement through ducts:** Reading διὰ τῆς <διὰ> τῶν πόρων with Rashed, Mugler, and Williams-1; Joachim-1 reads with the mss.

## Note 178
**In the way they say:** The reference is to Empedocles DK B84 = TEGP 151 F105 = *Sens.* 437$^ب$26–438$^a$2 and perhaps also Plato, *Ti.* 45b–46c. Both theories involve light rays emitted by the eyes passing through a transparent medium and being reflected back.

## Note 179
**Being a cause of coming to be [such-and-such]:** *Gennan*, an active infinitive, refers here not to a cause of unconditional coming to be, but to affecting (see *to gennan kai to poiein* at 327$^a$26) or causing to grow. I have added [such-and-such] to make this clear.

**An often-mentioned starting-point:** See 316$^b$21n49. This distinction between potentially and actually is indeed often mentioned by Aristotle, but its relevance to the claim that a body that is potentially F, when so affected as to become actually F, does so at each point at which it is potentially F, to the extent that it is potentially F at that point, is novel.

## Note 180
**Just like [veins of ores] stretching continuously in mines:** "Some translators speak of 'veins of susceptible stuff stretching continuously through the substance' of metals. . . . But after a short survey of ancient texts on the topic, and some conversations with metallurgists, I have not been able to find any phenomenon which plausibly matches this description. On the contrary, metals seem to be models of physical homogeneity. . . . So that it seems more plausible that μεταλλευόμενα [*metalleuomena*] here are the mines or deposits of ores or native metals. This meaning, though less frequent in the Aristotelian corpus than that of 'metals,' is well attested in Greek texts of the same period. If this is correct, the mention of 'veins' here would only provide a model for the spatial structure of the 'more susceptible' parts of a body (so that their form could resemble the Empedoclean pores [or ducts]), but should not be considered as a real example of such a difference of susceptibility in nature" (De Haas & Mansfeld (Crubellier), pp. 275–276).

## Note 181
**Grown together:** Growing together (*sumphuein*) is sometimes a process that can lead to such things as Siamese twins: "Most monstrosities (*terata*) are due to embryos growing together" (*GA* 773$^a$3–4). But more often, as here, it is a completely natural process (*Met.* 1014$^b$20–26), resulting in a natural unity.

**When grown together and one, each thing is unaffectable:** "It is evident, then, that in a way the capacity to affect and to be affected are one (for something is capable either by itself having a capacity to be affected or by another thing having the capacity to be affected by it), whereas in another way they are distinct. For the one capacity is in what is affected (for it is because it has in it a certain starting-point, and because the matter too is a certain starting-point, that what is affected is affected, and that one thing is affected by another; for what is oily is burnable, what yields in this specific way is crushable, and similarly in the other cases), whereas the other capacity is in what acts—for example, heat or the craft of building (the one in what is capable of heating, the other in what is capable of building). That is why insofar as it is naturally unified, nothing is affected by itself; for it is one, and not other" (*Met.* 1046ª19–29). Thus when a doctor treats himself, this involves his having in himself two distinct starting-points: one is the craft knowledge of medicine that he has in his understanding, which is the starting-point of his active capacity to produce curative movements in a diseased body (1032ª32–ᵇ14), and the other is the diseased condition in his body, which makes him a suitable case for medical treatment. Natural unity precludes the sort of complexity that having two such starting-points would require (1069ª5–14, 1070ª10–11, *Ph.* 227ª23–32).

## Note 182
**Having drawn distinctions at the start:** The reference is to the distinction drawn at the beginning of this chapter (326ᵇ29–31), which in turn refers us back to 316ª14–317ª17.

## Note 183
**A body or a plane that is indivisible:** Since we are looking at the view that bodies are divisible at some points and not at others, the body and plane referred to must be indivisible points within an otherwise divisible body. But such a point or plane would be a natural unity, and so would be unaffectable (327ª1), so that the body would not be affectable at every point, as the starting-point of the discussion requires (326ᵇ30–34).
**Neither would any magnitude be continuous:** Continuity presupposes divisibility at every point (325ª6n156), but the bodies under consideration, as not affectable at some points, are at those points indivisible.

## Note 184
**Even if it is not yet divided . . . :** Aristotle does not accept that all possibilities will at some time be actualized: "it is possible for this cloak to be cut up, but it will not be cut up but will wear out first" (*Int.* 19ª12–14). So we should not see him as appealing to that here. Instead, what the present claim is based on is the fact that indivisible atomic bodies, as in constant movement, are always affecting and being affected by each other, necessitating their actual division.

## Note 185
**As Democritus says:** Turning is position, contact is order (*Met.* 1042ᵇ11–15). Notice "position" and "order" in the next sentence (327ª19). See also 314ª18n7.
**Nor does it now have hard and solidified particles:** Reading οὐδε νῦν ὑπάρχει σκληρὰ with Rashed for Mugler, Joachim-1 οὐδ' ἐνυπάρχει τὰ σκληρὰ ("nor does it have within it what is hard . . .").

## Note 186
**For not every part . . . :** See 321ᵇ10–322ª33.

**By having changed intrinsically:** As when water increases in volume by becoming air. See 329ª9–29.

## Note 187
**At the start:** See 322ᵇ25–26.

## Note 188
**Those who say . . . :** The thinkers referred to include, in particular, Anaxagoras: "If we were to take Anaxagoras to say that there are two elements, what we took him to say would be most in accord with an account that he himself did not articulate, although he would necessarily have had to follow those who do advance it. For to say that at the start all things had been mixed is both strange on other grounds and because it follows that they must have been unmixed before the start, and because a random thing cannot naturally be mixed with a random thing, and in addition because affections—even [intrinsic] coincidents—would be separated from substances (for of the same things as there is mixture there is also separation)" (*Met.* 989ª30–ᵇ4). The two elements referred to are understanding (*nous*) and the primordial mixture, which contains an infinite number of homoeomerous things (985ª18–19, 988ª28), both apparently treated as material causes (989ª19–20), though earlier understanding is treated as an efficient and final cause (984ᵇ15–22). No doubt Aristotle saw it as having a tincture of each (988ª22–23).

## Note 189
**Puzzle:** An *aporêma*, in the technical sense, is "a dialectical deduction of a contradiction" (*Top.* 162ª17–18). Here, however, as often elsewhere, it seems to be just a puzzle. See *APr.* 71ª29, *APo.* 92ª29, *Ph.* 211ª10, *Met.* 1004ª34, 1011ᵇ6, 1077ª1.

## Note 190
**But rather that any part:** Rejecting with Rashed, Mugler, and De Haas & Mansfeld (Cooper), p. 318 n4 Joachim's addition of ὅτε post ἀλλ'.

## Note 191
**Lynceus:** Mythical prince gifted with superhuman sight.

## Note 192
**Convert:** The verb *antistrephein* is used to signify (1) a logical relation between propositions, so that, for example, the universal negative converts, because if no B is A, then no A is B (*APr.* 25ª5–6) and so on; (2) a logical relation between terms (51ª4–5), equivalent to counterpredication, where B is counterpredicated of A if and only if A is predicated of B and B of A; (3) the substitution of one term for another, without logical convertibility (*APr.* 64ª40); (4) the (valid) inference of (A admits of not being B) from (B admits of being A) (32ª30); (5) the substitution of the opposite of a premise for a premise (59ᵇ4); (6) an argument in which from one premise in a syllogism, and the opposite of the conclusion, the opposite of the other premise is deduced (2.8–10, *Top.* 163ª32–34); (7) at *Top.* 109ª10, and only

there it seems, A and B convert if and only if (B *belongs* to A) implies (A *is* B). Here, however, conversion seems to be affective reciprocity, so that A and B convert if and only if A affects and is affected by B and vice versa.

## Note 193
**That is why . . . :** See $324^b4$–6n146.

## Note 194
**The mastering one:** See $321^a35$n109.
**Chousin:** A *chous* (*choeusin* is the dative plural) was a measure of capacity ≈ 3.25 liters ≈ 0.86 gallons.

## Note 195
**Something intermediate and common:** Suppose that the things that are mixed are $M_1$ and $M_2$ and M the resulting mixture. What is "intermediate and common" is common not to $M_1$ and $M_2$ (since if they were already it, they could not become it), but rather to every particle of M, representing the outcome of the struggle for mastery of their more or less equal capacities. Call this common and intermediate feature C. Now pick some arbitrary region R of M. Any particle of $M_1$ in it will be C as will any particle of $M_2$. But there is no requirement that if X is in R and X is C, then X has particles of both $M_1$ and $M_2$ in it; X might be a transformed particle of $M_1$ alone, or of $M_2$ alone. See De Haas & Mansfeld (Cooper), pp. 322–323.

## Note 196
**Affecters that have a contrariety:** Affecters have the same matter ($328^a19$–22); matter is "as it were, the genus" ($324^b7$); "all contraries are in the same genus, and it is contraries that affect and are affected by each other" ($324^a1$–3).

## Note 197
**Viscous ones . . . :** Because, like olive oil and water, they are unmixable. See $330^a5$–6, *Mete.* $382^b16$.

## Note 198
**Play a double game:** The verb *epamphoterizein* is used to characterize ambiguous statements (Plato, *Rep.* 479c3) and to describe things that lie halfway between others. Thus "supposition (*hupolêpsis*) is that by which we play a double game (*epamphoterizomen*) with everything, as to whether it is so or not so" (†*MM* $1197^a30$–31), and water and air "play a double game," because they have tendencies to move up (relative to earth) and down (relative to fire) (*Ph.* $205^a28$). See also *Pol.* $1332^b1$–3.
**Recipient . . . form:** The recipient of, for example, pale is what the affection paleness belongs to (*Ph.* $186^a31$), or what "pale" is predicated of. Since "something's being pale . . . [is] a combination of surface and paleness" (*Met.* $1045^b15$–16), because surface figures in the definition of its essence, surface is the primary recipient of paleness. Surfaces, in turn, are the surfaces of substances, so that Socrates is also a recipient of paleness if his surface is a primary recipient of it. Here the

recipient, since it is of form, is matter: "where what is predicated is a form and a this something, the ultimate underlying subject is matter and material substance" (*Met.* 1049ᵃ35–36).

## Note 199
**All mixed:** Reading μιχθεὶς ἅπας with Rashed for Mugler and Joachim-1 καὶ μιχθεὶς ἄπεισι ("the tin, like some affection of the bronze that is without matter [of its own] pretty much vanishes and, after being mixed, departs").

## Note 200
**What is mixable is so in relation to a homonym:** The meaning here is that what is mixable is relative to something else which in that relation must also be called "mixable." On the more technical notion of a homonym, see 322ᵇ30n130.

# BOOK 2

## Note 201
**Air or fire:** "Anaximenes and Diogenes posit air as prior to water and as more than anything else the starting-point of the simple bodies. Hippasus of Metapontium posits fire, as does Heraclitus of Ephesus" (*Met.* 984ᵃ5–8).
**Something intermediate between these:** "Some make the underlying body one—either one of the three or something else that is denser than fire and rarer than air" (*Ph.* 187ᵃ14; also *GC* 332ᵃ21, *Met.* 988ᵃ30–31). The identity of these thinkers is unknown.

## Note 202
**Fire and earth:** Parmenides "posits two causes and two starting-points, hot and cold—in other words, fire and earth" (*Met.* 986ᵇ33–34). See 318ᵇ6-7n75.
**These and air as a third:** Supposedly, the tragedian Ion of Chios. See Philop. 207.19 = Williams-2, p. 117.
**Others these and water as a fourth:** "Empedocles, however, posits four things, positing earth along with those already mentioned as a fourth (for these, he says, always persist and do not come to be, except in quantity or smallness, aggregating into one and disaggregating from one)" (*Met.* 984ᵃ8–11). See DK B17 = TEGP 41 F20.

## Note 203
**Those . . . who posit a single matter beyond these:** The reference, as the identification of the single matter with "this unlimited" makes clear, is to Anaximander of Miletus (DK B1 = TEGP 1): "Or perhaps what is intrinsically an element is the unlimited or something else of that sort" (*Met.* 1052ᵇ10–11). See also *GC* 332ᵃ25.

## Note 204
**In the *Timaeus*:** See 50b–c (Appendix).
**It is impossible to call something . . . :** "As for that from which, as matter, they come to be, some, when they have come to be, are said not to be *that* but *thaten*—for example, . . . the statue is not said to be wood (*xulon*), but by derivation, wooden (*xulinos*), and brazen, not bronze, and stonen, not stone, and the house is said to be bricken but not bricks. But it is not the case either that a statue *comes to be* from wood, or a house from bricks, since if someone looked intensely, he would not say this unconditionally, because what something comes to be from must change, and not remain. That, then, is why we speak in this way" (*Met.* 1033$^a$5–23).
**The truest thing:** See 50b–c (Appendix).
**As far as planes:** See 53c–57d (Appendix).
**"Wet nurse":** See 49a (Appendix).

## Note 205
**Elsewhere:** In *Ph.* 1.6–9; about the elements in *Cael.* 3–4.

## Note 206
**Subject matter:** Here *to hupokeimenon* is not the underlying subject of predication, but the subject or subject matter of sight, namely, the affections (colors, shapes) that it alone can perceive—in other words, its so-called special or proper objects. That is why it is referred to as a *pathos* in the next sentence.
**[1] Sight is prior to touch . . . [2] but it is not an affection of tangible body insofar as it is tangible, but rather is in accord with something else, even if it happens to be prior in nature:** Aristotle sometimes gives epistemic prominence to sight for the variety of the things it makes accessible to us (*Sens.* 437$^a$5–7, *Met.* 980$^a$24–27). But other perceptual capacities seem sometimes to edge out sight for such prominence. Thus hearing is favored for its importance in learning and touch for exactness of its discriminations (*Sens.* 436$^b$18–437$^a$17, *DA* 421$^a$18–26). None of this, however, bears directly on our text, since what is at issue in it is *natural* priority, where X is naturally prior to Y if and only if X can exist without Y but not Y without X (see 315$^a$25n24). And this too raises immediate difficulties. For it is touch not sight that seems to have this sort of priority: "the primary sort of perception that belongs to all animals is touch" (*DA* 413$^b$4–5); "without touch none of the other sorts of perception is present, but touch is present without the others" (415$^a$3–5). As a next step ask: What visible objects do have natural priority of the relevant sort? And the answer is "the heaven and the most divine of visible things" (*Ph.* 196$^a$33–34), on which all coming to be and passing away ultimately depends, so that if they did not exist, it would not exist. See *GC* 336$^a$23–$^b$12. So the visual affections possessed by celestial objects that have the requisite sort of natural priority over tangible ones are in it. The point of [2], coming now to it, is to restrict the tangible affections definitive of body to the ones it has insofar as it is body. This excludes the naturally prior visual affections of the celestial objects, since it is not insofar as they are tangible that they have these: "It is not insofar as something is water or insofar as it is air that it is visible, but because there is a certain nature in

it that is the same in both of them and in the [eternal] body above [= ether]. And light is the activity of this, of the transparent insofar as it is transparent. But whatever this is present in, so potentially is darkness. For light is a sort of color of the transparent, when it is made actually transparent by fire or something of that sort, such as the body above. For one and the same also belongs to it" (*DA* 418$^b$7–13). The "something else" referred to in [2], then, is that "certain nature," which thus emerges as what is prior in nature.

## Note 207
**Coarse-grained fine-grained:** "What has small parts is fine-grained and what has large parts is coarse-grained" (*Cael.* 303$^b$26–27). It is misleading, therefore, to translate *pachus* as "dense" or "thick," and the corresponding verb *pachunein* as "thicken" or "increase in density."

## Note 208
**Heavy and light . . . :** Presumably because "if a heavy body is placed in contact with a lighter body the lighter body does not become heavier" (Williams-1, p. 158).

## Note 209
**They mix and change into each other:** "The mixing in question is of a different kind than the one presupposed in the discussion of *mixis* proper. A different simple body does not result from an equilibrium of opposed qualities (e.g., of hot and cold) but from a new combination of qualities, where one opposed quality is replaced by the other; for instance, when the hot and dry (fire) changes into the hot and moist (air)" (De Haas & Mansfeld (Frede), pp. 303–304).

## Note 210
**Hot and cold . . . :** "(i) Hot-cold and dry-moist [wet] are reciprocally active and passive in the sense that the *substratum*, which is hot, is *eo ipso* both alterative of, and liable to be altered by, that which is cold; whilst the *substratum*, which is moist, is *eo ipso* both alterative of the dry, and subject to its action. Each of these four qualities, within its own contrariety, is both active and passive in relation to its contrary. The hot and the cold, *qua* contraries informing the same matter, act and react on one another, and are each in turn both agent and patient. Each tends to assimilate its contrary to itself, and to be assimilated by it: and the result of this reciprocal action-passion is the *tempering* of both qualities, and their fusion in an intermediate quality, which is *less-cold-and-more-hot* than the original cold and *less-hot-and-more-cold* than the original hot. . . . By a similar reciprocal action-passion, the moist and the dry tend towards an intermediate or tempered state, in which *the dry* is more pliable and more cohesive by admixture of *the moist*. But this tempering of the dry by the moist requires for its completion the 'active operation' of the hot-cold (or of the tempered hot) in a sense in which we have now to consider. (ii) For although the reciprocal action-passion of the qualities within each contrariety is an essential condition of the emergence of a new ὁμοιομερές ['homoeomerous thing'], another kind of action-passion, *in which the hot-cold is*

*agent and the dry-moist is patient*, is also involved: and it is to this second kind of action-passion, where one contrariety is active and the other contrariety passive, that Aristotle is referring in the present passage.... The whole subject is worked out in [*Mete.* 4] with great elaboration" (Joachim-1, pp. 204–205).

**The disaggregating ... :** "It is ridiculous to assign a shape to fire only with a view to dividing; for it seems more to aggregate and bring together than to disaggregate. For it disaggregates things of different kinds, but aggregates those of the same kind. And while the aggregating is intrinsic to it (for bringing together and uniting are characteristic of fire), the disaggregating is coincidental (for it is in aggregating what is of the same kind that it removes what is alien). So either they should have looked toward both when they assigned [it a shape] or, better, toward the aggregating" (*Cael.* 307$^a$31–$^b$5). "They" are Plato, *Ti.* 56b (Appendix), and Democritus (see 326$^a$4–5n166). See also *Mete.* 378$^b$20–26.

**Things of the same kind ... :** No difference of meaning is intended between the terms *ta homogenê* and *ta homophula*.

## Note 211

**Defining mark:** A common meaning of the noun *horos*, from which the verb *horizesthai* ("define") derives, is "term," in the logical sense in which a syllogism has three terms. But often a *horos* is a definition or, as here, a defining mark (a boundary marker is a *horos*) that gives definition to what would otherwise lack it. See, for example, *Pol.* 1258$^a$18, 1267$^a$29, 1326$^a$35.

## Note 212

**In many ways:** Compare *Mete.* 379$^a$16–18.
**In the primary way:** See 329$^b$30–32.

## Note 213

**The elements:** That is, the elementary qualities: hot cold, wet dry. Elsewhere, these are referred to as causal factors (*Mete.* 378$^b$10–13) and as capacities (378$^b$29, 34, 379$^b$11).
**Contraries do not naturally pair:** Duplicates are excluded, along with contraries, at 331$^b$26–36.

## Note 214

**Some make them one ... :** See 328$^b$33–329$^a$5.

## Note 215

**Condensation and rarefaction:** "The starting-point of all affections is condensation and rarefaction; for in fact heavy and light, soft and hard, hot and cold, seem to be sorts of density or rarity. And condensation and rarefaction are aggregation and disaggregation, in virtue of which substances are said to come to be and pass away" (*Ph.* 260$^b$7–12).
**The rare and the dense, or the hot and the cold:** "But while the cold not only hardens but also condenses, the hot makes rarer" (*GA* 783$^a$37–$^b$2).
**The role of handicraftsmen:** Compare *Mete.* 384$^b$26–28, 388$^a$27, *GA* 730$^b$11–19.

## Note 216
**As Parmenides does with fire and earth:** See 318ᵇ6–7n75.

## Note 217
**As Plato does:** "Aristotle is not here attributing to Plato the doctrine of a triad of 'simple bodies' at all. All that he is saying is that the advocates of such a triad (e.g., Ion [329ᵃ2n202]) made one of the three a blend of the other two, 'just as Plato ἐν ταῖς διαιρέσεσιν [*en tais diairesesin*] makes the middle a blend'" (Joachim-1, p. 216).

**In the divisions:** The many interpretations of this phrase are cataloged by Migliori, pp. 230–231. Following Joachim-1 (who is followed also by Rashed, p. 158n5), I take the divisions to be "simply Aristotle's name for a famous passage in the *Timaeus* (35a ff.), where Plato describes the formation of the Soul. Plato there works with a triad, the third member of which is produced by blending the other two. God takes (a) the Indivisible and always Self-Identical Substance <Identity> and, blending it with (b) the substance ἡ περὶ τὰ σώματα γιγνομένη μεριστή ['the one that is divisible and comes to be in the corporeal realm'] <Otherness>, produces (c) a third kind of Substance. Next, God mixes together all three, viz. Identity, Otherness, and their Blend; and having done so, divides the whole resultant Substance into parts. The division—or rather the divisions, for Plato distinguishes in the whole process two successive operations—is introduced with the words ἤρχετο δὲ διαιρεῖν ὧδε ['this is how he began the division'] (35b), and is elaborately described. . . . It seems likely enough that this section of the *Timaeus* should have been quoted by Aristotle as αἱ διαιρέσεις ['the divisions']" (p. 217). Compare Aristotle's own description: "In the same way, Timaeus gives a natural scientific account of how the soul moves the body, since by its own movement it moves the body as well, because of being woven together with it. For when it had been constituted from the elements and divided into parts in accord with the harmonic numbers, in order that it might have a native perception of harmony and that the universe might move in harmonic revolutions, he bent the straight line into a circle, and, having divided the one circle into two, intersecting at two points, he again divided one of these into seven, the spatial movements of the heaven being regarded as the movements of the soul" (*DA* 406ᵇ26–407ᵃ2).

## Note 218
**As Empedocles does:** See 329ᵃ2–3.

**But he in fact leads them back to two:** "He was the first to say that the kinds of matter, the so-called elements, were four. Yet he does not *use* four but treats them as two only, fire by itself, on the one hand, and its opposites—earth, air, and water—taken as one nature, on the other (as we may gather from studying his verses)" (*Met.* 985ᵃ32–ᵇ3). See DK B62 = TEGP 125 F76.

## Note 219
**The simple ones:** The fire referred to as mixed is not Aristotle's own elemental fire, but *ordinary* fire, which is excess of hotness (330ᵇ25–26). It is mixed, not because,

like his elemental fire, it has two qualities, hot and dry (330ᵇ3–4), but because "flame is most of all fire, and flame is burning smoke, and smoke is composed of air and earth" (331ᵇ25–26). In the following text it is described as "what due to custom we call 'fire'": "At the center [of the universe] and around the center what is heaviest and coldest is set apart, namely, earth and water. Around these, and contiguous with them, are air and what due to custom we call 'fire,' but it is not fire; for fire is excess of hotness and a sort of boiling" (*Mete.* 340ᵇ19–23). Simple, or elemental, fire, on the other hand, is what, being like ordinary fire, is referred to as "fire-form," similarly in the case of air and the other elements (the words *puroeides* and *aeroeides* occur only here in Aristotle, though the latter also occurs in the pseudo-Aristotelian ††*Color.* 793ᵇ5). Similar considerations apply to the other elements. Notice "coarse-grained air" at *GA* 784ᵇ15.

## Note 220

**Nothing comes to be either from ice or from fire:** The fire referred to, since it is excess of hotness, is ordinary fire, not elemental fire (see previous note). For something to come from it, something contrary to it would have to mix with it, moderating its hotness. But it is too hot for that: "we do not say that wood has been mixed with fire, nor that it is being mixed when it burns, either itself with its very own parts or with the fire. On the contrary, we say that the fire comes to be and that the wood passes away" (327ᵃ10–13). Similarly, ice is too cold even to be combustible (*Mete.* 387ᵃ19). But see, for some apparent exceptions, *Mete.* 382ᵃ6–8n376.

## Note 221

**Two of each [pair] belong to each of the two places:** Reading ἑκάτερα τοῖν δυοῖν ἑκατέρου τῶν τόπων ἐστίν with Mugler and Joachim-1; Rashed reads ἑκάτερα τοῖν δυοῖν ἑκατέρου τῶν πρώτων ἐστίν ("and two each belong to the first ones"). The places referred to are the *proper places* of fire and earth respectively, which are the ones to which they naturally move if unimpeded, "whereas the others play a double game between up and down" (*Ph.* 205ᵇ28).
**The limit . . . the center:** That is, "those of the sublunary sphere" (Williams-1, p. 161).

## Note 222

**Earth is dry more than cold . . . :** "For insofar as they are capable of changing into each other they must participate in contrary qualities; but insofar as they are neighbors of each other it is necessary for them to have something in common. For example, fire is the neighbor of air, and, insofar as it is its neighbor, the two will have some quality in common, namely, heat. But insofar as either of them changes into the other, it is necessary that they should differ in another quality, wet and dry" (Philop. 230.14–20 = Williams-2, p. 141). Think of the series earth-water-air-fire as having earth, as more matter-like, at the bottom and fire, as more form-like, at the top. The transformations then lead back down in a circle. Thus what serves as form for an element is what distinguishes it from its neighbors. In the case of water, this is cold: "the dry and the wet are matter (for they are affectable), and of these earth and water are most of all the bodies (for they are determined by cold)" (*Mete.* 389$^a$29–32). For "water alone of the simple bodies is easily bounded" (334$^b$35–335$^a$1), and what bounds it, giving it form, is the cold that solidifies it. But what is selected as the form of an element in transformation is not responsible for all of its affections, since its matter too is the source of many of these: (1) "of the four elements earth is said to have the most special affections (*idiaitata*) of dry, water of wet" (*Mete.* 382$^a$3–4); (2) "the matter of which [the homoeomerous bodies] are composed is the wet and the dry, that is, water and earth (for each of these most clearly has each of the capacities), whereas the affecting ones are the hot and the cold (for these latter compose and solidify the latter from the former)" (388$^a$21–25). For further discussion, see Krizan, pp. 213–216. When cold is said to be a sort of matter (*Mete.* 389$^a$29), it is because "earth, water, and air . . . are matter for fire" (379$^a$14–16). Cold, after all, is just privation of heat.

## Note 223
**It has been determined previously:** Though the topic is briefly mentioned at 324$^b$15–16 and 329$^a$35–$^b$2, the reference is pretty certainly to *Cael.* 3.6.
**Alteration . . . :** That is, alteration of one primary body by another (taken as established in 2.2).

## Note 224
**Tokens:** *Sumbola* were originally two pieces of a bone or coin that uniquely fitted together, enabling a person with one to recognize a person with the other. Here Aristotle uses it to refer to a differentia shared by two consecutive elements, like the cold in earth and water. Thus when water becomes earth only one differentia has to be changed (dry to wet), which makes that change easier than one in which both differentiae have to be changed.

## Note 225
**The change . . . is not into each other:** That is, it is not reversible. See Gill, p. 71n43.

## Note 226
**Fire and ($kai_1$) water . . . earth and ($kai_2$) air . . . air and ($kai_1$) earth . . . fire and ($kai_2$) water:** $Kai_2$, as the next sentence shows, means "on one occasion X and on another occasion Y," and so has the force of "or."

## Note 227
**As we saw:** At 330$^b$3–4.

## Note 228
**Flame is most of all fire, and flame is burning smoke:** "Cases in which the underlying subject is hot in virtue of being affected also make it apparent that cold is not a certain nature but a privation. Maybe even the nature of fire may turn out to be something of this sort; for perhaps the underlying subject is smoke or charcoal,

smoke being always hot (for smoke is a vapor), whereas charcoal, when extinguished, is cold" (*PA* 649ª18–22). See also *Mete.* 387ᵇ29n425, 388ª2.

## Note 229
**One of the elements in each:** That is, one of the elementary qualities or tokens.

## Note 230
**Natural bodies:** That is, the so-called elements.

## Note 231
**There will, then, be some contrariety:** When something (for example, fire) comes to be from air, there will be a contrariety (a differentiating elemental quality), namely, hotness, one part (token) of which is possessed by air (hot, wet) and the other part (hot, dry) by fire.

## Note 232
**One of the contraries is a privation:** See 324ª2n143 (contraries), 318ᵇ16n76 (privation).

## Note 233
**Alone:** That is, without either the (positive) contrary or its privation.
**As certain people say:** For example, Anaximander. See 329ª12n203.

## Note 234
**If, then, nothing—at any rate, nothing perceptible—is prior to these:** The reference is probably to the matter that is inseparable from the so-called elements, since it is characterized as imperceptible at 332ª35. See also 329ª10–11 and 320ᵇ22–25.
**It would be all these:** Not, "these would be all things." See Rashed, p. 161n7.

## Note 235
**In the *Timaeus*:** See 54b–d (Appendix).

## Note 236
**Proved previously . . . :** See 331ª12–332ª2.

## Note 237
**Spoken about previously:** See 2.2–3.

## Note 238
**In the case of the extremes . . . :** If either earth or fire was the starting-point of the other elements, water and air, the latter would be earth + some token (elementary quality, differentia) or fire + some token. But since the elements change into each other, this is impossible, as was shown at 332ª12–18. If we argue in that way, however, it can seem unclear why "Aristotle confines this argument to the

'end-elements' [= extremes]. It would apply equally—if it applies at all—to whatever element is selected as ἀρχή ['starting-point'] of the rest" (Joachim-1, p. 227). But precisely because they are extremes, earth and fire are pure rather than mixed ($330^{b}33$–$331^{a}1$). And it is this fact that explains the restriction. For it is only in the case of an extreme that it alone—and not some mixture—is the starting-point of all the others.

## Note 239
**The way that it seems to some:** It is not clear to whom Aristotle is referring. Verdenius & Waszink, p. 60, conjecture that it is Anaximenes, citing DK A5 = TEGP 6: "[Anaximenes] says that air when it is thinned becomes fire, when it is condensed it becomes wind, then cloud, then, when still more condensed, water, then earth, then stones." For ease of reference only, let us call this *Anaximenes' Thesis*.
**Into each other:** Joachim-1 unnecessarily assumes a lacuna at this point. See Verdenius & Waszink, p. 60.

## Note 240
**This matter:** Namely, that on the assumption that the starting-point is an intermediate, the extremes do in fact change into each other, contrary to *Anaximenes' Thesis* (see previous note), since fire changes to water, and water to earth, and likewise earth will change to water, and water to fire ($332^{b}14$–30).

## Note 241
**Some contrariety . . . :** If F changes into X and X does not change into A, E, or W (since that would involve fire turning back), then there must be a new contrariety $C_1$, one token of which is possessed by F and the other by X.

## Note 242
**[1] Let K, then, belong to F, and Y to X. [2] Then K will belong to all of E, W, A, and F, since they change into each other. But [3] though in fact this has not yet been proved, at least it is clear that [4] if in turn X changes into something else, another contrariety will belong to both X and F (fire):** The crucial thing to remember is that Aristotle's target remains *Anaximenes' Thesis* (see n239) or more precisely that part of it (as yet unrefuted) which says that an intermediate M could serve as the starting-point for all the elements. (The other part claiming that the extremes do not turn into each other has already been refuted at $332^{b}14$–30.) Keeping that in mind, start with [4]. For F to turn into X, F and X must each have a token of $C_1$ (see previous note). For X to change into something else Y (without permitting any turning back), there must be a new contrariety $C_2$, one token of which is had by X and the other by F. Why? (i) Because $C_2$ is needed to enable the change of X into Y (just as $C_1$ was needed to enable the change from F into X), and (ii) because X and F are both M (albeit with different differentiae). So if X has $C_2$, M has $C_2$, and if M has $C_2$, F has $C_2$. That, in effect, is the base of the induction which will be used to draw a generalization of [2] as a conclusion.

## Note 243

**It is always the case . . .** : This is a generalization of [2], now drawn as an inductive conclusion from [4] (see previous note). Every contrariety in the (potentially) unlimited linear series of transformations will belong to the intermediate M that is the starting-point for all the elements. But because M is the starting-point of all of them, each of them is M (plus a differentia). Therefore, if the series of transformations does go on without limit, each element will have an unlimited number of contrarieties. But nothing can have both parts of a contrariety (both of a pair of contraries), let alone both parts of an unlimited number of them. Therefore, the linear series must stop.

## Note 244

**There will neither be a definition . . .** : This is because "a definition is a sort of number; for it is divisible, and indeed into indivisibles (for the accounts are not unlimited), and number is like that" (*Met.* 1043$^b$34–36; also 994$^b$16–24).

**If one is to have come to be from another . . .** : Suppose that at $t_1$ an element X in the unlimited series has a finite number of differentiae $D_n$, and so can be defined as $M + D_n$, and will have come to be at $t_1$. When at $t_2$ a new element is added to the linear series of transformations, that definition will be destabilized, since X will acquire a new differentia $D_z$ at that point, with the result that X will not have come to be at $t_1$ after all, since it did not have $D_z$ at $t_1$. $D_n$ is the "so-and-so many"; $D_z$ the "still more."

## Note 245

**All will be one:** For every element will be M + D, where D is the set of the unlimited differentiae.

## Note 246

**Empedocles:** DK B17.27 = TEGP 41.27 F 20.

## Note 247

**Cotyle:** A *kotule* is a liquid measure = 0.5 pints.

**[1] If it is with respect to quantity [that the elements are comparable], [2] it is necessary for there to be some same thing belonging to all the comparable elements by which they are measured—[3] for example, from one cotyle of water, ten cotyles of air might come:** The problem here is to explain the inference of [2] from [1] and [3] from [2]. "For why should we concede that if the quantity of A is comparable to the quantity of B, they must have a common substratum?" (Williams-1, p. 169). The answer lies in part in Aristotle's account of what a measure is and in part in his account of heaviness and lightness. "A measure is that by which quantity is known, and a quantity insofar as it is a quantity is known either by a one [or a unit] or by a number, and all number by a one, so that all quantity insofar as it is quantity is known by the one, and what quantities are primarily known by, this is itself one. . . . [And] the measure is always in the same genus as what is measured; for that of spatial magnitudes is a spatial magnitude, and in particular that of length is a length, that of a breadth a breadth, that of voiced sound a voiced sound, that of weight a weight, that of units a unit" (*Met.* 1052$^b$20–1053$^a$27). So start with an equality of one cotyle of water with ten cotyles of air. Then ask: What makes a cotyle a good measure of quantity for air and water? (Think: Why is volume a less good measure of how much ice-cream you have than mass or weight?) Ultimately, the answer will be that it is a good measure, everything else being equal, if when you put ten cotyles of air in one pan of a balance and one cotyle of air in the other, the balance (supposing it to be fair) will be in equilibrium. In this case the two are equally heavy. Now ask: What is heaviness? The "'unconditionally heavy' [is what] spatially moves downward or to the center" (*Cael.* 308$^a$30–31). But "each of the simple bodies has by nature a certain spatial movement (for example, fire upward and earth downward or toward the center)" (*Ph.* 214$^b$13–15). Hence earth is what is heavy and fire what is light (*GC* 319$^a$30–31). Now, when it comes to bodies that are mixtures of (so-called) elements, their spatial movement "is in accord with the simple body that is the mastering one in the mixture" (*Cael.* 269$^a$29–30). Air and water, to be sure, are not mixed in that way, yet, as intermediates, they are mixtures (*GC* 330$^b$34–331$^a$1), not of earth and fire, but rather of earth-form and fire-form (330$^b$24–25n219), which are precisely things that can be transformed into each other. So if one cotyle of water = ten cotyles of air, this entails, on Aristotle's view, that water can be transformed into air. And this in turn entails that there is something to serve as the underlying subject of that transformation.

## Note 248
**In quality . . .** : Reading ἐν μὲν ποιῷ with Mugler and Joachim-1; Rashed brackets as *lectio facilior*.

## Note 249
**It appears absurd . . .** : The argument draws on the same considerations as the earlier one, with hotness substituted for the heaviness (volume) measured by a cotyle (333$^a$20–22n247). If X units of F (fire) is as hot as nX units of A (air), there must be some same thing in both which, by being of the same kind, is the ground of their standing in this ratio. This will be the fire-form. But if it is present in both, they can change into each other. Hence the absurdity.

**For . . . this sort:** Reading τὸ γὰρ αὐτὸ πλεῖον τῷ ὁμογενὲς εἶναι τοιοῦτον ἕξει τὸν λόγον with Rashed, Mugler, Joachim-1; Williams-1 obelizes.

## Note 250
**Empedocles . . .** : DK B37 = TEGP 62 F37. Reading γένος with Rashed for Mugler and Joachim-1 δέμας ("Earth makes its own body grow"). "That is why, on the supposition that the primary body was something distinct, beyond earth, fire, air, and water, they [the ancients] gave the name *aithêr* ('ether') to the uppermost place, positing a name for it from the fact that, throughout eternal time, it is running always (*thein aei*)" (*Cael.* 270$^b$20–24). Primary body is for Aristotle the matter of the celestial spheres, which moves always in a circle.

## Note 251

**For the most part:** Aristotle associates what holds always with what holds by necessity: "'necessary' and 'always' go together (for what it is necessary for there to be cannot not be)" (*GC* 337$^b$35–36). He associates what holds for the most part (*hôs epi to polu*) with what rarely fails to happen (*Top.* 112$^b$10–11) and attributes its existence to matter: "Nature tends to measure comings to be and endings by the regular movements of these bodies [the sun and moon], but cannot bring this about rigorously because of the indefiniteness of matter, and because many starting-points exist which impede coming to be and passing away from being according to nature, and often cause things to come about contrary to nature" (*GA* 778$^a$4–9). Since the "indefiniteness of matter" seems to be a standing condition, while the "many starting-points . . . which impede" are not, we should presumably divide things up as follows. The indefiniteness of matter explains why laws or theorems of natural science hold for the most part, and so have contraries that are rarely true, while impediments explain why what otherwise would occur rarely may occur quite often. All human beings are bipeds, and this would remain true even if some freak accident or genetic disorder resulted in all or most human beings having only one leg. Nonetheless, it would still hold for the most part, since even under normal conditions a human offspring may be born with only one leg, simply due to facts about his father's seed (form) and his mother's menses (matter). See also *Met.* 6.2.

**By chance or by luck:** Unlike luck (*tuchê*), which in the strict sense is restricted to the subclass of what results from coincidental efficient causes that are "achievable by action" (*Ph.* 197$^a$36–$^b$3) and deliberate choice (*Met.* 1065$^a$30–32), chance (*automaton*) applies quite generally to the entire class, and so consists of all those things "whose cause is indefinite and that come about not for the sake of something, and neither always nor for the most part nor in an orderly way" (*Rh.* 1369$^a$32–34). Things that come to be by chance are sometimes said to come about spontaneously, or to be spontaneously generated. Often, however, as probably in the present discussion, luck and chance are treated more loosely as equivalent notions.

## Note 252

**Is it bone?:** "Empedocles says that bone exists as a result of its ratio, and this is the essence and the substance of the thing" (*Met.* 993$^a$17–18). See DK B96 = TEGP 114 F69, DK B98 = TEGP 115 F70. But "flesh and bone and things of that sort are parts of an animal" (*Ph.* 187$^b$18–19), moreover they are functional parts, so that they are bones only as long as they have their function: "if any bone were separate, it would not perform the function for the sake of which the nature of bones exists" (*PA* 654$^b$3–5). Hence having so many parts of water and so many of fire is not enough, as Empedocles thought, to make something a bone.

## Note 253

**The former is the cause of aggregation only . . . :** See 333$^b$20–23 for a correction.

## Note 254

**As Empedocles says:** See DK B8.3 = TEGP 32.3 F11 = Aristotle, *Met.* 1015$^a$2.

## Note 255
**"The name bestowed on them":** Compare, Empedocles DK B8.4 = TEGP 32.4 F11 = Aristotle, *Met.* 1015$^a$2a: "but 'nature' is the name bestowed on them by men."

## Note 256
**He says nothing about nature:** Although, the title of his work actually was *Peri Phuseôs* (*About Nature*).

## Note 257
**This cause is the well-being and good:** See 321$^b$1n109 on function.
**He gives the praise to mixing alone:** "If we were to follow and grasp the *thought* and not the inarticulate words of Empedocles, we would find that love is the cause of good things and strife of bad ones" (*Met.* 985$^a$4–7). See DK B17 = TEGP 41 F20, B21 = 45 F22, B35 = 51 F28, B122 = 183 F129, B115 = 25 F8.

## Note 258
**Yet, the elements . . . :** See 315$^a$3–8n20.
**By nature prior to the god:** The god = the divine sphere that love formed from the preexisting elements (DK B28–29 = TEGP 55 F30–32).
**Although they too are gods:** See DK B6 = TEGP 26 F9, where the elements are given the names of Olympian gods. Love and Strife are daemons at DK B59 = 119 F72–73, and Love is "Aphrodite" at DK B17.24 = 41.24 F20. Among the beings created by Love from the elements are other "long-lived gods" (DK B17.40 = 41.40 F20). Empedocles refers to himself, indeed, as a "deathless god" (DK B112.4 = 174.4 F120).

## Note 259
**The being for love . . . for strife:** The being for love = the essence of love (319$^b$4n86). If it is not the essence of love to move things in such a way that they aggregate, then it is possible for love not to move them in that way. But then we would need another cause to explain why it does in fact move them in that way (*Met.* 1071$^b$12–22).

## Note 260
**Defined:** (1) "A definition is an account that signifies the essence" (*Top.* 101$^b$38). (2) "A definition is composed of genus and differentia" (103$^b$15–16). (3) "There is nothing else in the definition except the genus that is mentioned first and the differentiae" (*Met.* 1037$^b$29–30). (4) "The ultimate differentia will be the substance of the thing and its definition" (*Met.* 1038$^a$19–20).
**Demonstrated:** To constitute a demonstration (*apodeixis*) a deduction must be a valid syllogism, whose premises meet a number of conditions. First, they must be immediate or indemonstrable, and so must be reached through induction. Second, our confidence in them must be unsurpassed: "Anyone who, on the other hand, is going to have scientific knowledge through demonstration must not only know the starting-points more and be more persuaded of them than of what is being proved, but also nothing else must be more persuasive or more known to him among the opposites of the starting-points from which there will be a deduction of

the contrary error, if indeed someone who has unconditional scientific knowledge must be incapable of being persuaded out of it" (*APo.* 72$^a$37–$^b$4). Finally, they must be necessary (and so, of course, true) in a special sense: the predicates in them must belong to the subjects in every case, intrinsically, and universally (73$^a$24–27). *In every case:* A predicate A belongs to every subject B if and only if there is no B to which it fails to belong and no time at which it fails to belong to a B: "for example, if animal belongs to every man, then if it is true to say that this thing is a man, it is also true to say that it is an animal, and if the former is the case now, the latter is also the case now" (73$^a$29–31). *Intrinsically:* A predicate A belongs intrinsically to a subject B just in case it is related to B in one of four ways: (i) A is in the account or definition of what B is, or of B's substance, or essence (73$^a$34–37); (ii) B is a complex subject φB$_1$, where φ is an intrinsic coincident of B$_1$—for example, odd number or male or female animal—and A is in the definition of φB$_1$'s essence; (iii) A just is B's essence; (iv) A is not a part of B's essence or identical to it but stems causally from it, so that being B is an intrinsic cause of being A (73$^a$34–$^b$24). *Universally:* A predicate A belongs to a subject B universally just in case "it belongs to it in every case and intrinsically, that is, insofar as it is itself" (73$^b$26–27).

**In an exact way:** In his focal discussion of *akribeia*, Aristotle makes clear that a science's degree of it is measured along three different dimensions: "One science is more exact than another, and prior to it, if it is both of the that and the why, and not of the that separately from the why; and if it does not have an underlying subject while the other does have an underlying subject (as, for example, arithmetic is more exact than harmonics); and if it makes fewer assumptions while the other makes some additional one (for example, arithmetic is more exact than geometry). By 'an additional assumption' I mean, for example, that a unit is a substance that does not have a position and a point is a substance that has a position—the latter depends on an additional assumption" (*APo.* 87$^a$31–37). The upshot is thus twofold. First, the most exact version or formulation of a science is the most explanatory one—the one consisting of demonstrations from starting-points. Second, of two sciences, formulated in the most exact way, one is more exact than the other, if it demonstrates facts that the other deals with but does not demonstrate. Because a natural science has to posit sublunary matter in addition to such starting-points, the strictly theoretical sciences (theology, astronomy, and mathematics) are more exact than any natural science. Hence it is among these that the most exact science will be found. And it will be the science that explains what the others treat as a fact or undemonstrated posit. *Top.* 111$^a$8–9 offers *saphês* ("perspicuous") as an equivalent.

## Note 261

**By force—that is (*kai*), contrary to nature:** (1) "By force and contrary to nature are the same" (*Cael.* 300$^a$23). (2) "What is forced [is] contrary to natural impulse" (*Met.* 1072$^b$12; also 1015$^b$15).

## Note 262

**The movement that love moves things with:** Love causes things to come together into one order, strife causes them to become many from one (DK B17.36–37 =

TEGP 41.36–37 F20). But when earth moves downward, it seems to move away from the other elements, and so in the direction of disaggregation. But movement toward disaggregation is caused by strife, which thus emerges as the cause of earth's downward movement in accord with nature. See $315^a3$–8n20.

## Note 263
**Nor is there rest:** Because "what is at rest . . . is what naturally moves but is not in movement when, where, or in the way it would naturally be so" (*Ph.* $234^a32$–33).

## Note 264
**He sometimes says . . . while at other times he says:** The contrast is that in the first case both events are the results of luck, whereas in the second there is the natural motion on the one hand, contrasted with a non-natural one.
**"It happened to run . . .":** DK 31 B53 = TEGP 97 F55 = Aristotle, *Ph.* $196^a22$–23.
**"Sank under the earth . . .":** DK B54 = TEGP 98 F56.

## Note 265
**He also says:** See $315^a3$–19.

## Note 266
**But of which of these . . . ?:** Reading τίνος with Rashed for Mugler and Joachim-1 τινος; Joachim-1 reads εἴ <γ'>; Rashed and Mugler εἴ. Joachim-1, followed by Williams-1, gives the meaning: "On the contrary these are the causes of particular movements, if, at least, that other is the starting-point." The argument is this: (1) Under love the cosmos would be as it now is under strife. (2) But love aggregates and strife disaggregates. (3) So there must be some further cause X to explain why these two causes produce similar effects. (4) But if X is then the starting-point of movement, it must be the cause of the movements caused by love and strife. (5) But these are contraries, since one is aggregating and the other disaggregating. (6) Therefore, X cannot be the cause of what love causes and of what strife causes. (7) Therefore, love and strife cannot be causes.

## Note 267
**But discussing these issues . . . :** Joachim-1 reads this sentence as the first of 2.7. The reference is to *DA* 1.4–5, especially $409^b23$–$410^a22$.

## Note 268
**The other necessarily follows:** See $314^b25$–$315^a3$.

## Note 269
**Except as bricks come to be from a wall:** That is, by disaggregation, just as the wall comes to be from the bricks by aggregation or composition ($334^a27$–28).
**It will be absurd:** See $333^b9n252$.

## Note 270
**When one of the two is fully actual . . . :** If X is fully actually hot, as fire is, X is fully potentially cold (that is, it is not to any degree actually cold, though it could become cold). But when X is neither fully hot nor fully cold, but somewhere in between, it is to some degree n potentially hot and to some degree m potentially cold. Where m = 2n, this means that X is twice as close to being fully hot as it is to being fully cold.

## Note 271
**In this way what comes to be . . . :** The matter M for element F (fire) and element E (earth) is the same ($334^b1-2$). If flesh G comes from mixing F and E, G ≠ F and G ≠ E, then G = M, since it seems that there is nothing else in the mixture for it to be identical to ($334^b4-7$). But there is an alternative possibility, namely, that G is not a mixing of the elements, but of the elementary qualities $H$ (hot) and $C$ (cold), which in pairs define the elements (F = $H$ + $dry$, E = $C$ + $dry$). For because these qualities come in degrees, the mixed quality that G has will be the resultant of their degrees of hotness and coldness, in the way described in the previous note, involving things that in a certain way are potentially. So the G that in this way comes to be is a mixture of elementary qualities. But a mixture of F and E also comes to be, and in it G = M.

## Note 272
**In our first investigations:** 1.7.

## Note 273
**The mean is of considerable extent and not indivisible:** Thus, though health, which "resides in wet things and dry ones, hot ones and cold ones, and (simply speaking) in all the primary constituents from which a living being is composed" (*Top.* $116^b18-20$), is "a balance of hot things and cold things" ($139^b21$), the same "balance does not exist in every healthy person, nor does the same one always exist in the same person, but it may be loosened to a certain point and still remain present, so differing in terms of more and less" (*NE* $1173^a23-28$).

## Note 274
**In the region of the mean:** We have just been told that it is when hot and cold "approach the mean," which is of considerable extent, that flesh and bone come from them. It seems reasonable, then, to take *kata mesotêta* here as referring to that region, in which both hot and cold are, so to speak, active in the mix. See Verdenius & Waszink, pp. 72–73, who make a similar point. The switch from *meson* to *mesotês* seems stylistic only.

## Note 275
**Proper place:** In the case of sublunary animals, up and down, front and back, right and left are not just spatially or relationally distinguished but functionally

*Note 276*

and absolutely so: "The part from which the distribution of nourishment and growth derives in each living thing is the up, while the last part it reaches is the down. The former is a sort of starting-point, the other a limit" (*IA* 705$^a$32–$^b$2). Similarly, the front is a starting-point, because it is where the perceptual organs are located (705$^b$10–13). Even in earthworms, where right and left are more difficult to distinguish perceptually, the functional difference between them still exists: "the starting-point from which movement derives is the same in all [animals], and by nature has its position in the same place; and the right is that from which movement derives" (706$^a$10–13). Thus human beings put their left foot forward, unless they accidentally do the opposite, since "they move not by the leg they put forward, but by the leg with which they step off" (706$^a$8–9). In the case of the universe, the same applies not just to right and left but to all six functionally defined directions: "There is no need to be puzzled, because the shape of the universe is spherical, as to how there can be a right and a left of it when all its parts are similar and all the time moving. Instead, we should understand that it is as if it were a thing in which there is a difference between right and left, even in their shapes, around which someone has placed a sphere. For it will then have the capacity corresponding to the difference, but would seem not to because of the uniformity of its shape. It is the same way with the starting-point of movement. For even if it never began moving, nonetheless it is necessary for it to have a starting-point from which it would have begun if it had begun moving, and, if it were to come to a stop, from which it would start moving again." (*Cael.* 285$^a$31–$^b$8). It is these functionally defined directions that determine unconditional or absolute locations or places in the universe: "every perceptible body is in a place, and the species (*eidos*) and differentia (*diaphora*) of place are up and down, before and behind, and right and left. And these are not merely relative to us or to position, but are also distinguished within the whole universe itself" (*Ph.* 205$^b$31–34). The place that is unconditionally up, for example, as opposed to being up relative to something else, is at the periphery of the universe; the one that is unconditionally down is at its center (*Cael.* 308$^a$17–29). It is absolute places, in turn, that figure in the essential definitions of the five elements, making them the closest analog of form that these elements possess: "this is what is being inquired into, namely, why it is that the light and the heavy do move to their own place. And the cause is that it is natural for them to be somewhere, and this is the being for the light and the heavy, the one being determined by up and the other by down (*Ph.* 255$^b$13–17). Thus earth, for example, is what is unconditionally heavy, since unless it is opposed, it naturally moves toward the place at the center. The center of the universe, therefore, is its *proper place*—the place where it would be unless something else prevented it.

## Note 276

**To the extent that substance . . . :** Not having a contrary is characteristic of substance (*Cat.* 3$^b$24–27; also *Met.* 1087$^b$2–3). But in that "they are composed of the contrary affections," there is a way in which the substances water and fire, earth and air, are contraries (*GC* 331$^a$1–3).

## Note 277

**Extreme contraries:** The extreme elements are earth and fire: "Earth and fire are the extremes and the purest, whereas water and air are intermediates and more mixed" ($330^b33–331^a1$). Analogously, the extreme contraries are the simple or unmixed ones, whose mixing, when it occurs in the mean region, produces flesh, bone, and the like ($334^b28–30$n273). So the pair of extreme contraries that is already present are those of earth (cold, dry) and those of water (cold, wet), and the other pair, required for change, is that of air (hot, wet) and that of fire (hot, dry).

## Note 278

**Farmers try to mix in something:** "Farmers mix in not just any random earth, but manure, which partakes of fiery and airy substances, and, having mixed, he says, use it in this way in watering" (Philop. 280.8–10 = Kupreeva, p. 72).

## Note 279

**Nourishment belongs with the matter . . . :** See $320^b34–322^a33$.

**As previous thinkers also say:** "But some people think that it is the nature of fire to be the unconditional cause of nourishment and growth; for among the bodies fire alone is something that is nourished and grows. That is why we might suppose that in both plants and animals it is this that performs the function. But, though it is in a way a contributing cause, it is certainly not an unconditional cause. On the contrary, it is rather the soul that is this. For the growth of fire is unlimited, as long as there is fuel, but there is a limit and an account of size and growth for things that are put together by nature; and these are characteristic of soul but not of fire, and of the account [= the form] rather than of the matter" (*DA* $416^a9–18$). The identity of the thinkers is not entirely clear, but most likely includes Heraclitus and Hippasus, who both favor fire as the starting-point. See $328^b34–35$n201.

**Fire alone and most of all belongs with form . . . :** Fire by nature spatially moves in a straight line toward the innermost surface of the sublunary sphere, which is the latter's defining mark or boundary. It thus encompasses the other sublunary elements in the way that the form (shape) of a matter-form compound encompasses the matter: "For as the matter and the unlimited are what are encompassed and inside, the form is what encompasses" (*Ph.* $207^a35–^b1$). In turn air encompasses water and earth, and water earth, making the latter most matter-like. See $330^b33–^a1$n221. Though it is likely that no more than this is involved in our text, there is a back story, for which, see Introduction, pp. liv–lxv.

## Note 280

**Each thing . . . :** That is, each element by nature moves toward its own proper place.

## Note 281

**The place around the center:** That is, the terrestrial or sublunary realm.

**Particular ones . . . universal ones:** The usual contrast is between particulars, as things that are severally one in number and jointly many (*Met.* $999^b34–1000^a1$), and universals, which belong to many numerically distinct particulars ($1038^{b}11$–12). But sometimes what is *kath' hekaston* is what is less universal than something else. Thus while true particulars are indefinable ($1039^{b}27$–29, $1040^{a}27$–$^{b}4$), it is "easier to define *to kath' hekaston* than the universal" (*APo.* $97^{b}28$), and a definition of a universal "divides it into *kath' hekasta*" (*Ph.* $184^{b}2$–3), where these are things that are particular in the sense of being "indivisible in species" (*PA* $644^{a}30$–31).

## Note 282
**The eternal and the primary things:** Namely, the celestial spheres, each of which is a matter-form compound that has ether (*aithêr*, primary body) as its matter.
**As matter ... as form:** The material cause and the formal cause, the latter of which will be identified with the final cause (see $335^{b}6$–7).

## Note 283
**The third starting-point:** That is, the efficient cause of movement. See $318^{a}1$–13.
**In the case of the primary things:** The primary things (the celestial spheres), as eternal and not subject to coming to be or passing away, have the sort of matter requisite for circular spatial movement alone, so that the efficient cause in their case is a cause of this sort of movement or change only. And that efficient cause is their understanding of the good and their desire for it: "There is something that is always moved with an unceasing movement, which is in a circle (and this is clear not from argument alone but also from the facts). So the primary heaven would be eternal. There is, therefore, also something that moves it. But since what is moved and moves something is something medial, there is something that moves without being moved, being eternal, substance, and activity. And this is the way the object of desire and the intelligible object move things: they move them without being moved. Of these objects, the primary ones are the same. For the [primary] object of appetite is the apparently good, and the primary object of wish is the really good. But we desire something because it seems [good] rather than its seeming so because we desire it" (*Met.* $1072^{a}21$–29). For these spheres are themselves living things: "We think about these stars as bodies only, that is, as units having a certain order, altogether inanimate. But we should conceive of them as participating in action and life" (*Cael.* $292^{a}18$–22). By contrast, in the case of sublunary matter-form compounds, including the elements, which do have the sort of matter requisite for it, their efficient cause is also a cause of coming to be and passing away. See $314^{b}26$–28n18.

## Note 284
**The cause as the for-the-sake-of-which ... :** "Nature is twofold, the one as matter and the other as shape, and since the latter is the end, and the other things are for the sake of the end, the cause in the sense of the for-the-sake-of-which must be the shape" (*Ph.* $199^{a}30$–32).
**This is the account of the substance of each thing:** "The for-the-sake-of-which and the account of the substance (these should be taken as pretty much one thing)" (*GA* $715^{a}4$–6; also *PA* $639^{b}11$–21).

## Note 285
**A third:** Reading τρίτην with Rashed for Mugler and Joachim-1, τὴν τρίτην ("the third").

## Note 286
**As Socrates says in the *Phaedo*:** It is probably passages like the following that Aristotle has in mind. "Nothing else makes something fine other than *that* fine [namely, the Form], whether by its presence or its being associated with it, or by whatever way or manner it comes to be added to it" (Plato, *Phd.* 100d); "You have no cause of coming to be two other than participating in twoness" (101c). It is unlikely, however, that these passages attribute *efficient* causal efficacy to Forms—something Aristotle has already acknowledged that Platonists do not do: "They neither take the Forms as matter for the perceptibles, and *the one* as matter for the Forms, nor these as the starting-point from which movement comes about (for they say that these are rather causes of immobility and of being at rest); instead, the Forms provide the essence for each of the other things, and *the one* provides it for the Forms" (*Met.* 988$^b$1–6). But, no doubt, it would not be entirely off base to describe them as, at any rate, *dreaming* of the efficient cause.

**Everything is said to be [what it is] . . . :** "The many things that have the same name as the Forms are [what they are] through participation in them" (*Met.* 987$^b$9–10).

## Note 287
**Others . . . :** It is unclear to whom Aristotle is referring. Among the various candidates are Empedocles (see 315$^a$21–23), Archelaus (to whom Plato is thought to refer at *Phd.* 96b; see Burnet, p. 96b3n), Parmenides (318$^b$6–7, 330$^b$13–19), the Atomists (see 315$^b$34–316$^a$2), and certain medical writers, such as Philistion of Locri (see Rashed, p. xlvi, and Solmsen, p. 346), who were influenced by Empedocles.

## Note 288
**Health-itself, scientific knowledge-itself:** That is, the Platonic Forms of these things.

## Note 289
**Essence:** *To ti ên einai* ("the what-it-was-to-be") is a phrase of Aristotle's coinage, of which "essence," from the Latin verb *esse* ("to be") is the standard translation. The imperfect tense *ên* ("was") may—as in the Latin phrase *quod erat demonstrandum* ("which was to be proved")—stem from an original context (such as a Socratic conversation) in which someone is asked to say or define what X is, and concludes by giving his answer in the imperfect tense to signal that he is giving the answer that was asked for (*ên* at *Met.* 1030$^a$1 may be a case in point). Apart from that, it seems to have no special significance, so we could equally well translate *to ti ên einai* as "the what-*is*-to-be."

## Note 290
**The capacities they assign to the bodies . . . :** Thinking that the capacities attributed to the elements could be the cause of coming to be would be like thinking

that the movements of the carpenter's instruments, without the form in his understanding to guide them, would be sufficient to cause the coming to be of beds, houses, and other such craft products. See *GA* 730$^b$11–23.

### Note 291
**Even fire itself is moved and affected:** See 322$^a$14–16, 323$^b$8–9. Hence it is not exclusively an active affecter, but admits of being controlled by, for example, a formative cause. See 330$^b$11–13.

### Note 292
**[1] In what way it moves it . . . [2] that [it is] worse than the instruments:** [1] is related to the criticism of these thinkers as making the capacities assigned to the (elementary) bodies too instrumental (see 336$^a$2n290). So the natural interpretation is to treat "the instruments (*ta organa*)" in [2] as referring back to the capacities attributed to the elementary bodies previously mentioned. This makes it plausible to understand "worse (*cheiron*)" as negatively comparing fire to those powers, and to be doing so in the terms already introduced: fire does not simply affect things, it is also affected by them (336$^a$6–7).

### Note 293
**We have spoken in universal terms . . . :** The reference is to the discussion in *Ph.* 2.3, 7 (the intervening chapters deal with luck and chance and whether or not they are causes).

### Note 294
**It has been proved . . . :** In *Ph.* 8.7–9.
**These things being so:** "Possibly Aristotle uses the plural ($^a$16 τούτων ὄντων) because he is thinking not only of the eternity of motion ($^a$15–16) but also of the 'inclination of the circle' which he will specify (36$^b$3–10) as the cause of the sun's alternate approach and retreat" (Joachim-1, p. 255).
**What is capable of causing coming to be:** Namely, the sun. Thus the cause of a human is, among other things, "the sun and its movement in an inclined circle" (*Met.* 1071$^a$15–16; also *Ph.* 194$^b$13).

### Note 295
**What was said previously:** In *Ph.* 8.7.

### Note 296
**What is the same . . . produces the same thing:** See *Mete.* 383$^a$7–8.
**Irregularity:** "Irregularity (*anômalia*) is sometimes a differentiation (*diaphora*) in the path of the movement (for a movement cannot be regular if its path is an irregular magnitude—for example, a broken line, a spiral, or any other magnitude that is not such that any random part fits on to any other random part). Sometimes, though, it lies neither in the place nor in the time nor in that to which, but in the manner, since sometimes the movement is differentiated by fastness and slowness;

for if its speed remains the same, it is regular, but if it does not, it is irregular. . . . Irregular movement, then, while it is one in virtue of being continuous, is less so, just as is the case with spatial movement in a broken line. And what is less so always involves an admixture of the contrary. But if every movement that is one admits of being both regular and irregular, movements that are contiguous but not the same in species cannot be one and continuous; for how could a movement composed of an alteration and a spatial movement be regular? For if a movement is to be regular it must fit together" (*Ph.* 228$^b$21-229$^a$6).

## Note 297

**The primary spatial movement:** The phrase *hê prôtê phora* usually refers to the movement of the primary heaven, the sphere of the fixed stars. But since the primary heaven has not been explicitly mentioned, and since "the movement in the inclined circle" is that of the sun, whose spatial movement has already been mentioned as producing coming to be and passing away (336$^a$16-18), it seems more natural, and more plausible, to take its reference here to be to the primary movement of the sphere of the sun—the second heaven (*Cael.* 285$^b$28). See next note.

## Note 298

**The spatial movement of the whole:** In cosmological contexts, "the whole (*to holon*)" usually refers to the primary heaven—the sphere of the fixed stars—which encompasses the whole universe. But it seems more natural here, given the contrast with "the inclination," to take it to be referring to *hê prôtê phora* (see previous note), and so to the movement of the whole sphere of the sun. This is how it is understood by Philoponus: "By 'the spatial movement of the whole' he does not mean the movement of the fixed [stars], as Alexander interpreted the phrase. . . . And he says that continuity belongs to this [spatial movement] because the whole sphere of the sun moves eternally, and its 'approaching' and 'retreating,' as he says, which is its irregularity, is due to the obliquity of the inclined circle. For it is because of this that the sun sometimes approaches and sometimes withdraws" (Philop. 291.18-28 = Kupreeva, p. 85). Williams-1 defends this view (pp. 188-191). Others, such as Joachim-1, p. 258, follow the Alexandrian alternative rejected by Philoponus. Following Philoponus, it goes without saying, does not preclude attributing ultimate causal responsibility to the primary heaven, and to its mover: Aristotle's primary god (*Met.* 12.7-10). Here just enough of the elaborate cosmology defended there (especially in 12.8) is exposed for present purposes: "as for the revolutions of the sun and moon, they may perhaps depend on other starting-points" (*GA* 778$^a$3-4).

## Note 299

**Because of the co-blending (*sugkrasin*) with each other:** Joachim-1 obelizes διὰ τὴν πρὸς ἄλληλα σύγκρασιν in part because σύγκρασιν seems not to appear elsewhere in Aristotle. *Krasis*, however, has an important role to play in his account of, at any rate, animal life spans (see previous note), and in fact κρᾶσιν is read here by ms. M$^1$ (not that we should put much weight on that). In any case, the co-blending must be understood as occurring in the matter mentioned in the next sentence ($336^{b}21$–24).

**Because the matter is irregular ... :** The question is, what exactly accounts for the irregularity or indefiniteness of matter? Insofar as an explanation is suggested in GC, it seems to reside in the fact that the ordinary so-called elements, such as fire and air, are mixed rather than pure ($330^{b}22$–23). Thus "flame is most of all fire, and flame is burning smoke, and smoke is composed of air and earth" ($331^{b}25$–26). And precisely because they, unlike such things as the fire-form ($330^{b}24$n219), are mixtures, one body of fire or air may differ from another. Now, in the case of colors, while many are constituted out of white and black in some definite ratio, others are constituted in "some incommensurable ratio of excess or deficiency" (*Sens.* $439^{b}30$). On the assumption that the same may be true of air and fire, we have our explanation of how matter's irregularity or indefiniteness should be cashed out: "the mean is of considerable extent and not indivisible" (*GC* $334^{b}28$–30n274).

**It is necessary ... :** The idea is not just that the elements change into each other, so that the passing away of one is the coming to be of another, but is rather to explain the difference in the speeds, so to speak, with which they do so. So, for example, if as a result of "co-blending" a quantity of ordinary air X is more liquid (wetter) than another quantity Y, X will take longer to pass away than Y, since passing away involves drying up (see $336^{b}20$–25n299). And because Y passes away more quickly, other things that rely on it will pass away more quickly too.

### Note 300

**Due to the cause we have mentioned:** At $318^{a}1$–27 the material cause is discussed, at $336^{a}32$–$^{b}3$, the efficient cause. The reference is probably to the latter.

### Note 301

**Nature always desires what is better:** (1) Many of the things Aristotle means by nature (*phusis*) are discussed in *Met.* 5.4. But he uses the term more widely than that discussion suggests. In the "primary and full way" a being that is or does something by nature has a nature—an internal starting-point of movement and rest ($1015^{a}13$–15; *Cael.* $301^{b}17$–18). The world of nature, investigated by natural science, is a world of such beings, all of which have perceptible matter as a constituent (*Met.* $1025^{b}30$–$1026^{a}6$). This world is roughly speaking the sublunary one. Beyond it lies the world of the heavens studied by astronomy and theology ($1026^{a}7$–22), where beings either have no matter, or matter of a different sort (*Cael.* $269^{b}2$–6, $270^{b}19$–25, *Mete.* $339^{b}25$–27). Although, strictly speaking, these beings do not have natures, since "nature is the proper order of perceptible things" (*Cael.* $301^{a}5$–6), Aristotle nonetheless speaks of them as if they do ($298^{b}23$). We use the term "nature" in a similar way when we speak of the nature of the numbers or the nature of fictional entities, not meaning to imply at all that these things are parts of the natural world (compare *Met.* $1078^{a}10$). (2) Sometimes, instead of using *phusis* to refer to the, or a *phusis of* X, Aristotle uses the term and its plural *phuseis* to mean something we translate as "a nature" (Greek has no indefinite article) or "natures." The thing or things referred to may or may not have natures in the strict sense; they are pretty much just entities of some sort. (3) He also speaks of *phusis* or *hê phusis* in agentive terms—for example, when he says, as he frequently does, that nature does nothing pointlessly (for example, *Cael.* 271ᵃ33, *DA* 415ᵇ16-17, 432ᵇ21, 434ᵃ31, *PA* 641ᵇ12-29) or that it does something correctly (*Cael.* 269ᵇ20), or for the best (288ᵃ3). Just as when he speaks of "the nature of the All" (268ᵇ11) or "the nature of the whole" (*Met.* 1075ᵃ11) it is not entirely clear how exactly or how literally these words are to be taken. He also speaks of it as having psychological attitudes, such as wish (*boulêsis*) (*Sens.* 441ᵃ3, *GA* 778ᵃ4, *Pol.* 1255ᵇ3)—though in these cases *bouleuesthai* is usually, and best, translated as "tend"—and, as here, "desire."

**Being is better than not-being:** An example: "It is clear that most human beings are willing to endure much misery in order to cling to living, on the supposition that there is a sort of joy in it and a natural sweetness" (*Pol.* 1278ᵇ28-30). But Aristotle is occasionally less sanguine: "Many things that happen are of the sort that cause people to give up their life—for example, diseases, excessive pains, or calamities. So it is clear that it might even from the start have been choiceworthy, because of these considerations at least, not to be born at all, if one were given the choice" (*EE* 1215ᵇ18-22). This thought has no parallel except in Aristotle's lost dialogue *Eudemus* or *On the Soul* (F44) where Silenus tells King Midas that "not to be born is best of all, and to be dead better than to be alive."

**Stated elsewhere:** At *Met.* 1003ᵃ33-ᵇ10, 5.7, 6.2, 7.1, 9.1, 9.10.

**Too far removed from the starting-point . . . :** The primary sort of being, on which all the others depend, is substantial being, since it alone is separable (see 316ᵇ3n42), and of substances the primary one is "the simple one and an activity" (*Met.* 1072ᵃ31-32). For the mark of an activity—an *energeia*—is that it is never on the way to an end, but at every moment fully achieving it, never becoming, always fully being (1048ᵇ18-36). This substance is Aristotle's primary god, which is "the active understanding of active understanding" (1074ᵇ34-35). (Notice "closest thing to being in the fullest sense" at *GC* 336ᵇ33.) And it, therefore, is "the sort of starting-point on which the heaven and nature depend" (*Met.* 1072ᵇ13-14). For it is the immovable mover of the primary heaven, and so of all the other celestial spheres, including that of the sun, on which sublunary coming to be and passing away depend (*GC* 336ᵃ32-ᵇ3). That is because the primary god—the activity of understanding or contemplating himself, which this god is—is the good that all other beings desire or aspire to: "If, then, that good state [of activity], which we are sometimes in, the [primary] god is always in, that is a wondrous thing, and if to a higher degree, that is yet more wondrous. And this is his state. And life too certainly belongs to him; for the activity of understanding is life, and his activity is that; and his intrinsic activity is life that is best and eternal. We say, then, that the god is a living being who is eternal and best, so that living and a continuous and everlasting eternity belong to the god, for this is the god" (*Met.* 1072ᵇ24-30).

The difference between god and these other beings is that he is always actively being the very thing that they aspire to be but are at different distances from reaching: "It seems that the good belongs without action to what is in the best state, to what is closest by means of one small action, and to what is further away

Note 301

by means of several actions. It is just as in the case of the body: one is in a good state without exercising, another by walking around a little, a third needs running, wrestling, and hard training, while to another again this good would not yet belong no matter how much exertion he undergoes, but rather a distinct one" (*Cael.* 292$^a$22–28). Thus the primary heaven achieves the good (to the extent that it can) by eternally revolving in a circle ("one small action"); the second heaven (the sphere of the sun), requires two actions; whereas sublunary things require yet more actions.

What is puzzling about this description is that it characterizes the primary god as possessing the good "without action," when we know that he is (engaged in) contemplative activity, which is itself a sort of action. To resolve the puzzle our first port of call must be the following text: "The [primary] god always enjoys a single simple pleasure; for there is not only an activity of moving but also an activity of immobility (*akinêsias*), and pleasure is found more in rest than in movement" (*NE* 1154$^b$26–28). Now, "in the case of what movement belongs to, immobility is rest" (*Ph.* 202$^a$5), but to the primary god, as we see, movement does not belong, so its immobility is not simply rest or lack of movement. Thus step one in the resolution of our puzzle is that god's immobility is not simply one of rest. That opens up the requisite possibility that it involves something else.

Second step: the paradigm cases of *actions*, as we understand them, are temporally extended bodily movements appropriately related to (perhaps by being caused by) beliefs, desires, and intentions. Hence "action" is clearly a somewhat misleading translation of *praxis*. Nonetheless, there is one type of action that *praxeis* seem to resemble quite closely, namely, so-called *basic actions*—actions we do directly without having to do anything else. This is especially true, if, as Aristotle himself seems to believe, these are thought to be *internal* mental acts of some sort: "we say that in the most controlling sense the ones who above all do actions, even in the case of external actions, are the ones who by means of their thoughts are their architectonic craftsmen" (*Pol.* 1325$^b$21–23). Like *praxeis*, in any case, these sorts of mental acts are not bodily movements and do not seem to take time to perform. Moreover, just as we do not perform basic actions by doing something else first, the same seems true of *praxeis*, so that a human being, for example, "is a starting-point and begetter of *praxeis* just as he is of children" (*NE* 1113$^b$18–19; also 1139$^b$5). So what we should say, then, is that the good belongs without *external* action to what is in the best state. But that, of course, is quite consistent with its not doing so without internal actions, such as the contemplative ones in which the primary god's life exclusively consists.

Third step: some actions are done both for their own sake and for the sake of other things, which may themselves be actions: "The activity of the practical virtues occurs in politics or in warfare, and the actions concerned with these seem to be unleisured and those in warfare completely so (for no one chooses to wage war for the sake of waging war, or to foment war either; for someone would seem completely bloodthirsty if he made enemies of his friends in order to bring about battles and killings). But the activity of a politician too is unleisured, and beyond political activity itself he tries to get positions of power and honors or, at any rate, happiness for himself and his fellow citizens—this being different from the exercise of politics and clearly something we seek on the supposition of its being different" (*NE* 1177$^b$6–15). Other actions or activities, by contrast, are done solely for their own sake, and these are the ones in which happiness consists: "Yet it is not necessary, as some suppose, for an action-involving (*praktikon*) life to be lived in relation to other people, nor are those thoughts alone action-involving that arise for the sake of the consequences of doing an action, rather, much more so are the acts of contemplation and thought that are their own ends and are engaged in for their own sake. For doing well in action is the end, and so action of a sort is the end too" (*Pol.* 1325$^b$17–21). In *Cael.*, Aristotle will rely on this very point: "What is in the best state, by contrast, has no need of action; for it is itself the for-the-sake-of-which; action, though, is always in two [varieties], namely, when it is the for-the-sake-of-which and when it is what is for the sake of that" (292$^b$4–7).

Putting the three steps together, the entire solution to our puzzle is now before us. That the good belongs without any action (that is, either an external action or one not exclusively an end) to what is in the best state. It is in this way that the primary god completes the whole.

## Note 302
**As has often been said:** Most recently at 336$^a$32–$^b$3.

## Note 303
**The spatial movement's being double:** See 336$^a$16–18, 336$^a$32–$^b$3.
**In the order:** See 336$^b$12.

## Note 304
**[1–5]:** The paragraph is a long protasis [1–4], with many sub-arguments, concluding finally with [5] the apodosis. With punctuation, it is possible to preserve its structure.
**[1]:** Reading τι with Rashed for Mugler, Joachim-1 τι τὸ κινοῦν ("some mover"). That the something is [1b] "immovable" indicates that it is the immovable mover, the primary god. Taken with the reference in [1c] to several circular spatial movements, this makes it likely that "elsewhere" in [1a] refers to the discussion in *Met.* 12.7–8, since it is in 12.8, in particular, that we learn how many celestial spheres there are, and why there are that many (1073$^b$39–1074$^a$14). It is also there that we learn [1c] about the unity of the universe that these spheres constitute. See Introduction, pp. xx–xxxv.
**[2]:** Since time and its relationship to movement are discussed exclusively in *Ph.* 4.10–14, to which [2a] clearly refers (see Philop. 301.2–3 = Kupreeva, p. 95), this is added evidence that the separate reference in [1a] is to the different discussion in *Met.* 12.7–8.
**[5]:** (1) "Just as what is in spatial movement and its spatial movement are together, so too are the number of what is in spatial movement and its spatial movement. For the number of the spatial movement is time" (*Ph.* 220$^a$1–4). (2) "Movement

too is continuous, then, in the way that time also is; for time is either the same thing as movement or an affection of it. But there is no continuous movement except movement in place, and of this only that which is circular is continuous" (*Met.* 1071$^b$9–11).

## Note 305
**Will be** and *is going to be*: Reading τὸ ἔσται καὶ τὸ μέλλον with Rashed and Mugler; Joachim-1 reads τὸ ἔσται καὶ τὸ μέλλει. The meaning is the same.

## Note 306
**Downward:** That is, toward the future.
**Unconditionally necessary . . . hypothetically so:** "The for-the-sake-of-which and the nobly good are found more in the works of nature than in those of craft. But what is of necessity does not belong in the same way to all the things that are in accord with nature. Yet pretty much everyone tries to refer their accounts back to it, without having distinguished in how many ways things are said to be necessary. Unconditional necessity belongs to the eternal things, while hypothetical necessity belongs even to things that come to be, as it does to the products of the crafts, such as a house and whatever else is of that sort. It is necessary that a certain sort of matter be present if there is to be a house or some other end, and *this* must come to be and be set in movement first, then *this*, and in this way successively up to the end and that for the sake of which each comes to be and is. And it is the same way too with things that come to be by nature. However, the mode of demonstration is different in natural science and the theoretical sciences. . . . For the starting-point in the latter is what is, in the former what will be. For [example,] 'since health or the human is such-and-such, it is necessary for *this* to be or come to be,' but not 'since *this* is or has come to be, *that* of necessity is or will be.' Nor is it possible to join together to eternity the necessity in such a demonstration, so as to say, 'since *this* is, therefore *that* is'" (*PA* 639$^b$18–640$^a$8).

## Note 307
**If it is of necessity, it is eternal:** "The things that are unconditionally necessary are all eternal, and eternal things cannot come to be or pass away" (*NE* 1139$^b$23–24).

## Note 308
**It cannot be rectilinear . . . :** Think of the chain of causes as starting now and leading down to the future; or starting now and going back up the chain toward the past. The argument is given in the following text: "For of medial things [in a series], since there is a last one and a prior one, the prior one must be the cause of the things that come after it. For if we had to say which of the three was the cause, we would say the first; for it is certainly not the *last*, for the final one causes nothing. But then it is not the medial one either, for it is the cause of only one thing (and it makes no difference whether there is one medial thing or more than one, nor whether they are unlimited or limited in number). But of series that are unlimited in this way, and of what is unlimited generally, all the parts are alike

medial things down to now, so that if indeed there is no first one, there is no cause at all" (*Met.* 994ª11–19).

## Note 309
**Not being limited:** Joachim-1 obelizes μὴ πεπερασμένης οὔσης. On the grammar of the sentence, see Rashed, p. 180n5.

## Note 310
**It makes no difference . . . :** That is, whether the circle consists of A causing B and B causing A, or because it consists of more things.

## Note 311
**On other grounds:** Namely, the ones provided in *Ph.* 8.7–9.
**The heaven:** "Let us first state what we say it is to be a heaven (*ouranos*) and in how many ways, in order that what we are inquiring about will become clearer to us. [1] In one way, then, we say that the substance belonging to the outermost revolution of the universe is a heaven, or the natural body that is on the outermost circumference of the universe; for more than anything else it is the last upper region that we usually call 'heaven,' the one in which we say that everything divine also has its seat. [2] In another way, it is the body that is continuous with the outermost circumference of the universe, in which we find the moon, the sun, and some of the stars; for we say that these bodies too are in the heaven. [3] Further, we say that the body that is encompassed by the outermost circumference is a heaven; for we are accustomed to say that the whole and the universe is a heaven" (*Cael.* 278ᵇ9–21). The reference here is to [1–2].

## Note 312
**The starting-point of the investigation . . . :** "It is the most natural function in those living things that are complete and not disabled or spontaneously generated, to produce another like itself—an animal producing an animal, a plant a plant—in order that they may partake in the eternal and divine insofar as they can. For all desire that, and it is for the sake of it that they do whatever they do by nature. . . . Since, then, they cannot share in what is eternal and divine by continuous existence, because nothing that admits of passing away can persist as the same and numerically one, they share in them insofar as each can, some more and some less. And what persists is not the thing itself but something like itself, not one in number but one in form" (*DA* 415ª25–ᵇ7).

## Note 313
**The movement follows along with the thing moved:** For the movement (the cyclical process) to be numerically the same, the thing (substance) in movement must be the same, since movements are ontologically dependent on substances: "But since some things are separable and others are not separable, the former are substances. And because of this the same things are causes of all things, because without substances, there are no affections or movements" (*Met.* 1070ᵇ36–1071ª2).

## Note 314
**If, though, these too are the same in number . . . :** "Having proved that the coming to be of the elements is accomplished when each of them passes away in number, but remains the same in form, he [Aristotle] now says that if someone said that these themselves, that is, the elements, remain the same in number {. . .} of whom Empedocles was one, it is to be replied that someone of that sort will be saying in effect that the elements are incapable of coming to be, not assuming, as we do, the substance to be capable of coming to be and of a sort that admits also of not being" (Philop. 314.3–8 = Kupreeva, p. 109).

## METEOROLOGY, BOOK 1

## Note 315
**[1–4]:** See Introduction, pp. xviii–xx.

## Note 316
**The primary element of the bodies:** The primary element is ether or primary body (*Cael.* 269$^b$4, 270$^b$2–3, 21), so that the bodies are the celestial ones (see *Mete.* 339$^a$19–20).
**The Milky Way . . . :** Discussed in 1.8 (Milky Way), 1.6–7 (comets), and 1.4 (shooting stars and meteors).

## Note 317
**We deliberately chose:** *Prohairesis*, which has the somewhat technical meaning of "deliberate choice" in Aristotle's ethical and political writings and elsewhere, also means "plan," which might seem to be its natural meaning here. But because "philosophy differs from dialectic in the way its capacity is employed, and from sophistic in the life it deliberately chooses" (*Met.* 1004$^b$23–25), and because "in dialectic a sophist is so called in virtue of his deliberate choice, and a dialectician is so called not in virtue of his deliberate choice, but in virtue of the capacity he has" (*Rh.* 1355$^b$20–21), it seems important to register that there may be more to *prohairesis* here, and in parallel contexts in other works, than "plan" or the like captures.

## Note 318
**We previously determined:** In *Cael.* 1.2.

## Note 319
**Air is nearest of all to fire, water to earth:** See *GC* 330$^b$30–331$^a$1.

## Note 320
**Continuous with the upper spatial movements:** Since there is no void. See *GC* 320$^b$27–28.

*It* must be considered the primary cause: As in *GC* 2.10, the reference is not to the immovable mover (the primary god), but rather, since it is itself in movement (next sentence), to the sphere of the sun.

## Note 321

**It has no end to the place of its movement . . . :** The place referred to is the proper place (see *GC* 334$^b$34n275), the one an element by nature moves to if not prevented. Because the primary body's movement is circular (*Cael.* 269$^b$4), it is always both at that place and in movement to it, and so its movement has no end, in the sense of a place where it naturally stops. Each of the sublunary elements, by contrast, has a proper place where it rests, separate from the other—earth at the center, surrounded by water, surrounded by air, surrounded by fire. Since no body is unlimited (see *Cael.* 1.7), these places too are limited.

## Note 322

**Come to be from each other:** See *GC* 331$^a$7–8, *Cael.* 3.6.
**Each is potentially present in the other:** See *GC* 334$^b$2–30.
**The same something underlies:** On the nature of this underlying thing, see *GC* 329$^a$24–26, and on its being presupposed by things coming to be from each other, 334$^a$16–18.

## Note 323

**Astronomical observations** (*theôrêmatôn*): A *theôrêma* is an object of contemplation (*NE* 1066$^a$26), so that *theôrêmata* (plural) are often theoretical views or speculations (*Div. Somn.* 455$^a$25, *Mete.* 345$^b$2), such as the mathematical speculations mentioned at *Met.* 1093$^b$15. But they can also be (perhaps theory-laden) observations, like the astronomical ones mentioned at *Mete.* 339$^b$8.
**The earth is far smaller even than some of the stars:** "The mathematicians who try to calculate the size of the earth's circumference say that it is about four-hundred-thousand stades. On the basis of these proofs, it is necessary not only for the mass of the earth to be spherical, but also for it not to be great in relation to the magnitude of the other stars" (*Cael.* 298$^a$15–20). The precise length of a stade is unknown, but if we assume a stade of approximately 0.09 of a mile, then 400,000 stades is roughly 36,000 miles. The actual circumference is approximately 25,000 miles. The mathematicians, whose astronomical speculations are referred to in our text, may include Archytas of Tarentum and Eudoxus.

## Note 324

**We have spoken previously:** See *Cael.* 1.2–3.

## Note 325

**Anaxagoras . . . :** See DK B2 = TEGP F2, also *Cael.* 302$^b$4, *Mete.* 339$^b$22–25, 369$^b$14–15. *Aithêr* seems to derive in fact from the verb *aithô* ("kindle," "light up"; passive: "burn"). See Chantraine, pp. 32–33.

## Note 326
**The body that is always running:** "As for *aithêr*, I'd explain it as follows: it is right to call it *aithêr*, because it is always running and flowing (*aei thei rheôn*)" (Plato, *Crat.* 410b).

**The same beliefs come about in cycles:** (1) "One must acknowledge that the same beliefs return to us not once or twice but an unlimited number of times" (*Cael.* 270$^b$19–20). (2) "We should take it, indeed, that pretty much everything else too has been discovered many times, or rather an unlimited number of times, in the long course of history. For our needs are likely to teach the necessities, and once they are present, the things that add refinement and abundance to life quite naturally develop" (*Pol.* 1329$^b$25–30). (3) "There is a tradition handed down from the ancients of the earliest times and bequeathed to posterity in the shape of a myth to the effect that the heavenly bodies are gods and that the divine encompasses the whole of nature. The rest of the tradition has been added later in a mythical way with a view to the persuasion of ordinary people and with a view to its use for legal purposes and for what is advantageous. For they say that these gods are human in form or like some of the other animals, and also other features that follow from or are similar to those just mentioned. But if we separate the first point from these additions and grasp it alone, namely, that they thought that the primary substances were gods, we would have to regard it as divinely (*theiôs*) said, and that while it is likely that each craft and each philosophy has often been developed as far as possible only to pass away again, these beliefs about the gods have survived like remnants until the present. In any case, the belief of our forefathers and of our earliest predecessors is to this extent alone illuminating to us" (*Met.* 1074$^a$38–$^b$14). The background explanation of this doctrine is presumably something like this: the world and human beings have always existed (*Mete.* 352$^b$16–17, *DA* 415$^a$25–$^b$7, *GA* 731$^b$24–732$^a$3) and human beings are naturally adapted to form largely reliable beliefs about the world and what conduces to their welfare in it (*Met.* 993$^a$30–$^b$11, *Rh.* 1355$^a$15–17).

## Note 327
**Those who say:** The identity of the thinkers is not entirely clear, but most likely includes Heraclitus (referred to at 339$^b$34) and Hippasus, who both favor fire as the starting-point. See *GC* 328$^b$34–35n201.

## Note 328
**We have also spoken about these matters previously:** *Cael.* 289$^a$13–33, 297$^b$30–298$^a$9.

## Note 329
**Intervals:** Namely, the ones between the celestial bodies.

## Note 330
**The co-ordinate bodies:** That is, the elements, in particular water and earth. See *GC* 315$^a$20–21.
**Heaven:** See *GC* 338$^a$18n311. Here the reference is [2] (≈ the sky).

## Note 331
**Yet allows that they are equal in capacity:** As Empedocles does. See *GC* 333ª18–20n246.

## Note 332
**Composed:** "The noun σύστασις [*sustasis*: translated as 'composition'] refers to a state of matter, which is often in the right or appropriate density or constitution for a certain outcome or has that appropriate constitution dissolved and destroyed by some external agency. It is used both for dry exhalations ... and wet exhalations. Dry συστάσεις are at the right density for ignition; a majority of the wet συστάσεις (eight of thirteen) concern reflection, for which the vapor has to attain the right density. The cognate verb συνίστασθαι can mean 'gather' (1.10.347ª27), and as such is similar to ἀθροίζειν [next note] (1.10.347ᵇ10 ...). More commonly, though, the verb refers to the process by which the wet exhalation turns into rain (though we should be wary of calling it 'condensation'). The noun, σύστασις, by contrast is never used to describe this process.... The sole cause of συνίστασθαι is the cold (1.9.346ᵇ29, 2.4.360ª1, 360ᵇ35, 6.364ᵇ27). The process of συνίστασθαι, then, is the opposite of διαλύεσθαι (2.2.355ª32) or διακρίνεσθαι ['disaggregate'] which can oppose or undo the process of συνίστασθαι (1.7.344ᵇ24, 345ª8, 8.346ª16)" (Wilson, p. 65).

## Note 333
**Gatherings:** "ἀθροίζειν [verb; *athroiseis* (singular: *athroisis*) is the nominal form] and its cognates generally refer to an intense gathering of a fluid material (i.e., not earth) as occurs with violent rain and wind (1.12.348ᵇ11 (twice), 22, 3.1.370ᵇ7, 371ᵇ1, 5), freezing (1.12.348ᵇ22), earthquakes (2.8.366ᵇ21, 367ª30, 368ᵇ4), mock suns (which explains why mock suns are white, 3.6.377ᵇ18). The Milky Way is an intense comet (1.7.345ª9, 1.8.346ª22). The term is not temperature related, so has nothing to do with 'condensation' of rain (i.e., the change of state from vapor to water). Because of its intensity, an ἄθροισις is better able to remain in its nature (2.2.355ᵇ26, 31, 2.5.361ᵇ18, 3.6.377ᵇ18). Conversely the lack of a single mass or gathering of water (2.2.354ᵇ6, 12, 13) on the earth's surface suggests the sea's instability" (Wilson, pp. 66–67).
**Where the rays already abate:** That is, in the earth's atmosphere.

## Note 334
**Vapor is disaggregated water:** "διάκρισις [*diakrisis*] accounts for changes from heavier elements to lighter elements (water to air; air to fire), perhaps as the material becomes less dense (1.3.340ª10, 8.345ᵇ34, 2.2.354ᵇ30). The διάκρισις of the air seems to be followed by an independent ignition (1.3.340ᵇ13, 341ª17). For a more violent rending of the dry exhalation ἀποσπᾶν (3.1.371ª32) and διασπᾶν (2.8.367ª29) are used" (Wilson, p. 67).

## Note 335
**For we say that [1] what is upper (*to anô*) and as far as the moon (*mechri selênês*) is [2] a body distinct from fire or air, but varying in itself in purity**

and freedom from admixture, and admitting of differences (*diaphoras echein*), especially [3] toward its limit on the side of the air, and the cosmos surrounding the earth: [2] refers to ether (primary body) and variations in it, especially as it gets closer to (roughly) the earth and its atmosphere. Hence [1] must refer to the upper region of the cosmos *down* as far as the moon (see Wilson, especially pp. 42–48). The fieriness of the lunar region is evidenced by the following texts: (1) "The outermost part of what is called 'the air' has the capacity of fire" ($345^b33$–34). (2) "The air . . . is composed of . . . vapor, which is wet and cold, . . . and smoke, which is hot and dry" ($360^a21$–25). (3) "The fourth genus [of animals], it must not be sought in these places [land, water, air], although there certainly wants to be one corresponding to fire in the order. . . . Instead, this fourth genus must be sought on the moon. For it appears to participate in [the body] at the fourth remove [= fire]" (*GA* $761^b15$–22). That is why "the heat and light from the stars come about when air is chafed by their spatial movement" (*Cael.* $289^a19$–21). For as the air mixed in with the ether explains, via friction, the heat from the stars, so the ether mixed in with the air explains their light: "It is not insofar as something is water or insofar as it is air that it is visible, but because there is a certain nature in it that is the same in both of them and in the [eternal] body above [= ether]. And light is the activity of this, of the transparent insofar as it is transparent" (*DA* $418^b7$–10).

Note 336
**Whatever other affections follow along with these:** See *GC* 2.2–3.

Note 337
**Movement and immobility:** Namely, the movement of the sphere of the sun (and the other celestial spheres) and the immobility of the primary immovable mover. See *GC* 2.10, especially, $336^b27$–34.

Note 338
**What due to custom we call "fire":** See *GC* $330^b21$–30n219.

Note 339
**Vapor's nature is wet and cold:** Reading ψυχρόν with Louis, Lee, and Webster for Fobes θερμόν: "vapor . . . is wet and cold" ($360^a23$); "the air contains large quantities of cold vapor" ($367^a34$).
**Exhalation:** "Aristotle does not maintain a strict nomenclature but uses the term ἀναθυμίασις [*anathumiasis*] generically to refer to both dry and wet exhalations (e.g., $1.4.341^b6$–8), and specifically for the dry exhalation alone (e.g., $1.4.342^a4$)" (Wilson, p. 52). See also $384^b33$n404.

Note 340
**A sort of fire:** "The outermost part of what is called 'the air' has the capacity of fire, so that when the air is disaggregated by movement, there is separated off a sort of composition (*sustasin*) which, we say, are comets" ($345^b32$–35).

## Note 341
**Except that part of it caught within the circumference...:** Because of the mountains and valleys on its surface, the earth is not a perfect sphere. The air caught in the valleys evens out the circumference by having as its radius "the distance from the center of the earth to the top of the highest mountains" (Lee, p. 21n*b*).

## Note 342
**[1] This air flows in a circle because it is drawn along by the circular spatial movement of the whole. For the fire is continuous with the upper element and the air is continuous with the fire. So their movement prevents them from being composed into water. [2] Instead, whenever any part becomes heavy the heat in it is squeezed out into the upper place and it spatially moves downward, but [3] other particles in turn spatially move upward together with the fiery exhalation, and [4] in this way it is continually the case that while one layer is always full of air and the other of fire, each of them is always coming to be one from the other:** Start with [4]: layer A is always full of air, layer F of fire. [3] explains why, when a part becomes heavy, heat is squeezed out of it. Call this heavy part P. This squeezed-out heat, because it is [2] squeezed into "the upper place" (here layer F) must be fire. This squeezed-out fire is the fiery exhalation that, because it moves upward, carries other parts upward with it to compensate for P, which as a result of having fire squeezed out of it, moves downward into layer A. Turn now to [1], which explains why and how P became heavy. Layer A is moving in a circle. As a result parts of it close to the boundary between layer A and layer F get mixed together into airy-fiery mixes. When the quantity of air in it exceeds that of fire, it becomes heavy, because air is heavier than fire. (If the quantities were equal, it would stay at the boundary.) It is a mistake, therefore, to say that before P became heavy it was air (Webster) or fire (Lee, p. 22n*a*). In all probability it was a mixture of the two.

## Note 343
**The works on perception:** No discussion of the felt heat of the sun, as such, is found in *DA* or *Sens.*, but we do find an account there of how we perceive hot and cold, and the heat of the sun is presumably a special case of these. See *Mete.* 382$^a$18–20n378.

**Heat is a sort of affection of perception:** The hot, for Aristotle, is what aggregates "things of the same kind" (*GC* 329$^b$26–27). Felt heat, by contrast, which is what we usually mean by "heat," is a perceptual quality.

# BOOK 4

## Note 344
**Book 4:** For persuasive defenses of the authenticity of this book, see Furley, pp. 132–148, and Lewis, pp. 3–9.

## Note 345
**Four causes have been distinguished:** See *GC* 329$^b$20–33, where the accounts referred to in the next sentence are also to be found.

## Note 346
**The species of the affectable ones:** See 4.2.

## Note 347
**The matter that underlies each nature . . . :** On the relevance of this to prime matter, see Introduction, pp. l–liv.

## Note 348
**Putrescence (*saprotês*) is the end of all these things:** Reading τούτων ἁπάντων with Webster and Louis for Fobes τῶν ἄλλων τούτων ("the others of these"), which Lee secludes.
**Unless something passes away by force:** That is, if they do not pass away in accord with nature. See *GC* 333$^b$26–29.

## Note 349
**In a special sense:** That is, when the wet (= what is being mastered in it) masters the dry (= what masters) (379$^a$10), so that it becomes wet—that is, begins to putrefy (379$^a$8–9).

## Note 350
**Matter for fire:** See *GC* 330$^b$21–30.

## Note 351
**Proper and natural heat . . . alien heat:** See *GC* 330$^a$12–24.

## Note 352
**Everything deficient in this sort of capacity is cold:** Because cold is by definition a privation of heat. See 380$^a$7–8, *GC* 318$^b$17n76.

## Note 353
**The mover does master:** That is, the cold, as greater than the heat of the surrounding air, masters it as a moving cause, and, keeping the thing frozen, prevents it from putrefying.

## Note 354
**Living things come to be in putrefying things . . . :** Aristotle thinks that insects (*HA* 539$^a$21–26), testaceans (547$^b$18–32), and eels (4.16) come about in this way.

## Note 355
**It remains to state the subsequent species:** See 378$^b$27–28.

## Note 356
**The opposing affectables:** Namely, the "passive" capacities, dry wet, which were also identified with matter at 378$^b$34.

## Note 357
**At that time it is useful . . . :** Wine must (a mixture of fresh grape juice, seeds, and stems) is useful because it is the first step in wine making. The pus that forms in boils tells us at a certain point that the boil is "ripe" and ready for lancing (380$^a$21). Since "the eye is healthy when it does not produce *lêmê*" (*HA* 633$^b$20–21), and *lêmê* means "eyesore" at *Rh*. 1411$^a$15, rheum's use, like that of pus, is probably diagnostic.

## Note 358
**The ratio:** See 378$^b$31–379$^a$1.

## Note 359
**Residues:** "By 'residue (*perittôma*)' I mean a leftover of the nourishment" (*GA* 724$^b$26–27). After eating, nourishment rises as vapor to the brain, where it is cooled and condenses into serum (*Mete.* 384$^a$16–17n399) and phlegm (384$^a$32n402). Unlike urine and stool, which are useless, these are (or are on the whole) useful.

## Note 360
**The same species (*idean*) [of ripeness]:** *Idea* here has the same meaning as *eidê* at 379$^b$17.
**As we said previously:** See 379$^b$14–18.

## Note 361
**Pneumatized things:** "Boiling is due to liquid being pneumatized (*pneumatoumenou*) by heat; for it gets swelled up because its mass becomes greater" (††*Resp.* 479$^b$31–32). The growth of eggs and grubs and the expansion of yeast in fermentation have a similar cause: "The growth of the egg is similar to that of larvae; for those animals that produce larvae also give birth to something small at first, which grows due to itself and not due to any attachment at all. The cause of this is quite similar to the very one in the case of yeast; for yeast too from being small becomes large as the more solid part liquifies while the liquid part becomes pneumatized. What crafts this in living things is the nature of the soul-involving heat, and in yeasts the heat of the humor (*chumos*) blended with it" (*GA* 755$^a$14–21). But what causes it to increase its mass and swell is the pneuma with which the heat imbues it. See Introduction, pp. lvi–lxv.

## Note 362
**The nature draws some of these into itself, while others it rejects:** Reading αὐτὴν for Fobes αὑτὴν. "This might mean: of ripening things, some are changed into a natural form, insofar as they are ripened, and the change into it is the natural end of their ripening. Others are rejected and excreted from the things which in accord with nature have them, like phlegm, pus, rheum, and excreta" (Alex., *In Mete.* 189.23–25 = Lewis, p. 78).

## Note 363
**Does not become coarse-grained:** That is, it does not form lumps or curdle in the way, for example, milk does. See *GC* 329$^b$20n207.

## Note 364
**Humors:** Aristotle uses the word *chumos* to refer to a number of apparently different things: (1) the "juice" in plants (*HA* 554$^a$13, 596$^b$17); (2) animal juices (556$^b$22, *PA* 676$^a$16); (3) the special object of taste (*DA* 418$^a$13), which is a sort of touch for Aristotle (414$^b$11); (4) a sort of seasoning that adds flavor (414$^b$13). The somewhat technical term "humor" seems to best capture its overall meaning.

## Note 365
**As was stated:** See 380$^a$23–25.

## Note 366
**The fire in the liquid:** That is, in the liquid in which the thing is being boiled.
**What is cooked on griddles is broiled . . . :** "The point here is that in roasted or fried things the internal heat is sealed in by the rapid cooking of the exterior surface" (Furley, p. 136); described at 381$^a$33–$^b$3.

## Note 367
**Olive oil by itself . . . :** See 383$^b$20–384$^a$2.

## Note 368
**Has already been stated:** See 380$^a$8.

## Note 369
**Is said to be burned:** "So we speak of *burning* porridge, which we *boil*" (Lee, p. 308n*a*).

## Note 370
**As we said:** See 379$^b$14–17, 380$^a$16–18.
**Due to craft . . . due to nature:** "We are accustomed to say that the producer, both in the case of what is by nature and what is from craft, is whatever it is that is capable of causing movement" (*GC* 335$^b$27–29).
**Craft imitates nature:** Also *Ph.* 194$^a$21–22, 199$^a$15–17, *Protr.* B13–14.

## Note 371
**As some people say:** It is not clear to whom Aristotle is referring—perhaps some Hippocratics. The connection to the discussion of digestion seems to be this: "if animals were generated in digestion, digestion would be σῆψις ['putrefaction'], and then it would be quite different from ἕψησις ['boiling']; so it is necessary to show that digestion is not σῆψις" (Webster, 381$^b$22n4).

**They come to be in the excreta:** The living things in question are probably "bowel or intestinal worms (*terêdones*)" (Alex. 197.15 = Lewis, p. 87), thought to "spontaneously generate" in the digestive process, whereas Aristotle thinks they come about in the excrement present in the lower intestine. See $379^b6$–8n354, $389^b5$–8.
**Upper intestines . . . lower ones:** Respectively, the stomach and the bowels.

### Note 372
**Spoken about elsewhere:** The reference is unclear.

### Note 373
**The opposite:** That is, potential.

### Note 374
**They are affected by each other:** For within their contrariety the affectables, the passive affections, affect each other. See *GC* $329^b24$–25n209.
**Each becomes a sort of glue to the other:** "In the skin of all animals there is a viscous liquid, less in some, more in others, for example, in the hides of oxen, out of which people make glue. And in some places glue is made from fish too" (*HA* $517^b28$–31).
**As Empedocles puts it:** DK B34 = TEGP 108 F6. See also, †*Pr.* 21.16–17.

### Note 375
**Earth is said . . . :** See *GC* $331^a3$–6n222.

### Note 376
**Here:** That is, in the sublunary realm.
**It is only in earth . . . :** "That winged creatures are also generated in earth is not difficult to recognize" (Alex. 199.23–24).
**Or fire:** Compare: (1) "In Cyprus, in places where copper ore is smelted, with more thrown in day after day, an animal comes to be in the fire, a little larger than a large fly, with wings, that can hop or crawl through the fire. . . . The salamander makes this clear, since it, so they say, by walking through the fire puts the fire out" (*HA* $552^b10$–17). (2) "If, then, ice is the solidification of wet and cold, fire will be the boiling of dry and hot. That is why nothing comes to be either from ice or from fire" (*GC* $330^b28$–30). (3) "Fire generates no animal, and none appears to be composed in wet or dry things under the influence of fire" (*GA* $737^a1$–3). (4) "The fourth genus [of animals] must not be sought in these places [land, water, air], although there certainly wants to be one corresponding to fire in the order. . . . Instead, this fourth genus must be sought on the moon. For it appears to participate in [the body] at the fourth remove [= fire]" ($761^b15$–22). A way to resolve somewhat the tensions between these claims is to recall that all of them, as belonging to natural science, rather than to a strictly theoretical one, hold only for the most part. But it is also important to remember that so-called (or nonelemental) fire's "underlying subject is smoke or charcoal," that "smoke is a vapor" (*PA* $649^a18$–22), and that vapor is "disaggregated water" (*Mete.* $340^b3$). We are in

an area, in other words, where "the more and the less and nearer and further make a wondrous difference" (*GA* 761ᵇ14–15).

## Note 377
**Replaced:** (1) "What can be pressed into itself and does not move to another place, which is precisely what the wet does, is soft" (*GC* 330ᵃ8–10). (2) "That place exists seems to be clear from replacement; for where there is now water, there, when the water has gone out as from a vessel, air is in turn present. Then some other bodies occupy this same place" (*Ph.* 208ᵇ1–4). In another sense, the verb can mean to compress (by surrounding), as at *Mete.* 347ᵇ6, 348ᵇ6, 16, 361ᵃ1, 382ᵇ10.

## Note 378
**Touch is what we use as a mean:** The mean mentioned is the perceptual mean, which is a constituent in a perceptual part that functions like a laboratory balance or weighing scale enabling it to detect differences in proper perceptibles, which activate it by tilting it, as it were, one way or another. See *DA* 423ᵇ27–424ᵃ10, Introduction pp. lxvi–lxvii.

## Note 379
**Two causes that have to do with the matter:** Reading περί with Louis for Fobes, Lee, Webster παρά ("two causes beyond the matter").

## Note 380
**As has been stated:** See 378ᵇ12–13.

## Note 381
**As was said previously:** Not so much said as presupposed at 347ᵇ2–7: "The north wind brings wintry weather. For it is cold, so it quenches the heat from exhalation . . . and due to its cold compresses and squeezes the heat," and also, perhaps, at 348ᵇ2–8.

## Note 382
**As was said:** See 382ᵇ16–18.

## Note 383
**Dissolve** (*luetai*): With occasional exceptions, such as 383ᵇ7, 12, dissolution and melting (*pêxis*) are not distinguished in 4.6–9.

## Note 384
**The same thing . . . :** Also *GC* 336ᵃ27–28.

## Note 385
**Water alone of the liquids . . . :** "Things that contain much earth are the ones that become composed and coarse-grained" (*GA* 735ᵃ37–ᵇ1). Since "all the definite

bodies here are not without earth and water" (*Mete.* 382ª4–5), any liquid other than (elemental) water will have some earth in it, and so will become coarse-grained (lumpy) if the water is boiled off, so that earthy solids in it get composed.

## Note 386
**Pliant:** *Hugros* usually means "liquid," or "wet," but also "soft," "pliant," "supple."

## Note 387
**The dross sinks down to the bottom:** In a modern blast furnace "the metal liquefies and the melted slag floats on top of it. But in the ancient furnace the slag would 'sink to the bottom' with the iron" (Lee, p. 329).

## Note 388
**Affected often . . . do not do this often:** "What Aristotle means is that while reheating was necessary . . . πολλάκις ["often"], it inevitably entailed some loss of metal and so was not repeated unduly . . . πολλάκις, not more often, we may suppose, than was absolutely necessary" (Lee, p. 329).

## Note 389
**Pyrimachus stone:** Apparently a sort of silex (especially quartz or flint).
**Millstones melt:** These were often made of lava of some sort, especially basaltic lava. See Melfos.

## Note 390
**Mud and earth (*gê*) both melt as well:** Reading τήκεται δὲ καὶ ὁ πηλὸς καὶ ἡ γῆ with Fobes and Louis; Webster and Lee seclude, as does Düring, who adds that the sentence "arouses suspicion, especially the senseless ἡ γῆ" (p. 85). If *gê* is elemental earth, Düring is clearly correct in his judgment, since only what contains water can melt (382ᵇ31–32), and elemental earth is water-free. But Aristotle is pretty clearly referring not to it but to so-called earth, since, as with millstones, pyrimachus stone, and iron, he is apparently basing his claim on observation of what happens to ordinary non-elemental earth, and, of course, to mud.

## Note 391
**Millstones:** Millstones melt in fire, but are not dissolvable in liquid. "Yet the μυλίαι of 383ᵇ12, having been solidified by heat (383ᵇ10), can hardly be the same as the μυλίαι of 383ᵇ7 which have solidified by cold (383ª26)" (Lee, p. 323nc).

## Note 392
**Soda:** Calcium carbonate.

## Note 393
**In water . . . but not in olive oil:** Because, while water is wet and cold, olive oil contains air (dry) and heat. See 383ᵇ30–31n395.

## Note 394
**That is also why . . . :** "Just as in dry things that have been burnt, such as ash, some fire is left behind in them, it is the same way too in wet things that have been concocted; for some part of the heat that was operative remains behind. That is why what is oily is light and rises to the surface in liquids" (*PA* 672$^a$5–9). The two views are consistent because the air in question has pneuma within it (notice *pneumatos* at *Mete*. 383$^b$26–27), and so contains heat. See 380$^a$23n361.

## Note 395
**It whitens . . . :** Compare: "For it is not only liquids composed of water and earthy material that get coarse-grained, but also those composed of water and pneuma—for example, foam becomes more coarse-grained and white, and the smaller and less clear the bubbles in it, the whiter and firmer the mass appears. Olive oil is affected in the same way; for on mixing with pneuma it gets coarse-grained, which is why the whitening [oil] becomes more coarse-grained—the watery material in it gets disaggregated by the heat and becomes pneuma" (*GA* 735$^b$7–16).

## Note 396
**As was said:** See 383$^a$13–14.

## Note 397
**Solidification, as was said:** See 382$^b$1.

## Note 398
**Wine, urine, vinegar, lye, and whey:** At 382$^b$13–15 these are forms of water, not because they are water and nothing else, but because they contain a preponderance of water.
**Lye:** Of wood ashes.

## Note 399
**But more so of earth in most cases:** "All milk is composed of a watery serum (*ichôra*) called 'whey' and a corporeal material called 'curd'; and the more curd there is the more coarse-grained the milk" (*HA* 521$^b$26–29). "Blood comes to be by concoction from serum" (521$^a$17–18). Serum is "the part of the blood that is watery, either because it is not yet concocted or because it has become corrupted" (*PA* 651$^a$17–18). The other part consists of fibers (*ines*), which are "in between sinew and blood-vessel" (*HA* 515$^b$27) and are "composed of earth" (*PA* 651$^a$7). See *Mete*. 384$^a$25–30.

## Note 400
**Fig juice:** The acidic juice of the fig tree is used like rennet to curdle milk in making cheese.

## Note 401
**They do not contain fibers:** "Modern accounts of blood plasma (the liquid in which blood cells and platelets are suspended) distinguish serum from proteins

called fibrins, which aid in clotting; and fibrin levels do vary from animal to animal" (Lennox, p. 201). *HA* 515$^b$32–33 suggests that Aristotle knew of some process for determining the fiber content of blood, "but the method is never described" (Lennox, p. 201).

## Note 402
**Serous:** Serum (*ichôr*) is the part of blood that is watery (see 384$^a$16–17n399).
**Phlegm:** Phlegm (*phlegma*) "is a residue from the useful nourishment: a sign of which is that when mixed with pure nourishment it is nourishing and is used up in cases of disease" (*GA* 725$^a$15–17). On residues, see 380$^a$2n359.
**The nature:** Since concoction is effected by the mastery of internal natural heat (379$^b$32–35), the nature in question must be that of the blood, and so of the animal whose blood it is. For *phusis* ("nature") in place of *thermotês* ("heat"), and corrected to the latter in some mss., see *PA* 671$^a$1–2.

## Note 403
**Water has no ways in:** See 385$^a$27–30.

## Note 404
**As has been stated elsewhere:** At *Mete.* 378$^a$18–31: "There are, we say, two exhalations, one vaporous and one smoky; and there are [correspondingly] two kinds (*eidos*) of things produced within the earth, 'fossils' and 'metals' [literally: things dug up and things mined]. The dry exhalation, by being fiery, produces all the 'fossils'—for example, all kinds (*genos*) of stones that are non-meltable, and realgar, ocher, ruddle, sulfur, and others of this sort. Most 'fossils' are colored dust or stone composed of this sort of thing—for example, cinnabar. Metals are products of the vaporous exhalation, and are all meltable or pullable—for example, iron, gold, and bronze. These are all produced by the enclosure of the vaporous exhalation, particularly within stones, due to the dryness in it squeezing it together and solidifying it."

## Note 405
**The special objects:** "By a 'special object (*idion*)' I mean whatever cannot be perceived by another perceptual capacity, and about which we cannot be deceived—for example, sight is of color, hearing of sound, taste of flavor, whereas touch has several different ones" (*DA* 418$^a$11–14).

## Note 406
**Drenchable . . . non-drenchable:** "It is not always easy to find words exactly covering the Greek words. . . . It is evident that τέγγεσθαι involves both βρέχεσθαι ('wet through') and μαλακώτερον γίνεσθαι ('become softer')" (Düring, p. 90). "In fact [*tegkton*] means 'capable of being drenched,' that is, able to be in the state of holding water internally. Some things melt, and so become liquid, while other remain solid, yet are made wet through and through (i.e., drenched). . . . [Thus] some things, upon being made wet, are not made wet through and through, but

melt. For something to be made wet through and through, for it to be drenched, it must remain solid. Of course, things are softened as a result of this drenching" (Lewis, p. 141n208).

## Note 407
**Non-viscous:** *Psathuron* means "friable" or "crumbly" but, when applied to liquids (as at †*Pr.* 927$^b$9–12), must be translated as "non-viscous."

## Note 408
**We have spoken in universal terms previously:** In 4.6–7.

## Note 409
**Iron, horn, and woods:** Retaining καὶ ξύλα ("and woods") with Fobes, Louis, and Düring; Webster and Lee (referring to 384$^b$15–16) seclude. Alexander makes our text consistent with 384$^b$15–16, by treating it as restricted in scope (in parallel with how Aristotle himself treats ebony): "*certain* woods (*xula tina*) are naturally bendable when heated and so softenable" (Alex. 215.19–20 = Lewis, p. 111).

## Note 410
**Harder than the [masses of] water:** Reading ὄντας δὲ σκληροτέρους with Lee for Fobes ὄντων σκληροτέρων, which "must be corrupt" (Webster, ad loc.). "Something with hard pores [or ducts] has pores which do not dissolve when a liquid enters them, but retain their shape and so hold the liquid" (Lewis, p. 141n211).

## Note 411
**In soda the ducts are throughout . . . :** "Soda has ducts throughout it, and these ducts interconnect with each other everywhere. That is why as soon as the water has been received, the parts of the soda are divided due to it. But in earth, though it has some ducts in such a way as to be throughout it, others lie so as not to meet and do not interconnect with each other. When, then, the water is received by the ducts that interconnect with each other and that are throughout it, it is melted, whereas when it is received by the ones that lie so as not to meet, it is drenched but not melted" (Alex. 216.1–7 = Lewis, pp. 111–112).

## Note 412
**Ducts:** A duct being a division in the thing at which shattering into the parts adjacent to it can occur.

## Note 413
**Soft:** Reading μαλακά with Webster and Lee for Fobes and Louis, μαλακτά ("softenable").

## Note 414
**Replacement:** See 382$^a$13–14n377.

## Note 415
**Pushing:** "Spatial movements caused by other things are of four species: pulling, pushing, carrying, and rotating. For all movements with respect to place are led back to these; for pushing along is a sort of pushing in which what is moving something away from itself follows it and continues to push it, whereas pushing away is when it does not follow what it has moved" (*Ph.* 243ᵃ16–21; also 244ᵃ7–8). Pushing in our text is like pushing along.

## Note 416
**Blow:** "A blow, though, does not come about without spatial movement" (*DA* 419ᵇ13).

## Note 417
**For sometimes . . . :** Reading ἐνίοτε γὰρ οὐ κενοί εἰσιν εἰς οὕς συνέρχεται, with Webster, Lee, Louis, and Düring; Fobes secludes.

## Note 418
**For a thing to be pulled . . . :** "Pulling is movement from something else to the puller itself, or to something else, when the movement of what is pulling is faster than the one that would separate the continuous things from each other, since it is this way that one is pulled along with the other" (*Ph.* 244ᵃ8–11). The continuous things are the puller and the thing it is pulling. The movement that would separate them is the natural resistance of the thing being pulled, which tends to disconnect it from what is pulling it.

## Note 419
**From liquid into (*eis*) air and wind (*pneuma*), capable of wetting things:** Webster secludes καὶ πνεῦμα. Düring's proposal to treat *eis* as locative seems inconsistent with the contrasting οὔτε πνεῦμα γίγνεται at 387ᵃ28–29. Vapor is capable of wetting things because it is "disaggregated water" (*Mete.* 340ᵇ3). On wind, see *GC* 318ᵇ29n79.

## Note 420
**Fumes:** Reading θυμιάματα with Lee for Fobes, Webster, Louis θυμιατὰ ("things capable of giving off fumes").

## Note 421
**By analogy, however, they are all in the same class:** "Of the animals, some have all their parts the same as each other, whereas some have different ones. Some parts are the same in form—for example, one human being's nose and eye are identical to another human being's nose and eye, one's flesh to the other's flesh, one's bone to the other's bone; and the same applies to the parts of a horse and of such other animals as we say are the same in form; for as the whole is to the whole, so each part is to each part. In other cases, though they are the same [in form], they differ

in excess or deficiency, namely, those whose genus is the same. By 'genus' I mean, for example, bird and fish, for each of these has differentiations with respect to its genus, that is, there are numerous species both of fish and of birds. Now, the differentiae of pretty much most of the parts in animals lie in the contrarieties of their affections, for example, of colors and shapes, in that some have the same ones to a greater degree others to a lesser one, and additionally in greater or fewer number, and larger or smaller size, and, in general, in excess or deficiency. Thus in some the texture of the flesh is soft, in others firm; some have a long bill, others a short one; some have many feathers, others few. Moreover, even in the cases we are considering, it happens that different ones have different parts—for example, some have spurs, others do not, some have crests and others do not. But (one might almost say) most of the parts, and those out of which the bulk of the body is composed, are either identical [in form] or differ by way of contrariety with respect to excess or deficiency; for greater or lesser [degree] may be taken as a sort of excess or deficiency. Some animals, however, do have parts that are neither the same in form nor [different] in excess or deficiency, but analogous—for example, as bone is to fish-spine, nail to hoof, hand to claw, feather to scale; for what the feather is in a bird, the scale is in a fish" (*HA* 486$^a$14–$^b$22).

## Note 422
**As Empedocles said:** DK B82 = TEGP 144 F96.
**Scales:** Reading λεπιδές with Louis and TEGP for Fobes λοπιδές.

## Note 423
**Because it is fat:** "Syrupy," as we might say.

## Note 424
**Stones:** Stones are non-combustible (387$^a$19), but are affected by fire in other ways.
**Anthrax:** "There is another kind (*genos*) of stone known as *anthrax*, which is wholly non-combustible, just as if it were naturally composed of contraries. Signets are carved from it. It is of red hue and when placed toward the sun produces the color of live charcoal" (Theophrastus, *De Lapidibus* 3.18 = Eichholz, p. 62). An *anthrax* is probably a ruby.

## Note 425
**The liquid contained in wood . . . :** Wood, as something splittable, has ducts running lengthwise throughout it, and it is in these that the liquid in it collects together (see 389$^a$19–21). When the wood is heated, therefore, this liquid is quickly available to produce flame. For "Liquid is the only nourishment for fire. . . . Flame comes about through the continuous [inter-]change of wet and dry" (355$^a$5–10).
**Whereas in bronze . . . :** The homoeomerous parts of bronze, like all homoeomerous bodies, are composed of (elementary) water and earth, but there is no water (liquid) collected together—no "free moisture" (Düring, p. 96)—in its ducts to produce flame.

## Note 426
**[Fumes] of things that burn very badly . . . :** For not having the dry in common as a "token" with fire, they change less quickly into fire: "For those that have tokens in relation to each other, the change is fast, for those that do not have them, slow, because it is easier for one thing to change than for many" (*GC* 331$^a$23–26).

## Note 427
**As we have said:** See 384$^b$7–385$^a$10.

## Note 428
**Metals:** See 384$^b$32n404. *Metalleuomena*, remember, are literally "things mined."
**Visceral body** (*splagchnon*): "Each of the other so-called viscera follows along with the heart. For they are composed of the same matter. For the nature of all of them is bloody, because they are situated on vascular channels and rivulets. So just as with silt in flowing water, these other viscera are like silt deposited by the flow of blood through the blood vessels. And the heart, being the starting-point of the blood vessels and having within it the primary capacity for crafting the blood, is itself for good reason composed of nourishment of that sort that it is a starting-point of. Why, then, the viscera are bloody in shape [= form], has now been stated, as has why they are in one way homoeomerous and in another non-homoeomerous" (*PA* 647$^a$34–$^b$9).
**Wood, bark, leaf, root, and things of this sort:** Wood and bark are homoeomerous, as are leaf and root at 389$^a$13, though non-homoeomerous apparently in the following text: "For even the parts of plants are instruments, although extremely simple ones—for example, the leaf is a covering for the pod and the pod for the fruit, and the roots are an analog of the mouth, since both take in nourishment" (*DA* 412$^b$2–4).

## Note 429
**Since these** (*tauta*) **are composed by another cause:** *Tauta* refers to the non-homoeomerous bodies (Alex. 219.20 = Lewis, p. 116). The other cause is the formal one. See 382$^a$27–$^b$1.
**Each most clearly has each of the capacities:** For "earth is said to have the most special affections of dry, water of wet" (382$^a$3–4).

## Note 430
**Of bodies that have been crafted:** For example, as the heart handicrafts the blood (*PA* 647$^a$34–$^b$9; quoted at *Mete.* 388$^a$17n428), or as the active capacities, hot and cold, handicraft the passive ones, wet and dry (*GC* 330$^b$13). See also *Mete.* 384$^b$26–28, 389$^a$28, *GA* 730$^b$11–19.

## Note 431
**As was stated previously:** At 382$^a$22–27.

## Note 432
**[1] Those that do not are composed of earth, or . . . [2] of earth and air (for example, wood):** [1] is problematic since it is difficult to see how a liquid could be composed of earth alone; as is [2] since wood is obviously not a liquid. That is why "Alexander explained ὑγρά as 'moist bodies' and believed that Aristotle thought of green wood. This explanation, taken isolated, is sound; Aristotle often indeed uses ὑγρόν ambiguously to denote elementary Moist, a liquid, or a moist substance in general. . . . But the context here undeniable demands that ὑγρά = liquids" (Düring, p. 98). The text, in any case, is unreliable, and we must suspect that "some reader before Andronicus added these definitions" (Düring, p. 99). On wood as composed of earth and air, see $384^b15$–16.

## Note 433
**Due to the smoke . . . :** Reading ὑπὸ τοῦ καπνοῦ with Düring for Fobes, Lee, Louis, ὑπὲρ τοῦ καπνοῦ. "Into the wine was often put various aromatic things, [such] as goat's-milk, whey cheese finely shred, spices, rose-leaves, violets, myrtle, aniseed or honey . . . forerunners to the vermouth of our time. When the wine-skins are kept hanging in the warm smoke . . . the wine is gradually dried up" (Düring, p. 99).

## Note 434
**In the case of the others:** For example, salt, soda.

## Note 435
**Frankincense . . . :** Reading λιβανωτοὶ δὲ καὶ τὰ τοιαῦτα παραπλησίως τοῖς ξύλοις ἀτμίζει with Fobes, Lee, Louis. Webster secludes, on the grounds that the sentence is "quite irrelevant to the context and may have been absent from Alexander's text." Düring considers it "a marginal note made by some reader after the time of Alexander" (p. 100). Notice, though, that frankincense is composed more of wood ($389^a14$).

## Note 436
**Serum:** See $384^a32n402$.

## Note 437
**Animals come to be in rotten things:** See $381^b9$–12n371.
**The presence of [alien] heat . . . :** See $379^a16$–22.

## Note 438
**The colliquescences:** Sometimes these are residues, as at *PA* $677^a13$, and so are non-concocted nourishment ($380^a2n359$). But sometimes the two are distinguished: "By 'residues' I mean what is left over from nourishment; by 'colliquescence' what is given off as a disaggregation from what is productive of growth due to its dissolution contrary to nature" (*GA* $724^b26$–28). Residues, such as stool and

urine, have natural exit points from the body, but for a colliquescence (sweat, for example) "no place has been assigned in accord with nature, rather it flows about in the body wherever there is a free passage" (725$^a$23–25).

## Note 439
**The account:** A *logos* is often Aristotle's way of referring to the form that the account defines (for example, *GC* 335$^b$6–7). But in light of *Mete.* 378$^b$31–379$^a$1 it may here be, in particular, a ratio (also *logos*). On substance, see *GC* 314$^b$14n14.

## Note 440
**A corpse . . . :** Since it can no longer perform the relevant functions. See *GC* 321$^b$1n109.

## Note 441
**[Fire's] function is yet less clear:** Aristotle's point may be that it is difficult to relate the matter of fire to its final cause (form, function). Whereas it is easier to do so in the case of flesh.

## Note 442
**Tension:** Tension (*tasis*) is an affection of, for example, sinews (*HA* 515$^b$15). The others mentioned are defined in *Mete.* 4.8, which lists eighteen together with their contraries.

## Note 443
**We must get a theoretical grasp on the non-homoeomerous ones . . . :** A project undertaken in *PA* 2–4.

# Further Reading

Detailed and regularly updated bibliographies of works on Aristotle's natural philosophy (compiled by István Bodnár) and on his philosophy generally (compiled by Christopher Shields) are available online at: https://plato.stanford.edu/entries/aristotle-natphil/ http://plato.stanford.edu/entries/aristotle/

*Thesaurus Linguae Graeca* (http://www.tlg.uci.edu) has excellent searchable Greek texts and English translations of Aristotle's writings, with linked dictionaries and grammars.

Editions of *On Coming to Be and Passing Away* and *Meteorology*, translations of them, and commentaries on them are listed under Abbreviations at the beginning of the present volume.

# Index

*Note:* In page numbers the initial 3 is omitted—for example, $314^a$ = $14^a$. Line numbers are to the Greek text and are approximate in the translation. References are typically to key doctrines or discussions in the text and associated notes. References in plain text are to *GC*, in italics to *Mete*.

Account (*logos*), $14^a3$n1, $17^a24$
  and a thing's nature, $79^b35$
  in unconditional coming to be, $78^b33$
  of the substance of each thing = the form, $35^b7$n284, $89^b29$
  one and the same as vs. one in, $20^b14$
  vs. luck, $33^b16$
  vs. matter, $90^b18$
  = substance, $90^a6$n439
Activity, actively (*energeia, kat' energeian*), $18^a20$
Actual, actuality (*entelecheia[i], entelecheia*), $16^b21$n49
  being vs. potential, $17^b17$
  body vs. potential, $20^a30$
  divisibility vs. potential, $16^b21$
  flesh vs. potential, $22^a11$
  in affecting and being affected, $26^b31$, $81^b27$
  in elemental transformation, $34^b9$, 21
  in growth, $22^a6$
  in mixing, $27^b23$, 29
  in unconditional coming to be, $17^b24$, $20^b19$
  magnitude vs. potential, $20^b26$
  substance vs. potential, $20^a13$
  vs. potential, $16^b21$, $17^b17$, $26^b31$; body, $20^a30$; degree of an elementary quality, $34^b9$
Affect (*poiein*)
  vs. being affected (*paschein*), $22^b10$
  vs. move, $23^a17$

Affecter (*poioun*)
  conversion between affected and, $28^a20$
  in the same genus as the affected (*pashon*), but in a different species, $24^a5$
  unaffectable, $24^a33$, $28^a21$
Affections (*pathê*), $14^b17$n16
  intrinsically, $19^b27$
Aggregation (*sugkrisis*)
  and disaggregation (*diakrisis*), $15^b8$; = passing away, $16^b34$
  = coming to be, $15^b20$, $16^b34$
  = mixing, $22^b8$
Air (*aer*)
  as element vs. as composite, $14^a26$
  fairly imperceptible, $19^b20$
  hot and wet, $30^b4$; in part hot and wet, in part hot and dry, $40^b24$
  like vapor, $30^b4$
  more a this something and a form than earth is, $18^b32$n79
  not simple, but mixed, $30^b22$, $31^a1$
  putrefies, $79^a15$
  so-called, $39^b3$, $40^b24$
  vs. air-form (*aeroeides*), $30^b24$n219
Aithêr, $33^b2$n250, $34^a1$
Alteration (*alloiôsis*), $19^b10$
  is with respect to the affections of tangible things, $31^a9$
  = coming to be? $14^a5$

195

## Index

Alteration (*alloiôsis*) (*cont.*)
    = when being X remains and the what-it-is, but an intrinsic affection that belongs to it previously did not belong to it, it has altered, 21$^b$4
    = when the change is in the affections and coincidental, 17$^a$37
    = when the underlying subject, which is perceptible, while remaining [the same], changes in its own affections, which are either contraries or intermediates, 19$^b$10
    ≠ coming to be, 19$^b$6
Amber (*êlektron*), 88$^b$18, 89$^a$13
Analogy, by (*kat' analogian*), 33$^a$28, 87$^b$3
Anaxagoras, 14$^a$12
    coming to be and passing away = alteration, 14$^a$13
Animal, 35$^b$32, 38$^b$8, 39$^a$7, 78$^b$31, 79$^b$6, 81$^b$9, 82$^a$6, 84$^b$31, 88$^a$16, $^b$22, 89$^b$5
    particular vs. universal, 22$^a$17
Anthrax, 87$^b$18n424
Appear to be so, things that (*ta phainomena*), 15$^a$4n19
Ashes (*tephra*), 87$^b$14, 89$^a$28, $^b$2, 3, 90$^a$23
Astronomical observations (*astrologika theôrêmata*), 39$^b$8n323

Bark (*phloios*), 84$^b$9, 88$^a$19, 89$^a$13
Being (*einai*) for X, 19$^b$4n86
    for love, strife (Empedocles), 33$^b$24
Being vs. non-being. See what is
Bendable (*kampton*) vs. non-bendable, 85$^b$27
Birdlime (*ixos*), 85$^b$5, 86$^b$14
Blood (*haima*), 84$^a$16n399, 25, 31, 89$^a$19, 20, $^b$9, 90$^b$16
Blow, a (*plêgê*), 86$^b$1
Body, bodies (*sôma*)
    composed by heat and cold, 84$^b$25
    composite, 35$^a$9
    co-ordinate, 40$^a$5
    definite, 82$^a$4
    determined by its own proper defining marks must be hard or soft, 82$^a$22
    elements of, 28$^b$32
    homoeomerous, 84$^b$31
    mixed, 34$^b$31
    natural, 32$^a$4
    perceptible, 28$^b$33, 29$^a$25
    potential vs. actual, 20$^a$30
    primary, 25$^b$18, (= ether), 40$^a$20
    simple, 30$^b$8, 31, 34$^b$32; all present in every composite one, 35$^a$9; imitate the circular spatial movement, 37$^a$3
    splitting of, 27$^a$15
Boil (*phuma*), 79$^b$31, 80$^a$21, $^b$13
Boiling (*zesis*), 30$^b$27
    par- (*molunsis*), 79$^a$2, $^b$14
Bone (*ostoun*), 14$^a$19, 33$^b$9n252, 34$^a$21, 79$^a$7, $^b$31, 80$^a$21, $^b$13, 85$^a$8, 87$^a$18, $^b$1, 88$^a$17, 89$^a$12, $^b$24, 90$^a$2, $^b$5
    comes to be from the elements, 34$^b$25
    dry, wet, and things of that sort, when in accord with the relevant mean, produce, 34$^b$29
    how it differs from other homoeomerous natural bodies, 85$^a$8
Bone marrow (*muelos*), 34$^a$25
Breakable (*katakton*) vs. non-breakable, 86$^a$9
Broiling (*optêsis*), 79$^b$13
    par- (*stateusis*), 79$^b$14

Capacity (*dunamis*), 22$^a$29n122
Category (*katêgoria*), 19$^a$11
    of being, 17$^b$6
Cause(s) (*aitia, aition*), 14$^a$2
    as matter, 18$^a$9, 35$^a$33; of things that come to be, $^b$5
    formal, 36$^a$2
    of contraries are contrary, 83$^b$16, 84$^b$2
    of earth and water existing in mixed bodies, 35$^a$4
    of a human always or for the most part coming to be from human, 33$^b$7
    of movement, 18$^a$1
    relation to effect, 83$^a$8, $^b$31
    = substance (essence), 33$^b$14
Chance (*automaton*) vs. luck (*tuchê*), 33$^b$6n251
Change (*metabolê*)
    mode (*tropos*) of vs. what it has to do with, 20$^a$16, 26
    natural, 78$^b$29

## Index

Cheese (*turos*), 84$^a$22, 24, 30, 88$^b$10
Coarse-grainedness (*pachunsis*), 29$^b$20n207
   comes about because of the exiting of water, 83$^a$11
   *See also* fine-grained
Cold (*psuchros*)
   as a sort of matter, 89$^a$29
   capable of affecting [only] as destructive or coincidentally, 82$^b$6
   determines earth and water, 89$^a$31
   is said to burn and heat, 82$^b$9
   more characteristic of affectable things, 82$^b$4
   solidifies and dries water, 84$^a$9
   = privation of heat, 18$^b$17n76, 80$^a$8, 81$^a$15
Combustible (*kauston*), 22$^a$11, 84$^b$16
   vs. non-combustible, 87$^a$17
Coming to be, unconditional (*genesis haplê*), 17$^a$17, 20$^a$13
   always as a result of something actually being [what it is], 20$^b$19
   and complete, 17$^a$17
   and natural, 78$^b$32
   cause of its always occurring, 18$^a$9, $^b$33
   is from unconditional not being, 17$^b$5
   is the work of the capacities that are capable of affecting and being affected, 78$^b$28
   the most common contrary of = putrefaction, 79$^a$3
   vs. partial (*kata meros*), 17$^b$35n68
   = the route that leads to unconditional being, 18$^b$10
   = when there is a total change from a *this* to a *this*, 17$^a$20n55
   ≠ aggregation, 17$^a$20
Completion (*teleiôsis*), 79$^b$18
   vs. incompletion (*ateleia*), 80$^a$31
Compressible (*pieston*) vs. non-compressible, 86$^a$29
Concoction (*pepsis*)
   forms of, 79$^b$12
   non- (*apepsia*), 79$^a$2
   of nourishment in the body is similar to boiling, 81$^b$7
   = completion due to the natural and proper heat that is produced from the underlying affectables, 79$^b$18
Condensation (*puknôsis*)
   and rarefaction (*manôsis*), 30$^b$10
Connate, grown together, cohere (*sumphues*), 27$^a$2n181
   water vs. brought in, 82$^b$11
Contact, make contact (*haphê, haptesthai*), 22$^a$32
   in the strict sense belongs to things that have position, 22$^b$33
   (physical) is between definite magnitudes whose extremities are together that are capable of moving and being moved by each other, 23$^a$10
   said of things in many ways, 22$^b$32
   = having the extremities together, 23$^a$3
Contiguous (*echomenon*), 17$^a$3n50
Continuous (*suneches*), 25$^a$6n156
Contrariety, contrarieties (*enantiôsis*)
   affection of a, 19$^b$21
   all underlying subjects are receptive of certain, 20$^a$5n93
   as forms and starting-points of perceptual body, 29$^b$9
   change of a, 19$^b$31
   mixable affecters are the ones that have a, 28$^a$32n196
   perceptible, 29$^a$10
Contrary, contraries (*enantia*), 24$^a$2n143
   are in the same genus, 24$^a$2; but unalike in species, 24$^a$6
   are what affect and are affected by each other, 24$^a$3
   columns of, 19$^a$15n82
   coming to be is to the, 24$^a$12
   composed of, 23$^b$29
   in species, 23$^b$33
   one is a privation, 32$^a$23
   pairings (*suzeuxeis, suzugiai*), 30$^a$34, 32$^b$3
   a single matter must always be supposed for, 14$^b$26n18
   vs. matter, 24$^a$22
Convert (*antistrephein*), 28$^a$19n192, 86$^b$24

*Index*

Co-blending (*sugkrasis*), 36$^b$21n299
Co-ordinate (*sustoichos*), 15$^a$21, 40$^a$5
Corn (*sitos*), 89$^a$15
Corpse (*nekros*), 89$^b$31
Craft (*technê*)
    imitates nature, 81$^b$6
    vs. nature, 35$^b$28, 31, 33, 81$^b$4
Crops (*karpoi*), 89$^a$15
Cuttable (*tmêton*) vs. non-cuttable, 87$^a$3

Deficiency (*endeia*), 80$^a$32
Define (*horisasthai*), 33$^b$25n260
Defining mark (*horos*), 29$^b$30n211
    proper, 82$^a$23
Deliberate choice (*prohairesis*), 39$^a$9n317
Democritus, 14$^a$21, 15$^a$35, $^b$6, 16$^a$1, 13
    on affecting and being affected, 23$^b$10
    on heaviness, 26$^a$9
Demonstrate (*apodeixai*), 33$^b$25n260
Determine (*horizein*)
    it is impossible for what does not master to, 80$^a$22
Differentia (*diaphora*), 14$^b$18n16
    of matter as signifying a this something vs. a privation, 18$^b$15n76
    of place, 23$^a$7
    primary, 23$^a$7
Diogenes, 22$^b$13
Dough (*stais*), 86$^b$14
Drying up (*auansis*), 79$^a$5
Drenchable (*tekton*)
    vs. non-drenchable, 85$^b$12n406
Ducts (*poroi*), 24$^b$26, 30, 35, 25$^b$2, 81$^b$1, 3, 85$^a$29, $^b$20, 25, 86$^a$15n412, $^b$2, 4, 5, 6, 9, 87$^a$2, 19, 21
    alternate, 85$^b$24
    how one should speak about, 27$^b$34

Earth (*gê*)
    and water present in all sublunary determined bodies, 82$^a$4
    at the center, 34$^b$32
    belongs to dry rather than to cold, 31$^a$4
    most especially dry, 82$^a$3, $^b$2, 88$^a$22

Easily bounded (*euoristos*), 28$^a$35
    vs. difficult to bound (*dusoriston*), 29$^b$32, 81$^b$29
    = divides easily into small particles, 28$^b$2
Ebony (*ebenos*), 84$^b$17
Element(s) (*stoicheion*), 14$^a$15
    compose the homoeomerous things, which in turn compose as matter all the works of nature, 89$^b$27
    of bodies, 28$^b$31, 33$^a$17
    primary (= ether), 39$^b$17
    simple bodies as, 30$^b$8
    so-called, 22$^b$2, 28$^b$31, 29$^a$26, 39$^b$5
    upper, 41$^a$3
    = elementary qualities, 30$^a$30, 31$^b$27
Empedocles, 14$^a$11, 81$^b$33
    on alteration and passing away, 25$^b$16
    on bone, 33$^b$9n252, 34$^a$27
    on comparability of elements, 33$^a$18
    on earth, water, air, and fire as elements, 29$^a$3, $^b$1, 30$^b$20
    on growth, 33$^a$35
    on movement, 33$^b$22
    on perception, 24$^b$33, 25$^b$6
    on soul, 34$^a$10
Essence (*to ti ên einai*), 35$^b$35n289
Exact way (*akribôs*), 33$^b$25
Excreta (*hupchôrêsis*), 80$^a$1, $^b$5
Exhalation(s) (*anathumiasis*), 40$^b$26, 27, 84$^b$33
Experience, lack of (*apeiria*), 16$^a$6

Fat (*piôn*), 87$^b$6
    = dry oily, 88$^a$7
Fiber (in blood) (*is*), 84$^a$28, 88$^a$17, 89$^a$20, 21
Fig juice (*hopos*), 84$^a$21n400, 89$^b$10
Fine-grained (*lepton*) and coarse-grained (*pachus*), 29$^b$20n207, 80$^a$24
Fire (*pur*)
    alone and most of all belongs with form, 35$^a$19n279
    alone does not putrefy, 79$^a$15
    alone of the simple bodies is nourished, 35$^a$17

## Index

animals not generated in, $82^a7$n376
function of, $90^a15$
in the liquid, $80^b17, 29$
proper, $79^b3$
vs. fire-form (*puroeides*), $30^b24$n219
= excess of heat vs. elemental fire, $30^b25$
= excess of hotness and a sort of boiling, $40^b22$
Flame (*phlox*), $87^b29$
   = burning smoke, $31^b25$n228
   = burning wind (*pheuma*) or smoke, $88^a2$
Flammable (*phlogistos*) vs. non-flammable, $87^b18$
Flesh (*sarx*), $14^a19, 34^a20, 25, 89^b24$
   comes to be from the elements, $34^b25$
   dry, wet, and things of that sort, when in accord with the relevant mean, produce, $34^b29$
   function of, $90^a14$
   how it differs from other homoeomerous natural bodies, $85^a8$
For-the-sake-of-which, the (*to hou heneka*), $24^b15$
   less clear in those cases where the matter has the greatest extent, $90^a3$
   = shape, that is, form, $35^b6$
Force, by (*bia[i]*)
   pass away by, $79^a6$
   = contrary to nature, $33^b26$
Form (*eidos*)
   as a starting-point of coming to be, $35^a30$
   in-matter, $21^b21$n114
   same in number vs. same in, $38^b13$
   taken together with the matter, $35^a16$
   vs. recipient, $28^b11$
Formal cause (*kata to eidos aitia*), $36^a2$
Forms (Platonic)
   vs. participants, $35^b12$
Frankincense (*libanôtos*), $87^b26, 30, 88^a3, {}^b20, 31$

Frost (*pachnê*), $88^b12$
Fumes, capable of giving off (*thumiaton*)
   vs. incapable of giving off, $87^a23$
Fuming (*thumiasis*)
   = the disaggregation due to burning heat of a compound exhalation of dry and wet, $87^a30$
Function, work (*ergon*), $21^b1$n109
   of the capacities capable of affecting and being affected, $78^b29$
   of flesh vs. of the tongue, $90^a14$
   of philosophy, $18^a6$
   they are all defined by their, $90^a10$

Gathering (*athroisis*), $40^a31$n333
Genus, kind (*genos*), $14^b4$n11
   ≈ matter, $24^b7$n147
God, the (*ho theos*), $36^b32$n301
Grain (*karpos*), $85^b19, 89^a15, 90^a23$
Growth (*auxêsis*), $14^a5$n2
   and withering (*phthisis*), $14^b15$n14
   -producer (*auxetikon*), $22^a12, 27$
   vs. nourishment, $22^a23$
   = the growth of a preexisting magnitude, $20^b30$
Gum (*kommi*), $88^b20$

Hail (*chalaza*), $88^b12$
Hair (*thrix*), $86^b14, 87^b1, 4, 88^a17, 89^a12, 90^b5$
Handicraft (*dêmiourgein*), $30^b13, 84^b26, 88^a27$n430, $89^a28$
Hard, hardness (*sklêron, sklêrotês*)
   determined relative to touch, $82^a18$
   does not come to be as a result of hard, $20^b21$
   due to solidification, $82^a25, 88^a28$
   unconditionally vs. in relation to something, $82^a15$
   vs. soft (*malakon*), $14^b19, 25$
   = that whose surface cannot be pressed into itself, $82^a11, 86^a23$
   + heavy, $15^a11$
   + softness = primary affections of a definite thing, $82^a9$

199

*Index*

Heat, hot (*thermotês, thermon*)
  alien, $79^a17$, $81^a23$, $89^a26$, $89^b2$
  and cold (*psuchron*), $29^b18$
  dry, $81^a23$, $82^b33$, $83^a2$, $^b10$, $84^b13$; contrary to wet cold, $83^b15$
  drying, $82^b17$
  external vs. internal, $80^b23$, $82^b18, 24$
  makes things more composed, denser, and drier, $80^a5$
  natural, $80^a20, 22$, $89^b9$, $79^b18$; deficiency of, $80^a32$
  proper, $79^b18$; vs. alien, $79^a17$, $89^b6$
  wet, $80^b13$
  = what aggregates things of the same kind, $29^b26$, $78^b22$
Heaven, the (*ouranos*), $38^a18$, $40^a6$
Heaviness (*baros*) and lightness (*kouphotês*), $23^a8$n133
Homoeomerous (*homoiomerês*), $14^a19$n8
  form and matter of, $21^b20, 31$
  universal seed-bed of, $14^b1$
  vs. non-homoeomerous, $21^b18$n114
Homonymously (*homônumôs*), $22^b30$n130
  a corpse is a human being, $89^b31$
Honey (*meli*), $83^a5$, $84^a15$, $85^b2$, $88^b10, 23$
Horn (*keras*), $83^a32$, $84^b1$, $85^b11$, $88^b31$, $89^a11$
Humor (*chumos*), $80^b2$n364, 32

Ice (*krustallos*), $25^a21$, $85^a32$, $^b7$, $86^a10$, $87^a19, 22$, $88^b11, 16$
  = excess of coldness, $30^b26$
Impression, an (*thlasis*)
  = a shifting downward of part of a thing's surface by a pushing or a blow, or, in general, by contact, $86^a18$
Induction (*epagôgê*), $78^b14$
Instrument, instrumental (*organon, organikos*), $36^a12$
  capacities causing coming to be as, $36^a2$n290
  craft-produced vs. natural, $81^a10$
Intermediate (*metaxu*), $24^a8$
Intrinsic (*kath' hauto*), $19^b27$n91

Iron (*sidêros*), $83^b4$, $84^b14$, $85^b11$, $86^b10, 33$, $88^a14$, $^b31$, $89^a11$
  wrought, $83^a32$
Irregularity (*anômalia*), $36^a30$n296

Kneadable (*pilêton*) vs. non-kneadable, $87^a15$

Lead (*molubdos*), $85^a32$, $89^a8$
Leather thong (*himas*), $86^b14$
Leucippus, $14^a12$, $15^b6$
  on affecting and being affected, $25^b11$
  on atoms and void, $25^a23$
Lime (*titanos*), $83^b8$, $89^a28$
Liquefaction (*hugrainesthai*), $82^b28$
Liquid(s) (*hugron*), $88^a29$
Logico-linguistic way (*logikôs*), $16^a11$n36
Lye (*konia*), $84^a13$, $89^a10, 27$
Lynceus, $28^a15$

Malleable (*elaton*) vs. non-malleable, $86^b18$
  = things part of whose surface is capable of simultaneously shifting both sideways and lengthwise due to the same blow, $86^b19$
Mania (*mania*), $25^a19$
Many ways, said of things in (*pollachôs legetai*), $22^b30$
  dry and wet are, $30^a12$
  rawness and ripeness are, $80^b3$
Marrow (*muelos*), $14^a20$, $89^b10$
Mass (*ogkos*), $21^a11$n105
Master (*kratoun*)
  = determine, $80^a23$
Mastering one, the (*to kratoun, to epikratoun*), $21^a35$n109, $28^a26$
Mathematical objects, $23^a1$n131
Matter (*hulê*), $14^b27$n18
  as a cause, $36^a14$
  as a starting-point of coming to be, $35^a30$
  can never exist without affections and without shape, $20^b16$
  common to distinct elements, $32^a18$
  corporeal and separable, $29^a9$
  differentiae of, $18^b14$n76

for the perceptible bodies (= elements) is not separable but always goes along with a contrariety, $29^a24$
in the extreme case is nothing beyond itself, $90^a5$
in the most strict sense = the underlying subject receptive of coming to be and passing away, $20^a1n93$
is irregular, and not everywhere the same, $36^b21n299$
natural = the underlying affectables, $80^a9$
of natural bodies, $32^a4$
perceptible vs. unapparent, $18^b20$
primary, $29^a23$
to be affected and to be moved is characteristic, $35^b30$
underlying, $28^b34$
= the capacities to be affected (wet, dry), $78^b33$, $82^a8$
= underlying affectables, $79^b19$
= liquid, $79^b33$
≈ genus, $24^b7$
Mean (*meson*, *mesotês*), $34^b27n273$
dry, wet, and things of that sort, produce flesh, bone, and the others, when in accord with the relevant, $34^b29$
Measure (*metrein*, *metron*)
it must be understood as if someone were measuring out water by the same, $21^b24n115$
quantity and, $33^a21n247$
Meltable (*têkton*) vs. non-meltable, $85^a21$, $87^b25$
Melting (*têxis*), $82^b30$
vs. meltable, $81^b28$
Metals (*metalleuomena*), $84^b32$, $88^a13$
See also mines
Meteorology (*meteôrologia*), $38^a26$
Methodological inquiry (*methodos*), $38^a25$
Milk (*gala*), $80^b8$, 32, $81^a7$, $82^b12$, $83^a22$, $84^a24$, 30, $88^a31$, $90^b2$
composed jointly of earth and water, $84^a16n399$
Millstones (*muliai*), $83^b7$
Mines (*metalleuomena*), $26^a35$

Mixable (*mikton*)
= easily bounded, and capable of being affected and of affecting, and is so with the sort of thing that is mixable [with it], $28^b20$
Mixing, mixture (*mixis*), $15^b4n27$
compound, $21^b1$
what masters what in a, $21^a35n109$
wine with water, $21^a33$
= aggregation, $22^b8$
= the unification of mixable things when they have been altered, $28^b22$
Most part, for the (*hôs epi to polu*), $23^a25$, $33^b5n251$, $87^a8$, $89^a26$, 27
Mover, the (*to kinoun*)
moved vs. immovable, $23^a12$
Myrrh (*smurna*), $88^b20$, $89^a13$

Nail (*onux*), $89^a12$
Name (*onoma*), $14^a6n2$
said in many ways, $22^a30$
Natural (*phusikos*)
productions, $15^b6$
Natural science, way appropriate to (*phusikôs*), $16^a11$, $35^b25$
Nature (*phusis*), $36^b28n301$
in all cases always desires what is better, $36^b28$
Nature, by (*phusei*), $14^a1n1$
as form and substance, $79^b25$
depart from their, $89^b11$
vs. from craft, $35^b28$
Necessary (*anagkaion*)
unconditionally vs. hypothetically, $37^b26$
Nourishment (*trophê*)
and growth, $21^a32$, $22^a23$
belongs to matter, $35^a15$
in fruit, $80^a12$
of each thing is by the very same things as it is composed of, $35^a10$
pipe (*aulos*) analogy, $22^a28$
≠ growth-producer in being, $22^a28$
≈ a contrary changing to the same form, $22^a1n118$

# Index

Oily (*liparos*), $87^b6$, $88^a8$
Old age (*gêras*), $79^a5$
Olive oil (*elaion*), $81^a8$, $82^b16$, $83^b14$, 28, $84^a16$, $85^b4$, $87^b7$, 10, 22, $88^a5$, 9, 32, $^b10$
    is most puzzling, $83^b21$
Order (*taxis*) of all things, $36^b12$

Parmenides, $18^b6$, $30^b14$
Passing away, unconditional (*phthora haplê*), $17^a17$
    and complete, $17^a17$
    cause of its always occurring, $18^a9$
    comes about when what is being determined masters what is determining it because of what encompasses them, $79^a11$
    = the route that leads to unconditional not being, $18^b10$
    = when there is a total change from *this* to *this*, $17^a20$
    ≠ disaggregation, $17^a20$
Perception (*aisthêsis*)
    has the capacity of scientific knowledge, $18^b23n78$
    in agreement with our arguments, $36^b16$
    overstepping and disregarding, $25^a13$
    that the simple bodies come to be is evident from, $31^a8$
    this coming to be of fire is also in agreement with, $31^b24$
Perspicuous way (*saphôs*), $22^b9$
Philosophy (*philosophia*), $18^a6n70$
Phlegm (*phlegma*), $84^a32n402$, $84^a32$, $86^b16$
Pitch (*pitta*), $82^b16$, $88^b5$, $87^b22$, $88^a4$
Place (*topos*), $23^a1n131$
    as a category, $17^b10$
    change with respect to, $14^b27$, $19^b32$
    intermediate between earth and heaven, $40^a5$, 18
    of the primary body at the center, $34^b32$
    position belongs to just those that also have, $23^a1$
    primary differentia of, $23^a6$
    proper (of elements), $34^b34n275$
    separable in account vs. separable in, $20^b24$
    two things cannot be in the same, $21^a8$, $^b16$
    what spatially moves changes its, $20^a20$
Plant(s) (*phuton*), $39^a7$, $78^b31$, $84^b31$, $88^a16$, 19, $90^a17$, $^b21$
    nourished by water, $35^a12$
Plastic (*plaston*) vs. non-plastic, $86^a28$
Plato, $15^a29$
    in the divisions, $30^b16n217$
    *Phaedo*, $35^b10$
    *Timaeus*, $15^b30$, $25^b25$, 32, $29^a13$, $32^a29$
Plenum (*plêres*), $25^a11$
    and ducts, $26^b8$
    being = total, $25^a29$
    *See also* void
Pneuma, $21^b9$, $87^a29$
    cooling of, $82^b30$
    in clay, $84^b21$
    in mist, $87^a25$
    water produced from, $83^b26$
    *See also* wind
Pneumatized (*pneumatikos*), $80^a23n361$, 29
Point (*stigmê*) vs. *sêmeion*, $17^a12n52$
Position (*thesis*)
    belongs to just those that also have place, $23^a1$
Pottery (*keramos*), $80^b8$, $83^a21$, 24, $^b11$, 20, $84^a34$, $^b2$, 19, $85^a30$, $^b9$, 28, $86^a11$, 18, 23, $^b26$, $88^a12$, 18
Primary things (*prôta*)
    = starting-points and elements, $29^a5$
Prior in nature, $15^a25n24$
    underlying subject of sight is, $29^b16$
Privation (*sterêsis*), $18^b16n76$, $32^a23$
Proportion, lack of (*asummetria*), $80^a32$
Pullable (*helkton*) vs. non-pullable, $86^b11$
    = things whose surface is capable of changing in the same plane, $86^b11$
Pushing (*ôsis*)
    = movement caused by a mover, which comes about due to [continuous] contact, $86^a33$

## Index

Putrefaction (*sêpsis*)
  products of, 89$^b$8
  = the most common contrary to unconditional coming to be, 79$^a$3
  = the passing away of the proper and in-accord-with-nature heat within a given wet thing due to alien heat, that is, heat from what encompasses it, 79$^a$16
Putrescence (*saprotês*), 79$^a$6
Puzzle (*aporia, aporêma*), 15$^b$19n29
  about the evaporation of wine, 88$^a$33
  about how something else comes to be from the elements, 34$^a$21
  about mixture, 27$^b$10
  about the nature of oil, 83$^b$20
  about so-called air, as to what we must take its nature to be, 39$^b$2
  about whether mixing is relative to perception, 27$^b$32
  as to the divisibility of bodies, 16$^a$14
  as to how on earth one should in fact speak about unconditional passing away and coming to be, 18$^a$11
  as to how unconditional coming to be and passing away is possible, 17$^b$18, 18$^a$11
  as to what it is that increases, 21$^a$29
  as to what the cause is of the unbroken continuity of coming to be, 18$^a$13
  as to whether coming to be = aggregation, 15$^b$19
  as to why what learns is not said to come to be unconditionally but to come to be scientifically knowledgeable, whereas what is born is said to come to be, 19$^a$9
  for those who posit a single matter for the elements, 34$^b$3
  wondrous, 17$^b$18
Puzzle-free (*euporos*), 15$^b$21
Pyrimachus stone, 83$^b$5

Rare (*to manon*) and dense (*to puknon*), 30$^b$11n215

Ratio (*logos*), 33$^a$34, $^b$11, 40$^a$11
  and a thing's nature, 79$^b$35
  in unconditional coming to be, 78$^b$33
  of hot to cold, 34$^b$15
  vs. luck, 33$^b$16
  *See also* account
Rawness (*ômotês*), 79$^b$13
  = contrary of ripeness, 80$^a$27
Ray(s) (*aktis*) reflected from the earth, 40$^a$29
Reasonable, reasonably (*eulogos, eulogôs*)
  for coming to be and passing away to be always continuous, and will never to fail to occur, due to the cause we have mentioned, 36$^b$27
  for coming to be to be in a circle, 38$^a$17
  for fire to heat and for cold to cool, 24$^a$9
  for large things to break up rather than small ones, 26$^a$26
  for what is to be the cause of the coming to be of what is not than for what is not to be it for what is, 36$^a$20
  more, 15$^b$32
  that air closest to what is spatially moving by force becomes most hot, 41$^a$27
  that the differentiae are allocated to the primary bodies, 30$^b$6
  that fire alone of the simple bodies is nourished, 35$^a$16
  that like is not affected in any way by like, 23$^b$19
  that more heat should be generated when the sun itself is there, 41$^a$24
Receptive of impressions (*thlaston*) vs. non-receptive of impressions, 86$^a$17
Reed (*kalamos*), 85$^b$27
Replacement (*antiperistasis*), 82$^a$12, 14, $^b$2, 86$^a$25
Residue (*perittôma*), 80$^a$2n359
Resolution (*analusis*), 29$^a$23
Resolve (*luein*), 16$^b$18
Rheum (*lêmê*), 79$^b$32n357
Ripening (*pepansis*), 79$^b$12, 80$^a$11
  what it is, 80$^a$25

*Index*

Salt (*hals*), $83^b13, 20, 84^a18, 85^a31, {}^b9, 16, 88^b13, 15, 89^a18$
Scientific knowledge (*epistêmê*), $35^b21$
Scientific knower (*epistêmôn*), $35^b22$
Sediment (*hupostasis*), $82^b14$
Seed (*spêrma*), $80^a14, 90^b16$
Semen (*gonê*), $19^b16n88, 89^a19, 22, {}^b10$
Separable (*chôriston*), $16^b3n42$
    body, $28^b35$
    from substance, $17^b10$
    matter, $29^a10$
    no affection is, $27^b22$
    non-, $27^b19$
Serum (*ichôr*), $89^a10$
    serous (*ichôreidê*), $84^a32n402$
Shape(s) (*morphê*)
    as a cause, $36^a14$
    differentiae of, $15^b36$
    in matter, $24^b5$
    matter can never exist without, $20^b17$
    of indivisible bodies (Democritus), $14^a23, 15^b7, 26^a15n170, {}^b1$
    vs. matter, $36^a14$
    = form, $35^a16, 21$
    ≈ essence, $35^b35$
Shatterable (*thrauston*) vs. non-shatterable, $86^a9$
Silver (*arguros*), $84^b32, 88^a14, 89^a7, 90^a17, {}^b12$
    quick- (*chutos*), $85^b4$
Sinew (*neuron*), $86^a14, 88^a17, 89^a12, 90^a19, {}^b5$
    how it differs from other homoeomerous natural bodies, $85^a8$
Smoke (*kapnos*), $87^b23, 24, 3, {}^b6, 89^a22$
    = fuming of woody materials, $87^b1, 88^a2$
Snow (*chiôn*), $88^b11$
Socrates, $35^b10$
Soda (*nitron*), $83^b12, 84^a18$
Soft (*malakon*)
    determined relative to touch, $82^a18$
    due to solidification, $82^a25$
    unconditionally vs. in relation to something, $82^a15, 86^b32$
    = that whose surface can be pressed in, but not by being replaced, $82^a11n377$

    = what can be pressed into itself and does not move to another place, which is just what the wet does, $30^a8$
    = what is capable of being pressed, $26^a14$
Softenable by heat (*malakton*) vs. non-softenable by heat, $85^b6$
Solidifiable (*pêkton*) vs. non-solidifiable, $85^a20$
Solidification, solidified (*pêxis, pepêgos*), $30^b27, 39^a4$
    a body that is determined by its own proper defining marks must be, $82^a23$
    softness and hardness are due to, $82^a25$
    vs. diffusion (*diachusis*), $82^a30$
    = a sort of drying, $82^b1, 84^a11$
Space (*chôra*)
    proper, $37^a9$
Special (*idios*), $20^b29$
Speculations (*theôrêmata*)
    about the upper place, $39^b37$
    astronomical, $39^b8n323$
Splittable (*schiston*) vs. non-splittable, $86^b26$
Sponge (*spoggos*), $86^a28, {}^b5, 7, 17$
Stalactites (*pôroi*), $88^b26$
Star(s) (*astêr*), $38^a21, {}^b22, 39^b9$
    air is between earth and the, $39^b32$
    heat from the, $40^a21$
    outermost, $39^b14$
    place intermediate between earth and the, $41^a11$
    shooting, $38^b23, 41^a33$
    spatial movement of the [fixed], $41^a22$
Starting-point (*archê*), $14^b16n15$
    of coming to be, $35^a26$
    of completion, $79^b21$
    of movement, $18^a1$
State (*hexis*), $24^b17n149$
Strict, strictly, controlling (*kuriôs*), $17^a33, 22^b33$
Substance(s) (*ousia*), $14^b14n14$
    as cause, $33^b14$
    more of a, $18^b15n76$
    nature as, $79^b26$
    potential vs. actual, $20^a12$

that are by nature composite, 28$^b$33
= a this something, 17$^b$32n67
≈ form, 18$^b$15n76
Successive (*ephexês*), 17$^a$9n51
Sun (*hêlios*)
   approach of, 36$^b$17
   Empedocles on, 15$^a$10
   heat generated by, *41$^a$13, 23*
   moves in a circle, 38$^b$3
Synonymous (*sunônumos*), 14$^a$20n8

Theoretical grasp on, get a (*theôrein*), 15$^b$19, 16$^a$32
Theoretical knowledge (*theôria*), 34$^a$15
Thisness (*to tode*), 17$^b$9n62
This something (*tode ti*), 17$^b$32n67
   as signified by the differentiae of matter, 18$^b$15
   things that signify vs. things that do not, 18$^b$1
   vs. affections, 17$^b$32
   vs. quality, quantity, etc., 19$^a$12
   = substance, 19$^a$12
   ≈ form, 18$^b$32n79
Tokens (*sumbola*)
   = shared differentia, 31$^a$23, 34, 31$^b$4, 32$^b$9
Touch (*haphê*), 19$^b$19
   hard and soft determined relative to, 82$^a$18
   not all contrarieties produce forms and starting points of body, but only those in accord with, 29$^b$10
   used as a mean, *82$^a$20n378*

Unaffectable (*apathês*), 23$^b$4
   affecters, 24$^a$33, 28$^a$21
   indivisibles are, 26$^a$1
   things capable of affecting that do not have their shape (form) in matter are, 24$^b$5
   when grown together and one, each thing is, 27$^a$1
Unconditional (*haplous*), 14$^a$7n3
   signifies what is first in each category of being, or what is universal and encompasses everything, 17$^b$5

Underlies, the thing (whatever it is) by being which it (*ho men gar pote on hupokeitai*), 19$^b$3n86
Underlying subject (*hupokeimenon*), 17$^a$23n56
   into which the elements are at last resolved, *39$^b$2*
Universal (*katholou*)
   definition, 23$^a$22
   denial of everything (= not being), 17$^b$12
   quantity taken, 22$^a$16
   starting-points of coming to be vs. particular ones, 35$^a$28n281
   vs. particular, 31$^a$20
Universal seedbed (*panspermia*), 14$^a$29
Universe, totality (*to pan*), 14$^a$8n4, 18$^a$18
Unlimited, the (*to apeiron*), 329$^a$12
   + the encompassing, 32$^a$25
Urine (*ouron*), *80$^a$1, $^b$5, 84$^a$13*

Vapor (*atmis*), *40$^a$34, 84$^a$6*
   = disaggregated water, *40$^b$3*
   = a disaggregation due to burning heat, from liquid [out] into air and wind, capable of wetting things, *87$^a$25n419*
Visceral body (*splagchnon*), *88$^a$17*
Viscosity, viscous (*glischrotês, glischron*), *82$^b$16*
   and brittle (*krauron*), 29$^b$20, 32
   vs. crumbly (*psathuron*), *87$^a$11*
Void (*kenon*)
   separable, 20$^b$27
   = space for body, 26$^b$19
   ≈ imperceptible body, 20$^b$2
   *See also* plenum

Water (*hudôr*)
   alone of the liquids does not become coarse-grained, *83$^a$12*
   alone of the simple bodies is easily bounded, 35$^a$1
   and earth present in all sublunary determined bodies, *82$^a$4*
   and liquefaction and solidification, 82$^b$28
   belongs to cold rather than to wet, 31$^a$4

*Index*

Water (*hudôr*) (*cont.*)
   brought in vs. connate, *82$^b$11*
   characteristically wet, *82$^b$3*
   cold more than wet, 31$^a$5n222
   contrary to fire, 31$^a$2, 17
   determined by cold, *89$^a$31*
   has the most-special affections of wet, *82$^a$3*
   incapable of giving off fumes but does evaporate, *87$^b$8*
   intermediate and more mixed than earth or fire, 31$^a$1
   matter for animal bodies, *82$^a$6*; for fire, *79$^a$16*
   nearest to earth, *39$^a$19*
   putrefies, *79$^a$15*
   ratio preservation when air comes from, *40$^a$11*
Wet, liquid (*hugron*)
   and dry (*xêron*), 29$^b$19
   = what is not bounded by any boundary of its own but is easily bounded, 29$^a$30, 78$^b$24

What is (*to on*) vs. what is not (*to mê on*), 18$^b$6n75
What is capable of being and of not being, 35$^b$5
What-it-is, the (*to ti esti*), 21$^b$3n110
Whey (*oros*), *81$^a$7, 82$^b$13, 84$^a$14, 20, 89$^a$10*
Wind(s) (*pneuma*), 18$^b$29n79, 38$^b$26, 41$^a$1, 88$^a$2
   = more a this something and a form than earth is, 18$^b$32
Wine (*oinos*), 21$^a$33, 24$^a$30, 28$^a$27, *82$^b$13, 84$^a$4, 13, 87$^b$9, 88$^a$33, $^b$2, 10, 89$^a$9, 27*
   sweet, *87$^b$9*
Wine must (*gleukos*), *79$^b$30, 80$^b$32, 84$^a$5*
Withy (*lugos*), *85$^b$28*
Wood, logs (*xulon, xula*), 16$^b$10, 22$^b$15, 35$^b$33, *84$^b$15, 85$^a$9, $^b$12, 86$^a$10, 27, $^b$19, 23, 26, 87$^a$7, 18, $^b$26, 27, 88$^a$2, 19, 31, $^b$32, 89$^a$2*
Wool (*erion*), *82$^b$12, 85$^b$14, 18, 86$^a$28, $^b$16, 25, 87$^a$18*
Work. *See* function

206